Post-Soviet Constitutions and Challenges of Regional Integration

This book explores the implications of European and Eurasian integration projects for the constitutional orders of post-Soviet countries. On the one hand, the process of Eurasian integration, culminating in the establishment of the Eurasian Economic Union (EAEU), led to the creation of new institutions and mechanisms influencing the domestic legal order of the participating countries. On the other hand, the process of European integration, epitomised through the European Union (EU), constitutes an important source of reference for domestic constitutional developments in the countries which recently concluded a new generation of Association Agreements with the EU. This book analyses the implications of both processes.

The book addresses the relevant experience of the countries from Central and Eastern Europe with transitional constitutionalism, mapping out the significance of European and Eurasian integration for protecting the rule of law in the post-Soviet space and identifying the constitutional implications and challenges of the EAEU and the new generation of Association Agreements. It also provides detailed country reports on national constitutional orders in the post-Soviet space and their adaptability to regional integration projects, authored by leading academics from the countries concerned, providing a number of general reflections about the evolution of post-Soviet constitutions in light of European and Eurasian integration projects.

Roman Petrov is Jean Monnet Chair in EU Law at the National University of 'Kyiv-Mohyla Academy', Ukraine.

Peter Van Elsuwege is Professor in EU Law at Ghent University, Belgium.

Routledge Research in EU Law

www.routledge.com/Routledge-Research-in-EU-Law/book-series/ROUTEULAW

Available titles in this series include:

EU External Relations Law and the European Neighbourhood Policy
A Paradigm for Coherence
Bart Van Vooren

The Evolving EU Counter-terrorism Legal Framework
Maria O'Neill

The Early Warning System for the Principle of Subsidiarity
Constitutional Theory and Empirical Reality
Philipp Kiiver

The European Constitution, Welfare States and Democracy
The Four Freedoms vs. National Administrative Discretion
Christoffer C. Eriksen

New Governance and the European Strategy for Employment
Samantha Velluti

Human Rights and Minority Rights in the European Union
Kirsten Shoraka

Centralized Enforcement, Legitimacy and Good Governance in the EU
Melanie Smith

EU External Relations and Systems of Governance
The CFSP, Euro-Mediterranean Partnership and Migration
Paul James Cardwell

Post-Soviet Constitutions and Challenges of Regional Integration
Adapting to European and Eurasian Integration Projects
Roman Petrov and Peter Van Elsuwege

Post-Soviet Constitutions and Challenges of Regional Integration

Adapting to European and Eurasian Integration Projects

Edited by Roman Petrov and Peter Van Elsuwege

Routledge
Taylor & Francis Group
LONDON AND NEW YORK

First published 2018 by Routledge

2 Park Square, Milton Park, Abingdon, Oxfordshire OX14 4RN
52 Vanderbilt Avenue, New York, NY 10017

Routledge is an imprint of the Taylor & Francis Group, an informa business

First issued in paperback 2019

British Library Cataloguing-in-Publication Data
A catalogue record for this book is available from the British Library

Library of Congress Cataloging-in-Publication Data
Names: Petrov, Roman, 1973–, author. | Elsuwege, Peter Van, author.
Title: Post-soviet constitutions and challenges of regional integration : adapting to European and Eurasian integration projects / Roman Petrov and Peter Van Elsuwege.
Description: New York : Routledge, 2018. | Series: Routledge research into EU law | Includes bibliographical references and index.
Identifiers: LCCN 2017038224 | ISBN 9781138101593 (hbk) | ISBN 9781315656847 (ebk)
Subjects: LCSH: Constitutional law—Europe, Eastern. | Constitutional law—Eurasia. | International and municipal law—Europe, Eastern. | International and municipal law—Eurasia. | Law—Europe, Eastern—International unification. | Law—Eurasia—International unification.
Classification: LCC KJC4445 .P48 2018 | DDC 342.4702—dc23
LC record available at https://lccn.loc.gov/2017038224

ISBN: 978-1-138-10159-3 (hbk)
ISBN: 978-0-367-87546-6 (pbk)

Typeset in Galliard
by Apex CoVantage, LLC

Contents

Contributors

Vera Axyonova is Postdoctoral Researcher and Assistant Professor at the Justus Liebig University Giessen and Visiting Lecturer at Fulda University of Applied Sciences, Germany. She was previously Hurford Next Generation Fellow with the Euro-Atlantic Security Initiative of Carnegie Endowment for International Peace and Associate Researcher with Europe-Central Asia Monitoring program at FRIDE, a European think tank based in Madrid. She completed her PhD in Political Science at Bremen International Graduate School of Social Sciences and holds an MA in Intercultural Communication and European Studies and a Diploma in International Relations. She is the author of *The European Union's Democratization Policy for Central Asia: Failed in Success or Succeeded in Failure?* (2014) and editor of *European Engagement under Review: Exporting Values, Rules, and Practices to the Post-Soviet Space* (2016).

Paul Blokker is Associate Professor and Jean Monnet Chair at the Institute of Sociological Studies, Charles University, Prague, Czech Republic. His publications include *New Democracies in Crisis? A Comparative Constitutional Study of the Czech Republic, Hungary, Poland, Romania and Slovakia*, Routledge (2013); 'EU Democratic Oversight and Domestic Deviation from the Rule of Law: Sociological Reflections', in C. Closa and D. Kochenov (eds), *Reinforcing the Rule of Law Oversight in the European Union*, CUP (2016); and, co-edited with Chris Thornhill, *Sociological Constitutionalism*, CUP (forthcoming, 2017).

Olga Burlyuk works as Assistant Professor at the Centre for EU Studies (CEUS), Ghent University, Belgium. Her research focuses on EU external relations, in particular its efforts to transform third states and societies through the promotion of democracy, the rule of law and human rights, as well as trade and development cooperation. The (Eastern) European neighbourhood, and specifically Ukraine, is her area of specialisation. Her publications appeared in the *Journal of Common Market Studies, East European Politics and Societies, East European Politics, Hague Journal on the Rule of Law*, and *European Journal of Law Reform*. She is currently co-editing a special issue on *Civil Society* *in Post-Euromaidan Ukraine*, scheduled to appear in *Kyiv-Mohyla Law and Politics Journal* in December 2017. Alongside her academic career, Olga is an active member of the Ukraine expert coordination group in Brussels and has offered expertise on Ukraine to the European External Action Service, European Parliament, European Network of Political Foundations, and other Brussels-based actors.

Laure Delcour is a Senior Research Fellow at Fondation Maison des Sciences de l'Homme, France. Her research interests focus on the EU's influence on domestic change in post-Soviet countries and region-building processes in the post-Soviet space. She recently published *The EU and Russia in their 'Contested Neighbourhood': Multiple External Influences, Policy Transfer and Domestic Change* (Routledge, 2017).

Rilka Dragneva is Professor of International Legal Studies at the School of Law, University of Birmingham, UK. Her main research interests focus on regional integration, EU external policy, legal reform and international diffusion of norms with a special reference to Eastern Europe. Her recent publications focus on Eurasian economic integration, its overlaps with EU's initiatives in the post-Soviet region, and implications for multilateral trade more widely. Her work has strong comparative and interdisciplinary elements. Her expertise in the field has enabled her to engage in interactions with policy-makers and leading think tanks, law reform technical assistance projects, and professional training activities.

Gaga Gabrichidze is Professor of Public International Law and EU Law at the New Vision University in Tbilisi, Georgia. From 2008 to 2011, he held the Jean Monnet Chair in European Law at the Tbilisi State University. He earned a PhD from the Tbilisi State University (2005) and also holds a Master in European Law from the Europa-Institut of the University of Saarland, Germany (2000). He had several visiting research fellowships at the University of Saarland (Germany), the University of Frankfurt (Germany) and the University of Vienna (Austria). His research primarily focuses on constitutional issues of EU law, as well as on legal approximation and migration law. He is a member of the editorial board of the *Georgian Law Review*. He is also founder and president of the European Union Studies Association (ECSA) in Georgia.

Narine Ghazaryan is an Assistant Professor in Law at the University of Nottingham, UK, School of Law. She specialises in EU external relations law. Her research interests include the European Neighbourhood Policy, democracy and human rights promotion in EU external relations and others. She published, amongst others, a monograph on the European Neighbourhood Policy and the democratic values of the EU with Hart Publishing in 2014.

Paul Kalinichenko holds a Doctor of Legal Science degree in International and European Law. He is Jean Monnet Chair and Professor of Integration and European Law at the Kutafin Moscow State Law University, Russia. He is also appointed as Head of the European Law Department of the Diplomatic Academy at the Russian Foreign Ministry and as Professor of the Higher School of

Economics (Moscow). His research activities essentially focus on EU external relations law, EU economic law and EU-Russia relations. He was engaged as a legal advisor in European law for the Ministry of Education and Science of Russia and for the Eurasian Economic Commission.

Maksim Karliuk is a Research Fellow at the HSE-Skolkovo Institute for Law and Development, National Research University Higher School of Economics (Moscow, Russia) and a Joint PhD candidate at Ghent University (Ghent) and Belarusian State University (Minsk). He holds an LLM in European Law from the College of Europe, Bruges Campus. His research interests include the institutional foundations of Eurasian integration and the latest creation thereof – the Eurasian Economic Union.

Zhenis Kembayev is Professor of Law at the KIMEP University in Almaty, Kazakhstan. He was a Fulbright Scholar at the Southwestern Law School (Los Angeles, USA) in 2003–2004 and an Alexander von Humboldt Fellow at the Saarland University and the Max Planck Institute for Comparative Public Law and International Law (Heidelberg, Germany) in 2007–2008. In 2015, Professor Kembayev was selected as a Jean Monnet Chair in European and International Law and in 2016 as a Weiser Fellow at the Center for Europe and Eurasia of the University of Michigan. His teaching activities include courses on public international law, EU law, constitutional law and legal theory. Professor Kembayev's research addresses various legal issues related to the regional integration processes in Eurasia within the Eurasian Economic Union and the Collective Security Treaty, the development of constitutionalism in Kazakhstan, the evolution of European integration and EU external relations law, as well as the Shanghai Cooperation Organisation.

Roman Petrov holds an LLM in EU Law (Durham University, UK, 1998), PhD in Law (National Academy of Science of Ukraine, 2000), PhD in Law (Queen Mary, University of London, UK, 2005) and doctoral habilitation (Institute of Legislation of the Parliament of Ukraine, 2014). He conducted post-doctoral research as Max Weber Fellow at the European University Institute (Italy, 2006–2008) and had visiting research fellowships at the University of Heidelberg (Germany), the University of Oxford (UK), Ghent University (Belgium), University of Latvia and Augsburg University (Germany). In 2015–2016 Dr. Petrov was holding a Foreign Chair at Ghent University (Belgium). He is founder and first elected president of the Ukrainian European Studies Association. Currently, Dr. Petrov is Jean Monnet Chair in EU Law and Head of the Jean Monnet Centre of Excellence at the National University of 'Kyiv-Mohyla Academy' in Ukraine. Areas of his research and teaching include EU law, EU external relations law, approximation and harmonisation of legislation in the EU, rights of third-country nationals in the EU, and legal aspects of regional integration in the post-Soviet area.

Mihaela Tofan is Associate Professor at the 'Alexandru Ioan Cuza' University of Iasi, Romania. Her teaching and research activities focus on EU law and its influence on Member States' legislation. Since 2010, she is Jean Monnet Professor in the field of EU law and, since 2016, she holds a Jean Monnet Chair in EU financial regulation. She was invited for teaching activities in various higher education institutions such as the State University of Chisinau (Moldova), University of Perugia (Italy), Arel University Istanbul (Turkey), Ca'Foscari University Venice (Italy), University of Bifrost (Iceland), National University of Kyiv-Mohyla Academy (Ukraine) and CDA College Larnaca (Cyprus).

Peter Van Elsuwege is Professor in EU Law and co-director of the Ghent European Law Institute (GELI) at Ghent University, Belgium. He is also Visiting Professor at the College of Europe (Natolin Campus). His research activities essentially focus on the law of EU external relations. Specific attention is devoted to the legal framework of the relations between the European Union and its East European neighbours. He is, amongst others, the author of *From Soviet Republics to EU Member States: A Legal and Political Assessment of the Baltic States' Accession to the EU* (Brill, 2008) and editor (together with R. Petrov) of the book *Legislative Approximation and Application of EU Law in the Eastern Neighbourhood of the European Union: Towards a Common Regulatory Space?* (Routledge, 2014). He is also an affiliated member of the Centre for the Law of EU External Relations (CLEER) at the Asser Institute (The Hague) and the Centre for Russian International, Socio-Political and Economic Studies (CERISE) at Ghent University.

Abbreviations

AA	Association Agreement
AP	Action Plan
ASEAN	Association of Southeast Asian Nations
CEEC	Central and East European Country
CEPA	Comprehensive and Enhanced Partnership Agreement
CES	Common Economic Space
CFSP	Common Foreign and Security Policy
CIS	Commonwealth of Independent States
CJEU	Court of Justice of the European Union
CoE	Council of Europe
CSTO	Collective Security Treaty Organisation
CU	Customs Union
CUP	Cambridge University Press
CVM	Co-operation and Verification Mechanism
DCFTA	Deep and Comprehensive Free Trade Area
DG	Directorate General
DSM	Dispute Settlement Mechanism
EA	Europe Agreement
EAEU	Eurasian Economic Union
EaP	Eastern Partnership
EBRD	European Bank for Reconstruction and Development
EC	European Community
ECAA	European Common Aviation Area
ECHR	European Convention on Human Rights
ECR	European Court Report
ECtHR	European Court of Human Rights
ECU	Eurasian Customs Union
EEA	European Economic Area
EEAS	European External Action Service
EEC	Eurasian Economic Commission
EECA	East European and Central Asia
EFTA	European Free Trade Association
EMAA	Euro-Mediterranean Association Agreement

EnC	Energy Community
EnCT	Energy Community Treaty
ENP	European Neighbourhood Policy
ENPI	European Neighbourhood and Partnership Instrument
EPCA	Enhanced Partnership and Cooperation Agreement
EU	European Union
EurAsEC	Eurasian Economic Community
FTA	Free Trade Area
ILO	International Labour Organisation
JHA	Justice and Home Affairs
MP	Member of Parliament
NATO	North Atlantic Treaty Organisation
NEC	Neighbourhood Economic Community
NGO	Non-Governmental Organisation
NIS	Newly Independent State
ODIHR	Office for Democratic Institutions and Human Rights
OECD	Organisation for Economic Cooperation and Development
OJ	Official Journal
OSCE	Organisation for Security and Cooperation in Europe
OUP	Oxford University Press
PACE	Parliamentary Assembly of the Council of Europe
PCA	Partnership and Cooperation Agreement
PHARE	Poland Hungary Assistance for Restructuring the Economy
RSFSR	Russian Soviet Federative Socialist Republic
SCO	Shanghai Cooperation Organisation
SEAEC	Supreme Eurasian Economic Council
TACIS	Technical Assistance to the Commonwealth of Independent States
TBT	Technical Barriers to Trade
TCS	Treaty on Collective Security
TEAEU	Treaty on Eurasian Economic Union
TEU	Treaty on European Union
TFEU	Treaty on Functioning of the European Union
UN	United Nations
USSR	Union of Soviet Socialist Republics
WTO	World Trade Organisation

Acknowledgements

This book is the result of a joint cooperation between the Jean Monnet Centres of Excellence of the National University of 'Kyiv-Mohyla Academy' (Prof. Roman Petrov) and Ghent University (Prof. Peter Van Elsuwege). As a follow-up to the previous edited volume, entitled *Legislative Approximation and Application of EU Law in the Eastern Neighbourhood of the European Union: Towards a Common Regulatory Space?* (Routledge, 2014), the editors organised a series of workshops in Kyiv and Ghent bringing together a number of leading scholars working on the implications of the processes of European and Eurasian integration for the legal orders of the post-Soviet countries. The present volume is the result of in-depth discussions on draft papers presented during those events. The organisers of the workshops, also being the editors of this book, would like to express their deep appreciation to all the contributors for their cooperation and commitment.

This project would not have been possible without the support of the Jean Monnet Programme of the European Commission and the Alexander von Humboldt Stiftung. The idea to work together on the topic of European and Eurasian integration bore fruit in the wake of the annual Jean Monnet conference in Brussels and the organisation of the workshops leading to the present book could benefit from the final support of the Jean Monnet Programme. Cooperation in preparation of this volume was also made possible thanks to the support of the Russia Platform of Ghent University and the Flemish Chamber of Commerce for Russia, Belarus and Kazakhstan, which kindly supported the organisation of the workshop 'The Eurasian Economic Union, a significant legal actor?' in Ghent on 2 December 2016. A special word of thanks goes to Prof. Marc Maresceau for his never-ending inspiration, Hannah Lovelock from Routledge and Jennifer Bonnar from Apex CoVantage, who guided us through the publication process. Last but not least, we would like to thank our families for kindly allowing us to concentrate our efforts on this publication.

Roman Petrov and Peter Van Elsuwege
October 2017

Introduction

Roman Petrov and Peter Van Elsuwege

The end of the Cold War period and the demise of the Soviet Union formed the start for a process of 'transitional constitutionalism'.[1] The experience of Western, liberal-democratic constitutionalism served as a model for the adoption of new constitutions and the establishment of new institutions, most notably Constitutional Courts. This implied a renewed emphasis on legalism and the rule of law in contrast to the ideological approach to the role of constitutions during the Soviet period. Despite the shared legacy of communism, domestic constitutional politics as well as external factors largely determined the post-communist transformation in the region under former Soviet dominance.

The countries of Central and Eastern Europe (CEECs) all embarked on a process leading to EU membership. This entailed significant constitutional developments requiring, amongst others, a different approach to sovereignty and statehood.[2] Moreover, the EU's political conditionality within the 'pre-accession process' pushed for enhanced democratic and rule of law structures. Nevertheless, recent developments in countries such as Hungary and Poland reveal the emergence of illiberal tendencies leading to a so-called 'rule of law crisis' in the EU. Whereas this evolution is not the focus of this volume, the experience of the CEECs is relevant for understanding the mechanisms and challenges surrounding the process of transitional constitutionalism. For this purpose, Paul Blokker analyses the constitutional trajectories of the CEECs in order to draw some lessons for the post-Soviet countries.[3]

So far, the process of constitutionalism in the countries of the former Soviet Union has attracted far less scholarly attention in comparison to the constitutional evolutions in Central and Eastern Europe. This may be due to the absence of an external factor, such as the prospect of EU membership, as well as the less ambitious domestic reform agenda in (a large part of) the post-Soviet area. Whereas an emphasis on constitutional reform somewhat logically followed from the CEEC's democratic transition after the 1989 revolutions,[4] the ideology-focused Soviet legal heritage complicated the introduction of genuine rule of law mechanisms in the post-Soviet states.[5] Notwithstanding multiple references to 'the rule of law' in their new constitutions,[6] most countries of the former Soviet Union followed a 'rule *by* law' paradigm implying a largely formalistic and instrumental approach to law as a source of power politics in largely authoritarian regimes.[7]

However, as observed by Olga Burluyk and Vera Axyonova further in this volume, it is becoming increasingly difficult to treat the post-Soviet states as a homogeneous group. Their distinct post-Soviet experiences, combined with the rediscovery of their pre-Soviet legacies, result in an increased differentiation as far as their constitutional cultures are concerned. Of particular significance is the influence of distinct regional integration processes. On the one hand, the process of Eurasian integration, culminating in the establishment of the Eurasian Economic Union (EAEU), led to the creation of new institutions and mechanisms influencing the domestic legal order of the participating countries (Armenia, Belarus, Russia, Kazakhstan and Tajikistan). On the other hand, the process of European integration, epitomised through the European Union (EU), constitutes an important source of reference for domestic constitutional developments in the countries which recently concluded a new generation of Association Agreements with the EU (Georgia, Moldova and Ukraine).

This book analyses the implications of both processes. Whereas the first part of the book addresses the relevant experience of the CEECs (Paul Blokker), the relevance of European and Eurasian integration for protecting the rule of law in the post-Soviet space (Olga Burlyuk and Vera Axyonova) and the constitutional implications and challenges of the EAEU and the new generation of Association Agreements (Rilka Dragneva); the second part of the book includes country-specific reports analysing the influence of the relevant regional integration processes for the constitutional orders of Ukraine (Roman Petrov), Georgia (Gaga Gabrichidze), Moldova (Mihaela Tofan), Armenia (Narine Ghazaryan and Laure Delcour), Belarus (Maksim Karliuk) and Kazakhstan (Zhenis Kembayev). The book concludes with a number of general reflections about the evolution of post-Soviet constitutions in light of European and Eurasian integration projects.

Notes

1 W. Sadurski, 'Transitional Constitutionalism: Simplistic and Fancy Theories', in: A. Czarnota, M. Krygier and W. Sadurski (eds.), *Rethinking the Rule of Law After Communism*, Budapest and New York: CEU Press, 2005, pp. 9–24; R. Teitel, 'Post-Communist Constitutionalism: A Transitional Perspective', *Columbia Human Rights Law Review*, 1994, 167–190.

2 See: A. Albi, *EU Enlargement and the Constitutions of Central and Eastern Europe*, Cambridge: Cambridge University Press, 2005. W. Sadurski, A. Czarnota and M. Krygier, *Spreading Democracy and the Rule of Law? The Impact of EU Enlargement on the Rule of Law, Democracy and Constitutionalism in Post-Communist Legal Orders*, Dordrecht: Springer, 2006.

3 See the contribution of Paul Blokker in this volume.

4 See the contribution of Paul Blokker in this volume.

5 F.J.M. Feldbrugge, G.P. Van Den Berg and W.B. Simons (eds.), *Encyclopedia of Soviet Law*, Dordrecht: Martinus Nijhoff, 1985 (2nd ed.).

6 See annex 1 to this volume.

7 On the difference between 'rule of law' versus 'rule by law' paradigms, see the contribution of Olga Burluyk and Vera Axyonova in this volume.

Part I

European and Eurasian integration initiatives

Constitutional challenges

1 The evolution of constitutionalism in the post-communist countries of Central and Eastern Europe

Some lessons for the post-Soviet space

Paul Blokker

Introduction

The centrality of legality, the rule of law, constitutionalism and human rights in the radical changes in the former communist countries of Central and Eastern Europe (CEE) since 1989 has been widely noticed and analysed.[1] There are three reasons of why one would want to refer to a distinctive post-communist experience with constitutionalism. First of all, all the constitutional orders in the region emerged after a prolonged experience with communism. Second, a good part of the countries in the region embarked on a process of obtaining membership in the European Union (EU), while others have become part of the EU 'neighbourhood' and of the Council of Europe (CoE), a process often referred to as the 'return to Europe'. Third, as of 2017, many countries appear to be in an ongoing process of some form of transformation, particularly visible in explicit 'counterconstitutional'[2] moves in Hungary and Poland, but equally expressed in more modest ways of 'illiberal' or 'counterconstitutional' practice elsewhere (e.g. Romania).[3]

The processes of constitutionalisation in the post-communist region are in a general sense characterised by a dual process, that is, the original turn to constitutionalism and human rights regimes is importantly related to *domestic* processes of change and dissidence, but at the same time *international* factors (in terms of actors, models, institutions) have played a highly significant role from the start, and most conspicuously with the rapprochement to the EU and the CoE, and subsequent membership.[4] Constitutionalisation in the post-communist region has seen the emergence of important and complex processes of domestic constitutional politics and conflict, in some cases already before 1989, while external actors and models have become increasingly prominent in the post-communist transformations.[5] In this, the significant role of external factors and actors can hardly be overstated. In the heat of the 'constitutional moments' of the early 1990s, European constitutional models (in particular, those of Germany and France) evidently played a major role in constitution-making processes, even if sometimes in the form of opaque practices of 'bricolage'.[6] The prominence of the EU enlargement process and its conditionality has to be duly acknowledged,[7] while also the role of the CoE, through the European Court of Human Rights (ECtHR) and increasingly the Commission of Democracy Through Law (Venice Commission), is evidently considerable in the processes of constitutionalisation in the region.

The chapter will start with a discussion of the post-1989 process of constitution-making, with an emphasis on the widespread adherence in the region to a model of legal or 'new' constitutionalism. Second, the EU enlargement process will be related to constitutional trajectories in Central and Eastern Europe, while, third, the role of the EU Charter of Fundamental Rights, and, fourth, the complex nature, and the persistence, of national sovereignty in the context of EU law will be discussed, on the basis of relevant judgments. Fifth, the recent illiberal developments and their significance for constitutionalism in some countries (Poland, Hungary) will be identified. In the concluding section, some potential lessons for post-Soviet neighbourhood countries will be outlined.

Post-1989 constitutionalisation

An emphasis on legal constitutionalism in the post-communist societies is not surprising in the light of a dissident emphasis on human rights and the language of legalism shared by communist reformers and opposition forces prior to 1989.[8] The emphasis on legalism, legal continuity and the rule of law can further be related to the fact that legalism was perceived as an antidote to the 'ideological'[9] or 'contradictory'[10] socialist legality of the communist regimes. The post-1989 'return' to constitutionalism and the rule of law or, at the very least, the rejection of the communist instrumentalisation of the law for political purposes, reconnected with a trend of globally emerging, 'new' constitutionalism. By the end of the 20th century, legal or new constitutionalism[11] had allegedly become predominant, even if not uncontested. In the post-communist democracies, the role of new constitutionalism has not least been seen as one of securing the transition to robust constitutional democratic orders.[12]

What makes new constitutionalism relevant in the post-communist situation includes, among others, the following dimensions: the (re-)establishment of sovereign, democratic orders grounded in the rule of law, the idea of constitutional law as a higher law (and thus particularly entrenched against the influence from politics), the idea of fundamental rights, and the idea of a guardian of the constitution in the form of a Constitutional Court. New constitutionalism provides one possible way of protecting societies from succumbing to totalitarianism and dictatorship. The emphasis, in this, is on written constitutions with an entrenched 'catalogue of rights', and a 'system of constitutional justice to defend those rights'.[13] The Constitutional Court plays a primary role in the protection of society in that it is an independent institution, which is not only regarded the ultimate guardian and interpreter of the constitution, but equally so of fundamental rights.

The first feature that characterises new constitutionalism is an understanding of constitutionalism as closely related to the ideas of politico-legal autonomy and state sovereignty.[14] New constitutionalism follows a traditional understanding of state sovereignty, that is, sovereignty as indicating the relative autonomy of the state from both the external world (external sovereignty) and the internal citizenry (internal sovereignty). Part of the ontology of new constitutionalism corresponds to 'constitutional nationalism', that is, the idea that sovereignty is grounded in a national state, which has the 'final word'.[15]

New constitutionalism is relevant in the new democracies in that the new constitutions adopted in the post-communist region have generally displayed a disproportionate 'souverainist' character. Anneli Albi has argued that a 'characteristic feature of the post-Communist constitutions of Central and Eastern Europe is that they are distinctively more protective of sovereignty than most constitutions in Western Europe'.[16] In the run-up to EU membership, Albi argued that, '[a]utonomous control or even statehood having been (re-) established merely a decade ago, Central and Eastern European countries (CEECs) operate firmly in the traditional language of sovereignty, independence, the ethnically defined nation-state and national self-determination'.[17] Regarding the latter point, 'Eastern European academic discourse as well as citizenship and language legislation tend to approach the nation through the ethnocultural concept of the homogeneous nation-state'.[18] The souverainist and ethno-nationalist dimensions have continued to play an important role in post-communist societies, as is particularly, but not only, evident in current developments in Hungary and Poland. This is so, even if the interpretation of sovereignty and statehood has become more complex in the context of EU membership (see below).[19]

The second feature – that of the constitution as the apex of the legal system – is a primary dimension in all of the post-1989 constitutions. New constitutionalism tends to endorse the constitution in the form of a higher law, that is, as a law that is situated 'above' ordinary laws and is more difficult to change by political means. In other words, such a law is entrenched. The level of entrenchment of the constitution, however, differs importantly between constitutions, and equally within the region. Entrenchment further also relates to judicial review in that the more difficult Constitutional Court decisions are to override, the more entrenched a constitution is. As Sadurski has argued,

> [t]he degree of "finality" of decisions of constitutional courts may then be measured by the degree of entrenchment of the constitution: the easier it is to amend the constitution, the less final are the court's decisions. On the one side of spectrum, there will be cases of an "absolute" entrenchment: when the constitution itself precludes a possibility of amending certain provisions. . . . On the other side of the spectrum, there will be constitutions that are weakly entrenched, that is, those that envisage a reasonably easy amendment process.[20]

The higher-law status has constitutionally been enshrined in the form of limitations of revision ranging from simple supermajorities (as in the case of Hungary a two-third parliamentary majority), to complex provisions regarding initiators of revision, parliamentary approval and ratification by means of a popular referendum (such as in the case of Romania).

The third feature, the idea of a set of essential individual rights, became an equally widely endorsed element of the constitutions in the new democracies, not least due to their accession to the Council of Europe as well as the EU Charter of Fundamental Rights. The communist constitutions had included ample catalogues of rights, without, however, granting these rights the status of individual entitlements. Rather, individual rights were benefits granted by the state to citizens who were supposed to fulfil a range of duties, and were anyway interpreted arbitrarily and always within the context of the socialist ideal.[21] A main aim in all constitutions in the region was to entrench rights so as to protect these from political interference and arbitrariness.

A fourth dimension is that of the role of Constitutional Courts. The post-communist countries adopted a more or less similar model of concentrated or centralised review, in which one singular institution has the responsibility and independent status to 'authoritatively scrutinise laws in terms of their constitutionality'.[22] In this respect, the most important of the judicial review powers is that of review in abstracto, that is, the power to review the constitutionality of laws without reference to a specific case. While, on the one hand, we could speak of a region-wide phenomenon, on the other hand, it is necessary to recognise relatively different trajectories and institutional make-ups in the various countries. Generally, there is no tradition of Constitutional Courts in the region (except for the Czechoslovak case, where such a court was established by the 1920 Constitution and operated from 1921 onwards). Many countries looked to Western Europe for inspiration. In one case, some form of legal constitutionalism emerged already before 1989, as Poland set up a Constitutional Tribunal in 1985, in an attempt to enhance legitimacy of the regime and reflecting a growing acceptance of a constitutionalist idea. The role and importance of Constitutional Courts differ throughout the region, as we will see below. While Hungary could boast one of the strongest courts in the world under Chief Justice Solyom in the 1990s, in Poland it took until the 1997 Constitution for a legal constitutionalist argument to prevail, while in Romania it was only with the 2003 amendments that the Constitutional Court gained a final say in matters of constitutionality. What is conspicuous in recent developments is the political reaction against the new-constitutionalist model, and the assault on Constitutional Courts by political governments, particularly evident in the cases of both Hungary (since 2010) and Poland (since 2015).[23]

The eastern enlargement of the EU

A conspicuous dimension of the constitutional trajectories of the post-communist countries is EU membership, at least with regard to the countries in the Central and East European region that, since the adoption of the Copenhagen criteria in 1993, could increasingly count on a perspective of future membership in the EU. While it is debatable whether a strong EU impact could be felt on domestic constitution-making processes already in the early 1990s,[24] with the *de facto* initiation of accession trajectories in 1997, the Copenhagen criteria regarding the stability of democratic and judicial institutions,[25] the rule of law, and human rights,[26] including minority rights, and the general adoption of the *acquis*, clearly became an increasingly significant factor in political transformation in the accession countries. The criteria regarding rights, and their application through the conditionality process, were often perceived as based on a double standard due to their emphasis on the safeguarding of minority rights as criteria for accession, which were however not present in the reference to rights in former Article 6(1) TEU, pertaining to existing EU Member States.[27]

It can, however, be equally argued that the practical implications of the Copenhagen criteria were not systematic and profound,[28] in that only Slovakia (in 1997) was ever given an overall 'negative grade', in particular with regard to its performance regarding the separation of powers and the independence of the Constitutional Court[29]:

> Although the institutional framework defined by the Slovak constitution responds to the needs of a parliamentary democracy where elections are free and fair, nevertheless the situation is unsatisfactory both in terms of the stability of the institutions and of the extent to which they are rooted in political life. Despite recommendations made by the European Union in a number of demarches and declarations, there has been no noticeable improvement.
>
> In the light of these considerations, the Commission concludes that Slovakia does not fulfil in a satisfying manner the political conditions set out by the European Council in Copenhagen, because of the instability of Slovakia's institutions, their lack of rootedness in political life and the shortcomings in the functioning of its democracy.[30]

The main mechanism of influence of the EU on domestic constitutionalisation was the political conditionality mechanism, which provides benchmarks for assessment of candidates' progress towards EU membership.[31] Political conditionality itself evolved in the course of eastern enlargement, as the second group of candidate states (Bulgaria and Romania) faced more extensive conditions, in particular related to judicial and anti-corruption reforms, taking the form of the Cooperation and Verification Mechanism (CVM) in 2006.[32]

In general, the argument has often been made that EU accession enhanced democratic and rule of law structures in the new Member States. It seems beyond doubt that the EU accession – in terms of a preparatory process with attached conditionality as well as the role of the EU as a 'democratic anchor' in a wider sense – has played a very significant role in the democratic transformation of the former communist countries. Many observers agree that the EU accession of the CEECs has in this involved the strengthening of democratic structures, at least in a formalistic-institutional sense. Thus, Spendzharova and Vachudova have argued that

> [t]he tremendous benefits of EU membership created political incentives to satisfy the EU's extensive membership requirements. These incentives, along with certain characteristics of the pre-accession process to reward progress and publicise shortcomings, create the EU's leverage on domestic reform. EU leverage has helped compel candidates to reform the state and the economy, improving the quality of democracy and the efficiency of state institutions in various ways.[33]

Sadurski has referred to this as a 'democracy dividend' of EU accession, while paying due attention to the diverse impact of EU conditionality on the various candidate countries. As he has argued, '[t]he interaction between the "external" factors of conditionality and the domestic calculus of the costs and benefits of transforming an institution (or adopting a rule) provides the best lens through which to evaluate the impact of "conditionality" on the speed, depth and resilience of adoption and maintenance of particular democratic rules or institutions in the candidate states'.[34] But other observers, while acknowledging the positive results, have also called attention for how EU accession has in some ways compromised democratic practices and the emergence of a constitutional-democratic political culture. As Přibáň argues, the 'conditionality process weakened democratic deliberation but strengthened democratic institutional designs'.[35] In other words,

> [f]rom the perspective of democratic constitutionalism, the Copenhagen criteria and the Commission's progress reports (designed with conditionality in mind) had very mixed results. EU membership was considered such a political priority in all candidate states that the laws were approximated without appropriate democratic deliberation and then justified as a historical necessity. The candidate states did not participate in the creation of the EU *acquis* and their contribution to the Europe agreements and conditionality documents was very limited.[36]

Some argue that the EU accession process has, however, also compromised democratic constitutionalism and the rule of law in the region.[37] It has become increasingly clear that a problematic and uneven institutionalisation of constitutional democracy has occurred. In procedural terms, many have argued that the EU accession process itself has been asymmetric, in that the EU mostly imposed its (rather vague) norms and values, without allowing for democratic interaction between the prospective states and the EU, nor within the domestic political arenas of the candidate countries.[38] Also, the accession process was dominated by the governments of the candidate states, whereas the parliaments were largely sidelined, and public debate was largely avoided, even in the context of the referendum on EU accession.

It has often been argued – and rightfully so – that the conditionality of the EU enlargement process is based on vague criteria, which in practice were often applied in non-homogeneous ways with regard to the various applicant countries.[39] But at the same time, distinct dimensions have been and are present in the EU's approach towards the institutionalisation of constitutional democracy in candidate countries, even if often articulated only in an implicit way.[40] One dimension is that the EU accession process has in some cases clearly contributed to the promotion of a distinct vision and 'template' of constitutionalism. This becomes visible not least through an emphasis on judicial independence, including that of Constitutional Courts. It can therefore be argued that at least partially the European integration process of the new Member States has emphasised the importance of independent, non-political institutions that safeguard the primacy of the constitution and of fundamental rights. One of the concerns of the EU was whether domestic judiciaries would have the capacity to enforce the EU *acquis* at the national level.[41] In this regard, the EU is part of a wider constellation of international actors (notably including the Council of Europe) that promotes a 'certain institutional-design template',[42] in which a rigid separation of politics and law, not least through judicial independence, plays a significant role. The European Commission further endorsed active Constitutional Courts that could play the role of arbiter in the often very conflictive form of parliamentary politics in the region.[43] In the case of Romania, such external EU influence is particularly evident.

In this case, the European Commission noted in its first Opinion on Romania's application for Membership of the European Union in 1997 that 'the Court's ruling that an act is unconstitutional is without effect if Parliament upholds its original decision by a two-thirds majority (Article 145 of the Constitution), which limits considerably the scope of the supervision exercised'.[44] The Commission in general stated: 'The fact that the Constitutional Court's rulings can be overturned by a two-thirds majority of Parliament is a major obstacle to genuine constitutional control in Romania'.[45] In 2012, a statement by the European Commission repeated similar views, this time in the context of a Romanian constitutional crisis in the summer of 2012. As conveyed in a press release on an encounter between the President of the Commission José Manuel Barroso, and the Romanian Prime Minister Victor Ponta,

> President Barroso expressed his serious concerns about recent political events in Romania in relation to the rule of law, the independence of the judiciary and the role of the Constitutional Court. He underlined that the necessary checks and balances in a democratic system must be guaranteed. President Barroso made clear that the Romanian Government must respect the full independence of the judiciary, restore the powers of the Constitutional Court and ensure that its decisions are observed, appoint an Ombudsman enjoying cross-party support, ensure a new open and transparent procedure for appointing a General Prosecutor and Director of the Anti-Corruption Directorate and make integrity a political priority.[46]

In January 2013, the European Commission repeated its views, and among other things stated that 'the place of the Constitution and the Constitutional Court has been restored in line with the Commission's recommendations. It is however essential that the President, the new government and parliament ensure the stability of the constitutional order, and all political parties should work to reduce the polarisation of the political system'.[47] In a recent ten-year review of the Cooperation and Verification Mechanism, the Commission emphasised the key role of the Romanian Court in upholding the independence of the justice system:

> The Constitutional Court has played an important role in further development of the rule of law and the consolidation of an independent justice system. Since the constitutional upheaval of 2012, many decisions of the Constitutional Court have contributed to upholding the independence of justice and have sought to provide solutions linked to the balance of powers and respect for fundamental rights that could not be solved by the justice system alone.[48]

To sum up, as many observers have argued, the process of Europeanisation is ambiguous in that the EU has worked both as a stabilising factor in the consolidation of constitutional democracies and as an undermining factor by hindering the maturation of democratic learning, capacities and behaviour.[49] The European integration process signified a stabilisation of national constitutional democracies, the rule of law and the protection of rights by means of the process of conditionality and the monitoring of harmonisation of the legal orders in CEE.[50] But the EU equally complicated the exercise of new-won democratic capacities by insisting on swift, instrumental and technocratic adoption of the EU *acquis* in the preparation to accession. This process was largely driven by executives and bureaucracies (for instance, in the form of special institutions, such as was the case in the Czech Republic), largely sidelining parliamentary debate about significant legal changes.[51]

The impact of the European Convention on Human Rights (ECHR)

The groundbreaking changes around the year 1989 had as one major effect a (gradual) rapprochement of many states in the East-Central European and Eurasian area towards the Council of Europe (CoE), resulting in a membership of the CoE of 47 Member States, comprising the whole of the continent with the exception of Belarus, and becoming part of the human rights regime around the European Convention on Human Rights (ECHR). The latter is by many observers understood as the most successful human rights system in the world, and the accession of post-communist countries to the ECHR is often understood as a highly significant dimension in their democratising trajectories. The ECHR has clearly become a major legal (or even constitutional) instrument in the context of domestic constitutional law and legislation,[52] and is increasingly perceived as possessing constitutional qualities.[53]As one observer argues regarding the Convention,

> this remarkable instrument of European law started conquering the countries of the old communist regimes in Central and Eastern Europe. Within less than a decade, the ECHR became an undisputed legal instrument in these states too and started influencing constitutional law as well as legislation and the judiciary.[54]

As the main guardian of the Convention within the CoE, the European Court of Human Rights (ECtHR) has increasingly taken up an assertive stance regarding constitutional law, or a 'role of policing national systems',[55] with a particular emphasis on basic fundamental rights protection of individuals, but increasingly also regarding issues of constitutional design, touching on issues of the design of democratic governance.[56] The ECtHR has developed an ambitious approach to both rights protection and democratic consolidation. The latter is particularly part of the agenda of the increasingly active Venice Commission or Commission of Democracy Through Law. Altwicker argues that the two dimensions together – of individual rights as well as constitutional design – render the Convention to function as 'minimum constitutional guarantees [. . .] safeguarding a minimum standard of constitutionality in the Council of Europe (CoE) states'.[57] The status of the ECtHR has in this clearly increased with the adoption of Protocol 11 in 1998. Any European state seeking democratic and international legitimacy has a strong incentive to join the CoE (as indeed verified in the rapid enlargement of the CoE after 1989), while now a condition of CoE membership is the acceptance of the compulsory jurisdiction of the ECtHR.[58]

Within the structure of the Council of Europe, one of the increasingly relevant bodies regarding constitutional reform is the so-called Venice Commission or European Commission for Democracy through Law, originally established to assist the post-communist countries in the early 1990s.[59] The Venice Commission particularly operates through its Opinions on constitutional reform, drafted by its experts and requested by Member States, but also by the Council of Europe itself or other international organisations. Conspicuous cases of such Opinions have in recent years included Hungary, Romania and Poland.[60]

Hungary has been frequently a case of attention for the Venice Commission since 2010, in particularly with regard to its highly contested new Fundamental Law and related cardinal laws.[61] Three of the Commission's opinions regard the Fundamental Law that became the new Hungarian Constitution in 2012. The first Opinion was requested by the Hungarian government and addressed the issue of the potential incorporation of the EU Charter of Fundamental Rights.[62] A second Opinion was requested by the Monitoring Committee of the Parliamentary Assembly of the Council of Europe, due to concerns regarding the Fundamental Law's procedures of adoption, that is, in a rapid and non-transparent fashion by a singular political majority, without the consultation of oppositional forces.[63] After the Fourth Amendment to the Fundamental

Law, a third Opinion was requested by the Secretary General of the Council of Europe,[64] raising matters of constitutional review, the operation of the judiciary, and constitutional checks and balances. A further Opinion on media legislation was adopted in 2015.[65]

The Romanian constitutional crisis in 2012, concerning the formal positions of, and relations between, the President and the Prime Minister, led to the request for an Opinion of the Venice Commission, also as a number of Constitutional Court judges had received threats.[66] The Commission criticised in its Opinion *inter alia* a number of controversial steps undertaken by the government and parliament (including a change in the referendum law) and called for a strengthening of the Constitutional Court's review competences regarding internal acts of the parliament.

A second recent opinion by the Venice Commission on Romania concerned a proposal to reform the Romanian Constitution. The reform attempt started in 2013, and by the end of the year the Ponta government produced a constitutional revision draft, which was submitted to the Romanian Constitutional Court as well as the Venice Commission in February 2014. The Constitutional Court raised several issues of constitutionality in its review of the amendment proposal, finding problems of unconstitutionality with the proposed changes to 26 articles of the 2003 Constitution. In the Opinion of the Venice Commission, it welcomed the reform as a potential response to the 2012 crisis, but also considered that 'only a limited part of the recommendations contained in the 2012 Opinion of the Venice Commission have been translated into amendments to the Constitution'. Furthermore, it regretted that 'following some initial positive steps indicating an option for an open and transparent approach, the revision process was lead in a less inclusive manner and did not entirely benefit of the timeframe available and the potential input of the various circles having shown interest, in the Romanian society, for the revision of the Constitution'.[67]

In the constitutional crisis that emerged in Poland at the end of 2015, the Venice Commission was asked to give an Opinion on the amendments, adopted in December 2015, to the Act on the Constitutional Tribunal.[68] This Act had been adopted on 25 June 2015 by the *Sejm*, had entered into force on 30 August 2015, and allowed the government to adopt five new judges at the very end of the government's mandate. The Polish President Duda (member of the conservative Law and Justice Party, PiS) refused to take the oaths of the elected judges, as according to him democratic rules had been violated. With the electoral victory of PiS in the October 2015 elections, the new government appointed five new judges close to PiS instead, creating great uncertainty about the composition of the Polish Tribunal. The Opinion had been requested by the Minister of Foreign Affairs of Poland, in December 2015. In its Opinion, the Venice Commission warned for the crippling of the Tribunal's effectiveness due to a weakening of checks and balances, human rights and the rule of law due to a malfunctioning Tribunal.

In a follow-up Opinion,[69] requested in July 2016 by the Secretary General of the Council of Europe, the Commission found some improvements to the Act in the light of its March 2016 Opinion, but at the same time stated that the effects of these improvements were limited, leading to ineffectiveness of the Tribunal and limiting its independence. The Commission noted that 'the Parliament and Government continue to challenge the Tribunal's position as the final arbiter of constitutional issues and attribute this authority to themselves'.[70]

Divided sovereignty?

A highly significant matter in the context of membership in the EU is the relation between national constitutional law and EU law. A key debate, and clearly not only in the new Member States, regards the so-called *Solange* story, referring to a series of judgments of the German Constitutional Court, in which it defined the relationship between EU law and the German Basic Law, as well as its own role in guarding this relationship. *Solange* means 'as long as' and refers to the observation by the German Constitutional Court (made in its 1974 *Solange I* ruling) that as long as EU law did not provide a level of protection equivalent to that provided by the German Basic Law, as well as a similar grounding in democratic legitimacy, the Court would continue to review EU law according to the standards of the Basic Law.[71] The *Solange* story is a more widespread attitude among courts in EU Member States (similar positions have for instance been taken up by the Italian Court), defending the qualified supremacy of national constitutional law, but it has to be noted that since its *Maastricht* ruling, the German Court admitted that EU law now provided an equivalent standard of rights protection as that of national constitutional law, and hence review would not be necessary anymore.

The *Solange* story is one with a distinctive meaning for the post-communist societies, in that for those countries that applied for EU membership, a peculiar paradox emerged: on the one hand, the collapse of communism meant the regaining, or in some cases establishing, of national sovereignty, whereas, on the other, the most promising way of safeguarding that sovereignty meant the integration into a supranational, post-sovereign structure, meaning the delegation or 'pooling' of part of the recently regained national sovereignty.

It is in the light of this paradox not surprising that the tendency in Central and Eastern Europe has been largely one of following the *Solange* story, that is, arguing in favour of a conditional supremacy of EU law, but always with the proviso that the essence of the national constitution and its grounding in democratic legitimacy have an ultimate overruling status. Sadurski argues that, in general, the approach of CEE Courts is the 'early' *Solange* attitude of the German Court, that is, the view that review according to national constitutional standards of EU law remains necessary. In this, it can be argued that, even since accession to the EU, and a general amendment of national constitutions to accommodate such membership, a continuous emphasis on national, democratic sovereignty remains evident.[72] The case law of three courts seem particularly important from the perspective of *Solange*, that is, those of the Czech Republic, Hungary and Poland.[73] I will focus here on the Czech and Hungarian cases.

In the Czech case, the *Solange* story become visible in a number of rulings by the Czech Constitutional Court, starting with the *Sugar Quotas III* judgment in 2006, and the subsequent *European Arrest Warrant* judgment of the same year. The Czech Court followed a rather mild and nuanced path immediately after accession. In the *Sugar Quotas III* judgment, it argued that '[a]ccording to the case-law of the European Court of Justice, where a matter is regulated solely by EU law, it takes precedence and cannot be contested by means of referential criteria laid down by national law, not even on the constitutional level'. At the same time, however, the Court stated that EU law cannot be 'in conflict with the principle of the democratic law-based state or that the interpretation of these factors may not lead to a threat to the democratic law-based state.[74] According to various scholars, similar reasonings could be found in later judgments, not least the *Lisbon I* and *II* judgments.[75]

What has surprised, and even shocked, many observers was the decisively more aggressive attitude of the Court in its more recent response to the *Landtová* judgment of the CJEU, in its own *Holubec* judgment (2011), on the issue of Slovak pension schemes. In *Holubec*, it argued that the CJEU's judgment was *ultra vires* in applying EU regulation wrongly.[76] On the one hand, the Czech Court restated its commitment to cooperation between Member States and the EU. On the other hand, however, it argued that the EU could not go against fundamental principles of the Czech Constitution or transgress the competences it was granted by the Czech state.[77] Indeed, Priban concludes that the recent jurisprudence of the Czech Court is 'a persuasive example of a general process in which Constitutional Courts adopt post-sovereign perspectives of a constitutional democratic state while keeping the semantics of constitutional sovereignty as their persisting point of reference and empowerment'.[78]

In the case of Hungary, the *Solange* story is less visible, and the case law of the Hungarian Court has been less outspoken on issues of priority of EU law and the standing of national constitutional norms. In Sadurski's view, in some of the Hungarian Court's judgments, an 'emphasis on national sovereignty is clearly identifiable'.[79] The most relevant judgment is the *Sugar Surplus Duty* case of 2004.[80] In this case, the Hungarian Court argued that Hungarian law, implementing two EU regulations, worked retroactively and hence was unconstitutional, violating the Hungarian Constitution's rule of law clause. The Court, however, treated the case as one purely pertaining to Hungarian law, avoiding any direct judgments on EU law. The Court emphasised the principle of legal certainty, which can be seen as a fundamental tradition in its jurisprudence; a 'favourite mantra'.[81] Critics of the Court's judgment argued that the judgment was of a 'parochial' nature and sensed an anti-European attitude.[82] At least in some readings of the judgment, it becomes evident that the Court articulated its own standing as a guardian of Hungarian constitutional democracy and as an umpire with regard to the validity of European law.

Admittedly, in contrast to the Czech case, more recent judgments – including the *Lisbon* judgment of the Hungarian court – have not strengthened a 'sovereignty-insistence',[83] not even under the new Fundamental Law of 2011, adopted by the Eurosceptic Fidesz government.

Recent constitutional crises

The most striking and problematic developments in recent years concern dramatic and rather systematic turns away from the construction of legal constitutionalism by some new Member States, and deviation from the principles of the rule of law, human rights, and democracy as enshrined in Article 2 (TEU). The most significant challenge to EU law is the outcome of profound political, legal and constitutional changes in Hungary, including the adoption of the new Fundamental Law in 2011.[84] Recently, Poland has developed a not dissimilar trajectory, in terms of deviating from the rule of law and democracy, in an ongoing political assault of the Polish government on the Constitutional Tribunal, and even the ordinary judiciary.

Hungary presents the most problematic case in terms of constitutional developments. The adoption of a new constitution – the Fundamental Law – in 2011 represents a strong break with its post-1989 democratic-constitutional trajectory.[85] Not only was the new constitution adopted in a highly problematic and partisan way, as also observed by the Venice Commission, but the constitution itself has been frequently depicted as 'unconstitutional', for its lack of checks and balances, and undermining of the rule of law, as well as strongly diminished fundamental rights guarantees (in particular after the Fourth Amendment in March 2013[86]).[87]

The Hungarian developments and its moving towards illiberal democracy and even authoritarianism have strongly affected its status as an EU Member State as well as its more general relation to European constitutional and human rights regimes. On various occasions, Hungary has clashed with EU law and the Charter. An early, significant case was that over the Hungarian Media Law, adopted in 2010. In this case, most prominently the freedom and pluralism of the press were at stake, and according to the then Commissioner Kroes, various EU standards were violated, not least Article 11 of the EU Charter.[88] In a more general sense, numerous experts have argued that Hungary violates Article 2 TEU on various grounds – according to Sadurski, Fidesz is 'blatantly and clearly violating certain principles of democracy and human rights protection'[89] –, and hence an Article 7 TEU procedure would be warranted.[90] The European institutions have, however, been slow and non-systematic in confronting Hungary with violations of Article 2 TEU.[91] In general, it can be argued that a political will to trigger Article 7 TEU is lacking in the EU, and that in particular the European People's Party has been reluctant to intervene.[92]

The situation within the EU has now become more complicated, with the emergence of a second country that defies EU standards of constitutionalism and the rule of law, Poland. Since the coming to power of the new government of the PiS in November 2015, EU fundamental democratic values and the rule of law have been put to the test, so much so that the European Commission has started an unprecedented 'rule of law dialogue' in January 2016.[93] The main developments that were deemed worrisome according to the Commission were the laws concerning the Constitutional Tribunal and changes in the law on Public Service

Broadcasters. The Act on the Constitutional Tribunal, adopted by the government in December 2015, changed the composition of the Polish Court as well as its rules of decision-making, making it *de facto* very difficult for the Court to operate (in March 2016, the Act was declared in part unconstitutional by the tribunal itself), while laws regarding the direct appointment of heads of public TV and radio were highly controversial.[94]

In June 2016, the Commission issued an Opinion,[95] in which it argued that it

> is of the opinion that there is a situation of a systemic threat to the rule of law in Poland. The fact that the Constitutional Tribunal is prevented from fully ensuring an effective constitutional review adversely affects its integrity, stability and proper functioning, which is one of the essential safeguards of the rule of law established in Poland.

The Commission subsequently published a Rule of Law Recommendation on 27 July 2016[96] in which it asked the Polish government to 'take appropriate action to address this systemic threat to the rule of law as a matter of urgency', ensuring the effective functioning of the Polish Constitutional Tribunal, within three months (a deadline which expired without action being undertaken). In a complementary Recommendation,[97] the Commission gave Poland two months of extra time, but also raised a number of additional issues regarding the rule of law. In the (unpublished) response of 20 February 2017, the Polish government dismisses a rule of law problem. Various constitutional scholars have argued, however, that the Polish government has ignored the calls by the Commission for a respect of the rule of law, and has rather engaged in 'court packing' with its own candidates, including the Court's President, the production of 'alternative facts', and further action threatening democratic constitutionalism in the country.[98]

Concluding remarks: some lessons for post-Soviet realities[99]

The constitutional experiences of the CEECs are of substantial relevance for the post-Soviet countries, not least regarding those countries that are part of the Eastern Partnership (EaP), some of which recently signed Association Agreements (AAs) with the EU. The EaP countries are expected to benefit from policies and instruments (the European Neighbourhood Policy (ENP), the Association Agreements) of which similar positive outcomes – stability, democracy, and the rule of law – are expected, as was the case with the accession trajectories of the CEECs from 1997 onwards, even if the AAs constitute an alternative to membership. The AAs include the 'standard reference to democratic principles, human rights, and fundamental freedoms', but also contain 'common values that go beyond classical human rights', including references to principles of sovereignty and territorial integrity, and the inviolability of borders and independence.[100]

As analysed by Roman Petrov,[101] the AAs constitute constitutional challenges for the association countries, not least because of challenges regarding the effectiveness and application of the agreements, and the need for a redefinition of the relation between national and EU law (relating to similar tensions with regard to post-sovereignty as faced by the CEECs and old Member States alike, as described above). But beyond the – in themselves complex – questions related to the *acquis*, i.e. the status and implementation of EU law in national systems, it can be argued that objectives related to the common principles and values of the EU face even more intricate obstacles. Despite the important changes that the AAs might bring about, it should be noted that the processes of constitutionalisation, democratisation and rule of law development in post-Soviet countries under the gaze of the European Union are bound to suffer from similar drawbacks as those that have become evident from the discussion of the Central and East European experiences.

This has, first of all, to do with the substance and logic of the EU association policy itself. The *teleologic* view behind both the enlargement and external policies of the EU is in clear need of revision, not least in the light of developments within *both* old and new EU Member States.[102] In part, enlargement and association are informed by the idea of what sociologists call 'modernisation', which separates solid and long-standing modern democratic states from 'less modern', 'traditional', or 'developing' societies. The logic and template of modernisation presupposes that the associated states need to follow the same logic and trajectory in democratisation and institutionalisation of the rule of law as those of so-called established democracies. There is much in this approach that is open to doubt and critique,[103] not least the a-historical and context-insensitive nature of these presuppositions. With regard to constitutions, this points to the fact that while, on the one hand, modern constitutions might to a great extent have become globally transferred 'commodities', on the other, this does not undermine the fact that constitutional orders also always contain 'items that defy commodification', are not (easily) marketable, and prove 'transfer-resistant'.[104]

Secondly, as particularly forcefully argued by Dimitry Kochenov,[105] the conditionality that was part of the eastern enlargement process, which is now also part of AAs with regard to post-Soviet countries, is unlikely to produce the beneficial outcomes that are expected, and hence to realise the 'modernisation' agenda in practice. In particular the domestic dimension related to non-*acquis*, common values, such as democracy, human rights and the rule of law, is unlikely to be significantly enhanced by the AAs. The one-sided legalistic[106] or rule-based[107] approach, informed by the modernist view that was already evident in the enlargement conditionality regarding East-Central Europe, has led to important failures, as not least shown by the contemporary developments in Hungary and Poland. It is even less likely to produce structural results in the EaP countries. EU policy is one-sided in the sense that 'we could be overestimating the importance of rules export thereby dangerously neglecting the value-side of the EU's emergence as an important player in the world of international law and policy'.[108] In addition, as recently argued by Martin Mendelski,[109] the effects of EU-driven constitutional and rule of law reforms are 'context-dependent' and the contexts of countries such as Ukraine or Moldova display highly problematic features, not least related to the type of 'agents' that are supposed to undertake structural reforms. Mendelski describes in this regard 'harmful competition between domestic oligarchs, increasing the politicisation and fragmentation of state structures . . . and a polarized society'.[110] In this, the conditionality process tends to stimulate an instrumental, rather than a normatively driven, engagement with reforms.

In sum, as I have argued elsewhere,[111] one needs to be wary of too optimistic expectations regarding the international transfer of constitutional-legal norms and designs, without structurally supporting (the learning processes of) societal and political forces that are to uphold institutions and without taking distinctive contexts and historical trajectories into due account. In addition, the legal-constitutionalist template that has been prominent in the Central and East European transformation processes suffers from potential defects that might produce *perverse* effects with regard to the institutionalisation of constitutional democracy and the rule of law (as arguably has become visible in Poland, and Hungary in particular).

Notes

1 See, for a sample of the sizeable literature: J. Elster, C. Offe and U.K. Preuss, *Institutional Design in Post-communist Societies: Rebuilding the Ship at Sea*, Cambridge: Cambridge University Press, 1998; W. Sadurski, *Rights Before Courts*, Springer, 2008; W. Sadurski, *Constitutionalism and the Enlargement of Europe*, Oxford: Oxford University Press, 2012; P. Blokker, *New Democracies in Crisis? A Comparative Constitutional Study of the Czech Republic, Hungary, Poland, Romania and Slovakia*, Routledge, 2013; A. Fruhstorfer and M. Hein (eds.), *Constitutional Politics in Central and Eastern Europe*, Springer, 2016; M. Hein, *Verfassungskonflikte zwischen Politik und Recht in Südosteuropa: Bulgarien und Rumänien nach 1989 im Vergleich*, Baden-Baden: Nomos, 2013; L. Morlino and W. Sadurski (eds.), *Democratization and the European Union: Comparing Central and Eastern European Post-communist Countries*, Routledge, 2010; K. Topidi and A.H. Morawa (eds.), *Constitutional Evolution in Central and Eastern Europe: Expansion and Integration in the EU*, Ashgate, 2013; B. Puchalska, *Limits to Democratic Constitutionalism in Central and Eastern Europe*, Ashgate, 2011; G. Skapska, *From 'Civil Society' to 'Europe': A Sociological Study on Constitutionalism After Communism*, Brill, 2011; A. Albi, *EU Enlargement and the Constitutions of Central and Eastern Europe*, Cambridge: Cambridge University Press, 2005; A. Arato, *Civil Society, Constitution, and Legitimacy*, Rowman & Littlefield, 2000; J. Přibáň, *Legal Symbolism: On Law, Time and European Identity*, Ashgate, 2007.

2 K. L. Scheppele, *Counter-Constitutions: Narrating the Nation in Post-Soviet Hungary*, Washington, DC: George Washington University, 2004.

3 B. Bugarič, 'A Crisis of Constitutional Democracy in Post-Communist Europe: "Lands in-Between" Democracy and Authoritarianism', *International Journal of Constitutional Law*, 13(1), 2015, 219–245. This is not at all to suggest that these practices are confined to post-communist Europe, as attested in developments in Western Europe and even the United States. The suggestion is rather that these practices in post-communist countries may have to do with some form of ongoing post-communist transformation.

4 Cf. K. Topidi and A. H. Morawa (eds.), *Constitutional Evolution in Central and Eastern Europe: Expansion and Integration in the EU*, Burlington, VT: Ashgate, 2013.

5 This is, for instance, forcefully argued by Bogdan Iancu regarding the case of Romania, B. Iancu, 'Constitutional Revision in Romania: Post-Accession Pluralism in Action', in: P. Blokker (ed.), *Constitutional Acceleration Within the European Union and Beyond*, Routledge, 2017.

6 *Ibid.*

7 D. Kochenov, *EU Enlargement and the Failure of Conditionality: Pre-accession Conditionality in the Fields of Democracy and the Rule of Law*, Kluwer Law International, 2008.

8 J. Přibáň, *Dissidents of Law: On the 1989 Velvet Revolutions, Legitimations, Fictions of Legality, and Contemporary Version of the Social Contract*, Aldershot: Ashgate; P. Blokker, *New Democracies in Crisis? A Comparative Constitutional Study of the Czech Republic, Hungary, Poland, Romania and Slovakia*, Routledge, 2013.

9 S. A. Arjomand, 'Law, Political Reconstruction and Constitutional Politics', *International Sociology*, 18(1), 2003, 7–32.

10 J. Přibáň and W. Sadurski, 'The Role of Political Rights in the Democratization of Central and Eastern Europe', in: W. Sadurski (ed.), *Political Rights Under Stress in 21st Century Europe*, Oxford: Oxford University Press, 2006, pp. 196–238.

11 S. A. Arjomand, 'Law, Political Reconstruction and Constitutional Politics', *International Sociology*, 18(1), 2003; A. Stone Sweet, 'Constitutions and Judicial Power', in: D. Caramani (ed.), *Comparative Politics*, Oxford: Oxford University Press, 2008, pp. 217–239.

12 B. Bugarič, 'A Crisis of Constitutional Democracy in Post-Communist Europe: "Lands in-between" Democracy and Authoritarianism', *International Journal of Constitutional Law*, 13(1), 2015, 219–245.

13 A. Stone Sweet, 'Constitutions and Judicial Power', in: D. Caramani (ed.), *Comparative Politics*, Oxford: Oxford University Press, 2008, p. 219.

14 Cf. U. Preuss, 'Disconnecting Constitutions from Statehood: Is Global Constitutionalism a Viable Concept?' in: P. Dobner and M. Loughlin (eds.), *The Twilight of Constitutionalism?* Oxford: Oxford University Press, 2010, pp. 23–48.

15 Cf. G. Frankenberg, *Autorität und Integration: Zur Grammatik von Recht und Verfassung*, Frankfurt am Main: Suhrkamp, 2003, p. 48.

16 A. Albi, 'Postmodern Versus Retrospective Sovereignty? Two Different Discourses in the EU and the Candidate Countries?' in: N. Walker (ed.), *Sovereignty in Transition*, Oxford: Hart, 2003, pp. 401–422; A. Albi, *EU Enlargement and the Constitutions of Central and Eastern Europe*, Cambridge: Cambridge University Press, 2005, p. 24.

17 A. Albi, 'Postmodern Versus Retrospective Sovereignty? Two Different Discourses in the EU and the Candidate Countries?' in: N. Walker (ed.), *Sovereignty in Transition*, Oxford: Hart, 2003, p. 401. One example is Poland. The new Polish Constitution was adopted only in 1997, after protracted debate and political strife. In one respect, the 1997 Constitution could be understood as relatively open, that is, in its understanding of (external) sovereignty and its explicit reference to international cooperation (see Albi *op. cit.*, p. 31). But in other respects, a souverainist dimension can be detected also in the Polish document. In particular, the preamble contains indications of perceptions of sovereignty that correspond more to a traditional, centralistic view of sovereignty embedded in a homogeneous Polish nation, referring, for instance, to the 'struggle for *independence* achieved at great sacrifice'. In addition, one could refer to, among others, Article 3 in the main text, 'The Republic of Poland shall be a *unitary* State', Article 4(1), 'Supreme power in the Republic of Poland shall be vested in the Nation', and Article 5 that starts with 'The Republic of Poland shall safeguard the *independence* and integrity of its territory. . . ' (emphasis added).

18 A. Albi, 'Postmodern Versus Retrospective Sovereignty? Two Different Discourses in the EU and the Candidate Countries?' in: N. Walker (ed.), *Sovereignty in Transition*, Oxford: Hart, 2003, p. 419.
19 J. Přibáň, *Sovereignty in Post-sovereign Society: A Systems Theory of European Constitutionalism*, Routledge, 2015, p. 27.
20 W. Sadurski, *Rights Before Courts: A Study of Constitutional Courts in Postcommunist States of Central and Eastern Europe*, Springer, 2008, pp. 80–81.
21 J. Kurczewksi and B. Sullivan, 'The Bill of Rights and the Emerging Democracies', *Law and Contemporary Problems*, 65(2), 2002, 254–255.
22 W. Sadurski, *Rights Before Courts: A Study of Constitutional Courts in Postcommunist States of Central and Eastern Europe*, Springer, 2008, p. 5.
23 B. Bugarič and T. Ginsburg, 'The Assault on Postcommunist Courts', *Journal of Democracy*, 27(3), 2016, 69–82.
24 According to Cristina Parau, transnational influence was already important in the early phases of post-communist transformation, C. Parau, 'Explaining Governance of the Judiciary in Central and Eastern Europe: External Incentives, Transnational Elites and Parliamentary Inaction', *Europe-Asia Studies*, 67(3), 2015, 409–442. Bogdan Iancu, in contrast, argues that such influence was however fragmentary, B. Iancu, 'Constitutional Revision in Romania: Post-Accession Pluralism in Action', in: P. Blokker (ed.), *Constitutional Acceleration Within the European Union and Beyond*, Routledge, 2017. Wojciech Sadurski argues that the influence of the Europe Agreements of the early 1990s was focussed on the market economy and stability and international security, and less prominently on issues of democracy and human rights, W. Sadurski, *Constitutionalism and the Enlargement of Europe*, Oxford: Oxford University Press, 2012, p. 56.
25 Cf. C. Dallara, *Democracy and Judicial Reforms in South-East Europe: Between the EU and the Legacies of the Past*, Springer, 2014.
26 Themselves more prominent in the EU process, not least through the European Charter of Fundamental Rights, see W. Sadurski, *Constitutionalism and the Enlargement of Europe*, Oxford: Oxford University Press, 2012.
27 Reference is made here to Article 6 of the pre-Lisbon TEU. The Treaty of Lisbon partly solved the discrepancy between pre-accession conditions and membership obligations through the introduction of a reference to 'rights of persons belonging to minorities' in Article 2 TEU. Cf. W. Sadurski, *Constitutionalism and the Enlargement of Europe*, Oxford: Oxford University Press, 2012, p. 58; C. Hillion, 'Enlargement of the European Union – The Discrepancy Between Membership Obligations and Accession Conditions as Regards the Protection of Minorities', *Fordham International Law Journal*, 27(2), 2003, 715–740.
28 Kochenov argues that the actual application of these criteria, in particular in the Commission's Annual Opinions, proved to be non-transparent and inconsistent, cf. D. Kochenov, *EU Enlargement and the Failure of Conditionality: Pre-accession Conditionality in the Fields of Democracy and the Rule of Law*, Kluwer Law International, 2012.
29 W. Sadurski, *Constitutionalism and the Enlargement of Europe*, Oxford: Oxford University Press, 2012, p. 58.
30 European Commission, *Agenda 2000 – Commission Opinion on Slovakia's Application for Membership of the European Union*, Brussels: European Commission, 1997, p. 130.
31 C. Dallara, *Democracy and Judicial Reforms in South-East Europe: Between the EU and the Legacies of the Past*, Springer, 2014.
32 Further details of the benchmarks involved and the progress reports issued can be found here: https://ec.europa.eu/info/effective-justice/rule-law/assistance-bulgaria-and-romania-under-cvm/cooperation-and-verification-mechanism-bulgaria-and-romania_en#criteria-for-assessing-progress.

33 A.B. Spendzharova and M.A. Vachudova, 'Catching up? Consolidating Liberal Democracy in Bulgaria and Romania After EU Accession', *West European Politics*, 35(1), 2012, 39–58.
34 W. Sadurski, 'Accession's Democracy Dividend: The Impact of the EU Enlargement upon Democracy in the New Member States of Central and Eastern Europe', *European Law Journal*, 10(4), 2004, 371–401.
35 J. Přibáň, 'Legal Cultures in Transition: A Systems-Theory Approach', in: A. Febbrajo and W. Sadurski (eds.), *Central and Eastern Europe After Transition: Towards a New Socio-Legal Semantics*, Ashgate, 2010, p. 21.
36 *Ibid.*
37 Cf. M. Mendelski, 'Europeanization and the Rule of Law: Towards a Pathological Turn', *Southeastern Europe*, 40(3), 2016, 346–384.
38 B. Iancu, 'Post-Accession Constitutionalism with a Human Face: Judicial Reform and Lustration in Romania', *European Constitutional Law Review*, 6(1), 2010, 28–58.
39 D. Kochenov, *EU Enlargement and the Failure of Conditionality: Pre-accession Conditionality in the Fields of Democracy and the Rule of Law*, Kluwer Law International, 2008.
40 Cf. K. Haukenes and A. Freyberg-Inan, 'Enforcing Consensus? The Hidden Bias in EU Democracy Promotion in Central and Eastern Europe', *Democratization*, 20(7), 2013, 1268–1296.
41 C. Parau, 'Explaining Judiciary Governance in Central and Eastern Europe: External Incentives, Transnational Elites and Parliament Inaction', *Europe-Asia Studies*, 67(3), 2013, 409–442.
42 C. Parau, 'The Dormancy of Parliaments: The Invisible Cause of Judiciary Empowerment in Central and Eastern Europe', *Representation – The Journal of Representative Democracy*, 49(3), 2013, 267–280.
43 K. Haukenes and A. Freyberg-Inan, 'Enforcing Consensus? The Hidden Bias in EU Democracy Promotion in Central and Eastern Europe', *Democratization*, 20(7), 2013, 1268–1296.
44 European Commission, *Agenda 2000 – Commission Opinion on Romania's Application for Membership of the European Union*, Brussels, 1997, p. 14.
45 European Commission, *Agenda 2000 – Commission Opinion on Romania's Application for Membership of the European Union*, Brussels, 1997, p. 15.
46 European Commission 'Meeting Between European Commission President, José Manuel Barroso, and Romanian Prime Minister, Victor Ponta', available at: http://europa.eu/rapid/press-release_MEMO-12-558_en.htm; European Commission Report from the Commission to the European Parliament and the Council on Progress in Romania under the Cooperation and Verification Mechanism, Brussels, 2012, emphasis added.
47 European Commission Report from the Commission to the European Parliament and the Council on Progress in Romania under the Cooperation and Verification Mechanism, Brussels, 2013, p. 3; emphasis added.
48 Report from the Commission to the European Parliament and the Council, *On Progress in Romania Under the Co-operation and Verification Mechanism*, COM(2017) 44 final, p. 5.
49 M. Mendelski, 'Europeanization and the Rule of Law: Towards a Pathological Turn', *Southeastern Europe*, 40(3), 2016, 346–384.
50 W. Sadurski, 'Accession's Democracy Dividend: The Impact of the EU Enlargement upon Democracy on the New Member States of Central and Eastern Europe', *European Law Journal*, 10(4), 2004, 371–401.
51 Cf. J. Přibáň, 'From "Which Rule of Law?" to "The Rule of Which Law?" Post-Communist Experiences of European Legal Integration', *Hague Journal on the Rule of Law*, 1(2), 2009, 337–358.

52 C. Grabenwarter, 'The European Convention on Human Rights: Inherent Constitutional Tendencies and the Role of the European Court of Human Rights', in: A. von Bogdandy and P. Sonnevend (eds.), *Constitutional Crisis in the European Constitutional Area*, Nomos, 2015, pp. 257–274; I. Motoc and I. Ziemele (eds.), *The Impact of the ECHR on Democratic Change in Central and Eastern Europe: Judicial Perspectives*, Cambridge: Cambridge University Press, 2016.

53 Cf. W. Sadurski, *Constitutionalism and the Enlargement of Europe*, Oxford: Oxford University Press, 2012; T. Altwicker, 'Convention Rights as Minimum Constitutional Guarantees? The Conflict Between Domestic Constitutional Law and the European Convention on Human Rights', in: A. von Bogdandy and P. Sonnevend (eds.), *Constitutional Crisis in the European Constitutional Area*, Nomos, 2015, pp. 344–363.

54 C. Grabenwarter, 'The European Convention on Human Rights: Inherent Constitutional Tendencies and the Role of the European Court of Human Rights', in: A. von Bogdandy and P. Sonnevend (eds.), *Constitutional Crisis in the European Constitutional Area*, Nomos, 2015, pp. 257–274.

55 W. Sadurski, *Constitutionalism and the Enlargement of Europe*, Oxford: Oxford University Press, 2012, pp. 3–4.

56 T. Altwicker, 'Convention Rights as Minimum Constitutional Guarantees? The Conflict Between Domestic Constitutional Law and the European Convention on Human Rights', in: A. von Bogdandy and P. Sonnevend (eds.), *Constitutional Crisis in the European Constitutional Area*, Nomos, 2015, pp. 344–363.

57 *Ibid.*, p. 333.

58 W. Sadurski, *Constitutionalism and the Enlargement of Europe*, Oxford: Oxford University Press, 2012, p. 5.

59 P. Craig, 'Transnational Constitution-Making: The Contribution of the Venice Commission on Law and Democracy', *UCI Journal of International, Transnational and Comparative Law*, 57(2), 2017, 57–86; J. Nergelius, 'The Role of the Venice Commission in Maintaining the Rule of Law', in: A. von Bogdandy and P. Sonnevend (eds.), *Constitutional Crisis in the European Constitutional Area*, Nomos, 2015, pp. 291–310; for a critical view, see M. De Visser, 'A Critical Assessment of the Role of the Venice Commission in Processes of Domestic Constitutional Reform', *American Journal of Comparative Law*, 63(4), 2015, 963–1008.

60 Opinions of the Venice Commission on constitutional reform can be found here: www.venice.coe.int/webforms/documents/?topic=4&year=all.

61 J. Nergelius, 'The Role of the Venice Commission in Maintaining the Rule of Law', in: A. von Bogdandy and P. Sonnevend (eds.), *Constitutional Crisis in the European Constitutional Area*, Nomos, 2015, pp. 291–310.

62 European Commission for Democracy Through Law (Venice Commission), Opinion on Three Legal Questions arising in the Process of Drafting of the New Constitution of Hungary, no. 614/2011, 28 March 2011.

63 European Commission for Democracy Through Law (Venice Commission), *Opinion on the New Constitution of Hungary*, no. 621/2011, 20 June 2011.

64 European Commission for Democracy Through Law (Venice Commission), *Opinion on the Fourth Amendment of the Basic Law of Hungary*, no. 720/2013, 14 June, 2013.

65 European Commission for Democracy Through Law (Venice Commission), *Opinion on Media Legislation (ACT CLXXXV on Media Services and on the Mass Media, Act CIV on the Freedom of the Press, and the Legislation on Taxation of Advertisement Revenues of Mass Media) of Hungary*, no. 798/2015, 22 June 2015.

66 P. Blokker, 'Constitution-making in Romania: From Reiterative Crises to Constitutional Moment?', *Romanian Journal of Comparative Law*, 3(2), 2013,

187–204; J. Nergelius, 'The Role of the Venice Commission in Maintaining the Rule of Law', in: A. von Bogdandy and P. Sonnevend (eds.), *Constitutional Crisis in the European Constitutional Area*, Nomos, 2015, pp. 291–310. European Commission for Democracy Through Law (Venice Commission), *Opinion on the Compatibility with Constitutional Principles and the Rule of Law of Actions Taken by the Government and the Parliament of Romania in respect of Other State Institutions and on the Government Emergency Ordinance on Amendment to the Law N° 47/1992 Regarding the Organisation and Functioning of the Constitutional Court and on the Government Emergency Ordinance on Amending and Completing the Law N° 3/2000 Regarding the Organisation of a Referendum of Romania*, no. 685/2012, 17 December 2012.

67 European Commission for Democracy Through Law (Venice Commission), *Opinion on the Draft Law on the Review of the Constitution of Romania*, no. 731/2013, 24 March 2014.

68 European Commission for Democracy Through Law (Venice Commission), *Opinion on the Act on the Constitutional Tribunal*, no. 833/2015, 11 March 2016.

69 European Commission for Democracy Through Law (Venice Commission), *Opinion on the Act on the Constitutional Tribunal*, no. 860/2016, 14 October 2016.

70 The Opinion also mentions that '[i]n a letter to the Commission, these judges [the judges appointed by the PiS government, pb] stated that they do not trust the Venice Commission and that they believe that the meeting would serve as a legitimisation of another unjustified, biased and negative opinion against Poland'.

71 W. Sadurski, *Constitutionalism and the Enlargement of Europe*, Oxford: Oxford University Press, 2012, p. 99.

72 J. Přibáň, *Sovereignty in Post-Sovereign Society: A Systems Theory of European Constitutionalism*, Routledge, 2015; J. Přibáň, 'The Semantics of Constitutional Sovereignty in Post-Sovereign "New" Europe: A Case Study of the Czech Constitutional Court's Jurisprudence', *International Journal of Constitutional Law*, 13(1), 2015, 180–199.

73 W. Sadurski, *Constitutionalism and the Enlargement of Europe*, Oxford: Oxford University Press, 2012.

74 2006/03/08 – Pl. ÚS 50/04: Sugar Quotas III.

75 J. Přibáň, *Sovereignty in Post-sovereign Society: A Systems Theory of European Constitutionalism*, Routledge, 2015; W. Sadurski, *Constitutionalism and the Enlargement of Europe*, Oxford: Oxford University Press, 2012.

76 J. Přibáň, *Sovereignty in Post-Sovereign Society: A Systems Theory of European Constitutionalism*, Routledge: 2015, 196; J. Zemánek, 'An "Entirely-Specific" Situation or a Routine Limitation of the National Autonomy? Slovak Pensions XVII of the Czech Constitutional Court', in: R. Arnold (ed.), *Limitations of National Sovereignty Through European Integration*, Springer, 2016, pp. 125–139.

77 *Ibid.*

78 J. Přibáň, *Sovereignty in Post-Sovereign Society: A Systems Theory of European Constitutionalism*, Routledge, 2015, p. 199.

79 W. Sadurski, *Constitutionalism and the Enlargement of Europe*, Oxford: Oxford University Press, 2012, p. 120.

80 Decision 17/2004 V. 25) AB (25 May 2004). Cf. A. Bragyova, 'No New(s), Good News? The Fundamental Law and the Europan Law', in: G.A. Tóth (ed.), *Constitution for a Disunited Nation: on Hungary's 2011 Fundamental Law*, Central European University Press, 2011, pp. 335–358.

81 W. Sadurski, *Constitutionalism and the Enlargement of Europe*, Oxford: Oxford University Press, 2012, pp. 115–116.

82 A. Bragyova, 'No New(s), Good News? The Fundamental Law and the Europan Law', in: G.A. Tóth (ed.), *Constitution for a Disunited Nation: on Hungary's 2011 Fundamental Law*, Central European University Press, 2011 pp. 335–358.

83 Cf. P. Kovacs, 'The Transfer of Sovereignty in the Case Law of the Hungarian Constitutional Court', in: R. Arnold (ed.), *Limitations of National Sovereignty Through European Integration*, Springer, 2016, pp. 109–124.
84 G. A. Tóth (ed.), *Constitution for a Disunited Nation: On Hungary's 2011 Fundamental Law*, Central European University Press, 2011; A. von Bogdandy and P. Sonnevend (eds.), *Constitutional Crisis in the European Constitutional Area: Theory, Law and Politics in Hungary and Romania*, Nomos, 2015; C. Closa and D. Kochenov (eds.), *Reinforcing Rule of Law Oversight in the European Union*, Cambridge: Cambridge University Press, 2016.
85 K. Kovács and G.A. Tóth, 'Hungary's Constitutional Transformation', *European Constitutional Law Review*, 7(2), 2016, 183–203.
86 As argued by Human Rights Watch in its review of the Hungarian situation, in particular after the Fourth Amendment, the new constitution of the Fidesz government is problematic 'in ways that weaken legal checks on its authority, interfere with media freedom, and otherwise undermine human rights protection in the country', see Human Rights Watch, *Wrong Direction on Rights: Assessing the Impact of Hungary's New Constitution and Law*, 2013, available at: www.hrw.org/sites/default/files/reports/hungary0513_ForUpload.pdf. See also the Opinion of the European Commission for Democracy Through Law (Venice Commission), *Opinion on the New Constitution of Hungary*, Adopted by the Venice Commission at its 87th Plenary Session (Venice, 17–18 June 2011), available at: www.venice.coe.int/webforms/documents/CDL-AD(2011)016-E.aspx.
87 B. Bugaric, 'Protecting Democracy and the Rule of Law in the European Union: The Hungarian Challenge', 2014, LEQS Paper No. 79/2014, p. 8.
88 F. Hoffmeister, 'Enforcing the EU Charter of Fundamental Rights in Member States: How Far Are Rome, Budapest and Bucharest from Brussels?' in: A. von Bogdandy and P. Sonnevend (eds.), *Constitutional Crisis in the European Constitutional Area*, Nomos, 2015, pp. 204–247.
89 Available at: http://verfassungsblog.de/rescue-package-fundamental-rights-comments-wojciech-sadurski/
90 B. Bugaric, 'Protecting Democracy and The rule of Law in the European Union: The Hungarian Challenge', 2014, LEQS Paper No. 79/2014, p. 15.
91 Cf. F. Hoffmeister, 'Enforcing the EU Charter of Fundamental Rights in Member States: How Far Are Rome, Budapest and Bucharest from Brussels?', in: A. von Bogdandy and P. Sonnevend (eds.), *Constitutional Crisis in the European Constitutional Area*, Nomos, 2015, pp. 204–247.
92 B. Bugaric, 'Protecting Democracy Inside the EU: On Article 7 TEU and the Hungarian Turn to Authoritarianism', in: C. Closa and D. Kochenov (eds.), *Reinforcing Rule of Law Oversight in the European Union*, Cambridge: Cambridge University Press, 2016, pp. 83–84.
93 I. P. Karolewski and R. Benedikter, 'Poland's Conservative Turn and the Role of the European Union', *European Political Science*, 2016, pp. 1–20.
94 I. P. Karolewski and R. Benedikter, 'Poland's Conservative Turn and the Role of the European Union', *European Political Science*, 2016, pp. 1–20.
95 Commission Opinion of 1 June 2016 regarding the Rule of Law in Poland, available at: http://eulawanalysis.blogspot.it/2016/08/commission-opinion-of-1-june-2016.html
96 2016/1374, of 27 July 2016, regarding the rule of law in Poland.
97 Commission Recommendation of 21 December 2016, regarding the rule of law in Poland.
98 K. Scheppele and L. Pech, 'Poland and the European Commission, Part III: Requiem for the Rule of Law', *VerfBlog*, 3 March 2017, available at: http://verfassungsblog.de/poland-and-the-european-commission-part-iii-requiem-for-the-rule-of-law/, DOI: http://dx.doi.org/10.17176/20170303-131734

99 The focus here is on the evolving relations with the EU.
100 R. Petrov, 'Implementation of Association Agreements Between the EU and Ukraine, Moldova, and Georgia: Legal and Constitutional Challenges', in: T. Kerikmae and A. Chochia (eds.), *Political and Legal Perspectives of the EU Eastern Partnership Policy*, Springer, 2016, pp. 153–166.
101 *Ibid.*
102 Cf. D. Kochenov, 'The Issue of Values', in: R. Petrov and P. Van Elsuwege (eds.), *Legislative Approximation and Application of EU Law in the Eastern Neighbourhood of the European Union: Towards a Common Regulatory Space?* Routledge, 2014, pp. 46–62.
103 See P. Blokker, 'Post-communist Modernization, Transition Studies, and Diversity in Europe', *European Journal of Social Theory*, 8(4), 2005, 503–525.
104 G. Frankenberg, 'Constitutions as Commodities: Notes on a Theory of Transfer', in: G. Frankenberg (ed.), *Order from Transfer*, Edward Elgar Publishing, 2013, pp. 1–28.
105 D. Kochenov, 'The Issue of Values', in: R. Petrov and P. Van Elsuwege (eds.), *Legislative Approximation and Application of EU Law in the Eastern Neighbourhood of the European Union: Towards a Common Regulatory Space?* Routledge, 2014, pp. 46–62.
106 P. Blokker, 'EU Democratic Oversight and Domestic Deviation from the Rule of Law: Sociological Reflections', in: C. Closa and D. Kochenov (eds.), *Reinforcing the Rule of Law Oversight in the European Union*, Cambridge: Cambridge University Press, 2016, pp. 249–269.
107 D. Kochenov, 'The Issue of Values', in: R. Petrov and P. Van Elsuwege (eds.), *Legislative Approximation and Application of EU Law in the Eastern Neighbourhood of the European Union: Towards a Common Regulatory Space?* Routledge, 2014, pp. 46–62.
108 *Ibid.*, p. 46.
109 M. Mendelski, 'The EU's Rule of Law Promotion in Post-Soviet Europe: What Explains the Divergence Between Baltic States and EaP Countries?', *Eastern Journal of European Studies*, 7(2), 2016, 111–144.
110 *Ibid.*, p. 113.
111 P. Blokker, *New Democracies in Crisis? A Comparative Constitutional Study of the Czech Republic, Hungary, Poland, Romania and Slovakia*, Routledge, 2013; P. Blokker, 'EU Democratic Oversight and Domestic Deviation from the Rule of Law: Sociological Reflections', in: C. Closa and D. Kochenov (eds.), *Reinforcing the Rule of Law Oversight in the European Union*, Cambridge: Cambridge University Press, 2016, pp. 249–269.

2 Protecting the rule of law in post-Soviet states

The relevance of European and Eurasian integration

Olga Burlyuk and Vera Axyonova

Introduction

The year 2016 marked a quarter of a century since the fall of the Soviet Union. The independent states that emerged have varied progress to declare, including on the rule of law protection track. This chapter examines rule of law developments in twelve post-Soviet states (excluding the Baltics) with the aim of revealing the role of European and Eurasian integration processes therein. In what follows, we identify major *regional tendencies* in rule of law protection and analyse *paradigmatic effects* of respective regional integration processes.

For the purposes of this chapter, the rule of law is understood as a coherent directing idea that law should serve its social goals by coordinating social relations, minimising arbitrariness and providing order in society.[1] According to a conceptual baseline on the rule of law, relevant aspects include the separation of power, judicial independence and a transparent legislative process.[2] Adopting such a broad definition of the rule of law at the start grants conceptual and analytical openness necessary for examining the rule of law as an element of the countries' post-Soviet domestic development and processes of European and Eurasian integration.

The analysis reveals that the influence of European and Eurasian integration processes on the development of the rule of law protection mechanisms in post-Soviet states is principally different. With regard to the objectives of influence, the European Union (EU) draws on the broader understanding of the concept used by the Council of Europe (CoE) and seeks to promote this understanding in the region. The Eurasian Economic Union (EAEU), on the contrary, does not see the promotion of the rule of law among its priorities, even *vis-à-vis* its Member States that generally follow the rule *by* law paradigm (reducing law to the legal texts and applying those formalistically and instrumentally to assert power), and moreover serves to safeguard authoritarianism.[3]

With regard to mechanisms of influence, the EU does not offer membership prospects to any of the twelve post-Soviet states. The Association Agreements (AAs) between the EU and the three post-Soviet states aspiring to EU integration (Ukraine, Georgia and Moldova) offer a platform for the EU to advance its normative objectives, including respect for the rule of law. In all other cases, the

EU lacks the legal basis and political leverage to do so. Either way, post-Soviet states find themselves on the receiving end of the EU's normative agenda. The EAEU, in turn, draws on previous post-Soviet integration efforts, and all members are active co-shapers of its normative foundations. Uploading their own norms to the EAEU level gives additional legitimation to what has been previously established domestically and creates altogether different dynamics of norm transfer. Overall, while post-Soviet states all share Soviet legacies and struggle with the introduction and consolidation of the rule of law, it is increasingly difficult to speak of them as a coherent group: the diverse post-Soviet paths of each country are defined by peculiar domestic political and constitutional developments, as well as the relatively different relevance and weight of European and Eurasian integration processes.

A long path to the rule of law protection covered to date and remaining systemic deficiencies

After 70 years of Soviet rule, which for most post-Soviet states were preceded by centuries of colonization by tsarist Russia, states that emerged from the collapse of the USSR entered the era of independence with remnants of the Soviet legal system. The impact of communism on legal systems and cultures of post-Soviet countries is captured sharply by Michael Newcity:

> To the degree that a modern legal consciousness akin to the Western legal tradition might ever have developed [in these states], those prospects were dramatically short-circuited by the Bolshevik Revolution.[4]

Under the Soviet regime, the principles of Western democratic law were not abused or put in abeyance in practice; they were fundamentally challenged normatively and theoretically.[5] The official legal doctrine was directed against the bourgeois 'legalistic worldview'. The Soviet positivist legal doctrine transformed law into a superstructure of the state and judiciary, an attachment of the party system. And while the ends of Soviet communism were different from those of tsarist Russia, attitudes to an absolutist state and the coerciveness of law were rather similar.[6]

The Soviet legal heritage complicated the introduction of rule of law protection mechanisms in post-Soviet states. Nevertheless, the far-reaching changes implemented in the last twenty-five years must be acknowledged. The post-Soviet countries not only drafted an astonishing volume of laws, but also established a great number of new legal and judicial institutions, adopted a bulk of material and procedural codes regulating previously non-existent matters and designed constitutional frameworks from scratch in the absence of recent or historical experiences with constitutionalism.[7] Significantly, post-Soviet states declared their formal commitment to the rule of law through their newly adopted constitutions and numerous international treaties. With or without an explicit reference to 'the rule of law', all of the respective constitutions contain clauses that pertain to the rule of law's conceptual baseline. Table 2.1 provides an overview of rule of law provisions in the constitutions of post-Soviet states, and Annex 1 at the end of this volume contains respective excerpts from the constitutions.

Accordingly, all twelve constitutions proclaim the supremacy of the constitution, six of them formally pledge allegiance to the rule *of* law principle and three to the rule *by* law, or the rule of the written law (Azerbaijan, Belarus and Russia). Two striking observations are due here: first, the list of 'rule of law' countries includes Georgia, Moldova and Ukraine, which traditionally have a better rule of law protection track-record; second, Belarus declares both the rule *of* law and the rule *by* law principles (see *infra*). Moreover, despite the inclusion of necessary provisions, post-Soviet constitutions differ considerably in stipulating the mechanisms necessary to safeguard the rule of law. Thus, while all constitutions without exception maintain the importance of an independent judiciary, some of them remain vague or ambiguous on the procedures that shall ensure this very independence, including the appointment, terms in office and dismissal of judges (e.g. constitution of Turkmenistan), and yet others basically grant major control powers over the judiciary to the President as head of the executive branch (e.g. constitutions of Armenia and Uzbekistan). All post-Soviet constitutions provide for a possibility of certain restrictions on human rights and fundamental freedoms in the case of martial law or a state of emergency, thus openly allowing concessions with respect to one of the key elements of the rule of law.

At the same time, however precise and conforming to the basic principles of the rule of law they might be, constitutional provisions do not guarantee effective application of laws in the post-Soviet countries. In fact, when it comes to actual practices, post-Soviet states score poorly on rule of law compliance regardless of how the evaluation scale is drawn. Table 2.2 below offers an overview of the respective countries' performance on major global indexes on the rule of law, democracy, corruption and governance. It also highlights the top and the bottom of the class in each category.

The usual package of rule of law deficiencies in these states includes problems with the functioning of the system of justice and concerns about the independence, impartiality, effectiveness and accountability of judiciary and law enforcement institutions; the functioning of administrative and regulatory institutions at national and local levels; deficiencies in material and procedural law, legislative gaps and the lack of consistency and coherence within and between laws; and the problems with the protection of human rights and fundamental freedoms. Either laws and institutions are lacking, or they exist but are of poor quality, or they are of sufficient quality but are not applied or enforced properly. Notably, those states that perform the worst generally score low on every index and every dimension of an index in Table 2. For example, Uzbekistan and Turkmenistan have very bad scores across the board. In turn, those states that perform comparatively well (for example, Georgia, Moldova and Ukraine) often score better on some indexes or dimensions of an index and worse on others. Like this, Ukraine scores better than

Table 2.1 Rule of law provisions in the constitutions of post-Soviet states

Country	*Rule of law provision with direct mentioning of the term*	*Supremacy of the constitution*	*Separation of power*	*Independence of the judiciary*	*Respect for fundamental rights*	*Equal rights/ Equality before the law*
Armenia	x	x	x	x	x	x
Azerbaijan		x	x	x	x	x
Belarus	x	x	x	x	x	x
Georgia	x	x	x	x	x	x
Kazakhstan		x	x	x	x	x
Kyrgyzstan	x	x	x	x	x	x
Moldova	x	x	x	x	x	x
Russia		x	x	x	x	x
Tajikistan		x	x	x	x	x
Turkmenistan		x	x	x	x	x
Ukraine	x	x	x	x	x	x
Uzbekistan		x	x	x	x	x

Source: Compiled by the authors (see also annex 1 and 2 to this volume). For this table, the latest versions of post-Soviet constitutions were reviewed, with all amendments currently in force. The authors analysed both English and Russian translations of respective constitutions. Varying combinations of keywords for each category listed have been used to identify the presence of the above rule of law elements in the examined documents.

Table 2.2 Countries' performance on global rule of law and governance indexes

Country	*WJP RoL Index 2016*[1] *(0 – lowest, 1 – highest)*	*FH Nations in Transit 2016*[2] *(1 – best, 7 – worst)*	*TI Corruption Perception Index 2015*[3] *(0 – highly corrupt, 100 – very clean)*	*Transformation Index BTI – The Status Index 2016*[4] *(# in the world, 1 – highly advanced democracy)*	*Worldwide Governance Indicators – Rule of Law 2015*[5] *(-2.5 – lowest, +2.5 – highest)*
Armenia	–	5.36	**35**	64	–0.34
Azerbaijan	–	**6.86**	29	95	–0.60
Belarus	**0.54**	6.64	32	99	–0.79
Georgia	**0.65**	**4.61**	**52**	**45**	**0.30**
Kazakhstan	0.50	6.61	28	85	–0.37
Kyrgyzstan	0.47	5.89	28	60	**–1.00**
Moldova	0.49	4.89	33	**47**	–0.40
Russia	**0.45**	6.50	29	81	–0.72
Tajikistan	–	6.54	26	109	**–1.01**
Turkmenistan	–	**6.93**	**18**	**116**	**–1.39**
Ukraine	0.49	**4.68**	27	**52**	–0.80
Uzbekistan	**0.45**	**6.93**	**19**	**115**	**–1.07**

Source: Compiled by the authors on the basis of data from respective indexes.

[1]See http://data.worldjusticeproject.org/
[2]See https://freedomhouse.org/report/nations-transit/nations-transit-2016
[3]See www.transparency.org/cpi2015#map-container
[4]See www.bti-project.org/en/atlas/
[5]See http://info.worldbank.org/governance/wgi/#reports

Moldova on the Freedom House Nations in Transit Index, and Moldova scores better than Ukraine on the Transparency International Corruption Perceptions Index and BTI Transformation Index. And while they have identical scores on the World Justice Project Rule of Law Index (WJP RoL Index), Ukraine performs better on the Fundamental Rights dimension, and Moldova on Order and Security.[8] Georgia currently performs best among post-Soviet states, and Russia sank into the club of the worst, with the same WJP RoL Index score as Uzbekistan (and other scores similar to those of Belarus and Central Asian states). Paradoxically, Belarus scores remarkably well on the WJP RoL Index (second after Georgia), its dramatic scores on all others indexes notwithstanding. The high score on WJP RoL Index is due to indicators of Order and Security, Criminal and Civil Justice – and, despite its poor results on Constraints on Government Powers, Open Government and Fundamental Rights.[9] The aggregate scores often give a more optimistic impression than the real picture in specific sectors.

Moreover, while Table 2 gives a *snapshot* of the situation as of 2015–2016, we also engaged in a *longitudinal* analysis beyond Table 2, comparing countries' results on respective indexes across time. It demonstrated that 'the worst-performing' states in the group (Belarus, Turkmenistan, Uzbekistan) are steadily the worst, while the 'best-performing' states (Georgia, Moldova, Ukraine) swing as pendulums between better and worse, and occasionally switch roles of 'the best pupil in the class'. Georgia is in the lead at present, but that can change quickly again. This stability or swinging could be linked to the effects of European and Eurasian integration processes at different points in time (see *infra*). Importantly, Russia's standing in various indexes has been worsening, reflecting the consolidation of Putin's regime.

Overall, due to resilient authoritarian power structures and corruption, post-Soviet states have problems not only with rule *of* law compliance, but even with rule *by* law compliance. Two paradoxes coined by Olga Burlyuk elsewhere capture systemic shortcomings in post-Soviet states and can be labelled as the 'façade arrangement paradox' and 'Brownian motion paradox'.[10] The *façade arrangement paradox* implies that, despite the existence of rule of law clauses at the fundamental constitutional level, the implementation of these clauses fails drastically in reality. Although some post-Soviet states have generally more liberal legal frameworks than others and their rule of law protection mechanisms satisfy a higher standard, as illustrated in Table 2, the difference between what is proclaimed and what is implemented in reality is evident in all post-Soviet states. The *Brownian motion paradox*, in turn, refers to an empirical observation that, in the field of rule of law reform, there is a lot of movement with doubtful progress or change to declare. This paradox is more relevant for those post-Soviet states that experience frequent changes of ruling elites, political instability and subsequent reform efforts (e.g. Ukraine, Georgia, Moldova) and is less or not at all relevant for those states that have consolidated authoritarian regimes (e.g. Azerbaijan, Belarus, Kazakhstan, Russia, Turkmenistan, Uzbekistan). While in the former group of states the problem rests with the lack of political will for continuous, long-term and durable change, in the latter it rests with the lack of political will for change as such.

Rudenko and Harutyunyan, among other scholars, examine the sources of challenges to the rule of law in the latter group of post-Soviet states, led by Russia, and identify the reasons behind what one calls "pseudo-rule-of-law" and the other calls "deformed constitutionalism".[11] Four main explanations can be synthesised here. First, there is an anti-Western sentiment and relativistic approach to human rights and democracy, with voices against the export of Western liberal values and arguments for an own "democracy model" (observed e.g. in Azerbaijan, Kazakhstan, Russia).[12] Second, the identification of the rule *of* law with the rule *by* law results in a "dictatorship of law".[13] Indeed, the concept "the rule of law" is relatively new and there was even no term for it in the Soviet Union. While the rule of law as an essentially contested concept is bound to have varied meanings and understandings,[14] the debate in post-Soviet states challenged its very utility, necessity and relevance.[15] In Russian, there are two different words for law and the written law as a legal act: *pravo* and *zakon*. This distinction is familiar to other languages and legal systems: the Roman *jus* and *lex*, the German *Recht* and *Gesetz*, the French *droit* and *loi*, and others. The Soviet ideology insisted – as a matter of legal theory – that *zakon* is *pravo* and that there is no *pravo* outside *zakon*. Consequently, the introduction of the rule of law into legal doctrines and systems of post-Soviet states translated into an opposition between the principles of the rule *of* law (*verkhovenstvo prava*) and the rule *by* law (*vekhovenstvo zakona*), the latter sitting firmly at the top. Importantly, the Council of Europe[16] and the Venice Commission[17] emphasised that the concept of *verkhovenstvo zakona* found in post-Soviet states is not a proper equivalent for the rule of law, that treating it as such runs contrary to the essence of the rule of law, and that *verkhovenstvo prava* is the only proper equivalent for the rule of law.

A third challenge to consolidating the rule of law in post-Soviet states is the instrumentalist approach to law. This means that law is frequently used as a tool to achieve political objectives, for instance through constitutional amendments.[18] This was the case, for example, when the constitutions of Kazakhstan and Belarus were revised through referenda, and reinterpreted by Constitutional Courts, so as to enable the re-election of the countries' sitting presidents for longer (Kazakhstan) or indefinite (Belarus) terms. In violation of the spirit of the rule of law, these decisions had been passed in seeming conformity with the constitutions and the law. While such practices are strongest in Belarus and Central Asia, they are not uncommon in other post-Soviet states too. An instrumentalist approach to law is a Soviet legacy that proves difficult to transform.

Finally, para-constitutional practices are a menace in the region: the ruling elites have mastered the skill of redesigning institutional structures "within" the limits of the constitutions, so as to by-pass them and reinforce the authority of certain branches of power as needed (typically, the president).[19] This way, the appearances are kept, and the domestic and foreign audiences are appeased. Deficiencies in popular and elite demand for law, or 'the bundle of attitudes and behaviour toward law as affected by historical experience, both personal and societal', appear to be of crucial importance.[20] Attitudes, perceptions and value patterns of the elites and wider population mediate the impact of legal texts and institutions and so constitute a major constraint on any meaningful rule of law reform. A deficit of legal culture at all levels is a general characteristic of post-Soviet societies, states and legal systems.[21]

A few words should also be said to explain the diverse standing of post-Soviet states in the rule of law and governance indexes (reviewed in Table 2.2) despite the commonality of Soviet legacies. It is becoming increasingly more difficult to treat post-Soviet states as a homogeneous group: while the shared Soviet legacies do account for a large number of similarities between the states, it is the distinct *post*-Soviet experiences of these states, combined with the rediscovery of their *pre*-Soviet legacies, that account for the current diversity among them. Many obstacles to reform in the region today are inheritances from the most recent past, or 'post-communism gone astray'.[22] Additionally, some post-Soviet states embarked on recovering their pre-Soviet past. For example, Georgia, Moldova and Ukraine repeatedly appeal to their historical links and in fact belongingness to the European legal tradition. Post-Soviet states further east – especially in Central Asia – cannot boast direct historical ties to European legal tradition and instead try to artificially create such links (e.g. by modelling their constitutions on Western prototypes), albeit with their own interpretations of law, which at times revives pre-Soviet legal practices and values rooted in Islam.[23] Therefore, while important similarities can be observed, each country provides a distinct context for scholars to analyse and for external actors to engage in.

To conclude, systemic shortcomings in the protection of the rule of law in post-Soviet states stem from deficiencies in the supply of law and problems connected to the shape of laws and legal institutions, as well as from deficiencies in the demand for law and its rule among local elites and the wider population. The willingness of the ruling political and business elites to sustain existing power structures and the tendency of the elites (including legal scholars and practitioners) to equate the rule *of* law with the rule *by* law pose significant obstacles to the protection of the rule of law in these states. It is in this domestic rule of law context that post-Soviet states embark on European and/or Eurasian integration.

The rule of law and adaptation to European integration processes

European integration processes are profoundly conducive to rule of law protection in the states involved. The rule of law as a pan-European principle is an inevitable element of a country's integration with the European Union and membership in the Council of Europe.[24] In fact, the rule of law has been visibly mainstreamed within both the EU[25] and the CoE[26] in the last twenty years. On the European continent and beyond, these two organisations promote the triptych of 'shared European values' – democracy, human rights and the rule of law – and pursue principally the same 'civilising mission', notwithstanding important differences in their established objectives.[27]

As for the concept of the rule of law, the EU and the CoE (as well as the Venice Commission and the United Nations) advocate for the existence of a consensus on the core meaning of the rule of law and a shared pre-understanding of its essential, unquantifiable elements.[28] As mentioned in the previous section, the Venice Commission has explicitly stated that a consensual understanding of the essence of the rule of law is to be distinguished from a distorted, purely formalistic understanding as "rule by law", "rule by the law" or even "law by rules" found in some former socialist states.[29] Within the EU legal order, the rule of law is defined as one of the EU's foundational values (Article 2 TEU). Moreover, it serves as a central variable in the context of EU external action (Article 21(2) b TEU) and specifically in its relations with neighbouring countries (Article 8 TEU). The European Commission identified six key principles constituting the core of the rule of law in the EU legal order: legality and legal certainty, the prohibition of arbitrariness of the executive powers, the existence of independent and impartial courts, guarantees of effective judicial review (inclusive of respect for fundamental rights) and equality before the law.[30] Despite the existing differences in the definition and interpretation of the rule of law, 'we can be certain of at least one thing: an oppressive legal order cannot satisfy the EU's understanding of the rule of law'.[31]

Given the above, it is especially unfortunate for the introduction and consolidation of the rule of law in post-Soviet states that throughout the 1990s and early 2000s "European integration" of the region was of low intensity, to say the least. Armenia, Azerbaijan, Georgia, Moldova, Russia and Ukraine have become members of the CoE in the mid-1990s. In the uncertain political context of the early 1990s, accession to the CoE was dominated by presumptions that 'compliance could be achieved within a reasonable time-frame with the good will of governments' and that 'admission would result in a continuing and indeed much stronger influence of the CoE than would be the case if the country were not a member'.[32] As a result, the said states became CoE members despite their poor compliance record at the time.[33] Norm acceptance, however, has not been followed by norm compliance, as the analysis in the previous section illustrates. As for Belarus and Central Asian states, they are not even members of the CoE.

The EU, in turn, 'neither played nor endeavoured to play a role in domestic change in the Soviet successor states' until its eastward enlargements in 2004 and 2007.[34] Throughout the 1990s, EU relations with former Soviet states in Eastern Europe and South Caucasus were overshadowed by the EU accession process of the Central and East European countries. Central Asia was almost completely missing from the EU radar at the time. Bilateral relations between the EU and post-Soviet states did not go beyond the conclusion of Partnership and Cooperation Agreements (PCAs) and minimal cooperation within the TACIS programme. With regard to the former, the PCAs with nine out of twelve states entered into force only towards the end of the 1990s. The signature of the agreement with Tajikistan was postponed until 2004 due to the civil war in the country (1992–1997), resulting in a belated ratification in 2005. The ratification of the PCAs with Belarus and Turkmenistan has even been postponed indefinitely.

All ratified PCAs contain a provision emphasising respect for the principles of democracy, human rights and international law, in accordance with the UN Charter, the Helsinki Final Act and the Charter of Paris for a New Europe. This clause could, in principle, serve as a tool for the EU to push for adherence to the above principles, as well as the rule of law. The EU could even go as far as suspending the PCAs in case of a breach of these principles by the partner countries. However, in practice, this has happened only once – in the case of Uzbekistan, in response to severe human rights violations and massacre of civilians in the city of Andijan in 2005; and even in this case the PCA suspension was only partial and quickly reversed.[35]

With regard to the TACIS programme, post-Soviet states received tiny amounts compared to the assistance provided to acceding states in Central and Eastern Europe or Western Balkans. The total budget of the TACIS programme at 7,567.8 million Euro (supporting 13 states, among them such large states as Russia and Ukraine) is *two-and-a-half times smaller* than the total budget of the PHARE programme at 18,673.1 million Euro (supporting 12 states, including such small states as Malta and Cyprus) and is *less* than the combined assistance budget for just two countries, Bulgaria and Romania (7,665.7 million Euro). Likewise, financial assistance to Ukraine (998.3 million Euro) in the period 1991–2006 was lower than to the Czech Republic (1062.2 million Euro) and slightly higher than to Lithuania (808.5 million Euro) and Slovakia (805.2 million Euro); while Kazakhstan (166.2 million Euro) received less than three times the assistance to Malta (57 million Euro).[36] Besides, within the entire period of the programme's implementation (1991–2006), South Caucasus post-Soviet countries received relatively less than East European ones, and Central Asian states received least of all: while Russia and Ukraine received 2,060.6 and 998.3 million Euro respectively, the five Central Asian states combined received as little as 536 million Euro (or 1/2 of Ukraine's and 1/4 of Russia's total).[37] What is more, the larger part of TACIS funds were used to promote economic liberalisation, ensure nuclear safety and modernise public administration, rather than to foster political and legal reforms that could lead to a true advancement of democracy and the rule of law.[38] The EU support in these areas was thus missing exactly in the period when it was most needed and when it could have been most effective, considering that post-Soviet states were at that time going through major political transformations and were more open to external normative influences.

Starting with the mid-2000s, the EU has topped up its engagement in the region and has become a key centre of gravity. The European Neighbourhood Policy (ENP) launched in 2004 and the Eastern Partnership (EaP) launched in 2008 gave new impetus, structure and funding to EU cooperation with East European and South Caucasus states. These policies are based on the principles of shared values, conditionality, joint ownership and differentiation.[39] Despite the initial intention to bring all states under one umbrella, the EU's relations with the respective states are subject to progressively more political and legal differentiation, also in what concerns the rule of law. It has been argued elsewhere that such variation in EU rule of law promotion approaches is not a problem in itself, as long as there is a shared understanding of the core meaning and essential components of the concept.[40] The EU relies on a variety of instruments and mechanisms to promote the rule of law abroad, including soft law (Action Plans and Association Agendas) and hard law instruments ("essential elements clauses" in bilateral agreements); unilateral (technical and financial assistance), bilateral (framework and sectoral agreements) and multilateral (regional platforms) instruments; as well as what scholars call "value diffusion strategy" (e.g. diplomatic measures and discursive practices).[41]

Ukraine, Moldova and Georgia have repeatedly voiced their European aspirations and have concluded far-reaching Association Agreements with the EU.[42] This implies that the Union has more leverage to influence rule of law developments in these states. In turn, EU rule of law promotion is more difficult and less developed with regard to non-associated EaP countries (Belarus, Armenia, Azerbaijan).[43] In both groups, however, the actual commitment to European values – whether rhetorical or legal – is not accompanied by practical compliance, as analysed in the previous section and the EaP European Integration Index.[44]

The EU's influence remains very limited in relation to the Central Asian states. With the exception of Kazakhstan that signed an Enhanced Partnership and Cooperation Agreement with the EU in May 2016, the EU's relations with Central Asian states are still regulated by the initial PCAs.[45] Neither are these states covered by EU neighbourhood policies. Without a strong leverage at hand, the EU has to rely primarily on dialogue with Central Asian governments when promoting the rule of law in the region. This dialogue has been considerably boosted since the launch of the EU-Central Asia Strategy for a New Partnership in 2007. This document suggested establishing two new dialogue formats: a multilateral Rule of Law Initiative involving all Central Asian states and bilateral annual Human Rights Dialogues between individual governments and EU officials, including discussions on the adherence to the rule of law. Both formats, however, have demonstrated mixed results to date. The Rule of Law Initiative, which was supposed to rely on the joint ownership of Central Asian governments and be driven by selected EU Member States, did not have an easy start. The interest in the dialogue process on both sides was modest at best, whereas Uzbekistan and Turkmenistan basically refused to endorse the rule of law agenda.[46] The Human Rights Dialogues offered an opening for the EU to discuss sensitive political issues with the Central Asian governments. Yet the dialogue process was not backed up by any mechanisms to ensure that the governments followed through with their commitments.[47] In addition to the dialogue instruments, the EU provides bilateral financial and technical assistance, for instance to support judicial reforms in Central Asian states. Yet this assistance is limited and has hardly any impact.[48]

Two additional remarks are due here. First, the EU and the CoE are *existing* organisations with elaborate value and legislative packages. This leaves post-Soviet states on the receiving end of the European normative agenda: they can accept, adapt or reject respective value systems. Second, the mounting problems with rule of law compliance among EU Member States (especially but not only Central and East European countries with a communist past) constitute an important recent development.[49] For one thing, this sends a negative signal to post-Soviet states and puts in question the EU's image as a rock-solid rule of law authority for the region. At the same time, it strengthens (semi-)authoritarian ruling elites of post-Soviet states in their arguments against European integration as a civilisational choice and European values as a value basis to strive for. Just like 'the rotten capitalism' in the Soviet ideology, the narrative of a 'decaying Europe' is taking shape in Russia and other states in the region.

By way of a general observation, it is progressively more difficult to speak of the relevance of European integration for rule of law protection in post-Soviet states as a homogeneous region or even to identify sub-regions/sub-sets of states therein: Belarus is an outlier in the 'Eastern Europe' block; Georgia is a front-runner in the "South Caucasus"; and the variation in the strength and nature of EU's engagement with states in "Central Asia" is striking despite the initially chosen "regional" approach.

The rule of law and adaptation to Eurasian integration processes

Ever since the dissolution of the Soviet Union, post-Soviet states have been involved in various regional (re-)integration projects, most of them under Russia's leadership and domination. The Commonwealth of Independent States (CIS), the Collective Security Treaty Organisation (CSTO), the CIS Free Trade Area, the Eurasian Economic Community (EurAsEc) are but a few examples of Russia's failed political and economic attempts at Eurasian integration.[50] Respective integration frameworks are generally characterised by path dependence, recurrent sovereignty sensitivities and frequent changes in design.[51] Importantly, also in the post-Soviet period, Russia's legal system (in particular, its material and procedural codes of law) has served as a model for other states in the region with less constitutional and legislative experience.[52]

The Eurasian Economic Union (EAEU), launched on 1 January 2015, consolidated the twenty-five years of post-Soviet integration and is much more solid than its predecessors.[53] Instead of consistently promoting rule-based integration, however, the EAEU increasingly turns into a foreign policy instrument serving Russia's objectives.[54] Despite the EAEU's declared objective to bring long-term economic benefits to its Member States, it is unlikely to do so: its members are neither wealthy, nor are their economies complementary. As a cherry on the cake, Armenia is the only customs union member in the world without a shared border with either of the other participants. This has made scholars argue that the EAEU is at least as much a political organisation as it is economic, if not more.[55] The institutional structure of the EAEU is more pyramidal and less horizontal, and its Member State compositions are less balanced compared to the EU. In terms of the type of competences granted, the degree of independence of the organisation's internal bodies, the development of a body of common law, and the availability of disciplinary and enforcement mechanisms, the EAEU is less of a supranational framework than its predecessors. It offers weak formal constraints to state sovereignty and reasserts intergovernmental modes of operation under Russia's domination.[56] Moreover, Russia has been using bilateral trade, security and migration ties with post-Soviet states – economic, political and military pressure – to complicate their European integration and conduce them towards Eurasian integration, putting in question both the EAEU's economic and voluntary nature.

The Treaty on the EAEU says *nothing* about the rule of law. Instead, it refers to a 'rule of constitutional rights and freedoms of man and national', as well as universal principles of international law.[57] Moreover, the Treaty stipulates, in a number of clauses, that a Member State may deny compliance with a Union's decision if 'its execution may prejudice the sovereignty, security and public order of the Member State or is contrary to its legislation'.[58] This way, the EAEU is designed to reinforce domestic public orders of its Member States, taking into account their security and sovereignty concerns. These preoccupations are not new. An analysis of the post-Soviet states' constitutions reveals that territorial integrity and national sovereignty are emphasised more strongly and frequently than adherence to the rule of law.[59] Moreover, the language of the constitutions is rather defensive, with direct references to defence and protection (e.g. Armenia, Article 8; Azerbaijan, Article 9; Ukraine, Article 17), 'defensive war' (Georgia, Article 98), 'external threat' and 'aggression' (Kazakhstan, Article 44; Kyrgyzstan, Article 14). Moldova declared 'permanent neutrality' (Article 142), which reads as a pre-emptive appeasement-of-the-aggressor strategy. In turn, Ukraine's constitution speaks of the 'indivisibility and inviolability' of its territory (Article 17), rather than more common 'integrity', addressing the centuries-long attempts to divide the country along various lines and foreseeing the violation of its territorial integrity two decades later. Overall, sovereignty clauses of post-Soviet constitutions read as shields against classical threats to the state authority and territory (originating from Russia and/or state-internal secessionist tendencies). They do not provide for a soft and gradual delegation of sovereignty through functional integration with international organisations.[60] These concerns with state sovereignty and territorial integrity were reignited by Russia's annexation of Crimea and led to insistence for additional requirements to constrain Russia's domination in the EAEU by the presidents of Kazakhstan and Belarus.[61]

The value system underlying Eurasian integration is based on adherence to the rule *by* law principle, if at all, and as such is not conducive to rule of law protection and notions such as separation of power, judicial independence, a transparent legislative process and respect for human rights. There was initial optimism that further legalisation and institutionalisation under the auspices of the EAEU may eventually strengthen the rule of law or, at least the rule by law, in the region.[62] However, the EAEU as it took shape in the Astana Treaty – and the Astana Treaty itself – is considered 'weak from an international, legal and constitutional point of view'.[63] Moreover, the Union's competences have been progressively reduced in the course of negotiations and drafting of the Treaty and are now 'down to zero'.[64] Consequently, the concept of 'the law of the Union' has but an organising and symbolic role, with little legal effect.[65]

Nevertheless, the Eurasian integration process bears a strong impact on domestic political developments in the post-Soviet space. All countries in the region are affected by it to different degrees and for different reasons.[66] Moreover, the process of Eurasian integration challenges the very idea that the EU is the sole actor able to promote 'conceptions of normal'[67] to the post-Soviet space. The universal applicability and acceptance of European norms is questioned, as the EAEU is ready to offer a viable alternative to those not interested in implementing democratic and rule of law reforms. This alternative, rooted in the constantly emphasised principle of respect for the sovereignty, culture and traditions of the Member States,[68] resonates better with the visions and expectations of the countries' authoritarian leaders, even if the price to pay is the increased influence of Russia as the key member of the Union.

Just as Russia did not take European integration processes seriously until the colour revolutions in early 2000s and the launch of the ENP and the EaP, the EU did not take the regional re-integration processes in the post-Soviet region seriously until the establishment of the EAEU. The EU's initial reaction has been cautious and hardened after Armenia's departure from the AA with the EU in favour of EAEU membership in September 2013[69] and Russia's annexation of Crimea in March 2014. There is no 'bloc to bloc' dialogue between the EU and the EAEU, as high-level engagement could only follow serious shifts in Russian policy towards Ukraine and other states in the region. Nevertheless, there are contacts between EU and EAEU officials 'at technical level'. These are believed to help inform future strategies and offer pragmatic short-term gains, at least in defining substance for future discussions.[70]

Geopolitically, the EAEU is an integration framework meant to sustain post-Soviet states' links to Russia and stop the advance of the EU into Eastern Europe and the Southern Caucasus as well as the advance of China to Central Asia.[71] However, 'the dream of a geopolitical Eurasia died in Ukraine', that is, with Russia's annexation of Crimea and the outbreak of violence in Ukraine's eastern provinces.[72] Russia's pressure has already served as an important driver of Ukraine's, Moldova's and Georgia's European integration: all three hurried to conclude the Association Agreements with the EU. Similarly, it may drive Central Asian states into the arms of China, which has greater economic clout in the region.[73] In the coming decades or even years, the definition of 'Eurasian integration' as a Russia-led process may be challenged, making the balancing act for Central Asian states ever more difficult.

Conclusions

The influence of European and Eurasian integration processes on the development of the rule of law protection mechanisms in post-Soviet states varies in several regards. First, when looking at the EU and the EAEU as poles of attraction and actors in their own right, they pursue very different objectives with regard to the promotion of the rule of law. The EU draws on the broader understanding of the concept used by the CoE, which incorporates the principle of an independent judiciary and respect for human rights, and seeks to promote this understanding both within and beyond its borders. The EAEU, on the contrary, does not see the promotion of the rule of law among its priorities, even *vis-à-vis* its Member States that generally follow the rule *by* law paradigm, if at all. Moreover, it is designed to have no effect on domestic political orders of participant states so that it safeguards authoritarianism.

Second, the mechanisms of influence of both entities are quite different. The EU does not offer membership prospects to any of the twelve post-Soviet states, including those aspiring for accession. Instead, its relations with the states are regulated by framework treaties, varying from Association Agreements with Georgia, Ukraine and Moldova, which stipulate normative approximation of the partner countries with the EU, to less ambitious Partnership and Cooperation Agreements with the rest. In the former case, the asymmetric partnership between the EU and the three associated states offers a platform for the EU to advance its normative objectives, including the rule of law. In the latter case, the EU lacks a strong legal basis and political leverage to do so. In any event, post-Soviet states find themselves on the receiving end of the EU's normative agenda, as they can react to the principles advanced by the EU only by either accepting, adapting or rejecting them. Thus, in the process of European integration, in which only a few post-Soviet states participate and only to a limited extent, these states become either compliant or non-compliant with the EU norms. The EAEU is quite different in this sense, as it draws on previous post-Soviet integration efforts. The five current members of the Union were all part of the USSR before, and now they are active co-shapers of norms represented by the EAEU. In fact, as the process of Eurasian integration has a comparatively short history, the normative foundations of its Member States have been formed before the EAEU was established. And now these norms can be uploaded to the EAEU level and shared by its members, producing an additional legitimation effect to what has been previously established domestically. This creates very different dynamics of norm transfer than in the case of the EU, which acts as an external norm promoter *vis-à-vis* post-Soviet countries. At the same time, the limits of the EAEU's influence are quite obvious. Former Soviet states not participating in the EAEU are excluded from both shaping and receiving common norms of this Union.

A general observation stemming from the analysis in this chapter and worth reiterating here is that, at the time of writing and with regard to the subject addressed, speaking of post-Soviet states as a group is justified and unjustified at the same time. It is justified to the extent that all states involved share Soviet legacies, have been exposed to European and Eurasian integration efforts and generally struggle with the introduction and consolidation of the rule of law. It is unjustified, however, as far as the diverse post-Soviet and post-post-Soviet paths in each country are defined by peculiar domestic political and constitutional developments and varying links with European and Eurasian integration processes.

Notes

1 Hill, *Rule of Law Inventory Report: Academic Part*, Hague, 2007, p. 12; B. Tamanaha, *A Concise Guide to the Rule of Law*, NYQueens, 2007, p. 1.
2 For a conceptual baseline on the rule of law, see Hill, *Rule of Law Inventory Report, op. cit.*, p. 12.
3 On the differences between 'rule of law' and 'rule by law' paradigms, see further in this contribution.
4 M. Newcity, 'Russian Legal Tradition and the Rule of Law', in J.D. Sachs and K. Pistor (eds.), *The Rule of Law and Economic Reform in Russia*, Oxford: Westview Press, 1997, pp. 41–53.
5 J. J. Linz and A. Stepan, *Problems of Democratic Transition and Consolidation: Southern Europe, South America, and Post-communist Europe*, Baltimore and London: The Johns Hopkins University Press, 1996, p. 249.
6 The details are familiar and well documented. For Western accounts of the Soviet law see volumes by Barry, *Toward the 'Rule of Law' in Russia? Political and Legal Reform in the Transition Period*, Armonk, NY: M. E. Sharpe, 1992; W. Butler, *Soviet Law*, London: Butterworth, 1988; J. Burbank, 'Lenin and the Law', *Slavic Review*, 54(1), 1995, 23–44; H. Collins, *Marxism and Law*, Oxford: Oxford University Press, 1982.
7 On the evolution of constitutionalism in post-communist countries, see also chapter 1 in this volume.
8 See full country profiles available at: http://data.worldjusticeproject.org/#/groups/MDA (Moldova) and http://data.worldjusticeproject.org/#/groups/UKR (Ukraine).
9 See the full country profile for Belarus available at: http://data.worldjusticeproject.org/#groups/BLR
10 O. Burlyuk, 'The Introduction and Consolidation of the Rule of Law in Ukraine: Domestic Hindrances at the Level of the Demand for Law', *Hague Journal on the Rule of Law*, 7(1), 2015, 1–25.
11 V. Rudenko, 'Demokraticheskoie verkhovenstvo prava i politicheskiie rezhymy (Rossiia i postsovetskie strany)', *Nauchnyi ezhegodnik Instituta filosofii i prava Uralskogo otdeleniia Rossiiskoi akademii nauk*, 13(4), 2013, 57–73; G. Harutyunyan, 'Deformatsii konstitutsionalisma v Evraziiskom prostranstve', *Evraziiskiy Yuridicheskii Zhurnal*, 26(7), 2010, 2–9.
12 Rudenko, 'Demokraticheskoie verkhovenstvo prava', 62–63; Harutyunyan, 'Deformatsii konstitutsionalisma', 5.
13 Rudenko, 'Demokraticheskoie verkhovenstvo prava', 63–64. See also Harutyunyan, 'Deformatsii konstitutsionalisma', 6; M. Koziubra, 'Dykhotomiia bukvy i dukhu prava: vynyknennia problemy, yii aspekty ta napriamy vyrishennia', *Naukovi Zapysky NaUKMA*, 77(3), 2008, 3–8.
14 W. B. Gallie, 'Essentially Contested Concepts', *Proceedings of the Aristotelian Society*, 56, 1956, 167–198; J. Waldron, 'Is the Rule of Law an Essentially Contested Concept (in Florida)?' *Law & Philosophy*, 21(2), 2002, 137–164.
15 For a discussion of the cold reception of the rule of law by Ukrainian legal scholars, see Burlyuk, 'The Rule of Law in Ukraine', 8–14; M. Koziubra, 'Pryntsypy verkhovenstva prava i pravovoi derzhavy: yednist osnovnykh vymoh', *Naukovi Zapysky NaUKMA*, 64(3), 2007, 3–9; M. Koziubra, 'Verkhovenstvo prava: Ukrainski

realii ta perspektyvy', *Pravo Ukrainy*, 3(6), 2010, 6–18. Legal doctrines and systems of other post-Soviet states have had comparable experiences.

16 The Council of Europe, PACE Resolution 1594, 'The Principle of the Rule of Law', 2007, paragraph 4.

17 The Venice Commission, 'Report on the Rule of Law', 2011, paragraphs 4, 15 and 33.

18 Rudenko, 'Demokraticheskoie verkhovenstvo prava', 64–66. See also M. Koziubra, 'Pravo, polityka, pravosuddia: zarubizhnyi ta vitchyznianyi dosvid vzaiemovidnosyn', *Naukovi Zapysky Na UKMA*, 38, 2005, 3–8.

19 Rudenko, 'Demokraticheskoie verkhovenstvo prava', 66–68; Harutyunyan, 'Deformatsii konstitutsionalisma', 7, 9.

20 K. Hendley, '"Demand" for Law in Russia – a Mixed Picture', *East European Constitutional Review*, 10(4), 2001, 72–77.

21 On constitutional idealism and nihilism in post-Soviet states and specifically Ukraine, see M. Koziubra, 'Konstytutsiinyi idealizm ta konstytutsiinyi nihilizm yak proiavy defitsytu pravovoi kultury', *Naukovi Zapysky Na UKMA*, 53, 2006, 3–7.

22 P. Kubicek, 'Problems of Post-Post-Communism: Ukraine After the Orange Revolution', *Democratization*, 16(2), 2009, 323–343.

23 See J. Beyer, *According to Salt: An Ethnography of Customary Law in Talas, Kyrgyzstan*, Martin-Luther-Universitat; D.E. Merrell, 'Islam and Dispute Resolution in Central Asia: The Case of Women Muslim Leaders', *New Middle Eastern Studies*, 2011, 1. Available at: www.brismes.ac.uk/nmes (accessed 28 December 2016).

24 O. Burlyuk, 'A Thorny Path to the Spotlight: The Rule of Law Component in EU External Policies and EU-Ukraine Relations', *European Journal of Law Reform*, 16(1), 2014, 133–153.

25 European Commission Communication, 'A New EU Framework to Strengthen the Rule of Law', (COM (2014) 158, 11 March 2014), 2014;O. Burlyuk, 'Inescapable Partners: The European Union and the Council of Europe as Rule of Law Promoters in Ukraine', in: V. Axyonova (ed.), *European Engagement Under Review: Exporting Values, Rules, and Practices to the Post-Soviet Space*, Stuttgart: Ibidem-Verlag, 2016, pp. 177–202.

26 The CoE, the OSCE and the UN, 'Multilateral organizations rule of law pledge', 2005; Council of Europe PACE Resolution, 'The Principle of the Rule of Law' (1594/2007), 2007; Rapporteur Group on Legal Co-operation, Report 'The Council of Europe and the Rule of Law: An Overview' (GR-J(2008)11), 2008; Venice Commission, 'Report on the Rule of Law' (2011–003.rev), 2011.

27 This has been indirectly acknowledged in the Memorandum of Understanding between the CoE and the EU, concluded on 23 May 2007.

28 European Commission Communication, 'A New EU Framework to Strengthen the Rule of Law'; PACE Resolution, 'The Principle of the Rule of Law'; Venice Commission, 'Report on the Rule of Law'; UNGA Resolution, 'On the Declaration of the High-Level Meeting on the Rule of Law at the National And International Levels' (A/Res/67/1, 2012), 2012; Joint EU pledge for a High-level meeting at the UNGA, when the said resolution was adopted.

29 Venice Commission, 'Report on the Rule of Law', 4–5.

30 Annex I to European Commission Communication, 'A New EU Framework to Strengthen the Rule of Law'.

31 L. Pech, 'Rule of Law as a Guiding Principle of the European Union's External Action', *CLEER Working Papers* 2012/3, 1–56 at p. 27.

32 V. Djeric, 'Admission to Membership of the Council of Europe and Legal Significance of Commitments Entered into by New Member States', *Zeitschrift Fuer Auslaendisches Oeffentliches Recht And Voelkerrecht*, 60(3–4), 2000, 605–629; A.

Dimitrova and J. Pridham, 'International Actors and Democracy Promotion in Central and Eastern Europe: The Integration Model and Its Limits', *Democratization*, 11(5), 2004, 91–112.

33 P. Jordan, 'Does Membership Have Its Privileges? Entrance into the Council of Europe and Compliance with Human Rights Norms', *Human Rights Quarterly*, 25(3), 2003, 660–688.

34 K. Wolczuk, 'Implementation Without Coordination: The Impact of EU Conditionality on Ukraine Under the European Neighbourhood Policy', *Europe-Asia Studies*, 61(2), 2009, 187–211.

35 V. Axyonova, *The European Union's Democratization Policy for Central Asia: Failed in Success or Succeeded in Failure?* Stuttgart: Ibidem, 2014, pp. 65–67.

36 European Commission, *Evaluation of PHARE Financial Assistance. Final Report*, August 2015, Annex 2, 110, Available at: https://ec.europa.eu/neighbourhood-enlargement/sites/near/files/pdf/financial_assistance/phare/evaluation/2015/20150806-phare-ex-post-evaluation-final-report.pdf (Accessed 22 May 2017); European Commission, *TACIS in Tables*, April 2007, p. 2 [on file with the authors].

37 European Commission, *TACIS in Tables*, p. 2; S. Urdze, *Die externe Demokratieförderung der EU in den zentralasiatischen Staaten*, Baden-Baden: Nomos, 2010, p. 103.

38 *Ibid.*, p. 105. For a general overview of TACIS support, see A. Frenz, 'The European Commission's Tacis Programme 1991–2006: A Success Story', 2007. Available at: https://eeas.europa.eu/sites/eeas/files/tacis_success_story_final_en.pdf (accessed 28 December 2016); R. Mogilevsky and A. Atamanov, 'Technical Assistance to CIS Countries', *CASE Network Studies & Analyses*, 396, 2008, 1–31.

39 O. Burlyuk, 'The Four Principles That Structure EU-Ukraine Cooperation, or the European Neighbourhood Policy "in a Nutshell"', *Ukrainian Journal of European Studies*, 2014, 31–42.

40 O. Burlyuk, 'Variation in EU External Policies As a Virtue: EU Rule of Law Promotion in the Neighbourhood', *Journal of Common Market Studies*, 53(3), 2015, 509–523; P. Van Elsuwege and O. Burlyuk, 'Exporting the Rule of Law to the EU's Eastern Neighbourhood: Reconciling Coherence and Differentiation', in: S. Poli (ed.), *The European Neighbourhood Policy – Values and Principles*, London and New York: Routledge, 2016, pp. 167–182.

41 O. Burlyuk, 'An Ambitious Failure: Conceptualising The EU Approach to Rule of Law Promotion (in Ukraine)', *Hague Journal on the Rule of Law*, 6(1), 2014, 26–46; M. Cremona, 'Values in EU Foreign Policy', in: M. Evans and P. Koutrakos (eds.), *Beyond The Established Orders: Policy Interconnections Between the EU and the Rest of the World*, Oxford: Hart Publishing, 2011, 275–315; L. Pech, 'Rule of Law as a Guiding Principle of the European Union's External Action'; A. Haglund-Morrisey, 'EU Value Promotion and the European Neighbourhood Policy', *Southeastern Europe*, 2007, 39–59.

42 The Association Agreements were negotiated since 2008, signed in 2014 and those with Moldova and Georgia fully entered into force in 2016; the AA with Ukraine fully entered into force on 1 September 2017.

43 Van Elsuwege and Burlyuk, 'Exporting the Rule of Law to the EU's Eastern Neighbourhood: Reconciling Coherence and Differentiation', *op. cit.*, pp. 173–176.

44 I. Solonenko (ed.), *European Integration Index for Eastern Partnership Countries*, Kyiv: International Renaissance Foundation in cooperation with the Open Society Foundations, 2012; I. Solonenko (ed.), *European Integration Index for Eastern Partnership Countries*, Kyiv: International Renaissance Foundation in cooperation with the Open Society Foundations, 2011.

45 As mentioned above, the PCA with Turkmenistan is yet to be ratified and hence not in force.
46 V. Axyonova, 'Promoting Justice Reforms in Central Asia: The European Union's Rule of Law Initiative as Part of a Comprehensive Democratization Strategy?' *Central Asian Afffairs*, 2016, 29–48.
47 V. Axyonova, 'The EU-Central Asia Human Rights Dialogues: Making a Difference?' *EUCAM Policy Brief*, 16, 2011. Available at: www.eucentralasia.eu/uploads/tx_icticontent/EUCAM-Brief-16.pdf (accessed 28 December 2016).
48 V. Axyonova, 'Promoting Justice Reforms in Central Asia'; Z. Kembayev, 'Partnership Between the European Union and the Republic of Kazakhstan: Problems and Perspectives', *European Foreign Affairs Review*, 2016, 185–203.
49 See also the contribution of Paul Blokker in this volume.
50 N. Popescu, 'Eurasian Union: The Real, the Imaginary and the Likely', *ISSUE Chaillot Papers*, 2014, p. 7. For an overview of the different milestones in the process of Eurasian integration, see *inter alia* Table 1 in L. Delcour et al., 'The Implications of Eurasian Integration for the EU's Relations with the Countries in the Post-Soviet Space', *Studia Diplomatica*, 68(1), 2015, 5–33; Z. Kembayev, 'Regional Integration in Eurasia: The Legal and Political Framework', *Review of Central and East European Law*, 41, 2016, 157–194; V. Fedorenko, 'Eurasian Integration: Effects on Central Asia', *Rethink Paper*, 2015, 3–6.
51 R. Dragneva, 'The Legal and Institutional Dimensions of the Eurasian Customs Union', in R. Dragneva and K. Wolczuk (eds.), *Eurasian Economic Integration: Law, Policy And Politics*, Cheltenham: Edwards Elgar Publishing, 2013, pp. 34–60.
52 B. Khashmatulla, 'Formirovanie i spetsyfika postsovetskih pravovyh sistem', in: B. Khashmatulla (ed.), *Sravnitelnoe pravovedinie,* Moscow: TransLit, 2008, Chapter 7.
53 Delcour et al., 'The Implications of Eurasian Integration', *op. cit.*; Dragneva, 'The Legal and Institutional Dimensions of the Eurasian Customs Union', *op. cit.*; R. Dragneva and K. Wolczuk, 'Russia, the Eurasian Customs Union and the EU: Cooperation, Stagnation or Rivalry?', *Chatham House Briefing Paper*, 2012, 11/2014; I. Dreyer and N. Popescu, 'The Eurasian Customs Union: The Economics and the Politics', *ISSUE Brief*, 2014, 11/2014.
54 Delcour et al., 'The Implications of Eurasian Integration', *op. cit.*, 6. This point was also argued by speakers at the Eurasian Economic Union workshop at Ghent University, 2 December 2016.
55 Popescu, 'Eurasian Union', *op. cit.* ; Delcour et al., 'The Implications of Eurasian Integration, *op. cit.* ; Dreyer and Popescu, 'The Eurasian Customs Union: The Economics and the Politics', *op. cit.*; V. Erokhin, 'Contemporary Reshaping of Eurasian Integration: Russia's Policies and Their Implication for the EU and Eurasec', *Procedia Economics and Finance*, 22, 2014, 402–411.
56 See the contribution of Rilka Dragneva, 'The Eurasian Economic Union: Balancing Sovereignty and Integration', in this volume.
57 Preamble and Article 3 "Basic Principles" of the Treaty on the EAEU, courtesy translation into English as available online on the UN web-site at: www.un.org/en/ga/sixth/70/docs/treaty_on_eeu.pdf (accessed 22 May 2017).
58 This or similar formulation is found in various articles and protocols of the Treaty on the EAEU.
59 For an overview of relevant constitutional provisions, see annex 2 to this volume.
60 An exception is Article 79 of the Russian Constitution. See, in this respect, the contribution of Paul Kalinichenko in this volume.
61 See the contribution of Rilka Dragneva in this volume; M. Laruelle, 'Kazakhstan's Posture in the Eurasian Union: In Search of Serene Sovereignty', *Russian*

Analytical Digest, 165, 17 March 2015. Available at: www.css.ethz.ch/content/dam/ethz/special-interest/gess/cis/center-for-securities-studies/pdfs/RAD-165-7-10.pdf (accessed 28 December 2016), pp. 7–10.

62 B. Azanov, 'Dogovor o Evraziyskom Ekonomicheskom Soiuze: kompleksnyi pravovoi analiz', *Evraziiskii iuridicheskii zhurnal*, 2014. Available at: www.eurasialaw.ru/index.php?option=com_content&view=article&id=6530%3A-i-ii-&catid=99%3A2010-06-02-08-56-30&showall=1 (accessed 9 March 2017).

63 P. Kalinichenko, 'The Eurasian "Bewitchery" of the Astana Treaty', *The Intersection Project*, 14 July 2015. Available at: http://intersectionproject.eu/article/russia-world/eurasian-bewitchery-astana-treaty (accessed 28 December 2016).

64 E. Bail'dinov, 'Dogovor o Evraziiskom ekonomicheskom soiuze: shag vpered, dva nazad', *Evraziiskii iuridicheskii zhurnal*, 2014, 10, 77, 25–33.

65 See the contribution of Rilka Dragneva, 'The Eurasian Economic Union: Balancing Sovereignty and Integration', in this volume.

66 See country reports in Part 2 of this volume.

67 I. Manners, 'Normative Power Europe: A Contradiction in Terms?', *Journal of Common Market Studies*, 40(2), 2002, 235–258.

68 Not only in the Preamble and Article 3 'Basic principles' of the Treaty on the EAEU, but also throughout its more technical articles.

69 See the contribution of Narine Ghazaryan and Laure Delcour in this volume.

70 For more on this, see Delcour et al., 'The Implications of Eurasian Integration', *op. cit.*, 13–14; Popescu, 'Eurasian Union', *op. cit.*, 41–42; International Crisis Group, 'The Eurasian Economic Union: Power, Politics and Trade', *Europe & Central Asia Report*, 240, 2016. Available at: www.crisisgroup.org/europe-central-asia/central-asia/eurasian-economic-union-power-politics-and-trade (accessed 28 December 2016).

71 Delcour et al., 'The Implications of Eurasian Integration', *op. cit.*, 12.

72 Popescu, 'Eurasian Union', *op. cit.*, 34.

73 S. de Jong, 'The Eurasian Economic Union and the European Union: Geopolitics, Geo-Economics and Opportunities for Europe', *SIEPS European Policy Analysis*, 2016:11epa, 2016, 1–12. Available at: www.sieps.se/sites/default/files/2016_11epa%20eng%20A4%20korr2.pdf (accessed 28 December 2016), 6–7.

3 The Eurasian Economic Union

Balancing sovereignty and integration

Rilka Dragneva

Introduction

On 1 January 2015, a new international organisation was launched in the post-Soviet space, the Eurasian Economic Union (EAEU). Building on the previous integration efforts of Russia, Belarus and Kazakhstan, the formation of an economic union signalled the advancement of the integration agenda and was described as 'epoch-making' by Russia's President, Vladimir Putin.[1] This 'deepening' of integration was to be accompanied by improved institutions, including the drafting of a comprehensive Treaty to raise the effectiveness of integration.

That such an 'improvement' would (and even should) strengthen the supranational nature of the project was a reasonable assumption. Firstly, in comparative regional integration terms, moves towards 'deep' integration have been associated with 'high' institutionalisation and legalization of cooperative efforts, including the corresponding handover of sovereignty to common bodies.[2] The introduction of EU-style juridicised forms of dispute resolution, in particular, has been found to correlate with the proposed depth of integration.[3] Secondly, the institutional design of previous post-Soviet integration regimes already charted a progressive and deliberate course towards the adoption of EU-style supranational features.[4] The emulation of such institutional templates was motivated by the fact that, despite its deficiencies, the EU was seen as the only successfully functioning model for deep integration, one built upon 'objective principles' transferable across borders.[5] Thirdly, criticisms of the early Eurasian regime pointed consistently to the need for a more coherent and expanded common regulation. Importantly, many of the predictions about the potential benefits of Eurasian integration were premised on issues, such as the removal of non-tariff barriers as key obstacles to internal trade.[6] Such an extensive regulatory harmonisation agenda, however, is conditional on effective regulatory institutions and robust guarantees for domestic implementation, something found to be problematic in the Eurasian context. Finally, the narrative about the importance of transfer of sovereignty in the context of the EAEU was emphasised by the project's political leaders in their dealings on the international stage. Vis-à-vis the European Union, for example, it was underlined that sovereignty was transferred to the institutions of the EAEU in a supranational fashion with the implication that trade relations should be regulated not at bilateral but at inter-bloc level.[7] The same position was followed in the context of Kazakhstan's WTO accession, where its undertakings are to be implemented by domestic but also EAEU bodies.[8]

What the Treaty on the EAEU adopted on 29 May 2014 delivered in terms of institutional design,[9] however, suggests that the deepening of economic integration was not accompanied by a clear consolidation of the level of pre-existing institutionalisation or its expansion. As early commentators pointed out, the Treaty was weak 'from an international, legal and constitutional point of view'.[10] In particular, despite the welcome codification of the legal basis of integration, the Treaty on the EAEU reversed the trend towards high institutionalisation, strengthening the protection of state sovereignty in line with traditional, intergovernmental patterns of interstate relations. Indeed, in the context of awakened sovereignty sensitivities, political leaders, such as the Kazakh President, were keen to underline that the new Treaty 'entirely excludes any kind of limitation or violation of Kazakh sovereignty. We have provided mechanisms excluding limitations or violation of our sovereignty at all levels.'[11]

This development presents an empirical and analytical puzzle in terms of the resulting balance between integration objectives and the institutional framework for their achievement. This balance is sufficiently precarious and opaque, allowing for different interpretations to be communicated to different political audiences. The implications are extremely important in terms of the need to clarify the domestic, and particularly constitutional, implications of membership in the EAEU. Scrutinising the balance between the form and substance of integration is also vital in assessing the viability of the EAEU regime and its institutional determinants. Yet, while the policy interest in the EAEU has been massive, the academic analysis of its legal aspects is in its infancy.[12]

In addressing this puzzle and filling an important gap in the literature, this chapter examines the degree to which the formal setup of the EAEU entails a limitation or transfer of its Member States' sovereignty to the common integration framework. Drawing on legal approaches to international organisations, the chapter starts by identifying a set of formal criteria to capture the key limits imposed by sovereignty on the transfer of state power to such organisations. The discussion then proceeds to provide an overview of the circumstances around the adoption of the EAEU Treaty, situating it against the background of previous integration efforts and key aspects of the wider regional context affecting Member States' preferences in relation to integration-sovereignty trade-offs. Given the fluid and complex narratives accompanying the launch of the EAEU, the analysis also draws on the drafting history of the Treaty.[13] Even though Armenia's membership was also actively negotiated during the spring of 2014, the EAEU Treaty was very much the product of Russia, Belarus and Kazakhstan, with Armenia's place defined as a country 'acceding' to this Treaty.[14] This was the same with the Kyrgyz Republic, which followed suit in joining the EAEU.[15] That is why here only the negotiating position of the three founding countries will be considered. Applying the formal criteria identified, the next four sections seek to discuss the extent to which the design of the EAEU calls for the members' sovereignty transfer and how the imposed limits to such transfer compare with the provisions of previous regimes. In conclusion, the chapter offers some explanations for the observed trajectory and discusses its potential implications.

Conceptualising the limits on sovereignty

International organisations are frequently classified as 'intergovernmental' or 'supranational'.[16] The conceptualisation of these labels in the literature has not entailed a universally accepted, bright-line definition. While the EU tends to exemplify the most 'supranational', highly institutionalised end of the spectrum, it is recognised that all organisations entail some erosion of absolute state sovereignty, with Member States voluntarily granting powers for the purposes of achieving the organisation's objectives. This erosion tends to be revealed in a range of 'mixed' characteristics with many organisations representing hybrid types. Nonetheless, these categories remain helpful for the analysis of the EAEU, particularly when the focus of analysis is placed on the dynamic mix of different limits (material as well as temporal) imposed by sovereignty on the transfer of state power from the state to the international organisation, delineated in the latter's constitutive treaties.[17]

First, such limits are reflected in the type of competences granted to an organisation. As observed by Martin Martinez, unlike supranational organisations, intergovernmental organisations have concurrent instead of exclusive competences, which tend to be exclusively listed in constitutive treaties and limited to a restricted set of substantive areas.[18]

Second, the degree of independence of the organisation's internal bodies is highly indicative of the limits on sovereignty. Intergovernmental organisations may have common bodies, but they are not independent of the Member States, particularly of their executive branches.[19] Notably, governments cannot be bound against their will and any binding decisions require unanimity. In supranational organisations, common bodies exhibit high independence from Member States – in terms of their composition, but more importantly, in terms of their decision-making powers. Critically, independent bodies can adopt decisions by majority vote, thereby binding some Member States against their will.

Third, sovereignty can also be limited by the development of a body of common law within an organisation. Establishing the autonomous nature of such an order in international organisations can be complex.[20] The EU's model has underscored the ability of the organisation to enact binding decisions directly applicable to Member States and its citizens.[21] Thus, the acts adopted by the common bodies of a supranational organisation, unlike international law proper, require no ratification or the application of another domestic procedure for its entry into the domestic legal order or its supremacy over contradictory domestic norms. In this sense, the state is bound a priori, regardless of the particular decision at stake and without the possibility of controlling its entry into the domestic legal order.

Fourth, often the most visible limit on sovereignty relates to the availability of disciplinary and enforcement mechanisms, allowing a member state to be compelled to comply with the decision of the common bodies, even if it opposes it. Supranational organisations like the EU vest extensive disciplinary powers with its permanent regulator, the European Commission, as well as binding dispute resolution powers with its Court. In intergovernmental organisations, states' compliance is encouraged primarily through diplomatic means and peer-pressure.

The above list is not necessarily exhaustive, but captures the most salient limits on the transfer of sovereignty. Importantly, as Martin Martinez points out, the imposed limits are rarely static, but tend to change over time.[22] Such a dynamic perspective is particularly suited to the analysis of the EAEU, and Eurasian integration frameworks more generally, characterised by path dependence, recurrent sovereignty sensitivities as well as frequent changes in design.[23] While the EAEU has been in existence for a very short time and the observations on its institutional practices are still limited, it builds on several preceding initiatives. For this reason, it is important to situate it in its historical and regional context.

Institutional and historical background of the EAEU

The EAEU is a new international organisation in the post-Soviet world, launched following the adoption of its founding Treaty. Yet, its genesis and institutional design cannot be understood without tracing its roots within previous integration efforts in the region. In fact, the EAEU inherited an already developed regime and is best conceptualised in terms of its 'constitutionalisation' and modification. Thus, the drafting of the new Treaty was an opportunity to organise and improve the pre-existing framework. At the same time, the new round of bargaining allowed Member States to revisit the terms of integration in line with their evolving priorities and the changing geopolitical context.

The EAEU was set up on the basis of the Customs Union (CU) and Single Economic Space (SES) between Russia, Belarus and Kazakhstan. After a quick inception, including the drafting of a package of constitutive agreements, the CU was launched in June 2010. It was envisaged as a treaty regime within an existing organisation, the Eurasian Economic Community (EurAsEC).[24] This formula allowed a core of 'willing partners' to move fast towards more advanced forms of integration by upgrading and supplementing the EurAsEC regime. Importantly, as will be illustrated in the subsequent discussion, this commitment had a certain novelty to it in providing for an improved institutional framework to enable effective integration. In doing so, the supranational templates of the EU, viewed as the most successful example of 'deep' integration, provided inspiration for institutional design and signalled some in-roads into limiting sovereignty to achieve the objectives set.[25]

At the same time, given the incremental and selective nature of the design process, the resulting CU regime exhibited important gaps.[26] The addition of a large number of new agreements led to a cumbersome and complex web of regulation, characterised by complex cross-references and inconsistencies. These faults were exacerbated by the fast speed of the developing integration agenda, allowing little time for careful drafting or attention to domestic implementation. In 2012, the CU was transformed into a SES by adding another set of agreements and implementing a partial institutional reform, including the creation of a new permanent regulator with enhanced powers, the Eurasian Economic Commission. At the same time, the transition to a Eurasian Union was already contemplated in December 2010 with the process accelerating fast, as will be discussed below.[27]

The design of the CU and SES exhibited one other very important shortcoming: its legal status. Being a treaty regime, the CU did not have a separate legal personality. Thus, for example, following Russia's accession to the WTO in August 2012, the Eurasian institutions were in charge of implementing important undertakings, in particular, Russia's tariff reduction schedule. Yet, those institutions had no representative powers before the WTO. Similarly, it was clear that 'actorness' on the global stage, including the international legal personality behind it, was particularly prized by the Kremlin. President Putin made no secret of his ambitions about Eurasian integration as a constitutive part of a new multipolar world and an equal partner of the EU.[28] This was also important in terms of the planned widening of the Eurasian project. In particular, serious overtures to solicit the membership of Ukraine were made as of the spring of 2011; these were followed by talks with Kyrgyzstan, the partner of the Customs Union trio in the EurAsEC, with whom formal accession talks were started in October 2011.

The terms and outlines of the proposed Eurasian Union were initially set out in a draft Decision of the Commission of the CU of May 2011. This document exposed some of the clear differences in the country's views on further integration: Kazakhstan preferred a purely economic integration framework, yet one falling short of a currency union, whereas Russia viewed the project as a pathway to a fully fledged union, including cooperation in defence, border management and foreign policy. As Cooper points out, Kazakhstan had major reservations to calling the new entity a 'union', preferring the name 'single economic space' instead.[29] The following months were key in putting the project in motion and agreeing on some of its fundamentals. Much is owed to the drive of Vladimir Putin and the priority given to the Eurasian project in the context of his bid for a third presidency. The broad consensus reached was reflected in the Declaration on the Eurasian Economic Integration adopted by the countries' Heads of State on 18 November 2011, which launched the SES but also announced the intention to create a Eurasian Economic Union. The document provided little detail, yet it was telling of the compromises that had already taken place by defining the project in primarily economic terms, while retaining the name 'union'. Critically, it was decided that such a union will be based on the codification of the legal basis of the Customs Union and SES to be completed by 1 January 2015. To this deadline, another was added soon: that a draft treaty on the EAEU be prepared by 1 May 2014.[30] This ambitious time-scale was clearly driven by the Russian side, with President Putin initially referring even to a launch in 2013.[31]

Following this decision, the preparation for the planned codification and new Treaty progressed at a fast pace. The draft, leaked by the Kazakh side in September 2013, revealed that a highly 'unionist' concept was initially developed, as the following analysis will demonstrate, including a parliamentary body, the Eurasian Inter-parliamentary Assembly. These proposals met a strong opposition, particularly in Kazakhstan. The Kazakh position reflected its underlying preferences for a purely economic agenda expressed previously, but also its concerns over the running of the integration process. Significantly, the Council of Heads of State of 24 October 2013 became a platform for unprecedentedly open criticism of Russia's dominance over the project, as will be discussed later.

The result was a significantly trimmed down revised draft, made public in the beginning of February 2014. The draft retracted many of the previous features, including the planned parliamentary assembly, and reflected the reassurances sought to maintain the purely economic nature of the organisation as well as guarantee the equality of Member States. Nonetheless, a range of difficult issues remained, as revealed in the intense negotiations over the spring of 2014 in the rush to meet the agreed deadline of 1 May 2014.

Critically, this process was overtaken by the political developments in Ukraine, resulting in a popular revolt, the collapse of President Yanukovich's regime and the formation of a new government at the end of February 2014. Although Belarus and Kazakhstan allied behind Russia in its reaction to the Ukrainian events, some differences emerged. During the summit of Heads of State of 5 March 2014, Lukashenka and Nazarbayev expressed concerns about Russia's lack of consultation and the military build-up in the Crimean region.[32] The following annexation of Crimea, formally supported or at least not publicly challenged, and the ethnic zeal it unleashed in Russia, however, clearly unsettled countries like Kazakhstan with large Russian minorities and reawakened sovereignty concerns.[33]

These developments, it can be argued, affected the negotiating context. Speaking soon after the annexation, the Kazakh President was keen to emphasise that '[As] far as our independence is concerned, it is a constant. Kazakhstan will not surrender to anybody even an iota of its independence. But some economic prerogatives we will transfer voluntarily to supranational organs'.[34] Importantly, the Kazakh side became more determined to ensure that such transfer remains 'voluntary' and conditional on Member States' consensus, insisting on explicit guarantees to assert sovereignty and appease domestic sensitivities.

Recognising Belarus's high dependence on Russia, President Lukashenka was more prepared to accept limitations of sovereignty.[35] As he famously put it, 'sovereignty is not an icon one needs to pray before'.[36] He was determined, however, to get a better price for its sacrifice, slowing down the Treaty completion marathon in order to achieve it. The negotiations focused on seeking to secure a free trade with no exemptions, including tariffs on energy, culminating in an ultimatum issued in late April that Belarus might not sign with the satisfactory resolution of the issue. The strategy delivered only partial results, yet the attached financial package was sufficient to secure Lukashenka's support for the final run-up now planned for the end of May.[37] It was these tensions that captured the headlines, yet behind the stage the push for greater intergovernmentalism in the final version of the treaty continued, as will be illustrated in the discussion below.

Competences

Regional organisations in the post-Soviet space have tended to have wide and far-reaching, yet not necessarily clearly specified, objectives. The CIS sought to promote cooperation in an open-ended range of areas: from the economy to various aspects of culture and social life. Yet, the tasks of the organisation were always limited to promoting cooperation with Member States in the lead. The latter's participation in any of these platforms was always selective, frequently subject to extensive reservations, and revocable.[38] The EurAsEC was similarly designed with an ambitious agenda in mind, starting with a customs union, yet in terms of decision-making practices, it never moved beyond being a framework for discussion and broad cooperation.[39]

The Customs Union launched in 2010 represented a break in this pattern in so far as it had clearly defined objectives with competences in the area of customs regulation vested with the common bodies of integration, particularly its permanent regulator. The resulting regime was one of partial attribution of powers, with some issues vested with CU authorities, but others requiring the action of national bodies. For example, a main criticism of the Code of the Customs Union was the large number of references to domestic law.[40] Ultimately, the division of competences between CU and domestic institutions was problematic. In fact, one of the strongest grievances of the EU at the time was about this, including the instrumental use of the competence issue by Russia: often trade restrictions were initiated by domestic bodies, yet for their lifting, the trade partner was referred to the customs union institutions.[41]

Being a treaty regime made it possible to easily add new objectives to the project. The most notable expansion of the scope of cooperation was the addition of the SES in 2012. While the goal of the SES was generally defined as the creation of a common market, in practice there was a package of 17 agreements dealing with different areas of cooperation (or aspects thereof in some cases), such as macroeconomic policy, competition, natural monopolies, movement of capital, public procurement, labour migration and statistics. The level of transfer of powers to the CU and SES bodies was very different across these areas. President Nazarbayev referred to the transfer of 175 national competences to the newly launched Eurasian Economic Commission.[42] Yet few of these competences were exclusive, particularly in view of the decision-making mechanism established, as will be discussed in the next section.

The concept of the EAEU as a new, fully fledged international organisation gave the opportunity to reconsider the objectives and scope of Eurasian integration. As discussed earlier, the compromise reached was for drafting a treaty on integration in purely economic matters. The scope of economic integration was to be delineated by the previously concluded agreements, which were to be codified. At the same time, there was much talk on the possible expansion of this scope, particularly in relation to a common currency. Yet, the association of a monetary union with a political union was too strong for Russia's partners.[43] Indeed, none of the drafts purported to define exhaustively the integration agenda, allowing for new areas of cooperation to be added by subsequent agreements. Similarly, it was clear that the leadership of Russia and Belarus remained amiable to integration spilling into areas of political and defence cooperation. This explains Kazakhstan's insistence on including in the final draft the specific designation of the EAEU as an international organisation for 'regional economic integration'.[44]

To secure the achievement of its objectives, the September 2013 draft Treaty attempted to provide a clear division between Union and national competences. The proposal referred to exclusive Union competences in relation to the customs union, customs administration, external trade policy, competition, technical standards, sanitary and phyto-sanitary measures. In relation to the areas falling within the SES agenda, the proposal was for a joint competence of the Union and the Member States. Purely domestic competences in these matters were defined as residual: when envisaged in an international agreement or not regulated by Union legislation at all.[45]

Despite the systematic clarity on this issue, this draft must have resembled too much the various versions for a Union Treaty to replace the USSR developed during 1991. Unsurprisingly, this was one of the areas of notable difference between the various drafts. The January version listed the areas of Union competence, leaving out the term 'exclusive' altogether. It also abandoned the term 'joint' competence. The result was a distinction between 'coordinated (*skoordinirovannuiu*), harmonised (*soglasovannuiu*), and 'when needed', unified (*edinuiu*) policy in the areas determined by the treaty and other international agreements'.[46]

The final Treaty, however, opted for a much more opaque approach to this matter. Article 5 (1) stated that '[T]he Union is endowed with competences within the limits established by this treaty and other international agreements concluded within the Union.' Thus, it refrained from spelling out clearly the areas of attributed competence, leaving those to be identified by what is a complex analysis of the Treaty, its voluminous appendices and any other agreements that may be added subsequently.

Article 5 (2) of the Treaty retains the reference to coordinated and harmonised policy, as defined in this Treaty and other agreements. Responding to the criticisms,[47] the Treaty provided legal definitions for the two terms: 'coordinated' is defined as policy based on common approaches approved by the bodies of the Union, and 'harmonised' as based on harmonised legal regulation, including by acts of the bodies, to the extent necessary for achieving the objectives of the union.[48] On the basis of these definitions, however, it is extremely difficult to establish clearly the differences between the two types of policies. This is not just because of the unfortunate, hasty drafting. Confusingly, many policies were referred to as 'coordinated (harmonised)'.[49] It is also clear that the designation of cooperation in certain areas as 'unified' or 'coordinated' was of particular sensitivity in the drafting process, ultimately resulting in the near elimination of the term 'unified' and the higher number of 'harmonised' policies.[50]

Delegation to common decision-making bodies

In the past two decades, delegation to common bodies came to be seen as an important pre-condition for successful integration in the post-Soviet space. This has been particularly so with regard to the expectations of an effective permanent regulator. On balance, while the design of the principal plenary, decision-making bodies of integration has been characterised by strong intergovernmental features, the design of the permanent regulator in successive post-Soviet integration projects demonstrated some inroads into limiting Member States sovereignty. Yet such limitations have never been without reservations.[51] The EAEU reproduces this pattern, while also seeking to address some of the asymmetry concerns arisen in the previous years.

As with its predecessors, the principal decision-making fora of the EAEU are its Councils. The Supreme Council (*Vysshii sovet*) consists of the Member States' Heads of State and is defined as the highest body of the Union.[52] The organisation also has a junior council, the Intergovernmental Council (*Mezhpravitel'stevennyi sovet*), consisting of the Heads of Government.[53] Similar to the plenary bodies of other international organisations, these Councils meet periodically: at least once or twice a year, respectively. Critically, no departure from unanimity takes place in the decision-making process. Decisions are adopted by consensus, with no sacrifice of state sovereignty.[54] Importantly also, no other body can constrain the decisions of the Supreme Council. As pointed out earlier, the plans to set up a Parliamentary Assembly within the EAEU never materialised in the face of Kazakhstan's strong opposition.[55] The Supreme Council can turn to the Court of the EAEU with a query, yet the Court's consultative opinions have only the status of recommendations.[56]

The permanently functioning body of the EAEU, the Eurasian Economic Commission, largely inherited the design of its predecessor. As already noted, in 2012 a new Eurasian Economic Commission replaced the first Commission of the CU.[57] The 2012 Commission was modelled on the EU Commission, with a developed organisational structure consisting of two tiers, a Council and a Collegium, and clearly associated with the deepening of the integration agenda accompanying the simultaneous launch of the SES. It is noteworthy that it was hailed as the first 'supranational, neutral from the Member States body, to which newer and newer competences will be transferred'.[58]

The EAEU Treaty defines the upper tier of the Commission, the Council, as the body providing 'the general regulation of integration processes as well as the general leadership of the activities of the Commission'.[59] Indeed, the Council is in charge of the most important decisions within the competence of the Commission. As with the higher Councils, the EEC Council consists of Member States' representatives, this time at the level of Deputy Heads of Government.[60] Similarly, this Council adopts its decisions by consensus.[61] If no consensus is achieved, the decision is referred to the higher councils.

The lower tier of the Commission is the only body that can be deemed to exhibit supranational features. Its members (also called Ministers) must be citizens of the EAEU's Member States and are nominated by those Member States. Indeed, Member States must be equally represented within the Collegium.[62] Yet the principles of their appointment and portfolio allocation provide for some independence from the Member States, as this act should be approved by the highest common body of the EAEU, the Supreme Council. The Collegium was envisaged as a developed professional bureaucracy, where the Collegium members should have professional qualification and experience suitable to their portfolio.[63] Importantly, the Treaty requires that, in exercising their powers, Ministers should remain independent of the Member States which nominated them and cannot seek or receive instructions from them.[64] Their independence should be underpinned by the fact that they cannot be recalled by their Member States before the expiry of their four-year term, except in specified circumstances and pursuant to a decision of the Supreme Council.[65]

Yet, contrary to the stated intentions, the experience of the 2012 Commission showed that the formal regime is not sufficient to guarantee the independent, professional functioning of the Collegium. Indeed, this has been an area provoking some of the most vocal criticisms of the Commission. The Kazakh President Nazarbayev spoke of the 'politisation' of this body, protesting particularly against Russia's influence over 'its' Ministers and Commission's civil servants.[66]

The concern for Russia's ability to dominate the Commission and its departments, seated in Moscow, led to the insistence for additional requirements to prevent undue influence. Consequently, the appointment of department heads and their deputies must be done on competitive basis, yet also follow the principle of equal member state representation.[67] In an effort to provide stronger guarantees for independence, an explicit rule was included that the civil servants of a Department cannot be members of one and the same member state. The appointment of the departments' staff should also be on competitive basis, yet it can reflect the Member States' financial contribution to the Commission, thus potentially allowing for a larger Russian representation. As with the Ministers, civil servants and other staff must be independent from the EAEU Member States.[68] Indeed, as an additional precaution, the explicit obligation of Member States to abstain from seeking to influence the way civil servants might fulfil their duties, was inserted.

Critically, the supranational nature of the Collegium has been best exemplified in its power to decide certain issues by a qualified majority, where every country (and a country's Minister) carries one vote.[69] Thus, there is the formal possibility for a decision to be taken against the will of a member state, thereby directly restricting its sovereignty. This change introduced with the 2012 Commission and retained in the Treaty, was a departure from the previous design of post-Soviet permanent regulators, characterised by weighted voting as the basis for distribution of votes, thereby favouring Russia as the strongest state and essentially guaranteeing it formal dominance over the regulator's decision-making.[70] The implications of qualified majority voting, however, remain highly limited.

Firstly, qualified majority voting in the Collegium is reserved to routine, non-controversial issues. Issues of potential sensitivity are vested with the Council which, as mentioned, decides by consensus. Indeed, the Regulation on the Eurasian Economic Commission lists 130 issues, such as the preparation of draft decisions of the higher Councils, approval of changes to import tariffs of sensitive goods, and the adoption of technical standards.[71]

Secondly, and most importantly, any member state can request that a decision of the Collegium it disagrees with, is repealed or amended.[72] This request is initially dealt with by the EEC Council, but if no consensus is achieved there, it can be taken to the Intergovernmental Council or the Supreme Council.

Thus, the possibility for qualified majority voting has important domestic constitutional implications. However, its significance is easily negated and no country can be bound against its will by a decision of the Commission. This is not just with regard to matters deemed as 'sensitive' by the Supreme Council in advance, hence included in the list of issues reserved for the Council of the Commission. It applies also on an *ad hoc* basis even with regard to operational, potentially non-controversial issues. In this sense, delegation to the Collegium is revocable. Its decisions will stand only when they are accepted *ex post* by all Member States. If they are not, the contested issue can be escalated to the highest level of decision-making and resolved within the complex context of political bargaining. Unsurprisingly, the Collegium's role has been described as a 'filter' and a body proposing drafts for the higher bodies, rather than exercising its own decision-making or executive powers.[73]

This outcome ensures that the legal constraints which are placed on sovereignty as a result of delegation are weak and that the importance of the Collegium as a regulatory body, including the efforts to provide formal guarantees for its independence, is diminished. It is noteworthy that the description of the 2012 Commission as a 'supranational body' has been abandoned in the new set-up. Thus, ultimately, the EAEU's mode of decision-making remains strongly intergovernmental as well as centred on the highest level of state authority.

Common legal order

The experience of the Commonwealth of Independent States (CIS) led to the emergence of a 'law of the CIS'.[74] Such a law, however, was decidedly a sub-group of international law. Furthermore, there was little 'common' about it given the variable number of signatories and uneven ratification of international agreements.[75] The decisions of the CIS principal decision-making bodies, its Councils, when they were of normative nature, also had the status of international agreements and were, thus, subject to ratification or other procedure for transformation into domestic law. While subsequent integration frameworks toyed with the idea of 'direct applicability', ultimately this was purely a declarative notion, an epitome of the symbolic emulation of EU-templates.[76] The 'international law' position was retained within the EurAsEC, whereby decisions were deemed to be implemented 'through the adoption of the necessary domestic normative acts in accordance with national legislation'.[77]

The design of the Customs Union represented a break in the pattern to the extent that it sought to provide an 'organised' international law regime. The founding agreement of the CU delineated its 'treaty basis' to be included in a designated 'list' adopted by the Council of Heads of State.[78] The requirement for a 'block' adoption of agreements, whereby they enter into force simultaneously in all Member States, ensured a new level of commonality. Given the incremental fit of the CU within the EurAsEC, however, no special provision was made to determine the status of the decisions of the Council. In so far as the rules pertaining to the EurAsEC framework continued to apply, formally they still had the status of international law. Confusingly, however, despite the important normative contents of some of them, Council decisions were not explicitly defined as belonging to the treaty basis of the CU.[79]

The status of the decisions of the permanent regulator, the Commission of the CU, however, represented a clear departure from the past regime, thus introducing a certain duality in the integration regime. The Commission's decisions were to formally enter into force within a month of their official publication and, as of that date, become binding on the Member States.[80] A Decision of the Council of Heads of State defined further that such decisions are subject to direct application in the Member States of the CU.[81] Importantly, it provided that their legal force within the domestic systems of the Member States will be equivalent to that of acts issued by the state organs competent to regulate the issues transferred to the Commission. This approach was retained in the design of the 2012 Eurasian Economic Commission. Furthermore, the decisions of this Commission were explicitly defined as being part of the treaty basis of the CU.[82]

As noted previously, from its very inception, the drafting of the EAEU Treaty was linked to the effort to codify the legal basis for integration.[83] In the short period of existence of the CU and SES, the international agreements underpinning them had proliferated. The attempt to order this treaty basis by delineating them in a Council-approved 'list' was implemented in a problematic way.[84] Importantly, this solution did not help eliminate the build-up of gaps and inconsistencies in the common regime. Ultimately, this was a fragmented regulatory regime and its complexity was found to be a key obstacle to realising its potential benefits.[85]

The EAEU Treaty delivered on the promise in the sense that it codified (and reworked to various degrees) a large number of agreements. This has not necessarily stopped the further proliferation of agreements, but has rationalised the legal basis hitherto. Introducing a welcome clarity, the Treaty provided that its provisions will prevail over any contradictory provisions of such additional agreements, thus asserting its primacy.[86] The EAEU Treaty also referred to a distinct 'law of the Union', consisting of the Treaty, international agreements concluded within the Union, international agreements with third parties and the acts of the Supreme Council, the Intergovernmental Council and the Eurasian Economic Commission, adopted within the scope of their competences.[87] Significantly, the Treaty also defined the legal hierarchy of the acts of the different bodies, whereby the decisions of the Supreme Council prevail over any contradictory decisions of the Intergovernmental Council and the Commission, and the decisions of the Intergovernmental Council prevail over contradictory decisions of the Commission.

Nonetheless, the status of the decisions of the bodies of integration did not change. The legal nature of the acts of the Supreme and Intergovernmental Councils remains firmly grounded in international law. This outcome was the result of a compromise during the negotiations, where another attempt to provide for directly binding acts of the Councils failed in favour of a strict intergovernmental solution. Article 7 (2) of the September draft envisaged a general provision to the effect that 'the legal acts of the Union are subject to a binding application, have direct effect on the territory of the Member States and have priority over the domestic legislation of the Member States.' Article 13 (1) of the January 2014 draft, however, sought a more nuanced approach and included a Russian proposal to distinguish between EU-style regulations (*dekrety*) defined as explicitly binding on Member States, and directives (*direktivy*) defined as providing common objectives to be achieved through the adoption of domestic laws, which were also met with opposition. The result was the fall-back to the pre-existing solution, with the Treaty stating that their decisions are implemented by the Member States in the manner provided by national legislation.[88] Thus, ultimately, the domestic effect of the decisions of the Councils remains determined by the status granted to international law in domestic constitutions and laws of treaties.

Similarly, the Treaty maintains the approach to the Commission's decisions developed previously. These decisions are defined as explicitly 'binding' on the Member States and subject to direct application (*neposredstvennoe primenenie*) within the territories of the Member States.[89] While the Regulation on the Commission is fairly detailed on the organisational aspects of this body, there is nothing on the nature of this direct applicability in the context of domestic law. One might assume that, at least in law, the inherited agreement on the domestic force of the Commission's decisions previously reached might stand. Yet, this whole area remains unclear and unresolved.

Thus, the direct applicability of the Commission's decisions would suggest a sustained move towards supranationality with important implications for domestic constitutional arrangements. Yet, as with qualified majority voting in the Collegium, the potential effect of this provision on the restriction of Member States' sovereignty should not be exaggerated. As discussed, any decisions opposed by a member state can be 'uploaded' to the higher bodies, thereby placed back within the framework of international law. In this sense, the introduction of the concept of a 'law of the Union' has an organising and symbolic role, but little effect on its legal nature. What remains critically important, then, is the domestic treatment of this law. It is noteworthy, that during the drafting of the Treaty this was another area of high sensitivity and at least Kazakhstan was highly committed to minimising the references to 'bindingness' and ensuring that the law of the Union cannot have a direct effect, therefore the admission of the acts of the bodies of integration should firmly remain subject to its own constitutional order.[90]

Enforceability

Post-Soviet integration has been characterised by weak disciplinary and enforcement mechanisms. Despite the fact that a permanent dispute resolution body was created, the Economic Court of the CIS, its design was problematic. Importantly, its rulings were not defined as binding; instead, it was provided that 'the state with respect to which a decision was adopted, ensures its implementation.'[91] Thus, implementation was a matter of the state's discretion. In the event of non-compliance, the only option for the aggrieved state has been turning to the Council of Heads of State, as the highest body of integration.[92] Given the consensus-based mode of decision-making, however, this has meant that decisions can be blocked by the unwilling party.

In effect, very few state disputes were brought before the Court during its existence, restricting its primary importance to issuing advisory opinions.[93] Ultimately, the rulings of the Court in these disputes were predominantly not complied with, resulting in further rounds of diplomatic negotiations. The Court itself has over the years become increasingly marginalised and paralysed.[94] Ultimately, state disputes have been the province of high-level diplomacy within the framework of the Council of Heads of State or outside the multilateral framework altogether. In the absence of voluntary compliance, traditional bilateral interstate relations, including the use of economic coercion, have prevailed.

The establishment of the Eurasian Economic Community, despite its greater ambition, did not depart from the CIS formula. The EurAsEC Treaty provided for the creation of a dedicated Court, yet in practice such a Court was not set up. Instead, the exercise of its competence was placed with the Economic Court of the CIS on the basis of a confusing and poorly stitched up regime.[95] Its rulings were similarly deemed to only recommend measures for implementation, supported by the voluntary undertaking that every member state obliges itself to implement the decision of the Court issued in a case it is a party to.[96]

The launch of the CU and SES represented a change in this trend in so far as it was accompanied by the effort to strengthen the disciplinary and enforcement institutions of integration. Notably, after more than a decade, the Court of the EurAsEC was finally set up as a dedicated court in 2012. Its revised Statute removed the formula 'recommended for implementation', explicitly stating that the Court's decisions are binding (*obiazatel'nye dlia ispolneniia*) on the parties to a dispute.[97] This language betrayed a clear attempt to signal a higher degree of supranationality of the regime. Yet, the legal meaning of bindingness within the domestic legal orders of the Member States remained their own constitutional matter. In cases of non-compliance, the only remedy at the level of the common regime was turning to the Interstate Council. Thus, high-level political bargaining remained the ultimate resort in seeking compliance with the Court's ruling.

Of further significance were the important enforcement powers granted to the Commission. Exhibiting some similarity with its EU counterpart, the 2012 Eurasian Economic Commission was given the power to issue notifications informing a member state of the need for mandatory compliance. According to Article 20 of the Treaty on the Eurasian Economic Community, if a state failed to comply, the Commission was given the right to lodge a complaint with the Court of the EurAsEC.

Thus, at least on a symbolic level, the regime of the CU and SES suggested a willingness to provide for a developed dispute resolution system centred on the Court of the EurAsEC with some emulation of the design of the Court of Justice of the EU.[98] While ultimately a member state could not be forced to comply against its will, the institutional framework seemed to suggest a common commitment to create an effective and legitimate dispute resolution body. Certainly, the practice of the Court revealed its efforts to establish itself as an authoritative and respected institution, but also to engage in judicial activism emulating its EU counterpart.[99]

The Treaty of the EAEU opted for the creation of a Court of the EAEU as a completely new body, introducing some changes in the previous regime. Yet many of these changes weakened this body, raising concerns about its independence and the overall effectiveness of its role.[100] The decisions of the Court were not deemed to be part of the 'law of the Union'. In addition, a special provision was inserted to the effect that 'the decision of the Court does not change and/or invalidate any norms of the law of the Union in force and the legislation of the Member States, nor create new ones.'[101] According to commentators, this was in direct reaction to the judicial activism shown by the Court of EurAsEC, particularly in its *Iuzhnii Kuzbass* case where it provided a wide interpretation of its competences, suggesting the ability to create Union law.[102]

Critically, also the disciplinary and enforcement powers of the Commission were reduced. While the September 2013 draft reproduced Article 20, placing it at the very beginning of the treaty, this provision did not survive in the final version. Thus, currently compliance with agreements or decisions remains voluntary, with remedies that can be pursued only through the traditional route of interstate relations. The EAEU Treaty is similarly careful to give a wide berth to Member States in case consultations and negotiations between them fail. Article

112 provides that a country can resort to the Court of the EAEU 'unless an agreement on the use of another mechanism is reached'.

Thus, there has been an effort to minimise the juridicisation of the overall regime, leaving Member States in full control of the implementation of their undertakings. While the scope of integration remains substantial, there is little to ensure that Member States will comply with its various complex requirements. Ultimately, if the commitment of the leadership of the respective country wanes or it fails to deliver on the implementation of the necessary domestic measures, the only remedy is the political pressure that might be exerted by its peers.

Conclusion

The EAEU came into being following a stream of preceding integration initiatives. The political narrative around its inception and launch sought to present it as the next logical step in the integration process. This advancement of the integration agenda also suggested a parallel strengthening of the common regulatory regime, with respective implications for the limitation of Member States' sovereignty. Yet, in essence, the EAEU is less of a supranational framework than its predecessors, offering weak formal constraints to state sovereignty and reasserting intergovernmental modes of operation. As this chapter demonstrated, this was exhibited in the reduction of the Treaty limits on members' sovereign powers (e.g. the removal of enforcement powers of the Commission), the opaque nature of transferred competences (e.g. in relation to many of the common policies), or the lack of effective guarantees for upholding the existing limits (e.g. in relation to the acts of the Commission or the status of the Court's decisions).

Explaining this development and its meaning in comparative regional integration terms deserves an extensive treatment, which is beyond the scope of this work. Yet, the drafting history of the Treaty suggests that the observed shift is closely related to the eruption of the Ukraine crisis. Sovereignty sensitivities have mattered in previous post-Soviet integration rounds with important implications for the weakness and poor effectiveness of design.[103] In the Customs Union format, however, many of these sensitivities were placated or sufficiently offset by the expected benefits of integration.[104] Although none of the envisaged limitations of sovereignty were absolute, many of the design features of that regime as well as the language of integration suggested the transfer of powers to the common framework with important domestic constitutional implications, even when these required further attention and elaboration. Following Russia's annexation of Crimea, however, security and sovereignty concerns were reignited, feeding old sensitivities and prompting new attempts to balance the costs and opportunities of integration.[105]

The resulting institutional set-up places a huge emphasis on the presence of effective domestic constitutional mechanisms to ensure the supremacy of the common regime. Even more importantly, progress in integration and the implementation of undertakings are critically dependent not on common rules constraining behaviour, but on commitment at the highest level of political decision-making.

Any limitation of sovereignty is voluntary applying not just at the founding of the organisation and endowing it with certain powers and rules, but also at every step thereafter: every measure is conditional on the member state's consent and can be revoked.

Whether an ambitious integration agenda, including large-scale regulatory harmonization, can be delivered in this way, remains to be seen. The odds are complicated by the fact that the compromise reached with the Treaty of the EAEU is not necessarily stable. While all Member States proceeded to ratify the Treaty in a rather uneventful manner, ensuring its entry into force on 1 January 2015 as planned, the fragile nature of their commitment was laid bare. For example, amidst continued spats with Russia's leadership on Kazakh statehood, President Nazarbayev asserted the revocability of the commitment made:

> If the rules which were previously established in the treaty are not fulfilled, then Kazakhstan has the complete right to end its membership in the Eurasian Economic Union. Astana will never be in an organisation which represents a threat to the independence of Kazakhstan.[106]

Reading such statements, it is not surprising that 'sovereignty' is used in relative terms. While the traditional notion has become a rarity in the modern interdependent world, post-Westphalian sovereignty has exhibited a range of normative, rhetorical and theoretical shades of meaning.[107] Yet, it is clear that in the Eurasian context the securitisation of sovereignty and emphasis on 'independence' have become prominent with judgment on economic issues following suit.

At the same time, the commitment of Member States even with regard to core and hitherto relatively uncontroversial common competences, such as the Customs Union, has been undermined by the nature of Russia's response to Ukraine's progress with its Association Agreement with the EU. In the absence of a consensus by Belarus and Kazakhstan to support the removal of the CU preferential trade regime with Ukraine, Russia preferred to proceed unilaterally. While such a unilateral course was formally approved by the partners,[108] this step only underscored the principle of revocability of joint undertakings when a country disagrees with a certain course of action and the ultimately intergovernmental nature of the overall regime. Subsequent developments related to the similarly unilateral imposition of economic sanctions to Ukraine and the EU and the resulting 'trade wars' within the EAEU, including the reintroduction of customs borders, confirm the weakness of the formal arrangements made and the relative and symbolic nature of Eurasian integration. It is unsurprising that Russia's partners, to the extent allowed by their economic interdependence, have been keen to diversify trade and pursue a more openly multi-vector course. It is also unsurprising that Kazakhstan's accession to the WTO has also led to the introduction of a special regime on commodities with import tariffs lower than those of the CU, including customs controls within the Union and further fragmentation of the common customs regime.[109] Thus, despite the continued lip service to an ambitious Eurasian integration agenda with the potential to deliver benefits to a market of 180 million people, the institutional design falls short of guaranteeing the implementation of commitments and preventing the unravelling of achievements.

Notes

1 'Putin: Peredacha polnomochii v EAES ne oznachaet utratu suvereniteta', *RIA Novosti*, 29 May 2014, available at: http://ria.ru/economy/20140529/1009842639.html (accessed 8 October 2016).

2 Whilst this is a complex and much debated issue, many have argued that depth of integration and legality are positively correlated. For an overview, see K. Raustiala, 'Form and Substance in International Agreements', *The American Journal of International Law*, 99, 2005, 581–614. Despite the fact that the terms 'institutionalisation' and 'legalisation' can have somewhat different connotations in international law and international relation discourses, here they are used synonymously. They are understood as concepts to describe a continuum of possible institutional design, with the 'high' end of the spectrum associated with EU-style supranational transfer of sovereignty to a common organisation, e.g. K. Abbott et al., 'The Concept of Legalization', *International Organisation*, 54(3), 2000, 401–419.

3 J. McCall Smith, 'The Politics of Dispute Settlement Design: Explaining Legalism in Regional Trade Pacts', *International Organisation*, 54(1), 2000, 137–180.

4 R. Dragneva and K. Wolczuk, 'EU Emulation in the Design of Eurasian Integration', in: D. Lane and V. Samokhvalov (eds.), *The Eurasian Project and Europe: Regional Discontinuities and Geopolitics*, London: Palgrave Macmillan, 2015, 135–152.

5 T. Valovaya, 'Eurasian Economic Integration: Origins, Patterns, and Outlooks', *EDB Eurasian Integration Yearbook*, 2012, 42–61; V. Gustov, 'Na puti k sozdaniiu tamozhennogo soiuza Evraziiskogo Ekonomicheskogo Soobshcjestva', *Evraziiskaia Integratsiia: Ekonomika, Pravo, Politika*, 3, 2008, 19–23.

6 E.g. D. Tarr, 'The Eurasian Economic Union of Russia, Belarus, Kazakhstan, Armenia and the Kyrgyz Republic: Can It Succeed Where Its Predecessors Failed?' *East European Economics*, 54(1), 2016, 1–22.

7 See, for example, the statement of Russia's Deputy-Prime Minister Shuvalov following the signing of the Treaty, 'Obshchee ekonomicheskoe prostranstvo s Evropoi teper' vozmozhno lish' v formate ES-EAES -Shuvalov', *Vedomosti*, 30 May 2014, available at: www.vedomosti.ru/politics/print/2014/05/30/27183511 (accessed 12 November 2016). Similarly, 'Evraziiskii soiuz predlagaet ES nachat' dialog o sozdanii oshchego ekonomicheskogo prostranstva', *TASS*, 26 October 2015, available at: http://tass.ru/ekonomika/2380019 (accessed 12 November 2016).

8 WTO, 'Overview of Kazakhstan's Commitments', available at: www.wto.org/english/news_e/news15_e/kazakhannex_e.pdf (accessed 13 October 2016). Kazakhstan became formally a member of the WTO on 30 November 2015.

9 The Treaty on the Eurasian Economic Union was signed by Russia, Belarus, and Kazakhstan on 29 May 2014 and entered into force on 1 January 2015.

10 P. Kalinichenko, 'The Eurasian "Bewitchery" of the Astana Treaty', *The Intersection Project*, 8 August 2015, available at: http://intersectionproject.eu/article/russia-euroep/eurasian-bewitchery-astana-treaty (accessed 12 December 2016).

11 'Dogovor o sozdanii EAES zakonodatel'no iskliuchaet narushenie suvereniteta – Miniust RK', *Tenge*, 26 May 2014, available at: http://tenge.me/?p=9546 (accessed 20 November 2016).

12 See, for example, E. Bail'dinov, 'Dogovor o Evraziiskom ekonomicheskom soiuze: shag vpered, dva shaga nazad', *Evraziiskii iuridicheskii zhurnal*, 10(77),

2014, 25–33; M. Karliuk, 'The Eurasian Economic Union: An EU-Inspired Legal Order and Its Limits', *Review of Central and East European Law*, 42(1), 2017, 50; Z. Kembayev, 'Sravnitel'no – pravovoi analiz funktsionirovaniia Suda Evraziiskogo Ekonomicheskogo Soiuza', *Mezhdunarodnoe pravosudie*, 2(18), 2016, 30–45, R. Petrov and P. Kalinichenko, 'On Similarities and Differences of the European Union and Eurasian Union Legal Orders: Is There the "Eurasian Economic Union Acquis" ?' *Legal Issues of Economic Integration*, 43(3), 2016, 295–308.

13 Two drafts of the Treaty are used in particular. The first one was posted by the Kazakh side on 10 September 2013, available at: http://kazenergy.com/ru/2012-09-05-04-11-04/2011-05-13-18-20-44/10777-2013-09-10–07–03–15.html. The second draft, dated 30 January 2014 and containing the comments, proposals and reservations of the three member state, was posted also by the Kazakh side, //palata.kz/ru/news/3129, followed by a publication on the web-site of the Russian Ministry of Economic Development on 12 February 2014, available at: http://economy.gov.ru/minec/about/structure/depSNG/doc20140212_1. Information is also drawn from conversations with senior officials of the Eurasian Economic Commission and interviews reported in the press.

14 Armenia signed an accession treaty on 10 October 2014, which entered into force on 2 January 2015.

15 The Kyrgyz Republic signed an accession treaty on 23 December 2014, coming into force on 12 August 2015.

16 E.g. J.H.H. Weiler, *Supranational Law and the Supranational System*, Ph.D. Thesis, Florence: EUI, 1982, Florence, available at: http://cadmus.eui.eu/handle/1814/4822 (accessed 15 October 2016); H. Schermers and N. Blokker, *International Institutional Law*, 3rd ed., The Hague, London and Boston: Martinus Nijhoff Publishers, 2001.

17 M. Martin Martinez, *National Sovereignty and International Organisations*, The Hague, Boston and London: Kluwer Law International, 1996.

18 *Ibid.*, at p. 72.

19 Schermers and Blokker, *op. cit.* note 16.

20 M. Sørensen, 'Autonomous Legal Orders: Some Considerations Relating to a Systems Analysis of International Organisations in the World Legal Order', *International & Comparative Law Quarterly*, 32, 1983, 559–576.

21 Weiler, *op. cit.* note 16.

22 Martin Matinez, *op. cit.* note 17.

23 R. Dragneva, 'The Legal and Institutional Dimensions of the Eurasian Customs Union', in: R. Dragneva and K. Wolczuk, (eds.), *Eurasian Economic Integration: Law, Policy and Politics*, Cheltenham: Edward Elgar, 2013, 34–60.

24 The Eurasian Economic Community was set up in October 2000 and united Russia, Belarus, Kazakhstan, Kyrgyzstan and Tajikistan. Its set up drew on a previous set of agreements and integration bodies between those countries, Dragneva, *op. cit.* note 23.

25 Valovaya, *op. cit.* note 5.

26 Dragneva, *op. cit.* note 23.

27 J. Cooper, 'The Development of Eurasian Economic Integration', in: R. Dragneva and K. Wolczuk (eds.), *Eurasian Economic Integration: Law, Policy and Politics*, Cheltenham: Edward Elgar, 2013, 15–33. The idea of the Union is traditionally attributed to Nursultan Nazarbayev, the President of Kazakhstan, presented in a speech at the Moscow State University on 29 March 1994. The focus here, however, is on the practical incarnation of the initiative within the Eurasian integration project.

28 V. Putin, 'Novyi integratsionnyi proekt dlia Evrazii – budushchee, kotoroe rozhdaetsia segodnia', *Izvestiya*, 4 October 2011. Notably, the value of international legal personality of integration platforms was also exhibited at the founding of the EurAsEC back in 2000, Dragneva and Wolczuk, *op. cit.* note 4.
29 Cooper, *op. cit.* note 27, at p. 29.
30 Decision Nr 21 of the Supreme Eurasian Economic Council, 19 December 2012.
31 N. Buckley, 'Putin Sets Sight on Eurasian Economic Union', *Financial Times*, 16 April 2011.
32 A. Klaskovskii, 'Putin vsypal Kievu, a zatylok cheshut I v Minske', *Naviny*, 5 March 2015, available at: http://naviny.by/rubrics/politic/2014/03/05/ic_articles_112_184790 (accessed 12 October 2016); N. Hayrumyan, 'Integration Talks Amid Ukraine Crisis: Leaders of Customs Union Member States Meeting in Moscow', *ArmeniaNow.com*, available at: www.armenianow.com/commentary/analysis/52454/armenia_customs_union_russia_membership_kazakhstan_belarus_lukashenko_nazarbayev (accessed 12 October 2016).
33 'Russia-Ukraine Crisis Alarms Central Asian Strongmen', *EurasiaNet.org*, 4 March 2014, available at: www.eurasianet.org/node/68104 (accessed 11 November 2016). D. Solovyov, 'As Kiev Looks West, Putin Turns East to Build Eurasian Dream', *Reuters*, 27 March 2014, available at: http://uk.reuters.com/article/uk-ukraine-crisis-centralasia-idUKBREA2Q0BW20140327 (accessed 11 November 2016).
34 'N. Nazarbaev: Kazakhstan ne otdast ni iotu nezavisimosti komu by to ni bylo', *Zakon.Kz*, 25 March 2014, available at: www.zakon.kz/4611637-n.nazarbaev-kazakhstan-ne-otdast-ni.html (accessed 12 November 2016).
35 M. Frear, 'Belarus: Player and Pawn in the Integration Game', in: R. Dragneva and K. Wolczuk (eds.), *Eurasian Economic Integration: Law, Policy and Politics*, Cheltenham: Edward Elgar, 2013, pp. 119–138.
36 'Suverenitet ne ikona', *Gazeta.Ru*, 24 October 2013, available at: www.gazeta.ru/business/2013/10/24/5722545.shtml (accessed 11 November 2016).
37 'Moskva nal'et Belarusi polstakana v dolg', *Naviny*, 9 May 2014, available at: http://naviny.by/rubrics/economic/2014/05/09/ic_articles_113_185443 (accessed 11 October 2016).
38 R. Dragneva, 'Is "Soft" Beautiful? Another View on Law, Institutions and Integration in the Commonwealth of Independent States', *RCEEL*, 29(3), 2004, 279–324.
39 M. Golovnin, 'Opportunities and Obstacles to EurAsEc Integration', *EDB Eurasian Integration Yearbook*, 2008, 38–53, available at: www.eabr.org/general/upload/docs/a_n1_2008_12.pdf (accessed 12 October 2016). Arguably, the most important contribution to integration was made by the Court of the EurAsEC, as will be discussed further below.
40 See, for example, V. Visloguzov, 'Kodeks razdora', *Kommersant*, 21 June 2010.
41 Interviews with DG Trade officials (April 2014) and EU's Trade Delegation in Moscow (November 2013 and March 2014).
42 V. Osipov, 'Evoliursiia evraziiskoi integratsii', *Kazakhstanskaia Pravda*, 1 January 2012, available at: www.kazpravda.kz/archives/view/141430 (accessed 12 November 2016).
43 While even a name for such a currency was floated, *altyn*, it was decided not to proceed in this direction at that point. Nevertheless, discussions on a possible transition to a monetary union continue. See, for example, A. Kim, 'Common Currency for the Eurasian Economic Union: Testing the Ground?' *Eurasia Daily Monitor*, 27 March 2015, available at: www.jamestown.org/programs/edm/single/?tx_ttnews%5Btt_news%5D=43712&cHash=965d3d424fe9325ed36b197d121ccf66#.VzgQ__krLIU (accessed 11 October 2016).
44 Article 1 (2) of the EAEU Treaty.

45 Article 5 of the September 2013 draft.
46 Article 5 of the January 2014 draft.
47 For example, see President Nazarbayev's comments at the December 2013 summit, 'Sochinitel'nyi Soiuz', *Gazeta.Ru*, 24 December 2013, available at: www.gazeta.ru/business/2013/12/24/5818017.shtml (accessed 10 September 2016).
48 Article 2 of the Treaty.
49 E.g. Article 86 (Transport), Article 94 (Agricultural policy).
50 'Unified' policies are only mentioned in Article 1. 'Obedinit'sia – ne znachit dogovorit'sia', *Kommersant*, 12 February 2014, available at: www.kommersant.ru/doc/2405918 (accessed 10 September 2016); 'Chto ne ustraivaet Kazakhstan v dogovore o Evraziiskom soiuze?' *Radio Azattyq*, 25 March 2014, available at: http://rus.azattyq.org/a/evrazijsky-soiuz/25308597.html (accessed 10 September 2016).
51 Dragneva, *op. cit.* note 23.
52 Article 10 of the EAEU Treaty.
53 Article 14 of the EAEU Treaty.
54 Article 13 (2) and Article 17 (2) of the EAEU Treaty.
55 The September 2013 draft referred to a Eurasian Inter-Parliamentary Assembly modelled on the Parliamentary Assembly of the Eurasian Economic Community.
56 Section 98 of Annex 2, Statute of the Court of the EAEU.
57 Cooper, *op. cit.* note 27. Treaty on the Eurasian Economic Commission, 18 November 2011.
58 See President Medvedev's statement, 'Vstrecha presidentov Rossii, Republiki Belarus', *I Kazakhstana*, 18 November 2011, available at: http://kremlin.ru/events/president/news/13581 (accessed 10 September 2016).
59 Section 22 of the Regulation (*Polozhenie*) on the Eurasian Economic Commission, Annex 1 to the TEEU ('The EEC Regulation').
60 Section 23 of EEC Regulation.
61 Article 18 (2) of the EAEU Treaty.
62 According to the latest developments, the Collegium consists of ten members, that is two from each Member States, Decision 23 of the Supreme Council, 16 October 2015.
63 Section 32 of the EEC Regulation.
64 Section 34 of the EEC Regulation.
65 Section 41 of the EEC Regulation.
66 President Nazarbayev referred to the participation of Russia's Ministers in meetings of the Russian government allowing them to receive guidance on specific issues. He also protested about the minimal time given to evaluate lengthy drafts prior to their tabling for approval. 'Kazakhstan nameren vstupit' v VTO do sozdaniia Evraziiskogo ekonomicheskogo soiuza – Glava gosudarstva', *Kazinform*, 24 October 2013, available at: http://inform.kz/rus/article/2599908 (accessed 10 September 2016).
67 Article 9 (2) of the EAEU Treaty. These civil servants are appointed by the Chairperson of the Collegium for a period of 4 years subject to requirements for professional qualification and experience. Tellingly, the importance of this provision is underscored by envisaging it in the Treaty itself rather than in the Annex 1 dealing with the composition and functioning of the Commission.
68 Section 56 of the EEC Regulation.
69 Section 21 of the EEC Regulation; Article 18 (2) of the EAEU Treaty.
70 Dragneva *op. cit.* note 23.
71 Appendix 1 to EEC Regulation.
72 Section 30 of the EEC Regulation
73 Bail'dinov, *op. cit.* note 12.

74 V. Kirilenko and Iu. Mishal'chenko, 'Pravo Sodrushestva Nezavisimykh Gosudarstv v sisteme mezhdunarodnogo prava', 2001.
75 Dragneva *op. cit.* note 38.
76 Dragneva and Wolczuk *op. cit.* note 4. The Treaty on the Customs Union and the Single Economic Space of 26 February 1999 provided for an 'EU-style decisions', binding in their entirety and subject to direct implementation by the Member States. The Agreement on the Legal Guarantees for the Formation of the Customs Union and the Single Economic Space of 26 October 1999, however, defined 'direct implementation' as requiring transformation into domestic law.
77 Article 14 of the Treaty on the EurAsEC. This view was also upheld in Consultative Ruling Nr 01–1/3–05 of the Economic Court of the CIS (sitting as a Court of the EurAsEC) of 10 March 2006, which stated that none of the Member States' constitutions provided for an act of international body to be a source of law within these countries without an act of domestic transformation.
78 Protocol on the Procedure for Entry into Force of the International Agreements Directed to Forming the Treaty Basis of the Customs Union of 6 October 2007.
79 Dragneva, *op. cit.* note 23.
80 Articles 7 and 8 of the Treaty on the Commission of the Customs Union of 6 October 2007.
81 Decision Nr 15 of the Council of Heads of State of 27 November 2009.
82 Article 5 of the Treaty on the Eurasian Economic Commission.
83 See, for example, Decision Nr 21 of the Supreme Eurasian Council of 19 December 2012.
84 Among other things, the last formally approved list was adopted in November 2009 and, despite the legal importance of the list, not updated thereafter, Dragneva, *op. cit.* note 26.
85 Interviews with senior officials of the Eurasian Economic Commission, November 2013.
86 Article 6 (3) of the EAEU Treaty.
87 Article 6 (4) of the EAEU Treaty.
88 Article 6 (1) of the EAEU Treaty. The Treaty defines a decision (*reshenie*) as an act of normative nature, distinguishing it from resolutions (*razporiazheniia*) as acts of organisational and administrative nature, Article 2 of the EAEU Treaty.
89 Section 13 of the Regulation on the EEC.
90 See, for example, Kazakhstan's proposal in the January 2014 draft stating that 'an act of the Union cannot repeal or change the national legislation of the Member States', Article 6 (3), which was not retained in the final version as a general provision, but clearly explains the compromise reached. The strength of Kazakhstan's sensitivity is evident in that it even objected to the Russian proposal that 'international treaties representing the law of the Union, which have entered into force, become binding on the Union and its Member States', Article 6 (2).
91 Article 4 of the Statute of the Economic Court of the CIS, 6 July 1992.
92 Article 18 of the CIS Charter provides that the Council can 'recommend to the parties an appropriate procedure or method of settling' the dispute.
93 R. Dragneva, 'The Legitimacy of International Trade Tribunals: The Case of Post-Soviet Regional Courts', in: H. Ruiz Fabri, R. Howse and G. Ulfstein (eds.), *International Trade Tribunals*, Cambridge: Cambridge University Press, 2017 (forthcoming).
94 Currently, only Russia and Belarus appoint regular judges to the Economic Court of the CIS. While the Court has continued issuing certain acts, their legitimacy and legality is highly questionable.
95 Dragneva, *op. cit.* note 93.

96 Article 6 (1) of the Statute of the Court of the EurAsEC, approved by Decision Nr 122 of the Interstate Council of EurAsEC, 27 April 2003.
97 Article 20, Statute of the Court of the EurAsEC, approved by Decision Nr 502 of the Interstate Council of EurAsEC, 5 July 2010.
98 A. Ispolinov, 'Pervye resheniia Suda Evrazes: teoretisheskie I prakticheskie voprosy iurisdiktsii', *Rossiiskoe pravosudie*, 6(86), 2013, 89–101.
99 This activism was revealed primarily in relation to appeals by commercial actors against the decisions of the permanent regulator, the Eurasian Economic Commission, *Ibid.*
100 Bail'dinov, *op. cit.* note 12; Karliuk, *op. cit.* note 12.
101 Section 102 of the Statute of the Court, Annex 2 of the EAEU Treaty.
102 Karliuk, *op. cit.* note 12; Kembayev, *op. cit.* note 12.
103 Dragneva, *op. cit.* note 38.
104 R. Dragneva and K. Wolczuk, 'Commitment, Asymmetry and Flexibility: Making Sense of Eurasian Economic Integration', in: R. Dragneva and K. Wolczuk (eds.), *Eurasian Economic Integration: Law, Policy and Politics*, Cheltenham: Edward Elgar, 2013, pp. 204–221.
105 M. Laruelle, 'Kazakhstan's Posture in the Eurasian Union: In Search of Serene Sovereignty', *Russian Analytical Digest*, No. 165, 17 March 2015, Centre for Security Studies, available at: www.css.ethz.ch/content/dam/ethz/special-interest/gess/cis/center-for-securities-studies/pdfs/RAD-165-7-10.pdf (accessed 12 September 2016).
106 'Nazarbaev zaiavil o vozmozhnom vykhode Kazakhstana iz Evraziiskogo soiuza', *Newsru.com*, 31 August 2014, available at: http://newsru.com/world/31aug2014/nazarbaev.html (accessed 10 September 2016).
107 See, for example, J. E. Thomson, 'State Sovereignty in International Relations: Bridging the Gap Between Theory and Empirical Research', *International Studies Quarterly*, 39, 1995, 213–233.
108 See Decision Nr 48 of the Supreme Eurasian Economic Council, 24 October 2013.
109 See Decision Nr 22 of the Supreme Eurasian Economic Council, 16 October 2015.

4 The Association Agreements between the EU and Georgia, Moldova and Ukraine

Constitutional issues of sovereignty and legitimacy

Rilka Dragneva

Introduction

The Association Agreements (AAs) signed in 2014 represent a radically new development in the relations between the European Union (EU) and Georgia, Moldova and Ukraine.[1] The Agreements do not lead to or prepare for membership in the EU, nor do they contain the promise of one. In this sense, they stop short of the extensive transfer of sovereign powers associated with membership in a supranational organisation, such as the EU.[2] Nonetheless, the AAs embody commitments which affect these countries' sovereignty in important ways. While the nature of the AAs as novel instruments aiming to deliver 'integration without membership' has attracted scholarly attention,[3] their consequences for the constitutional foundations of the partner countries merit further discussion.

In entering the AAs, the partners commit to a unique form of close and lasting relations with the EU.[4] In addition to enhanced political association, the AAs aim at advanced economic integration in setting up Deep and Comprehensive Free Trade Areas (DCFTAs). Thus, the Agreements deal not only with tariffs and other border issues. They reach deep into the regulatory fabric of a large number of sectors where, following the alignment with EU legislation, the objective is the gradual integration into EU's internal market. Furthermore, the AAs have an explicitly transformative dimension, seeking to 'support the Partner's efforts to complete the transition into a functioning market economy',[5] with domestic reform as a premise to successful implementation. Importantly, the AAs pursue these objectives on the basis of an innovative institutional regime, which provides for binding obligations, a comprehensive system of common bodies endowed with important powers and a developed system of disciplines. The economic integration aimed at by the DCFTAs is thus premised on a common legal space achieved through institutional mechanisms, characterised by some supranational elements. Significantly, reminiscent of the EU's enlargement policy, the institutional processes envisaged by the AAs exhibit asymmetric features, underscoring the differences in bargaining power between the EU and the partners.

Thus, it can be argued that, given their ambition in terms of objectives, substantive scope and institutional set-up, the AAs have significant and far-reaching implications for the constitutional and legal orders of the partner countries. These implications extend to both their 'internal sovereignty', associated with the supreme authority within a territory and a political community, and 'external sovereignty', associated with the participation of a state in the international order.[6] Internally, the AAs constrain the partners' decision-making capacity over key areas of the economy, evidenced in undertakings affecting the legislative, regulatory and judicial field. Externally, the most visible implications relate to the ability of the partner countries to engage in overlapping integration arrangements, something brought to light particularly by the case of Ukraine.[7]

Loss of sovereign powers has become the corollary of modern, interdependent international relations. Constitutionally, countries act as gatekeepers to such limitations. All partner countries following their post-Soviet independence proceeded to order the relationship between domestic and international law in their constitutions and laws on treaties.[8] Following the doctrine of 'monism', they generally provide that agreements that have been duly signed and transformed into domestic law assume an obligatory role within the country. Yet comparative experience shows that the constitutional conceptualisation of sovereignty in different countries can vary.[9] There are differences in the 'sensitivity' threshold at which a loss of policy discretion in the interdependent world becomes loss of sovereignty requiring constitutional protection and guarantees to ensure the voluntary and democratic nature of its limitation. Accordingly, there can be important country specificities in the conditions attached to the process of transforming international law into domestic law, the definition of international law for these purposes as well as its domestic effects. Furthermore, international agreements themselves can vary in their design characteristics, presenting specific constitutional challenges for the countries signing them. It is such features of institutional design that this chapter will focus on in exploring the AAs and their implications for the partner countries. In particular, the discussion will centre on key characteristics, such as the extent of international delegation, the scope of substantive commitments, and the mechanisms for monitoring and enforcing performance, including dispute settlement, which can be particularly costly in terms of sovereignty.[10]

While the main focus here is on sovereignty as a constitutional category, it should not be forgotten that it also has strong political dimensions and discursive value; it is a multi-layered concept played out in a certain historical context.[11] These dimensions were thrown into sharp relief when in November 2013 Ukraine's President Yanukovych abandoned the AA in favour of closer relations with the Customs Union between Russia, Belarus and Kazakhstan. Even though Ukraine had negotiated the Agreement over an extensive period of time and already initialled it, it was not only the economic benefits of the Agreement and its implementation costs that were in question. Pro-Russia politicians deemed the AA a betrayal of Ukraine's independence and an unconstitutional sacrifice of its sovereignty that will turn Ukraine into 'a colony of the EU'.[12] Subsequent events proved this to be the minority view, with Ukraine proceeding to the successful signature of the Association Agreement.[13] In light of this, the chapter will also consider the possible effects on political and popular notions of sovereignty in the AA context. Given the 'revenge of sovereignty' observed in EU Member States,[14] and internationally, the issue and its relation to the AAs may not be put to rest. In this sense, any limitations on sovereignty – even if not deemed as requiring constitutional responses in the short-run – may affect popular perceptions of legitimacy of far-reaching integration agreements, such as the AA.

The Association Agreements: historical and institutional context

The constitutional implications of the AAs are particularly notable against the background of previous relations between the EU and Georgia, Moldova and Ukraine. Despite their broad scope and objectives, these relations were developed within general, non-binding frameworks, imposing few restrictions on the exercise of sovereign powers. Examining this background is also important to understand the motivation of the partner countries in accepting, and indeed, demanding, a far-reaching agreement with the EU.

The main legal framework for dealing with the EU until the AAs took effect were the Partnership and Cooperation Agreements (PCAs).[15] The PCAs aimed at political dialogue and economic cooperation, yet were radically less ambitious than the AAs. In trade terms, these were agreements liberalising trade in goods by providing Most Favoured Nation (MFN) treatment within the framework of GATT.[16] This was not necessarily a major advancement of previous relations;[17] similarly, its liberalisation undertakings were limited.[18] With regard to the countries under discussion here, free trade was a long-term objective open only to Ukraine and Moldova.[19] The PCAs contained an evolutionary clause, whereby the parties undertook to consult further as to 'whether circumstances . . . allow the beginning of negotiations on the establishment of a free trade area'.[20] This was not the case with Georgia, whose Agreement had only a general clause on the possibility of developing the PCA.[21]

The PCAs dealt with economic cooperation in areas of mutual interest, such as customs, standardisation, industry, statistics, energy, agriculture and transport, yet there was little specificity or clear priorities for their advancement. Legislative approximation with the EU *acquis* was seen as an important factor in this process, aiming to bring the partner countries closer to the EU's internal market. This, however, was a voluntary undertaking embodied in 'best endeavour' clauses. While the legislative approximation clauses largely replicated those contained in the Association Agreements with the Central and East European countries, also known as the Europe Agreements, they were embedded in a 'softer' framework of disciplines and institutions.[22] The PCAs contained some elements of political and economic conditionality; however, it was one virtually impractical to activate. The PCAs set up Cooperation Councils as the main forum for consultation between the parties. These bodies had important powers in relation to implementation, monitoring and dispute resolution. Yet their impact was limited, given the ability to adopt only non-binding 'recommendations'. Importantly, the PCAs lacked the key driver behind the success of the Europe Agreements, that is, the promise of membership.[23]

Certainly for Ukraine, the institutional deficiencies of the PCA were leading to early demands for the improvement of the regime, which the EU was reluctant to accommodate.[24] The EU launched a number of political instruments to improve the effectiveness and development of relations with its Eastern neighbours. Yet these developments did not change the role of the PCA as the underlying contractual mechanism or the fundamental nature of the obligations arising from it. In 1999, the EU adopted a Common Strategy for Ukraine as part of its new foreign policy initiative with selected strategic partners.[25] This was a vague and incoherent framework, aptly described as an 'encyclopaedia of generalities'.[26]

In 2004, following its eastern enlargement, the EU launched its European Neighbourhood Policy (ENP),[27] aiming to ensure 'prosperity, security and stability' in its new neighbourhood.[28] The ENP proposed to do that by offering the partners 'more than partnership and less than membership', sharing everything but the institutions', as the Commission President Romano Prodi famously stated.[29] The cornerstone of this proposal was 'a common market embracing the EU and its partners'.[30] The new policy was also an opportunity to coordinate the various strands of cooperation based on diverse and disjointed instruments. This was seen as important also given that cooperation under the intergovernmental pillars of the EU, Common Foreign and Security Policy (CFSP) and Justice and Home Affairs (JHA) evolved outside the PCAs.[31] At the same time, the grand promise of a 'stake in the internal market' was insufficiently clear. According to some, it 'would require progressive convergence with internal market rules, coupled with stepped-up consultation and co-operation, as well as adaptation of institutional practices to EU standards.'[32] Importantly, this was to be a flexible policy developed bilaterally in country-focused Action Plans (APs) with specific priority areas for cooperation and reform outlined in each AP. This selectivity also extended to the legal approximation needed to accompany the process. Yet the template for legal approximation across the multiple areas was vague, ill-defined and unspecific, which created significant problems for implementation.[33]

At the same time, despite its generality and the political emphasis on partnership, the ENP embraced the strong conditionality approach, used in the eastern enlargement, thus underlying the asymmetry between the EU and the eastern partners.[34] Crucially, progress in cooperation was dependent on the progress in implementation of the agreed priorities and particularly in the area of legal approximation. Thus, the ENP formula complemented the PCAs in its ambition, but remained fundamentally a 'soft' framework. The Action Plans were adopted by the institutions set up under the PCA, namely the Cooperation Councils, thereby having a non-binding status.[35] Legal reform remained important, yet domestic commitment was compromised by the lack of clarity of benchmarks and the uncertainty of the rewards. Unsurprisingly, while some legal reform took place in the context of implementing the PCAs and the APs, the results were modest and patchy.[36]

For Ukraine, the context for advancing relations with the EU changed decisively following the Orange Revolution of 2004. Using the negotiations of the AP as a platform, Ukraine demanded closer and faster integration with the EU in the shape of a new agreement. Reluctantly, the EU conceded on starting work on a new agreement. The legal status of the new agreement was not clear at the start of the negotiations, so the term 'enhanced' was initially used. Only after the September 2008 EU-Ukraine summit was a consensus defining the agreement as an 'association' one finally reached.[37] Negotiations on the political part of the AA were launched as early as 2007. Negotiations on the DCFTA followed in the immediate aftermath of Ukraine's accession to the WTO in 2008. The promise of such an agreement was extended to Moldova and Georgia with the launch of the Eastern Partnership in 2009.[38] Importantly, the DCFTA negotiations with these countries did not start until February 2012, that is, in fact after the negotiations with Ukraine were completed in late 2011. There were some differences in the approach to the talks,[39] resulting in key differences of undertakings in some sectors. In terms of the main features of the institutions for integration, however, the AAs with Moldova and Georgia largely follow the template of Ukraine's AA, which is why many of the examples below will be illustrated with reference to this agreement.

The story of the signature and ratification of the AAs, particularly in the case of Ukraine, is told elsewhere and is beyond the scope of this discussion.[40] Nonetheless, it is important to point out three main dimensions of the partners' motivation in the build-up to the conclusion of the AAs, which help understand the willingness to accept the extensive commitments envisaged in it.

Firstly, from quite early on, the fundamental aspirations of the partners centred on membership in the European Union. In Ukraine these aspirations were magnified after the Orange Revolution, but remained an official state policy under successive leaderships.[41] Like Ukraine, Georgia also sought to include a 'membership perspective' into various EU policy documents, particularly after

Table 4.1 Milestones in concluding the Association Agreements between the EU and Georgia, Moldova and Ukraine

	Started DCFTA negotiations	*Agreement initialled*	*Agreement signed*	*Domestic ratification*	*Provisional application*	*Entry into force*
Georgia	Feb 2012	29 Nov 2013	27 June 2014	18 July 2014	1 Sep 2014	1 July 2016
Moldova	Feb 2012	29 Nov 2013	27 June 2014	2 July 2014	1 Sep 2014	1 July 2016
Ukraine	Feb 2008	19 July 2012	21 March 2014 27 June 2014	16 Sep 2014	1 Jan 2016	1 Sep 2017

the Rose Revolution in 2005–2006.[42] Given EU's reluctance to agree to such a demand, the prospect of 'association', including deep economic integration, was viewed as 'the second best' option. For Ukraine, for example, the insistence on the agreement being called an 'association' agreement was symbolic of its privileged relations with the EU. For the EU, however, it was important to underline its disassociation from membership, using the formula that the Agreement 'neither precludes nor promotes Ukraine's membership aspirations'.[43] Nonetheless, 'association' continues to be viewed as a stepping-stone to joining the EU: as President Poroshenko has often stated, in signing the AA, 'Ukraine is underlining its sovereign choice in favour of membership of the EU'.[44]

Secondly, while the EU increasingly resorts to exporting its single market *acquis* in its trade agreements with third countries,[45] extensive and binding undertakings in this field were seen by the partner countries as conducive to their modernisation. While the partners' enthusiasm for legislative approximation was not equal, the view that the EU's *acquis* can represent a ready-made blueprint for reform has been surprisingly popular.[46] This was particularly pronounced in the case of Ukraine, where the negotiating team took the opportunity to demand and agree on extensive commitments, thus binding the political elite to a system of external disciplines to achieve much needed domestic reforms.[47]

Finally, it should be remembered that the developing relations with the EU cannot be dissociated from the partners' effort to balance Russia's influence. Ukraine, Moldova and Georgia participated in Russia's economic integration projects in the post-Soviet space, yet were classified as 'minimalists' in terms of their interest in integration.[48] On balance, they were neither enthusiastic nor full participants, preferring selective engagement and limited constraints.[49] Notably, as early as October 1997, all three countries sought to form an alternative centre of integration by setting up another organisation (together with Azerbaijan), called GUAM Organisation for Democracy and Economic Development.[50] Thus, deepening relations with the EU was part and parcel of a multi-vector foreign policy approach in response to a geopolitical predicament. These calculations were reinforced for Georgia following the 2008 war with Russia and the occupation of Abkhazia and South Ossetia, and for Ukraine, following the annexation of the Crimea in March 2014. Even though Russia's influence remains important,[51] pursuing close relations with the EU continues to be a key factor in security terms, particularly in Ukraine and Georgia.

These dimensions, it can be argued, underpin the partners' motivation to enter into a far-reaching association agreement with the EU and accept its sovereignty implications.

Delegation to common bodies

The AAs introduce a common institutional framework representing a significant upgrade of the system of the PCAs. The decision-making bodies under this framework are the Association Council, the Association Committee and its subcommittees.[52] The EU-Ukraine AA also formalises the Summit meetings at the highest level of political decision-making. They take place once a year with the purpose of providing 'overall guidance for the implementation' of the Agreements and as 'an opportunity to discuss any bilateral or international issues of mutual interest'.[53] The AAs also set up two consultative bodies, the Parliamentary Association Committee and a Civil Society Platform, which can make recommendations to the Association Council. While they provide a forum for including representatives of the legislature and civil society, respectively, hence a wider societal dialogue on matters of the AA, it is yet to be seen whether they will be able to exercise any significant constraining power.

In terms of their composition, the Association Council and Committee are intergovernmental in nature. The Association Council meets at ministerial level and is composed of members of the EU Council and Commission and members of the government of the partner country. The Association Committee meets at the level of senior civil servants. In terms of their powers, however, these bodies exhibit important supranational elements. The Association Council is endowed with extensive powers in relation to supervising and monitoring the application and the implementation of the Agreement and is required to periodically review its functioning. These powers are not limited to the scope of the AAs: the Council can 'examine any major issues arising within the framework of this Agreement and any other bilateral or international issues of mutual interest.'[54] The Association Committee is the junior decision-making body, intended to assist the Association Council in the performance of its duties, including the preparation of its meetings. The AA vests various explicit powers with the Association Committee in its various configurations, such as the Trade Committee in the DCFTA chapter. In addition to the powers vested under the AAs, the Committee can also exercise any powers that the Association Council may delegate to it.

Among the most significant powers of the Association Council are those related to legislative approximation. The Association Council is a forum for exchange of information on legislative acts under preparation and in force in both parties, including any implementation, enforcement and compliance measures. It monitors the progress made under the Agreement and is the body competent to decide on the progress in integration. This is particularly relevant to the DCFTA chapter, where the promised access to the EU internal market is largely conditional on implementing the legislative approximation commitments undertaken by the partners, as will be discussed further below. Crucially, the Association Council also 'may update or amend the Annexes to this Agreement . . . taking into account the evolution of EU law and applicable standards set out in international instruments deemed relevant by the Parties'.[55] The far-reaching nature of these powers is underpinned by envisaging that the decisions of the Association Council and the Association Committee are binding on the parties.[56] In a clear departure from the PCA regime, this power allows the parties to develop their mutual relationship and scope of integration without the need to adopt a new international agreement. This is vital for ensuring the durability of the regime, something deemed as critical for a new agreement.[57]

Yet such Council decisions have profound domestic constitutional and legal ramifications. Decisions are to be taken by agreement between the parties, who undertake to take the appropriate measures to implement them. In formal terms, the consensus principle in adopting decisions upholds the sovereignty of the partners. This means that any party can block a decision it deems against its interest. The parity between the parties is underlined also by the requirement for alternating the chairmanship of the Association bodies.[58] Yet, as in other contractual settings, this does not necessarily eliminate the potential limitations and sensitivities that may result from the underlying inequalities of bargaining power between the EU and the partners.

At the same time, the binding nature of their decisions entails a restriction of sovereign powers. In respect of the EU legal order, the Court of Justice, ruling on the status of the decisions of the EU-Turkey Association Council, established that 'when, regard being had to their wording and their purpose and nature, as well as those of the association agreement, they contain a clear and precise obligation which is not subject, in its implementation or effects, to the adoption of any subsequent measure', such decisions can have direct effect.[59] In the case of the Europe Agreements, for example, it was clear that this was a complex constitutional issue in the Central and Eastern Europe countries (CEECs).[60] In those circumstances, 'bindingness' opened the question of the possibility of an act of an international body, such as the Association Council, to become part of the domestic legal order without the need for domestic ratification, usually reserved for the category of 'self-executing treaties', as well as of the place of those decisions within the domestic legal hierarchy.

As the subsequent chapters will show, this remains an important constitutional issue for Ukraine, Moldova and Georgia to address.[61] In this context, it is worth pointing out that there are no legal precedents these countries can draw on involving their own integration experience. While all three countries participated in post-Soviet integration projects, such as the Commonwealth of Independent States (CIS), none of the bodies set up within that organisation were vested with the powers to issue binding acts and the decisions adopted within it, if of normative character, had the status of international agreements.[62]

Scope of legislative commitments

A key feature of the AAs is the obligation to incorporate and apply a preselected part of the EU *acquis* by the partner countries. Thus, the partner countries largely undertake to follow a particular legislative agenda in terms of what laws they adopt, when, and the institutional bodies and procedures that must be put in place to implement them. The flip side of this undertaking is the relative loss of discretion or control over one of the key dimensions of internal sovereignty, that is, domestic law-making. In effect, what the AAs require is the widespread adoption of a foreign law, whereby few areas of domestic law-making remain untouched. Given the centrality of legislative approximation for the realisation of the objectives of the AAs and the DCFTA, in particular, it is important to outline the type of constraints imposed on domestic law-making and the system of disciplines attached to it.

The undertaking for legislative approximation under the AAs is extensive, covering a significant part of the EU's internal market *acquis*. This wholesale adoption is unprecedented outside the accession context, but also in comparison to the EU's trade agreements with third countries with the exception of the EEA.[63] Legislative approximation commitments are envisaged in most of the chapters of Title IV Trade and Trade Related Matters, or the DCFTA part,[64] and Title V dealing with Economic and Sector Cooperation.[65] Yet the nature of the undertaking differs significantly between chapters and countries, and has varying sovereignty implications. A comprehensive discussion of these variations is beyond the scope of this chapter. Instead, the focus will be on one primary example where a significant loss of domestic legislative and regulatory powers can be observed: that of Ukraine's obligations in the area of services.[66] This will illustrate the costliest implications for sovereignty, whilst also indicating some weaker forms of limitation.

First, Ukraine commits to adopting a list of specifically predetermined EU Regulations and Directives, subject to a strict timetable.[67] In addition to the legislative agenda, Ukraine needs to ensure the effective 'administrative capacity to enforce' this legislation and 'provide a satisfactory track record of sector-specific surveillance and investigation, prosecutions, and administrative and judicial treatment of violations.'[68] Thus, the obligation extends not only to reform of laws on the books, but fundamentally to delivering on the effective functioning of these laws.

As in the case of services, most chapters of the AA contain predetermined lists of EU legislation to adopt. Others, however, allow a greater autonomy for the partner country. For example, in relation to Ukraine's Sanitary and Phyto-Sanitary Standards (SPS) commitments, the AA provides a number of priority areas within which Ukraine needs to identify relevant EU legislation and then list a strategy for implementation. Yet, while this approach introduces flexibility allowing some control by the partner over which laws to adopt and when, this flexibility does not extend over the contents of the selected *acquis*. Similarly, it needs to be exercised within the institutional process set up by the Agreement: Ukraine's comprehensive strategy for implementation should be submitted for approval to the SPS Sub-Committee, thereby requiring the agreement of the EU side.[69]

Second, in implementing its services obligation, Ukraine subjects itself to a strict monitoring process, with strong asymmetric elements. For example, Ukraine is required to prepare a detailed roadmap and regularly report on its progress by submitting reports to the European Commission, followed by a transposition table to reflect the exact correspondence of the incorporated *acquis*. If the European Commission comes to a positive assessment of Ukraine's progress, it can propose to the Trade Committee that access to EU's internal market is granted. This is a prime example of the 'market access conditionality', applied in several chapters of the DCFTA,[70] whereby delivering on the legislative approximation undertaking is a formal precondition for the partners' enjoyment of the benefits of integration. As Van der Loo points out, this is unique relative to other trade agreements in that market access is tied to the country's track record in legislative approximation rather than on the country's mere commitment to it.[71]

The strict conditionality in this chapter is explained by the unprecedented level of integration granted to Ukraine and the need for the EU to ensure that the functioning of the internal market is not disturbed in this process. The decision to open the internal market is taken by a joint recommendation of the Association bodies, the Trade Committee in this case, by consensus. Yet, in the event of a failure to agree, there is little Ukraine can do given the dispute resolution process applying to legislative approximation under the DCFTA, as will be discussed below. A refusal by the EU to grant further access, which may or may not depend on Ukraine's actual implementation record, but reflect internal considerations or sensitivities, will not be deemed to be breach of its undertaking that can be challenged by Ukraine.

Furthermore, the credibility of the process may be put in question given that the standard for the implementation of the approximation commitment is not necessarily clear. As Van der Loo notes, the AAs refer to 'alignment with', 'achieving conformity with, 'incorporating into the legislation of' and other legal terms to convey the nature of the partners' obligation, thus, potentially contributing to differences in interpretation and standards of assessment.[72]

The undertakings in other sectors are not subject to such an enhanced monitoring and specific market access conditionality. Nonetheless, they are subject to the general monitoring process envisaged by the AAs to assess the approximation of Ukrainian law to EU law.[73] This empowers the Association bodies to use progress reports as well as new forms of assessment, such as 'on-the-spot missions', carried out by EU institutions as well as other actors, such as non-governmental bodies, supervisory authorities and independent experts. Similarly, all undertakings are conditional on the partner's adherence to a set of shared values. These values are most extensively defined in the case of Ukraine's AA and include respect for democratic principles, human rights and fundamental freedoms, the principle of the rule of law as well as 'respect for the principles of sovereignty and territorial integrity, inviolability of border and independence' as 'essential elements' of the Agreement.[74] The violation of these principles allows a party to take 'appropriate measures', including the suspension of their undertakings.[75]

Third, Ukraine's services undertakings have far-reaching sovereignty implications also because they extend beyond the scope of the EU *acquis* as identified prior to the signature of the AA. It also applies to new or amended EU legislation, thus ensuring the continued uniformity of the legal space underpinning this area of the internal market.[76] As noted, all Annexes to the AA can be updated or amended by the Association Council, taking into account the evolution of EU law.[77] Yet, this general provision does not turn the exercise of this power into a legal obligation. Similarly, while the Association Council can be a forum for exchange of information on future legislation, there is no binding requirement for the continuous tracking, notification or incorporation of new or amended legislation. The services chapter, however, adds its own complex procedure, whereby the Trade Committee is informed about new legislation, which is then added to the list and becomes subject to Ukraine's transposition. While all EU integration agreements include institutions that can update the scope of the relevant *acquis*, the partner's discretion is particularly limited prior to the internal market access being granted, with Ukraine having no ability to refuse to take on any modification of the corresponding EU law.[78]

Finally, an important aspect of Ukraine's undertaking relates to the need to interpret the transposed EU provisions 'in conformity' with the relevant rulings of the Court of Justice of the EU.[79] In effect, this is a far-reaching, binding obligation subject to which the partner cannot divert from the interpretations of the CJEU when applying and implementing the relevant laws. Ukraine has to ensure that courts rely on EU case law, without this case law being specifically notified or listed by a joint institution, as required in other integration agreements with the EU.[80] This effort to achieve uniformity of judicial interpretation is, again, linked to the depth of the access to the internal market provided. Yet, while the area of public procurement offers Ukraine a similarly extensive access, the obligation there is softer, with only 'due account' of the corresponding case law of the CJEU to be taken.[81] Other chapters, however, do not envisage such commitments at all. Thus, setting up the required domestic institutional process to ensure effective judicial harmonization will be a formidable domestic challenge. Yet, equally challenging may be to distinguish between the nature of the obligation in different sectors.

Clearly, there are significant constitutional implications in terms of the authorisation and implementation of the legislative approximation undertaking, as well as important legitimacy concerns that may arise in this process. As argued, the adoption of the EU *acquis* was seen by reforming elites as a template for modernisation to be implemented within a strict system of external disciplines. Yet the nature of emerging issues is not dissimilar from the ones raised in the context of the Eastern enlargement. The candidate countries had no input into drafting the legislation that they were required to adopt. Furthermore, this was legislation resulting from a particular intra-EU policy-making process and interest group input and therefore not necessarily suited to the candidates' particular problems or needs.[82] As the accession negotiations proved, the CEECs had little say on what they were required to adopt in preparation for accession, limiting bargaining largely to the matter of transition periods. Unsurprisingly, the EU was seen as acting as an explicitly 'hegemonic actor' in this context.[83] Despite the clear accession perspective provided to the CEECs, these were not simply theoretical grievances but gave rise to vocal sovereignty sensitivities and constitutional litigation in some of them.[84] Given the absence of a membership perspective and the even wider disparities in terms of economic political and economic development between EU members and the partners, such concerns may prove to be of even greater importance in Ukraine, Georgia and Moldova.

Dispute settlement

It can be argued that, given the complexity and durability of the regime set up by the AAs, the provisions on dispute resolution assume a particular significance. The AA delivers a complex system of mechanisms, depending on the type of dispute to arise, with varying sovereignty implications.

First, any disputes related to the non-DCFTA part of the Agreement, following a consultation period, are to be settled by a binding decision of the Association Council.[85] If the Council fails to reach a decision within three months, the aggrieved party is allowed to take 'appropriate' self-help measures, undertaking to prioritise such responses that least disturb the functioning of the AA. While this approach departs from the purely diplomatic solution common to simple free trade agreements,[86] it is still embedded in the intergovernmental institutional framework of the AAs.

Second, disputes concerning the interpretation and application of the provisions of the DCFTA, but not related to legislative approximation, are to be dealt with by a quasi-judicial model, inspired by the WTO Dispute Settlement Mechanism (DSM).[87] In the event of failure of consultations, the aggrieved party can request the establishment of an arbitration panel. The members of such a panel are chosen by the parties, or drawn (if no agreement can be reached) from a permanent list of panellists. The panel's ruling is binding on the parties, who undertake to comply with it, and there is no WTO-type appellate body that can be invoked. In the event of non-compliance, again there are certain self-help measures that the aggrieved party is allowed to take. Clearly, this solution entails a high degree of delegation and raises domestic constitutional issues in terms of the effect of the panel decisions. Yet, given that all partners are members of the WTO and subject to its DSM, despite the variations, the general issues raised under the AA are not unique. Importantly, the AAs explicitly state that the rulings 'shall not create any rights or obligations for natural or legal persons',[88] thus avoiding the possibility of granting direct effect to the DCFTA provisions.

Third, the most profound sovereignty implications are demonstrated in relation to disputes arising from the process of legislative approximation under the DCFTA.[89] In the event of a question on the interpretation of a provision of EU law, the arbitration panel must request the CJEU to give a preliminary ruling. As noted by commentators, this is a far-reaching provision in comparative terms, as it is an obligation not an option for the panel.[90] The ruling of the CJEU, then, is binding on the panel. The logic of requiring the CJEU to interpret the EU *acquis* is understandable: it ensures authenticity and follows the extensive nature of the legislative approximation undertaking of the partners in areas where deep access into the internal market will be granted. Yet, it also means that, be it only in relation to interpretation, the partners undertake to be bound by the decision of a foreign court without the ability to affect its composition, procedures or interpretative practice. This raises not only constitutional issues, but also possible sensitivities around the explicit acceptance of an external authority with the power to affect a wide range of undertakings.

Conclusions

It should not be a surprise that the constitutional implications of the AAs are extensive, given their integration ambitions and explicitly transformative agenda. The partner countries took on detailed commitments and accepted being bound by a system of disciplines which, despite formal parity in procedures, also reflects the EU's position of being able to deliver or withdraw the promised benefits of integration. The asymmetric and far-reaching nature of undertakings at the cost of sovereignty limitations can be explained by the EU's 'power of attraction' and the desire of these countries to follow its developmental model. Critically, it is also underpinned by those countries' geopolitical calculations and desire to balance Russia's extensive influence in the region. Thus, at the time of signing and ratifying the AAs, the limitations were clearly deemed to be acceptable, even if requiring some constitutional developments.

Yet it cannot be presumed that, given the complexity and demands of the AAs, the question of its implications for sovereignty, internal or external, will not resurface. The AAs promise important long-term benefits, yet they are premised on reforms which require a massive implementation commitment and entail short-term costs. While some of these costs may be off-set by capacity building measures and technical assistance, others – including costs related to the disruption of existing rent-seeking networks with access to powerful centres of political powers – will not. In this vein, of great importance is also the EU's credibility to deliver on its promises. The long delay of implementing the visa liberalisation plan, for example, has already dented public opinion in Ukraine, along with the EU's image in being able to deliver on restraining Russia's hybrid war advances and addressing Ukraine's territorial concerns.[91]

A further critical factor is Russia's continued geopolitical aspirations *vis-à-vis* the region. As mentioned, one of the most problematic questions presented by the AAs relates to their compatibility with other integration arrangements, particularly with Russia-led integration initiatives in the post-Soviet space. This does not necessarily present direct constitutional issues, being primarily a matter for resolving conflicts between international trade laws.[92] Yet, as Ukraine's case illustrates in the extreme, its geopolitical implications and relation to external sovereignty cannot be underestimated. Russia has already demonstrated its ability to use territorial disputes and economic penalties to increase the cost of EU integration. Certainly, the sanctions and other trade restrictions imposed by Russia on account of the countries' signing of the AA has hurt domestic producers,[93] particularly given their limited ability to reorient trade to the EU market in the short-run. Furthermore, it is clear that Russia continues to represent an alternative centre of attraction, at least in Moldova. Its new President Igor Dodon questioned the benefits of the AA, raising the possibility of scrapping it,[94] and proceeded to sign a cooperation memorandum, obtaining an observer status to the Eurasian Economic Union in April 2017.[95] It remains to be seen whether this will amount to a flexible diplomatic arrangement or is a precursor of a U-turn to come, as was the case with Armenia in 2013.

On balance, all these factors put pressure on the commitment to the AA. Thus, beyond the issue of the constitutional implications of the AAs, there remains the question about the extent to which the difficulties of implementation in combination with external factors may ignite latent sovereignty trade-offs, resulting in stalling the effectiveness of the agreement, or even a withdrawal from it.

Notes

1 Association Agreement between the European Union and the European Atomic Energy Community and their Member States, of the one part, and Georgia, of the other part, *OJ*, 2014, L 261/4; Association Agreement between the European Union and the European Atomic Energy Community and their Member States, of the one part, and the Republic of Moldova, of the other part, *OJ*, 2014, L260/4; Association Agreement between the European Union and its Member States, of the one part, and Ukraine of the other part, *OJ*, 2014, L 161.

2 For the constitutional implications of EU membership, see M. Martin Martinez, *National Sovereignty and International Organizations*, The Hague: Kluwer Law International, 1996; A. Albi, *EU Enlargement and the Constitutions of Central and Eastern Europe*, Cambridge: Cambridge University Press, 2005.

3 G. Van der Loo, P. Van Elsuwege and R. Petrov, 'The EU-Ukraine Association Agreement: Assessment of an Innovative Legal Instrument', *EUI Working Papers*, Law 2014/09; G. Van der Loo, *The EU-Ukraine Association Agreement and Deep and Comprehensive Free Trade Area*, Leiden and Boston: Brill Nijhoff, 2016.

4 This chapter uses the terms 'partners' or 'partner countries' to designate the three countries from the Eastern Partnership group of countries with which the EU has concluded Association Agreements.

5 E.g. Article 1.2 (d) EU-Ukraine AA.

6 T. Aalberts, 'Sovereignty', in F. Berenskoetter (ed.), *Concepts in World Politics*, Thousand Oaks, CA: Sage Publications, 2016.

7 G. Van der Loo and P. Van Elsuwege, 'Competing Paths of Regional Economic Integration in the Post-Soviet Space: Legal and Political Dilemmas for Ukraine', *Review of Central and East European Law*, 37, 2012, 421–447.

8 G. Danilenko, 'Implementation of International Law in CIS States: Theory and Practice', *European Journal of International Law*, 10, 1999, 51–69; W. Butler, *The Law of Treaties in Russia and the CIS*, Cambridge: Cambridge University Press, 2002.

9 It has been argued, for example, that in the early 1990s Central and European constitutions were distinctly more protective of sovereignty than most constitutions in Western Europe, following its forced subordination to the USSR, Albi, *op. cit.* note 2, pp. 24–25.

10 *E.g.* K. Abbott and D. Snidal, 'Hard and Soft Law in International Governance', *International Organization*, 3, 2000, 421–456; K. Raustiala, 'Form and Substance in International Agreements', *The American Journal of International Law*, 99(58), 2005, 581–614; B. Koremenos, 'Institutionalism and International Law', in J. Dunoff and M. Pollack (eds.), *Interdisciplinary Perspectives on International Law and International Relations*, Cambridge: Cambridge University Press, 2013, 59–82.

11 T. Aalberts, *op. cit.* note 6.

12 'V. Medvedchuk: soglashenie ob assotsiatsii s EC – soglashenie o kolonizatsii', *Kommersant' Ukraina*, Nr 204 (1907), 9 December 2013.

13 On the circumstances of Ukraine's signing of the AA, see R. Dragneva and K. Wolczuk, *Ukraine Between the EU and Russia*, Basingstoke: Palgrave Macmillan, 2015; G. Van der Loo, *op. cit.* note 3.

14 J. Shapiro and B. Lilly, 'Sovereignty's Revenge: The Power of Populism in the European Union', *Brookings*, 30 April 2015, available at: www.brookings.edu/blog/order-from-chaos/2015/04/30/sovereigntys-revenge-the-power-of-populism-in-the-european-union (accessed 23 May 2017).
15 Partnership and Cooperation Agreement between the European Communities and their Member States, and Ukraine, signed 14 June 1994, entered into force 1 March 1998 (*OJ*, 1998, L 49), Partnership and Cooperation Agreement between the European Communities and their Member States and the Republic of Moldova, signed 28 November 1994, entered into force 1 July 1998 (*OJ*, 1998, L 181), Partnership and Cooperation Agreement between the European Communities and their Member States, and Georgia, signed 26 April 1996, entry into force 1 July 1999 (*OJ*, 1999, L 205).
16 Not all goods were included in the PCA regime. In the case of Ukraine, textiles, steel, and nuclear materials were dealt with in separate agreements.
17 This was particularly where the EU had already extended its preferential treatment under the Generalised System of Preferences, e.g. World Bank, *Ukraine: Trade Policy Study, Volume 2: Main Report*, 16 November 2004, available at: https://openknowledge.worldbank.org/handle/10986/2194 (accessed 18 May 2017).
18 Despite its extensive commitments, the EU maintained a strong protectionist bias, A. Aslund and A. Warner, 'The EU Enlargement: Consequences for the CIS Countries', *Carnegie Endowment*, 2003, available at: http://carnegieendowment.org/files/wp361.pdf (accessed 16 May 2017).
19 This option was included in the PCA with Russia. For the negotiating background on this issue, see C. Hillion, *The Evolving System of European Union External Relations as Evidenced in the EU Partnerships with Russia and Ukraine*, Ph.D. Thesis, Leiden, 2005, p. 25.
20 Article 4 EU-Ukraine PCA, Article 4 EU-Moldova PCA.
21 Article 4 EU-Georgia PCA.
22 Hillion, *op. cit.* note 19.
23 In effect, following the Copenhagen European Council of June 1993, these became pre-accession agreements. See: K. Inglis, 'The Europe Agreements Compared in Light of their Pre-Accession Reorientation', *Common Market Law Review*, 37(5), 2000, 1173–1210.
24 K. Wolczuk, 'Ukraine's Policy Towards the European Union: A Case of "Declarative Europeanization"', 2004, available at: www.batory.org.pl/ftp/program/forum/eu_ukraine/ukraine_eu_policy.pdf (accessed 17 May 2017).
25 European Council Common Strategy of 11 December 1999 on Ukraine (*OJ*, 1999, L 331).
26 J. Hughes, 'EU Relations with Russia: Partnership or Asymmetric Interdependency?' 2006, available at: https://core.ac.uk/download/pdf/92752.pdf (accessed 18 May 2017).
27 European Commission, *European Neighbourhood Policy: Strategy Paper*, COM (2004) 373 final (12 May 2004).
28 European Council of 16 June 2006, Presidency Conclusions, Brussels, 10633/1/06 REV 1, para 57.
29 R. Prodi, 'A Wider Europe – Proximity Policy as the Key to Stability', Brussels, 5–6 December 2002, available at: http://europa.eu/rapid/press-release_SPEECH-02-619_en.htm (accessed 18 May 2017).
30 *Ibid.*
31 M. Cremona and C. Hillion, 'L'Union Fait la Force? Potential and Limitations of the European Neighbourhood Policy as an Integrated EU Foreign and Security Policy', *EUI Working Papers*, Law No. 39, 2006, available at: http://cadmus.eui.eu/handle/1814/6419 (accessed 18 May 2017).

32 M. Dodini and M. Fantini, 'The EU Neighbourhood Policy: Implications for Economic Growth and Stability', *Journal of Common Market Studies*, 44(3), 2006, 507–532.
33 A. Magen, 'The Shadow of Enlargement: Can the European Neighbourhood Policy Achieve Compliance?' *Columbia Journal of European Law*, 12, 2006, 383–427; R. Dragneva and K. Wolczuk, 'EU Law Export to the Eastern Neigbourhood', in P.J. Cardwell (ed.), *EU External Relations Law and Policy in the Post-Lisbon Era*, Berlin: Springer, 2011, 217–240.
34 J. Kelley, 'New Wine in Old Wineskins: Promoting Political Reforms Through the New European Neighbourhood Policy', *Journal of Common Market Studies*, 44(1), 2006, 29–55; Cremona and Hillion, *op. cit.* note 31; Magen, *op. cit.* note 33.
35 EU-Ukraine Cooperation Council, 'EU-Ukraine Action Plan', 21 February 2005; EU-Moldova Cooperation Council, 'EU-Moldova Action Plan', 21 February 2005, 'EU-Georgia Action Plan', 14 November 2006.
36 K. Wolczuk, 'Implementation without Coordination: The Impact of the EU Conditionality on Ukraine Under the European Neighbourhood Policy', *Europe-Asia Studies*, 61(2), 2009, 187–211; P. Van Elsuwege and R. Petrov (eds.), *Legislative Approximation and Application of EU Law in the Eastern Neighbourhood of the European Union*, London: Routledge, 2014.
37 Dragneva and Wolczuk, *op. cit.* note 13, 43; P. Van Elsuwege and G. Van der Loo, 'Continuity and Change in the Legal Relations Between the EU and Its Neighbours', in D. Bouris and T. Schumacher (eds.), *The Revised European Neighbourhood Policy*, London: Palgrave Macmillan, 2017, pp. 100–101.
38 *Joint Declaration, Eastern Partnership Summit*, 9 September 2008, available at: www.consilium.europa.eu/uedocs/cms_data/docs/pressdata/en/er/107589.pdf (accessed 22 May 2017).
39 K. Wolczuk et al., 'The Association Agreements as a Dynamic Framework: Between Modernisation and Integration', *EU-STRAT Working Paper* Nr. 4, forthcoming 2017.
40 Van der Loo, *op. cit.* note 3; Dragneva and Wolczuk, *op. cit.* note 13.
41 Dragneva and Wolczuk, *op. cit.* note 13.
42 L. Litra and I. Chkhiikvadze, 'EU Membership Perspective for Georgia, Moldova, and Ukraine: Impossible, Forgotten, of Hidden?' *Institute of World Policy*, 2016, available at: http://pasos.org/wp-content/uploads/2016/08/EU_Membership-_net_eng.pdf (accessed 20 May 2017).
43 Ukraine-EU Summit, Paris, September 2008. For more, see K. Wolczuk, 'A Dislocated and Mistranslated EU-Ukraine Summit', *ISS Opinion*, 17 October 2008, available at: www.iss.europa.eu/publications/detail/article/a-dislocated-and-mistranslated-eu-ukraine-summit (accessed 19 May 2017).
44 *BBC News*, 'EU Signs Pacts with Ukraine, Georgia and Moldova', 27 June 2014, available at: www.bbc.co.uk/news/world-europe-28052645 (accessed 20 May 2017).
45 A. Lazowski, 'Enhanced Multilateralism and Enhanced Bilateralism: Integration Without Membership in the European Union', *Common Market Law Review*, 45, 2008, 1433–1458.
46 Wolczuk et al., *op. cit.* note 39.
47 J. Langbein and K. Wolczuk, 'Convergence Without Membership? The Impact of the European Union in the Neighbourhood: Evidence from Ukraine', *Journal of European Public Policy*, 19(6), 2012, 863–881; Dragneva and Wolczuk, *op. cit.* note 13.
48 R. Sakwa and M. Weber, 'The Commonwealth of Independent State, 1991–1998: Stagnation and Survival', *Europe-Asia Studies*, 3, 1999, 379–415.

49 For example, Georgia and Ukraine never joined the Economic Court of the CIS, whereas Moldova formally withdrew from it in 2009. Georgia formally withdrew from the CIS following the 2008 war. For more on Ukraine's selectivity, see Dragneva and Wolczuk, *op. cit.* note 13.
50 For more on development of GUAM, see Zh. Kembayev, *Legal Aspects of Regional Integration Processes in the Post-Soviet Area*, Berlin and Heidelberg: Springer, 2009.
51 L. Delcour et al., 'The Implications of Eurasian Integration for the EU's Relations with the Countries in the Post-Soviet Space', *CEPS*, 30 September 2015, available at: www.ceps.eu/publications/implications-eurasian-integration-eu%E2%80%99s-relations-countries-post-soviet-space (accessed 22 May 2017); P. De Micco, 'When Choosing Means Losing: The Eastern Partners, the EU and the Eurasian Economic Union', *DG EXPO Policy Study*, March 2015, available at: www.europarl.europa.eu/RegData/etudes/STUD/2015/549026/EXPO_STUD%282015%29549026_EN.pdf (accessed 22 May 2017).
52 Arts. 460–470 EU-Ukraine AA, Arts. 400–410 EU-Georgia AA, Arts. 433–443 EU-Moldova AA.
53 Article 460 (1) EU-Ukraine AA.
54 Article 461.3 EU-Ukraine AA.
55 Article 463.3 EU-Ukraine AA.
56 Article 463.1 and 465.3 EU-Ukraine AA.
57 Dragneva and Wolczuk, *op. cit.* note 13.
58 Articles 462.3 and 464.3 EU-Ukraine AA.
59 Case C-192/89, *Sevince*, EU:C:1990:322, para 2.
60 A. Albi, *op. cit.* note 2, 43–44.
61 See the country reports in the second part of this volume.
62 R. Dragneva, 'Is "Soft" Beautiful? Another View on Law, Institutions and Integration in the Commonwealth of Independent States', *Review of Central and East European Law*, 29(3), 2004, 279–324.
63 Van der Loo, *op. cit.* note 3, 322–325.
64 In the EU-Ukraine AA these are the chapters on Technical Barriers to Trade, Sanitary and Phyto-Sanitary Measures, Customs and Trade Facilitation, Establishment and Services, Pubic Procurement and Competition.
65 These include cooperation in a large number of areas, such as science, technology, environment, and transport.
66 Particularly postal and courier service, electronic communications and financial services.
67 Appendix XVII EU-Ukraine AA.
68 Appendix XVII-6 EU-Ukraine AA.
69 Article 64 EU-Ukraine AA. In February 2016 Ukraine adopted a Comprehensive Strategy for Sanitary and Phyto-Sanitary Measures, which entails the adoption of 255 EU directives and regulations until 2021.
70 These are the chapters on Technical Barriers to Trade, Sanitary and Phyto-Sanitary Measures, Establishment and Services and Public Procurement.
71 Van der Loo, *op. cit.* note 3, 212–213.
72 Van der Loo, *op. cit.* note 3, 320–322.
73 Article 475 the EU-Ukraine AA.
74 Article 2 EU-Ukraine AA.
75 Article 478 EU-Ukraine AA.
76 On the importance of this consideration for the EU, see Lazowski, *op. cit.* note 45.
77 Article 463.3 EU-Ukraine AA.
78 Van der Loo, *op. cit.* note 3, 267–268.
79 Article 6 of Annex XVII EU-Ukraine AA.

80 Van der Loo, *op. cit.* note 3, 269.
81 Article 153.2 EU-Ukraine AA.
82 A. Evans, 'Voluntary Harmonization in Integration Between the European Community and Eastern Europe', *European Law Review*, 22, 1997, 201–220; H. Grabbe and K. Hughes, *Eastward Enlargement of the European Union*, London: Royal Institute of International Affairs, 1998; H. Grabbe, 'A Partnership for Accession? The Implications of EU Conditionality for the Central and East European Applicants', *EUI Working Paper No.* 99/1, 1999.
83 Grabbe, *Ibid.*, p. 20.
84 Albi, *op. cit.* note 2, pp. 56–66.
85 Article 477–478 EU-Ukraine AA.
86 E.g. J. McCall Smith, 'The Politics of Dispute Settlement Design: Explaining Legalism in Regional Trade Pacts', *International Organisation*, 1, 2000, 137.
87 Chapter 14, Title IV EU-Ukraine AA.
88 Article 321 (2) EU-Ukraine AA.
89 Article 322 EU-Ukraine AA. To reinforce the point, disputes on the extensive legislative approximation, required by Title V Economic and Sector Cooperation, remain outside this mechanism.
90 Van der Loo, *op. cit.* note 3, p. 297.
91 E.g. F. de Borja Lasheras, 'Ukraine's Rising Euroscepticism', *ECFR Commentary*, 22 December 2016, available at: www.ecfr.eu/article/commentary_ukraines_rising_euroscepticism_7208 (accessed 1 June 2017).
92 The AAs do not preclude 'the maintenance or establishment of customs unions, free trade areas or arrangements for frontier traffic except insofar they conflict with trade arrangements provided for in this Agreement,' e.g. Article 39 (1) EU-Ukraine AA. For more on this issue, see Micco, *op. cit.* note 51; Van der Loo, *op. cit.* note 3.
93 D. Cenusa et al., 'Russia's Punitive Trade Policy Measures Against Ukraine, Moldova, and Georgia', *CEPS*, 25 September 2014, available at: www.ceps.eu/publications/russia%E2%80%99s-punitive-trade-policy-measures-towards-ukraine-moldova-and-georgia (accessed 17 May 2017).
94 D. Dyomkin, 'In Russia, Moldovan President Says He May Scrap EU Trade Pact', *Reuters*, 17 January 2017, available at: www.reuters.com/article/us-russia-moldova-eu-idUSKBN151290 (accessed 1 June 2017).
95 See also the country report on Moldova in part 2 of this volume.

Part II

Constitutional orders of the post-Soviet countries and their adaptability to European and Eurasian integration

5 The constitutional order of Ukraine and its adaptability to the EU-Ukraine Association Agreement

Roman Petrov

Introduction

The constitutional system of Ukraine can be regarded as one of the most dynamic in the entire post-Soviet area. It took the Ukrainian political elites almost five years to agree on the text of the Constitution after gaining independence on 24 August 1991. After reaching a long awaited political compromise, the Constitution was adopted by the Ukrainian Parliament (*Verkhovna Rada*) on 28 June 1996 (last in the post-Soviet area). Its structure, objectives and basic principles echoed the constitutions of the Member States of the European Union.[1] In particular, it embedded separation of powers, protection of fundamental human rights and democratic freedoms. Therefore, at least on paper, the Constitution portrayed Ukraine as a modern European country that is eager to depart from its Soviet heritage and is ready to share international and European democratic values. However, Ukraine's newly established constitutional order did not enjoy relatively long stability. Since its adoption in 1996, the Constitution has been amended on numerous occasions. Initially adopted as the Constitution of a strong presidential republic it went through substantive revisions in 2004, in 2010 and in 2014. All these revisions took place in times of tense political crises in Ukraine and therefore reflected the will of the winning political establishment. The revision of 2004 coincided with the 'Orange Revolution' and was aimed at weakening the powers of the President in favour of the *Verkhovna Rada*. The revision of 2010 was initiated by the newly elected pro-Russian President Victor Yanukovych and was aimed at strengthening the powers of the President in line with the Constitution of 1996. The revision of 2014 took place immediately after the 'Revolution of Dignity' (*Maidan* Revolution) and recalled the format of the Constitution of 2004 with strong powers of the *Verkhovna Rada*.

In spite of many revisions and amendments, the constitutional provisions on sovereignty remained intact. Article 1 of the Constitution emphasises that 'Ukraine is a sovereign and independent, democratic, social, law-based state' and 'the sovereignty of Ukraine extends throughout its entire territory'.[2] Article 5 of the Constitution uncompromisingly states that '[t]he people are the bearers of sovereignty and the only source of power in Ukraine.' The President is the 'guarantor of state sovereignty and territorial indivisibility of Ukraine, the observance of the Constitution of Ukraine and human and citizens' rights and freedoms'.

The procedure to amend the constitutional provisions on state sovereignty is rather strict. Article 156 provides that amendments to Chapter 1 (General Principles) may be submitted only either by the President or by no less than two-thirds of the constitutional composition of the Ukrainian Parliament and on the condition that it is adopted by no less than two-thirds of the constitutional composition of the Ukrainian Parliament (300 members out of 450), and is approved by an all-Ukrainian referendum designated by the President. Article 157 provides that the Constitution cannot be amended if 'the amendments foresee the abolition or restriction of human and citizen's rights and freedoms, or they are oriented toward the liquidation of independence or violation of the territorial indivisibility of Ukraine'. These provisions were regarded as a formal reason to decline the invitation of the Russian government to join the emerging Eurasian Economic Union (EAEU) in 2013.[3] In theory, these provisions could play the same role in case the constitutionality of further integration with the EU would be challenged. So far, there has been no discussion on this issue among the Ukrainian political elites. However, these arguments may emerge once Eurosceptic and pro-Russian political forces in Ukraine endeavour to question the constitutionality of Ukrainian commitments regarding the adaptation of the EU *acquis* as provided in the EU-Ukraine AA. It is not excluded that the Constitutional Court of Ukraine could be asked to rule on the constitutionality of some provisions of the EU-Ukraine AA. For instance, it may be asked to rule on the binding force of decisions of the EU-Ukraine Association Council[4] and on the obligation of the EU-Ukraine joint arbitration panel to abide by rulings of the Court of Justice of the EU (CJEU) on interpretation of the relevant EU *acquis*.[5]

Application of international law in the legal system of Ukraine

The Ukrainian Constitution recognises the binding effect of international agreements within the national legal order, but deliberately excludes internationally recognised principles of international law as binding in the Ukrainian legal system.[6] Therefore, it can be argued that, from a formal point of view, the Ukrainian Constitution was drafted as less receptive to the influence of international law than, for instance, the Constitution of Russia.[7] However, this gap is consistently rectified by the gradual Europeanisation of the Ukrainian legal system, and of the Ukrainian judiciary in particular.[8] Article 9 of the Ukrainian Constitution provides that:

> International treaties that are in force, agreed to be binding by the Verkhovna Rada of Ukraine, are part of the national legislation of Ukraine. The conclusion of international treaties that contravene the Constitution of Ukraine is

possible only after introducing relevant amendments to the Constitution of Ukraine.[9]

In accordance with the Ukrainian Constitution, only duly ratified international agreements can be considered as an intrinsic part of the Ukrainian legal order. Within the hierarchy of sources of the Ukrainian legal order, duly ratified international agreements occupy a layer below the Ukrainian Constitution and above Ukrainian secondary legislation. It means that even a duly ratified international agreement cannot overrule conflicting provisions of the Ukrainian Constitution and general principles of law enshrined therein. However, in case of conflict with secondary legislation relevant provisions of a duly ratified international agreement prevail. This approach has been further formalised in Ukrainian legislation and case law of the Constitutional Court of Ukraine.[10]

Nevertheless, it should be emphasised that the application of international law within the Ukrainian legal order is not coherent. First, there is no settled practice on application of provisions of international agreements and their place within the Ukrainian legal order. Before the *Maidan* Revolution in 2014, the Ukrainian judiciary was reluctant to refer to international agreements in their judgments and there was no formal recognition of their direct effect within the Ukrainian legal order.[11] However, since 2014, the situation is gradually changing. The judicial reform caused by the implementation of the essential elements of the EU-Ukraine AA (ensuring the rule of law, strengthening the judiciary, improving its efficiency, safeguarding its independence and impartiality, and combating corruption)[12] triggered a rise of judicial activism among Ukrainian judges to refer to international law and decisions of international courts (mainly decisions of the European Court of Human Rights (ECtHR)) in their judgments. Two reasons for the observed increase of judicial activism can be highlighted. One reason is increased competitiveness and transparency of the Ukrainian judiciary caused by its ambitious reforms in 2015–2017.[13] Another reason is the fact that, since 2014, international organisations (UN, OSCE, Council of Europe, EU and others) have been consistently investing into teaching and training Ukrainian judges in foundations of international law and case law of the ECtHR).[14] However, it must be admitted that the Ukrainian judiciary still does not apply provisions of international agreements and international law principles, including ECtHR judgments, in a completely systematic and coherent manner but rather sporadically and selectively to suit the needs of argumentation in a particular case.[15]

In order to ensure efficient application of the ECHR and case law of the ECtHR, the Ukrainian Parliament issued a Law 'On execution of judgments on application of practice of the ECtHR' in 2006.[16] This law unequivocally confirms that the ECtHR judgments regarding Ukraine are binding and must be executed on the territory of Ukraine as a matter of priority.[17] Accordingly, the law ensures efficient enforcement of the ECtHR judgments, compensations and revisions of the Ukrainian court decisions related to or caused by the ECtHR judgments. Furthermore, the law states that the Ukrainian judiciary is bound to apply the ECtHR case law as a source of the national legal order.[18] The authorised governmental body of Ukraine (Representation of Ukraine in the Council of Europe) is obliged to perform regular monitoring of national legislation and practices in line with the ECHR and case law of the ECtHR.[19] Hitherto, the Constitutional Court of Ukraine and Ukrainian general courts frequently referred to the ECtHR case law and recognised the binding character of the ECtHR judgments in their decisions.[20]

The Ukrainian administrative and constitutional judiciary constitutes a judicial review of legislative and executive acts. The administrative judiciary has a competence of judicial review of legislative and executive acts of the government and municipalities as well as acts and failure to act by the Ukrainian Parliament and President of Ukraine. Judicial review of the constitutional acts, international agreements and interpretation of the Constitution falls within the jurisdiction of the Constitutional Court.

In our opinion, the current position with regard to the application of international agreements and other sources of international law does not encourage the Ukrainian judiciary to include references to the EU *acquis* in their decisions. A major challenge concerns the effective implementation of the Energy Community Treaty (EnC) and the EU-Ukraine Association Agreement (AA) within the Ukrainian legal order. In particular, it is not yet clear if the Ukrainian judiciary regard decisions of the EU-Ukraine common institutions set up under the AA and the Treaty of the EnC as sources of national law. In our opinion, the adoption of a specialised law similar to the Law 'On execution of judgments on application of practice of the ECtHR' could ensure the effective implementation of the respective agreements in the legal system of Ukraine. Ukrainian administrative courts already introduced references to the case law of the CJEU without, however, providing legal reasoning behind it.[21] This approach caused some confusion within the Ukrainian judiciary, who in many instances mistakenly referred to the CJEU cases as ECtHR cases. In response, in 2014 the High Administrative Court of Ukraine stated that Ukrainian administrative courts may not refer to the doctrines and principles as developed in the CJEU case law as a source of law but as an argumentation and 'persuasive source of reference' regarding 'harmonious interpretation of national legislation of Ukraine with established standards of the EU'. In the opinion of the High Administrative Court, this practice is justified by the need of the effective implementation the EU-Ukraine Association Agreement.[22]

Impact of the EU-Ukraine Association Agreement on the Ukrainian legal system

The EU-Ukraine AA is destined to have a profound effect on the Ukrainian legal system for several reasons. First, it has already triggered and is likely to trigger further profound constitutional amendments aimed at ensuring that Ukraine effectively shares the EU's common democratic values and implements the EU-Ukraine AA. Second, provisions of the EU-Ukraine AA and the relevant EU *acquis* must be effectively applied by the Ukrainian judiciary raising the issue of direct effect within the Ukrainian legal system. Third, the decisions of the common institutions set up under the EU-Ukraine AA will become part of the national legal system and find effective application by the national executive and judiciary.

Constitutional amendments

One of the first 'post-Maidan' constitutional amendments took place in June 2016 when the *Verkhovna Rada* adopted the 'Law on amending the Constitution of Ukraine (as to justice)'.[23] These constitutional amendments were proposed by President Poroshenko in light of the fight against corruption and the independence of judiciary in Ukraine. The constitutional amendments sparked considerable public debate in Ukraine and beyond. Externally, the European Commission for Democracy through Law (Venice Commission) two times scrutinised the draft amendments for their compliance with European standards and issued several important reservations.[24] Internally, on the one hand, the draft amendments were criticised for giving extended powers to the President of Ukraine to influence the appointment of judges, narrowing the scope of judges' immunity, and for keeping a complicated system of specialised courts in Ukraine. On the other hand, the position of the Office of the President of Ukraine was that the constitutional amendments were crucial to achieve the objectives of the EU-Ukraine AA regarding sharing common values, fighting corruption and improving access to judiciary. In particular, the constitutional amendments ensure that Ukraine observes the essential elements of the EU-Ukraine AA (respect for the principle of the rule of law)[25] and meets the objectives of Title III of the EU-Ukraine AA on justice, freedom and security which call Ukraine to consolidate the rule of law, to improve the efficiency of the judiciary, to safeguard its independence and impartiality, and to combat corruption.[26]

The official position of the EU institutions regarding the constitutional reform in Ukraine was rather supportive. The annual report on the progress of implementation of the EU-Ukraine AA hailed the constitutional amendments of 2016 as legislation, which 'strengthen judicial independence and [reorganises] the court system, by streamlining the judicial instances (from four to three) and by subjecting the sitting judges to examinations and mandatory electronic asset declarations'.[27] Furthermore, it must be acknowledged that the most recognised impact of the EU-Ukraine AA[28] on the constitutional reform in Ukraine can be seen in revised Article 124 of the Constitution, wherein it is stated that 'Ukraine may recognise the jurisdiction of the International Criminal Court as provided for by the Rome Statute of the International Criminal Court'. This amendment overrules the Decision of the Constitutional Court of Ukraine from 2001, which explicitly considered the recognition of the jurisdiction of the International Criminal Court as incompatible with the national Constitution and, therefore, made the ratification of the former by the Ukrainian Parliament impossible.[29] The wording of revised Article 124 of the Ukrainian Constitution opens a possibility for the Ukrainian Parliament to ratify the Rome Statute in the near future.

However, the ratification of the Rome Statute is likely to be postponed until the eventual implementation of the 'Minsk II Agreement' regarding the military conflict in the East of Ukraine (Donbass area) caused by the aggression of Russia in Ukraine. In particular, the sides of the conflict must ensure an effective ceasefire and effective control by Ukraine of its Eastern border with Russia and guarantee the amnesty of illegally armed belligerents. These actions must take place before the ratification of the Rome Statute in order to avoid entrenching a legal war between the government of Ukraine and the Russian government and governments of the self-proclaimed separatist republics in the East of Ukraine.

Further constitutional reforms took place in 2017 and targeted reform of the Ukrainian judiciary in line with the objective of the EU-Ukraine AA to strengthen efficiency, impartiality and independence of the Ukrainian judiciary.[30] A new law on the status of the Constitutional Court of Ukraine encourages the constitutional judges to enhance the quality of their judgments and grants Ukrainian nationals the right to access the Constitutional Court with 'constitutional complaints'.[31] Furthermore, the constitutional reform strengthens the efficiency of the Ukrainian judiciary by introducing electronic distance access to judiciary proceedings via a unified informational system and simplifying trial proceedings in order to decrease the workload of Ukrainian judges.[32]

Application and direct effect of the EU-Ukraine AA in the Ukrainian legal order

The Ukrainian judiciary already occasionally referred to fundamental principles of EU law and some elements of the EU *acquis* as well as to case law of the CJEU before the signature of the EU-Ukraine AA.[33] A combination of external and internal factors may explain this observation. First, since 2004 Ukraine's pro-European foreign policy has been underpinned by the national programme for approximating Ukrainian legislation to EU law. It served as a very important encouragement for few Ukrainian judges with expertise in EU law to refer to relevant EU *acquis* in their decisions. Second, the EU has been offering results-oriented technical and financial support to the Ukrainian judiciary. This support caused serious internal institutional reforms within the Ukrainian judiciary, such as the establishment of the system of administrative courts. According to the case law of Ukrainian courts, mostly administrative judges have been inclined to pioneer the application of the EU *acquis* within the Ukrainian judiciary.[34] A third factor was the increased transparency of the Ukrainian judiciary. The national registry of Ukrainian case law was launched in 2006 and found positive feedback among the Ukrainian legal community. Judges and lawyers were regularly informed about developments in EU law via workshops and courses at Ukrainian legal higher education institutions. The law 'On the All State Programme on the adaptation of Ukrainian legislation to EU laws' of 2004 encouraged the Ukrainian judiciary to use the EU *acquis* as an important source of reference.[35] This law, which is already out-dated today, envisages the export of the whole 'accession *acquis*' into Ukraine's legal system.[36]

There is a long track of applying the EU *acquis* by the Ukrainian judiciary (including the Constitutional Court of Ukraine) as a persuasive source of law before the signature of the EU-Ukraine AA. For example, the Ukrainian courts recognised priority of the EU-Ukraine AA's predecessor (EU-Ukraine PCA) over conflicting provisions of national law.[37] Furthermore, in cases related to state liability, the Ukrainian administrative courts have imported from the EU legal system the concept of legal certainty, previously unknown to the Ukrainian legal system. For example, in the *Person v Kiev City Centre for Social Assistance* case,[38] the Administrative Court of the Kiev District provided that the rights of the disabled to claim social and financial assistance from the State flow from the principle of legal certainty. It means that a State cannot justify its failure to guarantee constitutional rights by the absence of a specific national law. For this purpose, the Administrative Court of the Kiev District referred to the CJEU judgment in the *van Duyn v the Home Office* case,[39] wherein it is specified that nationals may rely on the State's obligations, even in cases when these obligations are provided in law without direct effect. Furthermore, Ukrainian courts developed the principle of legitimate expectations in the case of *Person v Darnitsa District of Kiev Center for Social Assistance*,[40] concerning the rights to benefits of those who took part in the operation during the Chernobyl catastrophe. The Kiev District Administrative Court provided that the principle of state liability to offer compensation to those involved in the Chernobyl disaster flows from the *van Duyn v Home Office* case. In particular, the Administrative Court of the Kiev District stated that if the State formally acknowledged its commitment to offer compensation to those involved in the Chernobyl disaster, it could not refer to its own failure to fulfil its commitments in order to avoid liability, which would also violate the legitimate expectations of Ukrainian nationals.

Such bold judicial activism of administrative judges, previously unknown for a post-Soviet legal system, was not welcomed by all representatives of the Ukrainian establishment. The government of Ukraine under President Yanukovich questioned case law of the administrative courts related to compensation to those involved in the Chernobyl disaster in the Constitutional Court of Ukraine. In the judgment of 25 January 2012, the Constitutional Court overruled the established case law of the administrative courts on the ground that social support of Ukrainian nationals guaranteed by the Constitution of Ukraine must be provided in line with the financial capacities of the state in accordance with the principles of proportionality and justice.[41] The Constitutional Court did not consider the relevance of the principle of legal certainty at all but referred to selected decisions of the ECtHR in justification of its own position. This controversial decision of the Constitutional Court was widely criticised by the expert community in Ukraine and even by some judges of the Constitutional Court in their special opinions for lack of reasoning, pro-governmental position and misleading references to the case law of the ECtHR.[42] The situation went even worse when the Highest Disciplinary Body for judges in Ukraine opened a disciplinary procedure against those administrative judges who referred to case law of the CJEU in their decisions related to the compensation to those involved in the Chernobyl disaster.

Further dramatic political events in Ukraine and the *Maidan* Revolution in 2013–2014, which led to the signature of the EU-Ukraine AA in June 2014, reinvigorated the debate on the application of the EU *acquis* and case law of the CJEU by the Ukrainian judiciary. At the end of 2014, the High Administrative Court decided to interfere and to fill in this gap in a traditional way for post-Soviet courts – to issue an informational letter to all administrative judges in Ukraine.[43] Therein the High Administrative Court of Ukraine stated that EU founding treaties do not bind Ukraine and, therefore, EU law and case law of the CJEU cannot be considered as part of the Ukrainian legal system.[44] Furthermore, the High Administrative Court confirmed that 'legal positions as they are formalised in decisions of the CJEU can be taken into consideration by administrative courts as argumentation, reflection regarding harmonious interpretation of Ukrainian legislation in line with established standards of the EU legal system, but not as a legal foundation (source of law) of a situation that caused a legal dispute'.[45]

This statement on behalf of the High Administrative Court of Ukraine played a dubious role. On one hand, it repudiated any formal grounds for Ukrainian judges to apply various sources of the EU *acquis* in their decisions. On the other hand, it gave a green light for Ukrainian judges to refer to general principles, doctrines and case law of the CJEU as a persuasive source of interpretation in their decisions. Unfortunately, the High Administrative Court did not go far and kept silent on the issues of application of the EU *acquis* referred to in the text of the EU-Ukraine AA and of binding decisions of the EU-Ukraine Association Council. Ironically, new constitutional amendments of 2016 envisage the abolishment of the High Administrative Court in favour of the single Supreme Court of Ukraine, thereby undermining the value of this information letter of the High Administrative Court of Ukraine for the Ukrainian judiciary.[46] The newly formed Supreme Court has not yet expressed its position on legality of references to the case law of the CJEU in judgments of the Ukrainian courts. Nevertheless, the issue of the application of the case law of the CJEU and the EU *acquis* is pending and must be clarified by the Supreme Court in the near future in order to ensure effective application and implementation of the EU-Ukraine AA.

Beyond any expectation the clarification of the High Administrative Court of Ukraine on application of CJEU case law found wide support among judges of common and administrative courts in Ukraine. In the period of 2015–2016, Ukrainian general, specialised and high courts referred to the EU-Ukraine AA and case law of the CJEU in dozens of their decisions.[47] In most cases Ukrainian judges who already possess considerable experience and knowledge in application of the ECHR and case law of the ECtHR strengthened their argumentation with frequent references to the EU *acquis* and the EU-Ukraine AA, in particular in decisions concerning protection of fundamental human rights in Ukraine. For instance, since 2015 most decisions of administrative courts on rights of pensioners provide a standard statement that the court applies the principle of rule of law in line with case law of the ECtHR and the CJEU. In these cases, Ukrainian judges cite the information letter of the High Administrative Court of Ukraine on taking into account the case law of the CJEU as a source of argumentation concerning harmonious interpretation of Ukrainian law with the EU *acquis*.[48] Some judges went even further and considered the entry into force of the EU-Ukraine AA in Ukraine as an obligation for applying the EU common values in Ukraine.[49] References to the EU-Ukraine AA and relevant EU *acquis* found application in cases regarding Ukrainian natural persons and companies who claimed the direct effect of these provisions in cases concerning paying customs duties when crossing Ukrainian border;[50] supply and trade of natural gas;[51] definition of origin of goods (honey);[52] or the legality of legislative drafts by the President of Ukraine.[53] However, the Ukrainian courts have not yet recognised (mainly avoided the recognition of) the direct effect of provisions of the EU-Ukraine AA in their decisions. In particular, the issue of direct effect of the EU-Ukraine AA may find a particular relevance in case of possible litigation on correspondence of Ukrainian laws and other legal acts to the objectives, principles and 'essential elements' of the EU-Ukraine AA before the Constitutional Court and general courts. Among the most recent examples are the Executive Order of the President of Ukraine on banning the Russian social networks (on the matter of national security and sanctions against the Russian Federation caused by the annexation of Crimea in 2014 and military aggression in the East of Ukraine)[54] and Law of Ukraine on banning the St. George (Guards') Ribbon (as propaganda of the Russian military aggression in the East of Ukraine).[55] These legislative acts raise some concerns regarding their compliance with the objectives of the EU-Ukraine AA, in general, and freedom and expression and the principle of proportionality (as they are applied and interpreted within the ECHR and the EU Charter of Fundamental Rights), in particular.[56]

Application of decisions of the EU-Ukraine common institutions

The EU-Ukraine AA established a specific institutional framework (Association Council, Association Committee and Parliamentary Assembly), which is characterised by the competence to issue decisions and legal acts of binding nature. The prime objective of the Association Council is to supervise and monitor the AA within the 'framework of regular meetings between the representatives of the Parties.'[57] For this purpose, the Association Council has the power to take decisions which are binding upon the parties. This power can be delegated to the Association Committee which assists Ukraine in achieving the results of the association.[58]

The binding force of decisions and acts of the EU-Ukraine joint institutions is new for the Ukrainian legal system and therefore their legal effect is not yet clarified. Hitherto, neither the EU-Ukraine Association Council nor other common institutions issued any decisions of binding nature yet. Therefore, there was no reason for the Ukrainian judiciary to clarify their position on this complicated issue. In the meantime, the Ukrainian Parliament and the government are working on a draft law to regulate all legal issues related to the implementation and application of the EU-Ukraine AA. Unfortunately, this draft law has not yet been proposed even for a first reading in the Ukrainian Parliament. According to this draft law, decisions of the EU-Ukraine common institutions will not be directly applicable but will be enforced similar to international agreements. In particular, the draft law considers binding decisions of the EU-Ukraine common institutions either as international agreements,[59] or as national laws, or as secondary acts depending on their content. In the former two cases, the binding decisions of the EU-Ukraine common institutions must be regarded as part of the national legal system which takes precedence over conflicting national legislation but not the Constitution. In the latter case, it will be regarded as a secondary legal source of the Ukrainian legal system. The draft law obliges the Ukrainian judiciary to apply these decisions as sources of law. Non-binding recommendations of the EU-Ukraine common institutions can be used as a source of interpretation of Ukrainian legislation and international obligations of Ukraine.

Conclusion

To conclude, in this chapter we set out a number of considerations which lead us to believe that the objective of effective implementation of the EU-Ukraine AA enhanced the adaptability of the national constitutional order to the European integration project and European common values. Internally, Ukraine went through a dramatic transformation from a country which pursued a multi-vector foreign policy aimed at appeasing two conflicting integration projects (European and Eurasian) to a country with a firm pro-European policy as cemented in the EU-Ukraine AA. Externally, Ukraine committed itself to the demanding conditionality and monitoring processes envisaged in the EU-Ukraine AA in return for better access to the EU internal market, establishing a Deep and Comprehensive Free Trade Area and abolishing the visa regime with the EU.

The EU-Ukraine AA established a sustainable institutional and legal framework for application of the EU *acquis* including the CJEU case law and comprehensive legislative approximation between Ukrainian and EU law. However, the institutional reforms that have already taken place cannot be regarded as fully sufficient. The Ukrainian Parliament failed to establish substantive and procedural foundations for the application and implementation of the EU-Ukraine AA in the legal order of Ukraine. However, this gap is being partially filled by a surprising judicial activism in Ukraine. The Ukrainian judiciary already started referring to the EU-Ukraine AA and relevant EU *acquis* thereby laying a foundation for the regular application of general principles of EU law in applying provisions of the EU-Ukraine AA. Undoubtedly, this is a great challenge for the Ukrainian legal system. A significant role in this process is expected from the Constitutional Court, which must eventually clarify the status of the EU-Ukraine AA within the Ukrainian legal order.

Furthermore, the Ukrainian Constitution has already been amended in order to encompass specific requirements of the EU-Ukraine AA (such as ratification of the Rome Statute and access to judiciary) and further amendments related to the implementation of the EU-Ukraine AA may be expected (such as strengthening the role of international law within the legal system of Ukraine, reference to the EU's common values, acknowledging and formalising the potential transfer of some of Ukraine's sovereign powers to supranational international organisations).

Looking at the pattern of adaptability of the Ukrainian constitutional order to the European integration project more widely, we may conclude that the external factors (such as the aims of the EU-Ukraine relations, including potential membership in the EU, introduction of the visa-free regime and others) play a catalyst role for constitutional change.

Notes

1 For example, R. Rezie, 'The Ukrainian Constitution: Interpretation of the Citizens' Rights Provisions', *Case Western Reserve Journal of Int'l Law*, 31, 1999, 169. R. Petrov and A. Serdyk, 'Ukraine: A Constitutional Design Between Façade Democracy and Effective Transformation?' in: L. Morlino and W. Sadurski (eds.), *Democratization and the European Union*, Routledge, 2010, pp. 170–193.
2 Article 2 of the Constitution of Ukraine available at: www.president.gov.ua/en/content/constitution.html (accessed 22 June 2017).
3 Article 157 of the Constitution of Ukraine, available at: www.justice.gov/sites/default/files/eoir/legacy/2013/11/08/constitution_14.pdf (accessed 22 June 2017).
4 Article 463(1) EU-Ukraine AA, *OJ*, 2014, L 161/1.
5 Article 322(2) EU-Ukraine AA, *OJ*, 2014, L 161/1.
6 R. Petrov and A. Serdyk, 'Ukraine: A Constitutional Design Between Façade Democracy and Effective Transformation?' in: L. Morlino and W. Sadurski (eds.), *Democratization and the European Union*, Routledge, 2010, pp. 170–193.
7 See the contribution of Paul Kalinichenko in this book.
8 R. Petrov and P. Kalinichenko, 'The Europeanization of Third Country Judiciaries Through the Application of the EU Acquis: The Cases of Russia and Ukraine', *International and Comparative Law Quarterly*, 60(2), 2011, 325–353.
9 Full text in English is available at: www.president.gov.ua/en/content/constitution.html (accessed 22 June 2017).
10 Article 19(2) of 'Law on International Agreements of Ukraine', 19 June 2004, No 1906-IV. Decision of the Constitutional Court of Ukraine on the Statute of the International Criminal Court on 11 November 2001, Case No 1–35/2001.
11 *Supra* note 8.
12 Articles 2 and 14 EU-Ukraine AA, *OJ*, 2014, L 161/1.
13 Among these reforms were: elimination of high specialised courts with subsequent sacking of all judges who worked in these courts and introduction of a transparent system of selection of judges of common courts and the Supreme Court of Ukraine in 2016–17. Detailed knowledge of the ECHR and the case law of the ECtHR are among key criteria of eligibility of newly appointed judges in Ukraine, more information is available at: http://vkksu.gov.ua/ua (accessed 22 June 2017).
14 For example, the OSCE has drafted a comprehensive handbook for Ukrainian judges on application of decisions of the EctHR, available at: www.osce.org/uk/ukraine/232716?download=true (accessed 22 June 2017). The Supreme Court of Ukraine launched a substantive handbook on the ECHR and database on the relevant case law of the ECtHR for the Ukrainian judges, available at: www.scourt.gov.ua/clients/vsu/vsu.nsf/(documents)/04041CB11A2E814EC2257F9900411906 (accessed 22 June 2017).

15 *Supra* note 8. For instance, Decision of the Constitutional Court of Ukraine on the Pension Fund of Ukraine on 25 January 2012, No 1–11/2012.
16 Law (Zakon) of the *Verkhovna Rada* of Ukraine 'On Execution of Judgments on Application of Practice of the ECtHR', 23 February 2006, No 3477-IV.
17 *Ibid.*, Article 2.
18 *Ibid.*, Article 17.
19 *Ibid.*, Article 18.
20 For example, Decision of the Highest Specialised Civil and Criminal Court of Ukraine (*Y. Lutsenko case*) on 19 February 2013, No 5–915. Analysis of case law of the Ukrainian courts, available at: www.reyestr.court.gov.ua (accessed 22 June 2017), indicates a steady increase of references to the case law of the ECtHR by Ukrainian judges since 2014.
21 *Supra* note 8.
22 Information Letter of the High Administrative Court of Ukraine on 18.11.2014 No. 1601/11/10/14–14.
23 Law of Ukraine 'On amending the Constitution of Ukraine (as to justice)' of 2 June 2016 № 1401-VIII.
24 The reservations concerned mainly the scope of judges' immunity and preserving the balance of power in the procedure of appointment of judges and prosecutors (election of the Highest Law Council, which is responsible for the appointment of judges (qualified majority voting) and right of the Ukrainian Parliament to veto the appointment and removal of the General Prosecutor of Ukraine). European Commission for Democracy through Law (Venice Commission), Opinion №803/2015 of 26 October and of 3 December 2015.
25 Preamble, Article 1(2)(e) and Article 2 EU-Ukraine AA, *OJ*, 2014, L 161/1.
26 Article 14 EU-Ukraine AA, *OJ*, 2014, L 161/1.
27 Joint Staff Working Document 'Association Implementation Report on Ukraine' (SWD(2016) 446 final).
28 Article 8 EU-Ukraine AA, *OJ*, 2014, L 161/1.
29 Decision of the Constitutional Court of Ukraine on the Statute of the International Criminal Court on July 11 2001, Case No 1–35/2001. Therein the Constitutional Court of Ukraine stated that in accordance with the Rome Statute the International Criminal Court complements the system of national judiciary. For example the International Criminal Court may exercise its jurisdiction on territories of the countries which are Parties to the Rome Statute. It contradicts the Title VIII 'Judiciary' of the Constitution of Ukraine which (Article 124) provides that 'delegation of competences of national judiciary is not permitted'.
30 Article 14 EU-Ukraine AA, OJ, 2014, L 161/1.
31 Articles 56, 89, 90 of Law (Zakon) of the Verkhovna Rada of Ukraine 'On the Constitutional Court of Ukraine', 13 July 2017, No 2136-VIII.
32 Draft Law 6232, 23 March 2017, No 2077-VIII.
33 R. Petrov, 'Regulatory Convergence and Application of EU Law in Ukraine', in: P. Van Elsuwege and R. Petrov (eds.), *Legislative Approximation and Application of EU Law in the Eastern Neighbourhood of the European Union: Towards a Common Regulatory Space?* Routledge, 2014, pp. 137–158.
34 *Supra* note 8.
35 Law of the Verkhovna Rada of Ukraine 'About the All State Programme of adaptation of Ukrainian legislation to that of the EU', 18 March 2004, No. 1629-IV.
36 The main objective of this law is the 'alignment of the Ukrainian legislation with the *acquis communautaire*, taking into consideration criteria specified by the EU towards countries willing to join the EU'.
37 Judgment of the High Commercial Court of Ukraine on 2 February 2005, No. 12/267. Also Judgment of the High Commercial Court of Ukraine on 25

March 2005 (Closed Stock Company 'Chumak' v Kherson Custom Office), No. 7/299. Also Judgment of the High Commercial Court of Ukraine on 22 February 2005 ('Odek' LTD v Ryvne Custom Office) No. 18/303.

38 Judgment of the District Administrative Court of Kiev on 25 November 2008, No. 2/416. Apparently, this judgment became pattern for subsequent decisions by Ukrainian administrative judges, see: Judgment of the District Administrative Court of Kiev on 24 November 2008, No. 5/503. Judgment of the District Administrative Court of Kiev on 1 December 2008, No. 5/451. Judgment of District Administrative Court of Kiev on 10 November 2008, No. 5/435.

39 Case 41/74 van Duyn v Home Office, EU:C:1974:133.

40 Judgment of the District Administrative Court of Kiev on 26 June 2008, No. 4/337.

41 Decision of the Constitutional Court of Ukraine on January 23 2012, Case No 1–11/2012.

42 For example, see Special Opinion of the Judge of the Constitutional Court Viktor Shishkin on Decision of the Constitutional Court on January 23 2012, Case No 1–11/2012.

43 Informational Letter of the High Administrative Court of Ukraine on November 18 2014, No 1601/11/10/14–14.

44 Law of the Verkhovna Rada of Ukraine 'About the All State Programme of adaptation of Ukrainian legislation to that of the EU', 18 March 2004, No. 1629-IV.

45 *Supra* note 40.

46 Law (Zakon) of the Verkhovna Rada of Ukraine 'On Judicial System and Status of Judges', 06 December 2016, No 1774-IV.

47 Detailed information on case law of the Ukrainian judiciary can be available at: www.reyestr.court.gov.ua (accessed 22 June 2017). For example, the analysis of decisions of Ukrainian courts issued in 2014 and in 2016 indicates significant rise in references to the EU-Ukraine AA and various sources of EU acquis (fundamental principles, secondary acts, case law of the CJEU).

48 For example, Judgment of the District Court of the city of Chernigyv on 26 June 2016, No. 750/5197/16-a.

49 For example, Judgment of the Interdistrict Court of the City of Kolomya on 07 July 2016, No. 346/3499/16-c contains a rather emotional passage 'The Court notes that after the signing of the Association Agreement with the European Union by the President of our country, and after the ratification by the supreme legislative body (the Verkhovna Rada Ukraine), Ukraine, as a state aspiring the full membership in the EU, must respect private property rights of every person as a basic tenet and a cornerstone of European values and inviolable foundation of the EU, which must by complied by all Member States and by associated countries.'

50 Judgment of the Appellate Court of the region of Lviv on 06 April 2016, No. 33/783/241/16.

51 Judgment of the District Administrative Court of the city of Kiev on 13 April 2016, No. 826/594/16.

52 Judgment of the District Court of the city of Tsyrypinsk on 29 April 2016, No. 664/906/16-c.

53 Judgment of the High Administrative Court of Ukraine on 26 April 2016, No. 800/251/16.

54 Executive Order (Ukaz) of the President of Ukraine on 15 May 2017, No. 133/2017.

55 Law of Ukraine 'Amending the Administrative Code regarding the ban on production and propaganda of the St. George (Guards') Ribbon' on 16 May 2017, No. 2031-VIII.

56 P. Van Elsuwege, 'Ukraine's Ban on Russian Social Media: On the Edge Between National Security and Freedom of Expression', *VerfBlog*, 2 June 2017, available at: http://verfassungsblog.de/ukraines-ban-on-russian-social-media-on-the-edge-between-national-security-and-freedom-of-expression (accessed 22 June 2017).

57 Article 463(1) EU-Ukraine AA, *OJ* 2014, L 161/1.

58 Article 465(2) EU-Ukraine AA, *OJ* 2014, L 161/1.

59 Within the issues related to political, territorial, human rights, participation in international unions and organisations, collective security, usage of Ukrainian territory and natural resources, military assistance and deployment of Ukrainian troops abroad (Article 3(2) of Law of Ukraine on International Treaties).

6 The constitutional order of Georgia and its adaptability to the EU-Georgia Association Agreement

Gaga Gabrichidze

Introduction

Prior to the signing of the EU-Georgia Association Agreement (AA), the difference in interpretation of the relevant provisions of the Georgian Constitution gave rise to a lively debate as to who has the authority to sign the agreement for Georgia, the President or the Prime Minister.[1] This discussion, which ultimately was pragmatically resolved rather than conclusively clarified, is only one of many issues that arise from a constitutional perspective.

Clarifying the division of competences between the Parliament and the President was one of the objectives of an extensive revision of the Constitution which has recently been undertaken. A package of constitutional amendments has been elaborated by the State Constitutional Commission which was created by the Parliament of Georgia on 15 December 2016 and tasked to prepare constitutional amendments before 30 April 2017. Based on the draft prepared by the Commission, the Parliament of Georgia initiated the constitutional amendments on 1 May 2017 and adopted them on 13 October 2017.[2] The constitutional changes will take effect immediately after the President of Georgia (elected in the next presidential election, which will be held in 2018) takes the oath of office. Along the issue of competences, the constitutional revisions concern the mode of election of the Parliament and the President. However, the constitutional provisions concerning the relationship between international law and national law remained largely unaffected during the process of constitutional revision.

The aim of this contribution is to clarify the relationship between the EU-Georgia AA and the Constitution of Georgia. Specifically, the place of the AA within the Georgian domestic legal order as well as its scope of application will be examined and the question will be addressed whether the implementation of the agreement may cause some constitutional problems. The issue of direct applicability will also be discussed. Finally, specific suggestions for constitutional reform allowing a solution for the problematic issues discussed in the contribution will be put forward.

The relationship between international law and Georgian law

The Georgian Constitution provides for specific provisions to ensure compliance of Georgian legislation with the international legal obligations of Georgia.

The Constitution not only indicates that it is 'the supreme law of the State' and, accordingly, all other legal acts shall comply with the Constitution.[3] It also expressly provides that the legislation of Georgia shall comply with the universally recognised principles and rules of international law. Furthermore, international agreements shall take precedence over domestic normative acts unless they conflict with the Constitution or the Constitutional Agreement of Georgia.[4]

The Constitution, on the one hand, declares the compatibility of Georgian legislation (of which the Constitution itself is as integral part) with universally recognised principles and rules of international law. On the other hand, within the hierarchy of norms, it places international treaties below the Constitution and above domestic laws and statutes. Hence, the wording of these provisions indicates that the Constitution differentiates between the legal position of universally recognised principles of international law, on one hand, and norms of international treaties, on the other hand.

There seems to be general agreement in the literature that international treaties rank below the Georgian Constitution. On the contrary, there are different opinions concerning the relationship between the Constitution and universally recognised principles and rules of international law.[5] However, this topic is less relevant in the context of this contribution.

The above-mentioned provisions of the Constitution recognise international treaties as an integral part of the Georgian legislation by defining their legal relationship with normative acts existing at national level. This clear expression of the hierarchy of norms – including international agreements – in the Georgian legal order is important. It implies that the Constitution proceeds from a monist approach with respect to international agreements.[6]

This approach finds more concrete expression in other acts of Georgian legislation. For instance, the Georgian Law on Normative Acts not only distinguishes between legislative and subordinate normative acts[7] but also explicitly indicates that constitutional agreements and international agreements and treaties are to be considered as normative acts.[8] Following this logic, international treaties should be included either on the list of legislative normative acts or on the list of subordinate normative acts. However, that is not the case.[9] The legislation separately regulates the status of international treaties in the Georgian legal order. In particular, the law on Normative Acts specifies the status of international treaties laid down in the Georgian Constitution and establishes their hierarchical position below the Constitution and the Constitutional Agreement and above laws of Georgia, including organic laws.[10]

Application of the EU-Georgia Association Agreement

The AA is an international treaty and rights and obligations deriving from it are of an 'international law' nature. Whereas the substantive content of the AA is largely based on EU law, this connection has been established on the basis of international law. Thus, the question of whether the norms of the AA do have direct effect in the domestic legal system should be answered by taking into account the respective constitutional system of the associated countries. Besides, since the Association Council is an institution established under the AA, the question of the legal effect of its decisions should be considered in view of the legal effect of international legal norms in the national legal system.

The Georgian Constitution provides the mechanism which Georgia has chosen to give effect to international law in its national jurisdiction. As mentioned above, according to the Georgian legislation, it is not required to adopt a special legal act, which would recognise an international treaty as a national normative act. If a provision of international law is binding on Georgia, it automatically acquires domestic validity. In other words, as soon as Georgia has ratified or acceded to an international agreement, that international law becomes an integral part of Georgian law.

The Georgian legislation establishes the preconditions for the application of norms of international treaties within the domestic legal order. Of particular significance is the law on International Treaties of Georgia, which explicitly stipulates that 'treaties are an integral part of the legislation of Georgia'.[11] Accordingly, provisions of officially published treaties determining the specific rights and obligations and not requiring adopting specific acts within the domestic legal order, shall be directly applicable in Georgia.[12] This means that norms of duly ratified treaties can potentially be invoked by legal persons and individuals before the Georgian courts and the courts can apply them directly.[13]

In the context of automatic incorporation and direct effect of international legal norms into the Georgian legal order, the competent authority to interpret provisions of the AA becomes particularly important. The Court of Justice of the European Union (CJEU) is not the judicial body in charge of settling disputes which may arise from the application of the Agreement in Georgia. However, under the AA, the arbitration panel, which may be established for the purpose of dispute settlement,[14] shall request the CJEU to give a ruling on the question if the dispute concerns the interpretation and application of a provision of the EU-Georgia AA which imposes upon a party an obligation defined by reference to a provision of EU law. The ruling of the CJEU shall be binding on the arbitration panel.[15] Taking into account the specific focus of this procedure, which essentially aims at guaranteeing the autonomy of the EU legal order,[16] it does not include the authority to decide on the direct applicability of a norm in the Georgian legal order. The latter is reserved for domestic Georgian courts.[17]

Transfer of sovereign powers

The membership in international organisations, or relationship to international organisations in whatever form, is constitutionally based on provisions regulating the process of ratification of international treaties.[18] The conclusion of the EU-Georgia AA is no exception.

There is no express provision in the Georgian Constitution allowing for the transfer of sovereignty to international bodies. The Constitution determines the scope of the exercise of sovereignty by explicitly stating that 'state authority shall be exercised within the ambit of the Constitution'.[19] This provision can be understood as a general norm, which in principle prohibits transfer of sovereignty, unless any other provision of the Constitution explicitly permits such transfer. On the other hand, it can also be defined as a preventive measure for avoiding disputes over competences between different state institutions. In contrast to this general norm, there could be a more concrete reference to transfer of legislative power with regard to the Georgian Parliament. However, the Constitutional norm, according to which 'the Parliament of Georgia . . . shall exercise legislative power', [20] gives no reason for asserting that the Parliament of Georgia exclusively has legislative power. All the more so since, in cases determined by the Constitution, the President of Georgia may also issue decrees having the force of law.[21] Furthermore, the Constitution establishes a list of fields which fall within the exclusive competence of the supreme state authorities of Georgia,[22] but this is done in the context of defining the division of competences between the central government and the autonomous entities and there is no reason to assume that this provision establishes the substantive content of the barriers for the transfer of sovereign powers to international institutions. Concerning this matter, it is noteworthy that the Georgian Constitution contains no provisions establishing substantive barriers with regard to amendments of the Constitution. Title VIII of the Constitution defines the procedural requirements only for changes to the Constitution.[23] The issue of limits to the transfer of sovereignty has been widely disregarded within the academic literature about Georgia so far.[24]

In practice, such transfer can be carried out on the basis of an international treaty concluded with an international organisation. Considering that there is no express limitation in the Constitution with regard to transfer of sovereign powers, procedural and competence rules for concluding such international treaties might give a reasonable reference with respect to the delegation of sovereign rights. In particular, the Georgian Constitution not only includes a general reference concerning the ratification of treaties and international agreements,[25] but also includes a list of international agreements where the duty of ratification is explicitly mentioned. This is the case for international treaties which a) envisage Georgia's accession of an international organisation or interstate alliance; b) are of a military nature; c) concern the territorial integrity or change of the state borders; d) concern the borrowing or lending of money by the State; e) require change of domestic legislation or adoption of laws necessary for the fulfilment of international obligations undertaken.[26]

In our opinion, this list of subject matters may be considered as the framework for determining which international agreements are most relevant from the point of view of sovereignty. Accordingly, the position of the Georgian Parliament with regard to the transfer of sovereignty, which may be expressed either through ratification or non-ratification, is constitutionally not limited and is subject only to formal procedural rules. Thus, the above-mentioned provision not only contains competence and procedural rules but also has substantial value, taking into consideration its effect on the transfer of sovereignty.

System of judicial review

The Constitution conferred a broad authority of judicial review to the Constitutional Court, which is described as the 'judicial body of constitutional control'.[27] Adjudication on the constitutionality of international treaties falls, *inter alia*, within its competence.[28] Whereas the Constitutional Court generally considers and adjudicates upon conformity with the Constitution of normative acts in force, constitutional control of international treaties may also be possible before their ratification.

If a constitutional submission has been lodged with the Constitutional Court, the respective treaty shall not be ratified until the Constitutional Court passes its judgment.[29] A constitutional submission can be lodged regarding the constitutionality of those international treaties or particular provisions thereof, which are subject to ratification. In any event, it shall be lodged before their ratification.[30] In contrast, a constitutional claim shall be lodged regarding the constitutionality of an international treaty which is already ratified or of a treaty which is not subject to ratification.[31] Besides, a constitutional submission regarding constitutionality of an international treaty already in force shall be lodged by a common court if the court finds that there is a sufficient ground to consider a provision of the relevant treaty, which the court must apply when resolving the case, to be fully or partially non-compliant with the Constitution.[32] Upholding a constitutional claim, as well as recognition as unconstitutional of an international treaty or certain parts thereof on the basis of a constitutional submission of a common court, shall result in annulment of the international treaty or certain parts thereof in respect of Georgia, whereas on the basis of a constitutional submission, recognition of an international treaty or certain parts thereof as unconstitutional shall result in the inadmissibility of ratification of the international treaty or agreement.[33] In practice, the Constitutional Court of Georgia only once had to decide on the constitutionality of an international agreement. The constitutional submission lodged by a district court questioned the constitutionality of an article of the international agreement concluded between Georgia and the International Committee of the Red Cross. In its decision the Constitutional Court did not follow this view.[34]

The signature conflict: constitutional controversy regarding the signature of the Association Agreement

As already mentioned in the introduction, the signature of the EU-Georgia AA has been the subject of lively constitutional discussions. Naturally, the debate was based on the provisions as they existed before the 2017 revision of the Constitution. In particular, the question had arisen as to who had the authority to sign the agreement on behalf of Georgia: the President or the Prime Minister. The origin of the dispute was a difference in interpretation of their respective scope of competences as determined by the Constitution. The latter, on the one hand, provides that the President of Georgia is the Head of the State of Georgia[35] who shall represent Georgia in foreign relations.[36] On the other hand, it also determines that the Government of Georgia shall be the supreme body of executive power to implement the internal and foreign policy of the country.[37] Furthermore, the Prime Minister and ministers shall represent Georgia in foreign relations within their competence.[38]

The administration of the President pointed out that even if the role of the President in the Georgian political system is quite modest, it is still more than representative and ceremonial. In particular, specific provisions of the Constitution show that representation in foreign relations on the part of the President is not a mere formality. For instance, the President of Georgia shall conduct negotiations with other countries and international organisations and conclude international treaties.[39] Besides, if the treaty is signed by the President, the President of Georgia shall apply to the Parliament of Georgia for ratification, denunciation, and annulment of the particular treaty.[40]

On the other hand, representatives of the Government claimed that, according to the Constitution, acts of the President must be agreed with the Government. In particular, the President may conduct negotiations and conclude international treaties only 'in agreement with the Government'.[41] Besides, as almost all legal acts of the President, the act of the President on applying to the Parliament for ratification of an international treaty requires the countersignature by the Prime Minister.[42]

Based on this position, the Government had decided that the Prime Minister would sign the Association Agreement. In response, the President adopted a decree, according to which the President had decided to delegate his authority as a one-time measure to the Prime Minister. The decree was based on the Law on International Treaties of Georgia. The latter provides that, when a treaty falls within the powers of the President, he/she shall grant full powers by issuing an edict that requires a countersignature of the Prime Minister.[43] With this step, the Administration of the President underlined that it maintained its view that under the Constitution the signature of this comprehensive agreement falls under the authority of the President. The explanation of the reasons for delegating the authority has also been given. In particular, the Administration of the President, referring to the fact that the government authorised the Prime Minister to sign the agreement, argued that the authority has been delegated by the President in order for the Prime Minister to execute the right of signing of the agreement in a way that would not question the legitimacy of signature either now or in the future.[44]

The government also insisted on its standpoint. As mentioned above, the act of delegation of authority was done through a presidential order, which requires the countersignature of the Prime Minister.[45] Such a step would be tantamount to accepting that the President had the prerogative to sign the Association Agreement. Consequently, the Prime Minister declared that he needed no additional authority to sign the agreement[46] and refused to countersign the presidential decree. The EU-Georgia AA was eventually signed by the Prime Minister on 27 June 2014.

It is clear the Constitution offered the parties to this dispute a certain margin for interpretation. On the one hand, it is a fact that the President had the authority to conclude international treaties even if only in agreement with the Government. The question might be asked, which international treaty can be so important and comprehensive that it should be signed by the formal Head of the State, when not the Association Agreement?!

On the other hand, the text of the Constitution clearly indicates that concluding and signing an international treaty by the President of Georgia is only possible in agreement with the Government. This consent should be given prior to the conclusion of a treaty. Otherwise, the presidential legal act of signing would domestically take legal effect only after the Prime Minister would countersign it.[47] Obviously, this would lessen the legal significance of the act of signature. If the approval from the side of the Prime Minister is given prior to the signing by the President, there will be no need for the countersignature as, according to the Constitution, countersignature shall not be required for the legal acts of the President of Georgia that have been issued on the recommendation of the Government or that have been preliminarily approved by the Government.[48]

In any case, it would seem to be difficult to interpret the Constitution in such a way that the President is allowed to sign an international treaty without agreement of the Government. The Constitution not only expressly provides that the President has the authority to sign but, significantly, as it also explicitly points out, the exercise of this authority is subject to the consent of the Government. It can be assumed that the relevance of this issue resulted from the political constellation with difficult interinstitutional and interpersonal relations between the President's office and the Government rather than from the legal differences.

The significance of EU law for decisions of the Constitutional Court of Georgia

In general, Georgian courts may refer to provisions of legally effective international agreements concluded by Georgia, since they constitute an integral part of the Georgian legal system.[49] As mentioned above, such agreements belong to normative acts of the Georgian legal system[50] and are situated between 'normal' laws and the Constitution.[51] By far the most mentioned international treaty in decisions of Georgian courts is the European Convention on Human Rights (ECHR).[52]

With the aim to provide the judges and lawyers and all the interested persons with information about the practice of the European Court of Human Rights (ECtHR), its approaches and the case law, the Human Rights Center of the Supreme Court of Georgia annually publishes the digest of the decisions and judgments delivered by the ECtHR. It also prepared and published the thematic directory which reflects the Strasbourg court's most important decisions and judgments.

The Association Agreement is also an international treaty duly ratified by the Georgian Parliament and, consequently, an integral part of the Georgian law. It has, as well as all other international treaties, precedence over Georgian laws but not over the Constitution. The same was the case with the Partnership and Cooperation Agreement (PCA) which was concluded between the EU and Georgia and constituted the legal basis for their relations before the entry into force of the Association Agreement. However, no references to the PCA can be found in decisions of Georgian courts.[53] This can notably be explained by the fact that this agreement – in contrast to the ECHR – contained hardly any provisions which could qualify for direct applicability.[54]

On the other hand, occasional references can be found to different sources of EU law that do not have any direct legal link to the Georgian legal system.[55] The analysis of the case law shows that in most cases Georgian courts refer to EU (legal) acts in order to reinforce their own legal positions.[56] For example, in a judgment of the Constitutional Court of Georgia a reference to the European Parliament Resolution of 18 January 2001 'On the visa regime imposed by the Russian Federation on Georgia' can be found.[57] It was used by the Constitutional judges as a source of reference for the human rights situation in the breakaway regions of Abkhazia and South Ossetia. In another decision, the Constitutional Court referred to the EU's practice in relation to consumer protection to conclude that state intervention in this area is justified under constitutional law.[58]

Furthermore, one case should be emphasised where the court uses a European legal norm and relevant decisions of the European Court of Justice for the purposes of interpretation of facts of the case. In particular, in one of its decisions the chamber in civil matters of the Supreme Court of Georgia had to explain the definition of an investment.[59] The court based its interpretation on EU law and referred for this purpose to EU Directive 96/9[60] and several decisions of the European Court of Justice.[61]

What made the courts to mention legal acts of the EU in their decisions? The fact is that Georgian courts were not required to apply EU law since there was (and still is) no obligation to do so under the legal framework of EU-Georgia relations. Such references may therefore be explained only by the perception of the EU as a kind of 'normative power[62] that exports its norms and values abroad. In this case, EU law is perceived as a model to be followed, irrespective of its formal status of 'bindingness'. However, it seems that the model character of EU law is not a sufficient explanation for the practice of Georgian courts to refer to EU legal acts. As mentioned above, such references are made, at least in most cases, when a judge tries to justify his/her own legal position. If we were in general to accept the model character of EU law, we would have to assume that Georgian courts would interpret a legal situation in conformity with EU law even when EU norms would not strengthen their own opinion but would be entirely contrary to it. However, such evidence is hard to find. It is clear that Georgian courts refer to EU norms in order to enhance the persuasiveness of their decisions through the authority of the EU.[63]

Arguably, the significance of EU law will only increase now that the AA has entered into force. So far, the Constitutional Court already made one explicit reference to the AA. In its Decision of 31 July 2015, the Court concluded that employees have the right to receive compensation in the event of unlawful termination of an employment contract. To reach this conclusion, it referred, *inter alia*, to Articles 228 and 229 of the AA and stated that these provisions recognise and protect standards established by the International Labour Organisation (ILO).[64]

Of course, in contrast to national courts of EU Member States, Georgian courts do not have any obligation to interpret national law in conformity with EU law. There is no provision in the legal framework of EU-Georgia relations that would oblige Georgian courts to opt in their search for an interpretation in conformity with EU legal norms.[65] Nevertheless, it should be taken into account that, by ratifying the Association Agreement, the Georgian Parliament has undertaken to approximate large parts of Georgian law to that of the EU. Thus, it would be logical to argue that Georgian laws, which were approximated to EU legal norms, should be interpreted in conformity with the latter. Obviously, the goal of legal approximation cannot be fully achieved if the approximation process is limited to creating norms complying with EU law without the effective interpretation and implementation of these norms.

Conclusion

The open attitude of Georgia towards the international legal order affects its approach to the legal instruments and concepts related to EU-Georgia relations. From the point of view of Georgian constitutional law, there are no major obstacles for the process of European integration. It is noteworthy that there are no express substantive limitations for the transfer of sovereignty in the Georgian Constitution and also no substantive barriers for the change of constitutional provisions. The fact that hardly any attention has been paid to these issues in the academic literature might be linked to the lack of relevance of such provisions in the previous practice of Georgia with regard to concluding international agreements. However, the conclusion of the EU-Georgia Association Agreement changes the situation fundamentally. Therefore, it might be expedient, despite the present integration-friendly attitude, to create a constitutional basis for either general international integration or, more specifically, European integration. This would prevent interpretations which would call into question the legality of steps towards further European integration. A first move in this direction is the recently adopted amendment to the Constitution, according to which 'the constitutional bodies shall take all available measures within their competence to ensure Georgia's full integration into the European Union and the North-Atlantic Treaty Organisation'.[66]

As to the issues of direct applicability of provisions of the Association Agreement and decisions of the Association Council, as well as the issue of interpretation of Georgian legal norms in conformity with EU law, the attitude of Georgia will most likely be defined by the case law of the Constitutional Court. The main challenge for the Constitutional Court will be to deal with the nature and substance of the provisions of the AA and their effect on the Georgian legal order.

Notes

1 See further in this contribution for more details about the background of this discussion.

2 The adopted constitutional amendments in Georgian language can be found on the following website: http://www.parliament.ge/ge/ajax/downloadFile/74766/.

3 Article 6.1 (future Article 4.4) of the Constitution of Georgia. 'Sakartvelos Parlamentis Utskebebi', 31–33, 24/08/1995.

4 Article 6.2 (future Article 4.5) of the Constitution of Georgia. The Constitutional Agreement is an agreement which governs relations between the State of Georgia and the Apostolic Autocephalous Orthodox Church of Georgia. It was concluded in 2002 on the basis of Article 9.2 (future Article 8) of the Constitution of Georgia.

5 See I. Putkaradze, The Universally Recognized Norms of International Law and the Protection of the Citizens' Political-Economic and Social-Cultural Rights and Freedoms at the Constitutional Court of Georgia. 'A Person and a Constitution', No. 3, 1998, where the author is of the opinion that whilst establishing principles and norms of the Constitution, the people and the state are bound by the universally recognised rights and freedoms, as directly acting law; K. Korkelia, '*Customary International Law in the Legal System of Georgia*', in: K. Korkelia and I. Sesiashvili (eds.), *Georgia and International Law*, Tbilisi:Gyla, 2001, pp. 62–80, where in the author's opinion, international law, in particular in the form of the universally recognised principles and norms, among those protecting and regulating human rights, stand lower than the Constitution of Georgia; I. Kurdadze, 'Stages of Development of Scientific Concepts on Correlation Between International and Domestic Law and Contemporary Events', *Journal of International Law*, 2008, 21–32. The author argues in favour of the primacy of universally recognised principles of international law over the Constitution.

6 Cf.: K. Korkelia, 'International Law in the Georgian Legal Order', *The Journal of East European Law*, 6(4), 1999, 387–388.

7 Article 7.1 of the Law of Georgia on Normative Acts. 'Sakartvelos Sakanonmdeblo Matsne', 33, 09/11/2009.

8 Article 7.1 of the Law of Georgia on Normative Acts.

9 According to Article 7.2 of the Law of Georgia on Normative Acts, types of legislative acts of Georgia are: a) the Constitution of Georgia, the constitutional Law of Georgia; b) organic laws of Georgia; c) law of Georgia, decrees of the President of Georgia, the Rules of Procedure of the Parliament of Georgia.

10 Article 7.3 and 7.5 of the Law of Georgia on Normative Acts; Article 6.2 of the Law of Georgia on International Treaties of Georgia. 'Parlamentis Utskebani', 44, 11 November 1997.

11 Article 6.1 of the Law of Georgia on International Treaties of Georgia.

12 Article 6.3 of the Law of Georgia on International Treaties of Georgia.

13 In practice, this only concerns the application of the European Convention on Human Rights. See, for example, Decision of the Tbilisi City Court, N3/2058, 10 October 2007.

14 Article 248.1 of the EU-Georgia AA.

15 Article 267 of the EU-Georgia AA.

16 See also, with respect to the EU-Ukraine AA, G. Van der Loo, *The EU-Ukraine Association Agreement and Deep and Comprehensive Free Trade Area: A New Legal Instrument for EU Integration Without Membership?* Leiden and Boston: Brill Nijhoff, 2016, pp. 296–301.

17 In the case law of Georgian courts, the issue of direct applicability of international norms has so far only played a role with respect to the European Convention on Human Rights. Like courts of other European countries, Georgian courts most often apply their norms as a tool for interpreting national norms. The cases of independent application of norms of the European Convention on Human Rights by Georgian courts are quite rare. See, for example, the above-mentioned Decision of the Tbilisi City Court, N3/2058, 10 October 2007. For more details see K. Korkelia, *How to Secure Protection of Human Rights Under the European Standards in Georgia*, Tbilisi: TSU University Press, 2010, p. 44.
18 Article 47 (future Article 65) of the Constitution of Georgia. According to Article 47.2 (future Article 65.2) of the Constitution, it shall also be obligatory to ratify an international treaty or which envisages Georgia's accession to an international organisation or interstate alliance.
19 Article 5.1 (future Article 4.4) of the Constitution of Georgia.
20 Article 48 (future Article 36.1) of the Constitution of Georgia.
21 According to (Article 73.1 i) of the Constitution of Georgia, the President may issue decrees having the force of law during a state of emergency or martial law that shall be valid until the end of the state of emergency or martial law. According to the amended version of this provision (future Article 71.3), the President may issue such decrees only on the recommendation of the Prime Minister.
22 Article 3.1 (future Article 7.1) of the Constitution of Georgia.
23 Article 102 of the Constitution of Georgia provides for that a draft law on revision of the Constitution may be submitted by more than half of the total number of MPs or not less than 200,000 voters. Following the public discussions, the draft law revising the Constitution shall be deemed adopted if it is supported by not less than three-fourths of the total number of MPs of Georgia at two successive sessions of the Parliament of Georgia after an interval of at least three months. According to the amended version of this provision (future Article 77), the public discussions will be followed by the system of plural voting, under which the draft law shall deemed adopted if a majority of two-thirds of two convocations of Parliament vote for the bill. A single convocation of Parliament can also adopt the draft law on revision of the Constitution if three-fourths of its members support it.
24 See, for example, the following general works on Georgian constitutional law: A. Demetrashvili (ed.), *Textbook on Constitutional Law*, Tbilisi: Holivudi, 2005; A. Demetrashvili, I. Kobakhidze, *Constitutional Law*, Tbilisi: Inovatsia, 2010.
25 According to Article 65.1 (future Article 47.1) of the Constitution of Georgia, the Parliament of Georgia, acting by a majority of its members, shall ratify, denounce, and annul international treaties.
26 Article 65.2 (future Article 47.2) of the Constitution of Georgia.
27 Article 83.1 (future Article 59.2) of the Constitution of Georgia.
28 Article 89.1 e (future Article 60.4 e) of the Constitution of Georgia.
29 Article 65.4 (future Article 47.4) of the Constitution of Georgia. It should be noted that 'a constitutional claim' is also mentioned along with 'a constitutional submission' in this article. However, considering the provision of Article 38.2 of the Organic Law of Georgia on the Constitutional Court of Georgia, according to which a constitutional claim shall be lodged either prior to ratification of the relevant treaty or when the relevant treaty is not subject of ratification, it is unclear, under which circumstances Article 65.4 of the Constitution would be of relevance for constitutional claims.
30 Article 38.2 of the Organic Law of Georgia on the Constitutional Court of Georgia. 'Parlamentis Utskebani', 001, 27/02/1996.
31 Article 38.2^1 of the Organic Law of Georgia on the Constitutional Court of Georgia.
32 According to Article 19.2 of the Organic Law of Georgia on the Constitutional Court of Georgia, if, while considering a particular case, a common court

concludes, that there is a sufficient ground to deem the law or other normative act, applicable by the court while adjudicating upon the case, fully or partially incompatible with the Constitution, the court shall suspend the consideration of the case and apply to the Constitutional Court. The consideration of the case shall be resumed after a judgment on the issue is adopted by the Constitutional Court.

33 Article 23.5 of the Organic Law of Georgia on the Constitutional Court of Georgia.

34 Decision of the Constitutional Court of Georgia, N 8/177/2, 21 May 2002. The case concerned the constitutionality of Article 3 of the 'Headquarters Agreement between the Republic of Georgia and the International Committee of the Red Cross' ratified by the resolution of the Parliament of Georgia of 16 October 1996, according to which the International Committee of the Red Cross enjoys immunity from any form of court and administrative activities, with Articles 42.1 and 82 of the Constitution of Georgia stating that 'Everyone has the right to apply to a court for the protection of his or her rights and freedoms' and that 'Acts of a court shall be binding for all state bodies and persons on the whole territory of Georgia.' The Constitutional Court concluded that Article 3 of the above-mentioned agreement does not imply an absolute immunity of the International Committee of the Red Cross and, therefore, it does not restrict the constitutional right to appeal to court. Thus, the disputed norm does not contradict the Constitution of Georgia.

35 Article 69.1 (future Article 49.1) of the Constitution of Georgia.

36 Article 69.3 (future Article 49.3) of the Constitution of Georgia.

37 Article 78.1 (future Article 54.1) of the Constitution of Georgia.

38 Article 78.4 of the Constitution of Georgia. According to the revised text of the Constitution, the Prime Minister represents Georgia in foreign relations and concludes international treaties on behalf of Georgia. See future Article 55.3 of the Constitution of Georgia.

39 Article 73.1 a) of the Constitution of Georgia. The revised Constitution emphasises a privileged role and function of the Government of Georgia in conducting international negotiations, entering into international treaties and exercising representative powers. For the President, the Government's consent will be required for not only negotiating with foreign States and international organisations, entering into international treaties and accepting ambassadors and other diplomatic representatives, but also for exercising representative powers in foreign relations. See future Article 52.1 a) of the Constitution of Georgia.

40 Article 65.1^1 of the Constitution of Georgia.

41 Article 73.1 a) of the Constitution of Georgia.

42 Article 73^1 (future Article 53) of the Constitution of Georgia.

43 Article 13.2 of the Law of Georgia on International Treaties of Georgia.

44 Special statement of the President's parliamentary secretary of 27 June 2014. Available at: www.president.gov.ge/ge/PressOffice/News?p=8815&i=1

45 Article 13.2 of the Law of Georgia on International Treaties of Georgia in connection with Article 73^1 of the Constitution of Georgia.

46 Available at: www.civil.ge/eng/article.php?id=27272

47 cf.: Article 73^1 of the Constitution of Georgia.

48 Article $73^1.3$ of the Constitution of Georgia

49 Article 6.1 of the Law of Georgia on International Treaties of Georgia.

50 Article 7.1 of the Law of Georgia on Normative Acts.

51 Article 6.2 (future Article 4.5) of the Constitution of Georgia; Article 7.3 of the Law of Georgia on Normative Acts.

52 Concerning application of the European Convention on Human Rights see: K. Korkelia, 'Application of the European Standards on Human Rights in

the Georgian Practice', *Constitutional Law Review*, 2010, 21–37. Available at: www.constcourt.ge/files/Journal_EN.pdf (accessed 10 March 2016).

53 For the application of EU law by the Georgian judiciary see G. Gabrichidze, 'Legislative Approximation and Application of EU Law in Georgia', in: P. Van Elsuwege and R. Petrov (eds.), *Legislative Approximation and Application of EU Law in the Eastern Neighbourhood of the European Union – Towards a Common Regulatory Space?* London and New York: Routledge, 2014, p. 188.

54 Concerning the question of the place of the European Convention on Human Rights in the Georgian legal system see: A. Phirtskhalashvili, *Schutzpflichten und die horizontale Wirkung von Grundrechten in der Verfassung Georgiens vom 24. August 1995: eine vergleichende Untersuchung der staatlichen Schutzpflichten aus der Europäischen Menschenrechtskonvention und der georgischen Verfassung unter besonderer Berücksichtigung der deutschen Schutzpflichtenlehre*, Potsdam: Universitätsverlag Potsdam, 2010, p. 109 et seq.

55 Decisions of the Constitutional Court of Georgia are available on the internet at: www.constcourt.ge/index.php?lang_id=ENG&sec_id=74 (accessed 15 March 2016). Decisions of the Supreme Court of Georgia are available on the internet at: http://prg.supremecourt.ge (accessed 15 March 2016).

56 For more details see: G. Gabrichidze, 'Auswirkung der Beziehungen zwischen Georgien und der Europäischen Union auf die georgische Judikative', *Zeitschrift für Europarecht*, 15(6), 2013, 136–142.

57 Decision of the Constitutional Court of Georgia, N 1/5/224, 16 November 2004.

58 Decision of the First Panel of the Constitutional Court of Georgia, N 1/1/374, 379, 9 February 2007.

59 Decision of the Supreme Court of Georgia, N AS-1210–1139–2012, 2 May 2013.

60 Directive 96/9/EC of the European Parliament and of the Council of 11 March 1996 on the legal protection of databases. Official Journal L 077, 27 March 1996, 0020–0028.

61 The judgments of the Court of Justice of the European Union mentioned in this decision are as follows: Case C-46/02, *Fixtures Marketing Ltd v. Oy Veikkaus Ab*, EU:C:2004:694; Case C-203/02, *British Horseracing Board v William Hill*, EU:C:2004:695; Case C-338/02, *Fixtures Marketing Ltd v. Svenska Spel Ab*, EU:C:2004:696.

62 See J. Manners, 'Normative Power Europe: A Contradiction in Terms?' *Journal of Common Market Studies*, 40(2), 235–258.

63 See G. Gabrichidze, 'Legislative Approximation and Application of EU Law in Georgia', in: P. Van Elsuwege and R. Petrov (eds), *Legislative Approximation and Application of EU Law in the Eastern Neighbourhood of the European Union – Towards a Common Regulatory Space?*, London/New York: Routledge, 2014, 188.

64 Decision of the Constitutional Court of Georgia, N 2/3/630, 31 July 2015.

65 Unlike to the practice of the Supreme Court of Georgia to inform judges on the case law of the European Court of Justice, the Supreme Court does not yet pursue activities aiming at explaining the issue of application of EU law and providing references to the CJEU's case law.

66 Future Article 78 of the Constitution. This amendment was part of the constitutional amendments package adopted by the Parliament of Georgia on 13 October 2017. For the English version of Article 78 of the Constitution see: European Commission for Democracy through Law (Venice Commission), 'Georgia. Draft Revised Constitution', CDL-REF(2017)027, Strasbourg, 17 May 2017.

7 The constitutional order of Moldova and the challenge of multi-vector integration

Mihaela Tofan

Introduction

Moldova occupies a special position among the countries of the post-Soviet space. On the one hand, the country has a long-term interest in close relations with the EU.[1] This resulted in the conclusion of an Association Agreement (AA) and the establishment of a visa-free regime for short-term travel in 2016. On the other hand, Moldova also pursues a special relationship with the Eurasian Economic Union (EAEU), which is based upon the conclusion of a Memorandum of cooperation[2] and the acquisition of an observer status in April 2017.[3] President Igor Dodon even suggested that Moldova may consider full membership in the EAEU if the AA with the EU does not lead to the expected results.[4]

Clearly, the development of close legal and political relations with both the EU and the EAEU raises significant constitutional questions related to the issue of national sovereignty and the status of international law in the domestic legal system. In order to tackle these issues, this chapter starts with a brief outline of the national constitutional system before clarifying the relationship with international law and the implications of multi-vector integration (i.e. with both the EU and the EAEU).

The national constitutional system of the Republic of Moldova

The Republic of Moldova was one of the first Soviet republics to proclaim its independence on 23 July 1990 and to leave the USSR in the aftermath of the *coup d'état* in Moscow in August 1991. The adoption of a new constitution on 27 August 1994 was a crucial step towards cementing Moldova's newly acquired independence and confirming its future as a European country that shares international and European democratic values.[5]

Similar to any European constitution the Constitution of Moldova guarantees the protection of human rights; formalises the principle of market economy; introduces the respect for human dignity; proclaims the rule of law; formalises the principles of separation and balance of powers and eligibility and accountability of the authorities and independence of judiciary.[6]

Moldova is a classical parliamentary republic, with the Parliament as the supreme representative body of the people of Moldova and the sole legislative authority of the state. The Moldovan unicameral legislature is composed of 101 members.[7] The executive in Moldova includes a mixed system of governance (dual executive consisting of the President and the government (Prime Minister and the Council of Ministers)).[8] The Moldovan justice works on the basis of a traditional three-level system with lower courts, courts of appeal and the Supreme Court. The Constitutional Court of Moldova possesses the exclusive competence of judicial review of the constitutionality of laws and other acts (decisions of the Parliament, decrees of the President of Moldova, governmental acts and international agreements). Furthermore, it enjoys the following powers: interpretation of the Constitution; confirmation or invalidation of results of referendums and of parliamentary and presidential elections; approval of legality of the dissolution of Parliament and the impeachment of the President and legitimacy of the interim President's actions.[9] The role of constitutional justice in Moldova is to ensure respect for the Constitution, for democratic principles and fundamental rights, towards the consolidation of democracy and social progress.[10] Therefore, the Constitutional Court plays an essential role in ensuring the interpretation of the EU-Moldova AA and is likely to address the constitutionality of the possible termination of this agreement and potential accession of Moldova to the EAEU.

The relationship between international law and domestic law

The constitutional system of Moldova is considered to be one of the most 'international law friendly' in the post-Soviet era as far as the relationship between international law and national law is concerned.[11]

As the highest representative institution, the Parliament has full competence to ensure the application of international law within the legal order of Moldova,[12] and to decide on ratification, acceptance, approval or accession of Moldova to international treaties and international organisations.[13] Furthermore, the Constitutional Court is empowered to review the constitutionality of laws and international treaties to which Moldova is a party.[14] Nevertheless, the Constitution of Moldova cannot be regarded as a classical monist constitution because it does not ensure the direct applicability of all universally recognised principles and norms of public international law and international agreements within the national legal order. Duly ratified international treaties that contain provisions which conflict with the Constitution, will trigger either the repeal of these provisions or the amendment of the relevant provisions of the Constitution.[15]

The Constitution unequivocally confirms that Moldova is bound by the established norms and principles of international law. For instance, Moldova must respect the Charter of the United Nations and international treaties to which it is a party. Relationships between Moldova and other countries must be in line with unanimously accepted principles and norms of international law.[16] Hence, the Constitution imposes a general commitment on Moldova to respect universally recognised principles and norms of public international law in its domestic and foreign policies.

However, the distinctive feature of the Constitution of Moldova within the post-Soviet area is that it recognises the absolute priority of public international law in the field of the protection of fundamental human rights over conflicting national legislation (but not the Constitution).[17] It implies that the Moldovan legislature, executive and judiciary must interpret and enforce constitutional rights and freedoms of Moldovan nationals in accordance with the Universal Declaration of Human Rights and with conventions and international treaties to which Moldova is a party.[18] The respect of ECtHR jurisdiction is insured, but there are still gaps in applying the ECHR as a general and mandatory source of law in Moldova.[19] The Supreme Court frequently states that, in cases of conflict between national legislation and international treaties in the field of fundamental human rights and liberties, the latter prevails.[20] For example, the Supreme Court has been consistent on recognising supremacy of the ECHR over conflicting provisions of national legislation.[21] A national law on application of international treaties clarifies the limits of direct application of international treaties in domestic law: 'the provisions of the international treaties (enforced in Moldova) that by the formulation are likely to apply in legal relations without adopting special laws, are directly applicable and enforceable in the legal system of the Republic of Moldova'.[22]

Further references to primacy of international treaties over conflicting provisions of national legislation are present in national codes and laws (Civil Code, Civil Procedure Code, Penal Code, Criminal Procedure Code, Family Code, etc.). For example, the relevant provision of the Moldovan Civil Code provides that 'if the treaty to which Moldova is party establishes other provisions than those stipulated in the civil national regulation, the provisions of the international treaty shall apply'.[23]

The foregoing indicates that the international law friendly approach of the Constitution of Moldova can be a great asset for the effective implementation of the EU-Moldova AA. The political objectives and essential elements of the EU-Moldova AA correspond to the constitutional principles in Moldova. It equips the Constitutional Court with discretion for interpreting the EU-Moldova AA in conformity with the Moldovan Constitution. Furthermore, Moldovan domestic courts can interpret conflicting provisions of national law in favour of the relevant provisions of the EU-Moldova AA, especially with respect to the protection of human rights and democratic freedoms.

Balancing between the European Union and the Eurasian Economic Union

European integration remains a key foreign policy priority for Moldova. It is the obvious fruit of the soft power of attraction of the European common values and principles (individual freedom, equality and social justice, respect for human rights and freedoms, principles of democracy) and an essential consequence of social, labour and cultural integration of the people of Moldova in the EU.[24] In particular, Moldova's close historical, linguistic and cultural links with Romania determine the country's pro-European orientation. On the other hand, the Soviet legacy also plays an important role in the Moldovan society.[25] The tension between both factors of Moldova's identity became obvious in the constitutional discussions regarding the name of the official state language.

Whereas Article 13 (1) of the Constitution proclaims that '[t]he State language of the Republic of Moldova is the Moldovan language based on the Latin alphabet',[26] the Constitutional Court decided in 2013 that this provision is superseded by the 1991 Declaration of Independence, which identified Romanian as the official language.[27] This decision is not without controversy, particularly because the promotion of a separate Moldovan linguistic identity is a legacy of the Soviet past. It has been found that the Moldovan language is mostly supported by the rural population and parts of the post-Soviet political elite.[28]

Significantly, the controversy regarding the name of the official state language – Moldovan or Romanian – also appeared in relations with the EU. In 2007, European Commissioner Ferrero Waldner unequivocally stated that 'Moldovan' – and not Romanian – is the official language of the Republic of Moldova. She based her conclusion on the text of the Moldovan Constitution and the sovereign right of every state to determine its official language.[29] Moreover, the 'Moldovan language' was referred to in the Partnership and Cooperation Agreement (PCA) and, therefore, part of the *acquis* and binding on all EU Member States (including Romania which joined the PCA through the conclusion of a protocol under Article 6 (2) of the Accession Act). However, the Association Agreement (AA), which was concluded after the 2013 Moldovan Constitutional Court Decision, no longer refers to the Moldovan language.[30] Hence, it appears that the constitutional developments in Moldova tacitly resulted in the dropping of Moldovan as a separate language in EU-Moldovan relations.

Arguably, the AA opens a new era for EU-Moldova cooperation confirming the country's 'European choice' based upon a commitment to the shared values of democracy, respect for human rights and fundamental freedoms and the rule of law.[31] Moreover, the EU-Moldova AA emphasises that regional stability, security and democratic development in the region and, in particular, the peaceful settlement of regional conflicts are among the guiding principles of the agreement.[32] The agreement further highlights the Parties' commitment to a sustainable solution to the Transnistrian issue, in full respect of the sovereignty and territorial integrity of Moldova as well as to facilitating jointly post-conflict rehabilitation.[33] This is a very important element of the political cooperation between the EU and Moldova since it provides the legal and political ground for a gradual settlement of the Transnistrian problem and engagement of the key international actors into the peace building process and territorial integrity of Moldova.

However, the European common values have not always been positively perceived by the mainly rural population of Moldova with strong Orthodox traditions. As a consequence, the issue of Moldova sharing European common values, especially regarding the protection of sexual and ethnic minorities, became controversial and was cleverly exploited by anti-European political parties.[34] Furthermore, in 2015–2016 the Moldovan society was shaken by notorious corruption scandals associated with ruling pro-European parties.[35] These events brought thousands of Moldovans to the streets for mass protests. Consequently, following the presidential election in November 2016, outspoken pro-Russian politician Igor Dodon was sworn in as President of Moldova on 23 December 2016. There is no immediate threat for the pro-European foreign policy of Moldova and, consequently, for the EU-Moldova AA, since the President's powers in relation to foreign affairs are considerably limited by the Parliament. For instance, the President can negotiate and sign an international agreement with obligatory approval of the Parliament and cannot terminate it without the Parliament.[36]

Nevertheless, the consequences of this election became quickly visible. In April 2017, Moldova was granted observer status by the EAEU. This status does not come close to full membership. For instance, it does not entail a right to take part in the decision-making process and access to official meetings of the EAEU institutions is only possible by invitation.[37] The decisions adopted in the EAEU framework are not binding for the observer country. Nevertheless, the EAEU Treaty imposes a binding obligation ('loyalty clause') on the observer state 'to refrain from any action that may infringe the interests of the Union and its Member States, as well as the object and purpose of this Treaty.'[38] Arguably, this loyalty commitment may potentially cause conflicts with Moldova's obligations under the EU-Moldova AA. For example, the extensive list of 'essential elements' in the EU-Moldova AA may conflict with potential deepening of the political and security cooperation under the framework of the EAEU. Furthermore, future external agreements of the EAEU and decisions of the EAEU Court may contradict the objectives of the EU-Moldova AA. Therefore, the decision of President Dodon to obtain observer status in the EAEU is questionable from a constitutional perspective. In particular, the question arises whether this action was within the President's constitutional powers. Articles 60, 86 and 135 of the Constitution are explicit about the President's competence to negotiate and conclude international treaties, but only the Parliament may enforce them. Since Moldova has not yet applied for full membership in the EAEU and did not become a party to the Astana Agreement, the fact of obtaining observer status in the EAEU can still be considered as constitutional. However, the hypothesis of full membership in the EAEU certainly falls beyond the President's competence and will require parliamentary endorsement. Eventually, this situation may become a reality if, in the course of the forthcoming parliamentary elections in 2018, pro-Russian political forces take the majority in the Parliament and initiate a so-called 'Molexit' from the AA with the EU.

In order to pave the ground for the forthcoming parliamentary elections and strengthening his constitutional powers, President Dodon recently initiated a number of controversial legislative initiatives. First, in February 2017 he presented a draft law to supplement the Constitution in order to enlarge his powers to dissolve the parliament.[39] Second, a reform of the electoral legislation in Moldova was discussed in April 2017. In essence, the reform implies the introduction of a mixed electoral system with 50 Members of Parliament (MPs) to be elected by a proportional closed-list system in a nationwide constituency and 51 MPs elected in separate constituencies under a plurality system.[40] This initiative has been heavily criticised by the Council of Europe, the OSCE and the EU.[41] While accepting that the choice of an electoral system is a sovereign decision of a state, the three organisations raised several concerns. In particular, the lack of prior consultation with relevant stakeholders, the risks of influence on candidates and the excessive thresholds for parliamentary representation may undermine the country's democratic system. In this respect, the European External Action Service (EEAS) already recalled that 'democracy and the rule of law are at the core of our Association Agreement.'[42] Moldova is, therefore, expected not to implement the proposed revision of the electoral legislation and to cooperate closely with the Council of Europe and its Venice Commission. Hence, the further evolution of this discussion is a first important test case for analysing the impact of the AA on crucial domestic evolutions in Moldova.

Decisions of the EU-Moldova Association Council in the Moldovan legal order

The institutional structure of the EU-Moldova AA replicates other EU association agreements. The EU-Moldova AA empowers the Association Council to issue binding decisions and non-binding recommendations.[43] The EU-Moldova Association Council is assisted by the Association Committee, which is composed of the parties' senior officials and may be granted by the former the competence to issue binding decisions.[44] Furthermore, the EU-Moldova AA establishes the Parliamentary Association Committee that is the platform for cooperation between the Members of the European Parliament and the Members of the Moldovan Parliament. The Parliamentary Association Committee may issue non-binding recommendations.[45]

The Moldovan legal order does not provide any clear answer regarding the legal force of the acts issued by the Association Council, Association Committee or by the Parliamentary Association Committee within the national legal order. Following the constitutional provisions and the law on international treaties the binding decisions of the EU-Moldova common institutions must be incorporated into the national legal order either through implementing acts (laws, ordinances, decisions) or through a special law on application of the EU-Moldova AA. So far, no legal acts of this kind have been drafted and enforced in Moldova. This has not been overtly problematic because the meetings of the EU-Moldova Association Council have not yet led to the adoption of any binding decisions.

Compatibility between the EU-Moldova Association Agreement and the Constitution

Notwithstanding its general 'international law friendly' approach (cf. *supra*), the Constitution of Moldova also includes a number of specific sovereignty clauses.

Article 2, for instance, provides that the national sovereignty belongs exclusively to the people of Moldova, who shall exercise it directly and through its representative bodies in the ways provided for in the Constitution. Furthermore, no private individual, no part of the people, no social group, no political party or other public organisation may exercise state power in its own name. Usurpation of state power constitutes the gravest crime against the people. The Constitution is the supreme law of the land what means that no law or other legal act, which contravenes the Constitution, has legal power.[46] Article 10 of the Constitution expressly provides that the constitutional foundation is the unity of Moldova as the common and indivisible homeland of all its citizens. The Constitution further recognises and guarantees the right of all citizens to preserve, develop and express their ethnic, cultural, linguistic and religious identity. Finally, Article 11 of the Constitution proclaims the permanent neutrality of Moldova and prohibits the stationing of troops of other states in its territory.

The Constitutional Court considered the interaction between the national constitution and the EU-Moldova AA for the first time on 9 October 2014.[47] In particular, the Constitutional Court addressed the correlation between national constitutional principles, i.e. the principle of sovereignty and the principle of respect for international law, in relation to the law on the ratification of the EU-Moldova AA.[48] In essence, the Constitutional Court argued that the right of the state to assume international commitments is an inherent element of state sovereignty, which can be manifested externally by establishing collaborative relationships with other countries and international entities on the basis of international agreements.

Further, the Constitutional Court concluded that the delegation of certain powers to designated international institutions by concluding international agreements does not imply the simultaneous transfer of national sovereignty. According to the Constitutional Court, such international agreements are conventions by which the sovereign state accepts that another authority or institution may exercise certain powers within the framework of the agreement in a manner provided in the international agreement itself. Therefore, the Constitutional Court considered the complaint that the EU-Moldova AA limits Moldova's sovereignty as groundless. The signing, the ratification and the entry into force of the EU-Moldova AA does not affect the supremacy of the Constitution or the sovereignty of the Republic of Moldova and does not undermine the nature of the Constitution as an expression of the will of the nation and supreme law of the state.

The Constitutional Court further stated that the EU-Moldova AA promotes political association and economic integration between Moldova and the European Union, based on common values such as respect and promotion of the principles of sovereignty and territorial integrity, the inviolability of borders and independence of Moldova, democracy, rule of law and respect for human rights and fundamental freedoms. Therefore, in the opinion of the Constitutional Court, the purpose and objectives of the EU-Moldova AA are in line with Article 1 of the Constitution.[49] Hence, this judgment implies that there is no urgent need for domestic constitutional reform in order to ensure the effective implementation of the EU-Moldova AA.

However, in case the Moldovan Parliament decides to adhere to the Astana Agreement and to acquire the full membership in the EAEU it would imply the eventual denunciation of the EU-Moldova AA following the procedure in Article 460 of the agreement.[50] The full membership of Moldova in the EAEU will imply the transfer of some of its sovereign powers to the EAEU's supranational institutions (Eurasian Economic Commission), recognition of the EAEU's exclusive and shared external competence[51] and abidance by decisions of the EAEU's institutions as it has been confirmed by recent case law of the EAEU Court,[52] which is incompatible with Moldova's commitments under the EU-Moldova AA (especially in light of the far-reaching obligations of legal approximation with the EU *acquis* and the functioning of the DCFTA with the EU).

Concluding remarks

It can be concluded that Moldova is a very special case within the group of post-Soviet countries. First, the constitutional system of Moldova is one of the most international law–friendly among these countries. Second, arguably, Moldova is the most EU integrated country of the Eastern Partnership. It has close social, historical and cultural (common language) links with an EU Member State (Romania). Furthermore, it was the very first post-Soviet country to acquire the visa-free regime with the EU in 2016. However, Moldova also was the first country of the Eastern Partnership to bring to power a pro-Russian President who brought this country to observer status in the EAEU and suggested to abandon the association relations with the EU.[53] Nevertheless, all these conflicting features make the Moldovan case extremely interesting and provoking from a political and academic perspective. On the one hand, the EU-Moldova relations display the considerable achievements of economic, political and legal integration of a post-Soviet country under the framework of the Eastern Partnership to the EU (visa-free regime and limited access to the EU internal market). On the other hand, these gains failed to become an ultimate 'success story' of the Eastern Partnership due to popular disappointment caused by the failure of the Moldovan pro-European government to ensure the rule of law and combat corruption. As a result, the Moldovan case perfectly displays all economic, political and cultural dilemmas of the post-Soviet countries, which experience growing geopolitical pressure of two conflicting integration blocks (EU and EAEU).

This challenging future puts forward several issues for further consideration. The first issue is the future constitutional reform in Moldova. The analysis of the relevant provisions of the Constitution and national law indicate that the objectives of the EU-Moldova AA are in line with the constitutional principles of the Moldovan legal order. The Constitutional Court clearly expressed its view that there is no need to either revise or amend the sovereignty clauses in the Constitution, as they are consistent with the EU-Moldova AA.

The second issue is Moldova's simultaneous integration with the EU and the EAEU. Although there are no legal impediments for Moldova to pursue association relations and to maintain the functioning of the DCFTA with the EU, on the one hand, and to exercise political, economic and legal cooperation with the EAEU, on the other hand, parallel integration in the EU and EAEU structures is not possible due to several legal reservations. In particular, full participation in the customs union established under the EAEU is incompatible with the commitments under the DCFTA.

It is quite feasible for Moldova to keep the *status quo* by continuing its active participation in the Eastern Partnership and ensuring effective implementation of the EU-Moldova AA and the DCFTA. Moldova may just keep its observer status in the EAEU, thereby avoiding a potential transfer of sovereign competences to the institutions of the EAEU. Alternatively, Moldova may terminate the EU-Moldova AA and join the Astana Agreement in order to obtain full membership in the EAEU. However, this action will unavoidably raise new constitutional questions regarding the compatibility of such undertaking with the constitution's sovereignty clauses. The issue of transfer of sovereign competences is likely to result in a national referendum.[54] Furthermore, the 'EAEU *acquis*' is predominantly economically oriented and therefore omits the human rights and common values dimension. It implies that, in the case of Moldova's accession to the EAEU and departure from the Association Agreement with the EU, Moldovan nationals may experience a gap in the protection of their fundamental freedoms. Consequently, potential integration of Moldova in the EAEU almost unavoidably leads to a plethora of constitutional challenges before the Constitutional Court and further amendments to the Constitution.

Notes

1 A. Khvorostiankina, 'Legislative Approximation and Application of EU law in Moldova', in: P. Van Elsuwege and R. Petrov (eds.), *Legislative Approximation and Application of EU Law in the Eastern Neighbourhood of the European Union: Towards a Common Regulatory Space?* Routledge, 2014, p. 159.

2 Memorandum of cooperation between Eurasian Economic Commission and the Republic of Molodva, available at: https://docs.eaeunion.org/docs/ru-ru/01413501/ms_05042017 (accessed 21 June 2017). 'Moldova Granted Observer Status in Eurasian Union', *Euractiv.com*, 19 April 2017, available at: www.euractiv.com/section/europe-s-east/news/moldova-granted-observer-status-in-eurasian-union (accessed 21 June 2017). Also see 'Igor Dodon Signs Memorandum of Cooperation with the Eurasian Economic Commission', available at: www.presedinte.md/rus/comunicate-de-presa/igor-dodon-si-tigran-sargsyan-au-semnat-la-chisinau-memorandumul-de-cooperare-intre-comisia-economica-euroasiatica-si-republica-moldova (accessed 21 June 2017).

3 Decision of the Supreme Eurasian Economic Council, 'On Request of the Republic of Moldova to Obtain the Observer Status in the Eurasian Economic Union' on 14 April 2017, No. 6 available at: https://docs.eaeunion.org/docs/ru-ru/01413582/scd_17042017_6 (accessed 21 June 2017).

4 'Moldovan President Hopes to Cancel EU Association Agreement', *Euractiv.com*, 17 January 2017, available at: www.euractiv.com/section/enlargement/

news/moldovan-president-hopes-to-cancel-eu-association-agreement (accessed 21 June 2017). Eventually, President Dodon is planning to enlarge his constitutional power in order to dissolve the Parliament of Moldova which may stand on his way to terminate the EU-Moldova AA. See: European Commission for Democracy Through Law (Venice Commission), Proposal by the President of the Republic of Moldova to supplement the Constitution in order to enlarge powers of the president to dissolve parliament, Opinion No. 886/2017, Strasbourg, 23 May 2017, available at: www.venice.coe.int/webforms/documents/?pdf=CDL-REF(2017)026-e (accessed 21 June 2017).

5 For instance, Article 1 (3) of the Constitution proclaims that 'Moldova is a democratic state, governed by the rule of law, in which the dignity of people, their rights and freedoms, the free development of human personality, justice and political pluralism represent supreme values that shall be guaranteed.'

6 Article 6 of the Constitution of Moldova, available at: www.presedinte.md/eng/constitution (accessed 21 June 2017).

7 Article 60 of the Constitution of Moldova, available at: www.presedinte.md/eng/constitution (accessed 21 June 2017).

8 'Constitutional history of Moldova', available at: www.constitutionnet.org/country/constitutional-history-moldova (accessed 21 June 2017).

9 Article 4 of the Law 'On the Constitutional Court' (No. 317/1994), available at: http://lex.justice.md/md/311650 (accessed 21 June 2017).

10 Article 135 of the Constitution of Moldova, available at: www.presedinte.md/eng/constitution (accessed 21 June 2017).

11 N. Osmochescu, 'The Application of International Law in Republic of Moldova's Legal Order: Theoretical and Practical Aspects', in: V. Cojocaru, D. Sarcu-Scobioala and V. Zagaria (eds.), *Interaction of the National Legal System with International Legal System: Challenges and Solutions*, Chisinau: Tipografia Centrala, 2015, p. 5.

12 Article 60 of the Constitution of Moldova, available at: www.presedinte.md/eng/constitution (accessed 21 June 2017).

13 Article 11 of Law 'On International Treaties in Moldova' no. 595-XIV, 24th September 1999, available at: http://lex.justice.md/index.php?action=view&view=doc&id=311696 (accessed 21 June 2017).

14 Article 135(1)(a) of the Constitution of Moldova, available at: www.presedinte.md/eng/constitution (accessed 21 June 2017). A. Baiesu, 'Interaction of Constitution and International Law: The Jurisprudents Solutions of Constitutional Court of the Republic of Moldova', in: V. Cojocaru, D. Sarcu-Scobioala and V. Zagaria (eds.), *Interaction of the National Legal System with International Legal System: Challenges and Solutions*, Chisinau: Tipografia Centrala, 2015, p. 25.

15 Article 8(2) of the Constitution of Moldova, available at: www.presedinte.md/eng/constitution (accessed 21 June 2017).

16 Article 8 of the Constitution of Moldova, available at: www.presedinte.md/eng/constitution (accessed 21 June 2017).

17 Article 4(2) of the Constitution of Moldova, available at: www.presedinte.md/eng/constitution (accessed 21 June 2017).

18 Article 4(1) of the Constitution of Moldova, available at: www.presedinte.md/eng/constitution (accessed 21 June 2017).

19 Decision of the Parliament of the Republic of Moldova no. 1298 of 1997, available at: http://lex.justice.md/index.php?action=view&view=doc&lang=1&id=307753 (accessed 21 June 2017).

20 Report of the Moldovan Supreme Court for 2014, available at: http://jurisprudenta.csj.md/search_plen_csj.php?id=71 (accessed 21 June 2017).

21 For instance, Judgment of the Supreme Court of Moldova 3/2014, available at: http://jurisprudenta.csj.md/search_hot_expl.php?id=181 (accessed 21 June 2017).

Judgment 1/2011 the Supreme Court of Moldova, available at: http://jurisprudenta.csj.md/search_hot_expl.php?id=135 (accessed 21 June 2017), provided that the right of liberty of meetings and associations must be applied and interpreted in accordance with the ECHR because the relevant provision of the Constitution (Article 40) is too brief and laconic to prevail over the ECHR.

22 Article 20 of Law 'On International Treaties in Moldova' no. 595-XIV, 24th September 1999, available at: http://lex.justice.md/index.php?action=view&view=doc&id=311696 (accessed 21 June 2017).

23 Article 7 of the Civil Code of Moldova, available at: http://lex.justice.md/md/325085/ (accessed 21 June 2017).

24 For instance, according to official statistics 319 000 Moldovans (out of 1 272 800 active Moldovans) worked or looked for job abroad (predominantly in the EU Member States) in 2016, available at: http://statbank.statistica.md/pxweb/pxweb/ro/30%20Statistica%20sociala/30%20Statistica%20sociala__03%20FM__03%20MUN__MUN070/MUN070100.px/table/tableViewLayout1/?rxid=2345d98a-890b-4459-bb1f-9b565f99b3b9 (accessed 21 June 2017).

25 For an account on the background of Moldova's complex history and identity, see: C. King, *The Moldovans: Romania, Russia and the Politics of Culture*, Stanford: Hoover Institution Press, 1999.

26 It is noteworthy that – in addition to the single official state language – Article 13 (2) of the Moldovan Constitution recognises and protects the usage of Russian as well as other languages of national minorities. See: www.presedinte.md/eng/constitution (accessed 21 June 2017).

27 Decision of the Moldovan Constitutional Court No. 36 on 5 December 2013, available at: www.constcourt.md/ccdocview.php?tip=hotariri&docid=476&l=ro (accessed 21 June 2017).

28 According to Federica Prina, 'communists have tended to refer to the state language as "Moldovan", nationalists and unionists (those who sought unification with Romania) have referred to it as "Romanian"'. See: F. Prina, 'Linguistic Justice, Soviet Legacies and Post-Soviet Realpolitik: The Ethnolinguistic Cleavage in Moldova', *Journal of Ethnopolitics*, 14(1), 2015, 52–71. See also A. Iavorschi, 'The Problem of National Identity in the Republic of Moldova: Moldovanism and Romanianism', *Oikonomia Journal of Ethics and Social Sciences*, 2012, available at: www.oikonomia.it/old/pages/2012/2012_ottobre/pdf/08_spazio%20aperto_arina.pdf (accessed 25 June 2017).

29 Answer given by Mrs. Ferrero-Waldner on behalf of the Commission to written question No E-5014/07 (regarding the Commission's position on the 'Moldovan language' being made the official state language), 19 December 2007.

30 Article 465 AA defines all EU languages as authentic texts, but in contrast to Article 104 of the PCA, the Moldovan language is not mentioned.

31 See preamble of the EU-Moldova AA, *OJ*, 2014, L 260/1.

32 Articles 2 (4) and 8 (1) of the EU-Moldova AA.

33 Article 8(2) of the EU-Moldova AA.

34 For example, see 'European Values versus Traditional Values and Geopolitical Subtext in Moldova', available at: http://humanrights-online.org/en/european-values-versus-traditional-values-and-geopolitical-subtext-in-moldova/ (accessed 21 June 2017).

35 A. Rettman, 'Pro-Russia Protesters Storm Moldova Parliament', *EU Observer*, 21 January 2016, available at: https://euobserver.com/foreign/131938 (accessed 21 June 2017).

36 Article 86 (1) of the Constitution of Moldova provides that: 'The President of Moldova Shall Be Empowered to Hold Official Negotiations, Conclude

International Treaties on Behalf of the Republic of Moldova and Submit Them, in the Manner and Period Prescribed by Law, to Parliament for Ratification', available at: www.presedinte.md/eng/constitution (accessed 21 June 2017).

37 According to Article 109 of the Astana Treaty (EAEU Treaty), available at: www.eaeunion.org/?lang=en#info (accessed 21 June 2017), any country may apply for an observer status in the EAEU. This status is granted by the Supreme Council of the EAEU and implies that representatives of the observer country may be present at the meetings of the EAEU institutions by invitation only (sic!) and to request documentation that is not confidential. The observer status does not give a right for the third countries to take part in the decision-making process in the EAEU.

38 Article 109(5) of the EAEU Treaty, available at: www.eaeunion.org/?lang=en#info (accessed 21 June 2017).

39 See: European Commission for Democracy Through Law (Venice Commission), Proposal by the President of the Republic of Moldova to supplement the Constitution in order to enlarge powers of the president to dissolve parliament, Opinion No. 886/2017, Strasbourg, 23 May 2017 available at: www.venice.coe.int/webforms/documents/?pdf=CDL-REF(2017)026-e (accessed 21 June 2017).

40 See: Joint Opinion of the European Commission for Democracy Through Law (Venice Commission) and the OSCE Office for Democratic Institutions and Human Rights (ODIHR) on the draft laws on amending and completing certain legislative acts (electoral system for the election of the parliament), Strasbourg/Warsaw, 19 June 2017, Venice Commission Opinion No. 884/2017 and ODIHR Opinion Nr. ELE-MDA/308/2017, available at: www.jurnal.md/files/pdf/default.pdf (accessed 25 June 2017).

41 Statement of the Spokesperson of the EEAS on the Venice Commission and OSCE Office for Democratic Institutions and Human Rights' Opinion on a draft revision of the electoral legislation of the Republic of Moldova, available at: https://eeas.europa.eu/delegations/moldova_en (accessed 21 June 2017).

42 *Ibid.*

43 Article 436 of the EU-Moldova AA, *OJ*, 2014, L 260/1.

44 Article 437 of the EU-Moldova AA, *OJ*, 2014, L 260/1.

45 Article 440 of the EU-Moldova AA, *OJ*, 2014, L 260/1.

46 Article 7 of the EU-Moldova AA, *OJ*, 2014, L 260/1.

47 Judgment of the Moldovan Constitutional Court on 9 October 2014, available at: www.constcourt.md/ccdocview.php?tip=hotariri&docid=511&l=ro (accessed 21 June 2017).

48 Law No. 112 of 2 July 2014 'On Ratification of the EU-Moldova Association Agreement', available at: http://dcfta.md/lege-nr-112-pentru-ratificarea-acordului-de-asociere-intre-republica-moldova-pe-de-o-parte-si-uniunea-europeana-si-comunitatea-europeana-a-energiei-atomice-si-statele-membre-ale-acestora-pe-de-alta-parte (accessed 21 June 2017).

49 Article 1 of the Moldovan Constitution reads: 'Republic of Moldova is a sovereign, independent, unitary and indivisible state; it is a state of law, democratic, in which human dignity, rights and freedoms, free development of human personality, justice and political pluralism represent supreme values and are guaranteed', available at: www.presedinte.md/eng/constitution (accessed 21 June 2017).

50 Article 460 (2) AA provides that '[e]ither party may denounce this agreement by notifying the other Party. The Agreement shall terminate six months from the date of receipt of such notification.'

51 According to Article 7(1) of the Astana Treaty (EAEU Treaty), available at: www.eaeunion.org/?lang=en#info (accessed 21 June 2017), the EAEU 'the Union shall have the right to engage in international cooperation with states, international

organizations, and international integration associations and independently or jointly with the Member States conclude international treaties therewith on any matters within its jurisdiction'.

52 P. Kalinichenko, 'A Principle of Direct Effect: The Eurasian Economic Union's Court Pushes for More Integration', *VerfBlog*, 16 May 2017, available at: http://verfassungsblog.de/the-principle-of-direct-effect-the-eurasian-economic-unions-court-pushes-for-more-integration (accessed 21 June 2017).

53 'Moldova President Dodon to EU Council President Tusk: I Will Support Cancelling the Association Agreement in a Referendum', available at: www.moldova.org/en/moldova-president-dodon-eu-council-president-tusk-will-support-cancelling-association-agreement-referendum (accessed 21 June 2017).

54 Article 75(1) of the Moldovan Constitution provides that 'Problems of Utmost Importance Confronting the Moldovan Society and State Shall Be Resolved by Referendum', available at: www.presedinte.md/eng/constitution (accessed 21 June 2017).

8 From EU integration process to the Eurasian Economic Union

The case of Armenia

Narine Ghazaryan and Laure Delcour

Introduction

As a small constituent of the so-called 'shared' or currently 'divided'[1] neighbourhood between Russia and the European Union (EU), Armenia seemingly successfully pursued a policy of complementarity[2] with both regional actors for most of its independent existence. The EU-Armenia relations were to advance further with the negotiation of an Association Agreement (AA) promising closer political and economic ties with the Union. The European integration course, however, came to an abrupt end when the national government announced its withdrawal from the project in September 2013 prior to the Eastern Partnership (EaP) Vilnius summit where the agreement was to be initialled.[3] The country's leadership simultaneously declared its intention to embark on an alternative integration process – accession to the Russian-led Eurasian Customs Union (ECU) and Common Economic Space[4] – under explicit pressure from Russia. The ECU and the relevant Common Economic Space were upgraded to a Eurasian Economic Union (EAEU) with a signature of a relevant agreement in May 2014 which replaced over 100 agreements, laying the basis for the former two entities. Armenia previously had only an observer status in the Eurasian Economic Community, which existed between 2000 and 2014, and did not express much interest in becoming a member of the latter or its anticipated successor organisations. Having withdrawn from the EU integration course in September 2013, hasty measures were undertaken for the country's accession to the rival project. On 24 October 2013, a Declaration of the Heads of States of the Republic of Belarus, Republic of Kazakhstan, Russian Federation and the Republic of Armenia on the participation of the Republic of Armenia in the Eurasian integration process was adopted, followed by the Decision of the Supreme Eurasian Economic Council on an accession roadmap in December 2013.[5] In May 2014, a treaty on Armenia's accession to the EAEU was signed paving the way for the country's membership on 2 January 2015.[6]

As a result of this major shift in Armenia's political life, the country faces a two-track process of reluctant integration to EAEU and disintegration from the previous EU-oriented course. This process raises issues of legislative and institutional nature as provisions should be made to accommodate Armenia's accession to an alternative trade block. At the same time, the country faces the legacy of years of legislative approximation with the EU *acquis communautaire*. What should happen to the outputs of the EU integration process that has been cut short? What impact, if any, would Armenia's Eurasian integration process have on its WTO obligations? In addition to these questions, another important issue is the future of Armenia's cooperation with the EU. Following the announcement on withdrawal from the AA, the Armenian Government noted that the country would be in favour of signing another – less ambitious – agreement with the EU.[7] Since the new agreement had to take into account Armenia's membership in the EAEU, the negotiations were opened in December 2015[8] and finalised in February 2017. The Comprehensive and Enhanced Partnership Agreement (CEPA) was initialled one month later in Yerevan.[9] In addition to the bilateral cooperation, the prospect of EU cooperation with Armenia through the EAEU should also be considered, even though it appears unlikely at present.

Armenia, therefore, should be seen as a unique case study of parallel processes of political and economic integration and disintegration. It is for this reason that the chapter deviates somewhat from the format of the other country reports presented in the volume. Against this background, the next section overviews the reversal of the EU integration process, including the impact of the EAEU accession on Armenia's WTO commitments. Next, the legislative and institutional aspects of the new economic integration course are considered, including the status of the EAEU legislation in the Armenian legal order. The final section concerns the current and future prospects of EU-Armenia cooperation. The chapter concludes with a brief summary of findings.

The wider narrative of reversing the process of EU integration and Armenia's accession to the EAEU

Armenia offers an unprecedented example of (dis-)integration with the EU under the European Neighbourhood Policy (ENP)/EaP.[10] Between 2010 and 2013, the country has engaged into substantial reforms in line with EU demands as part of negotiations for an Association Agreement and a Deep and Comprehensive Free Trade Area (DCFTA). Prior to that, attempts at legislative approximation were undertaken within the frame of the PCA relevant provisions.[11] These efforts came to an abrupt end following the declaration of Armenia's Government's intention to join a rival Eurasian integration project. This decision seemingly put an end to the EU integration process in Armenia, given that membership in the EAEU precludes the conclusion of a DCFTA.[12] One of the main reasons for this is that the membership of the EAEU entails an imposition of common external tariff which is incompatible with the abolition of tariffs envisaged under the DCFTA. This section seeks to explore both the reasons that prompted Armenia to give an unprecedented impetus to integration with the EU when the EaP was launched in 2009 and the factors that steered the country away from EU integration and toward the Eurasian project in 2013–2015. It also scrutinises the extent to which Armenia has actually reversed the process of EU integration and engaged with Eurasian integration.

The narrative guiding EU integration: the need for modernisation

Despite Armenia being regarded as a 'hesitant' ENP partner in the mid-2000s,[13] it subsequently launched major institutional and policy reforms to deepen EU integration. Upon the conclusion of the ENP Action Plan in 2006, the country introduced an institutional mechanism which gave a prominent role to the Ministry of Economy for coordinating the activities related to EU integration.[14] In the late 2000s, Armenia selectively adopted EU demands under the ENP Action Plan. For instance, while it introduced significant reforms in the migration area, the country's compliance was assessed as shallow in the case of energy and anti-corruption policies.[15]

However, the narrative about EU integration changed in the early 2010s. The EU's offer under the EaP was welcomed in Yerevan. For South Caucasus countries, the EaP held significant promise as it offered greater proximity with the EU by extending tangible incentives – enhanced contractual framework, DCFTAs and visa liberalisation – that hitherto had been on the table with Ukraine only. The Armenian authorities, in particular, perceived the EaP as an opportunity to carry out their own reform agenda. Economic modernisation indeed emerged as an imperative in light of the country's increasing vulnerability after the Russian-Georgian conflict, the failed rapprochement with Turkey and the global economic and financial crisis.[16] Domestic pressure for reforms also increased in the wake of the deep political crisis that followed the 2008 presidential elections and the post-electoral crackdown on opposition demonstrators.[17]

Against that backdrop, the Armenian authorities regarded reforms as a *sine qua non* both for ensuring their own political survival and for reducing the country's regional vulnerability. They also viewed the EU *acquis* as a template for modernisation, and a consensus emerged among domestic actors on the benefits of closer relations with the EU.[18] Therefore, in contrast to some other EaP countries, the Armenian narrative on EU integration was premised neither upon an aspiration to join the EU, nor even upon a shift in the country's geopolitical orientation. Instead, it emphasised the EU's role domestically, as highlighted by President Sargsyan in 2011:

> We have stated more than once that European direction is our priority. In recent years, we have registered considerable success in that area. [The EU] has not only become one of our most important partners in the world but also plays a significant role inside Armenia, assisting us in the implementation of the reforms and in strengthening economic and overall stability of the country.[19]

Armenia's interest in the EU's model translated into substantial domestic change in line with EU templates in a process of 'silent Europeanisation'.[20] In fact, Armenia quickly caught up with Georgia and Moldova in the negotiations for a DCFTA. However, in some sectors (for instance energy) the country's efforts to initiate reforms consistent with EU demands were short-lived due to the increasing pressure of Russia.[21] Perhaps paradoxically, Armenia's efforts to reduce its vulnerability by becoming more competitive and diversifying its foreign policy stumbled against the strategic use of this vulnerability by its main ally, the Russian Federation.

From EU to Eurasian integration: security as an overarching priority

While the Armenian authorities regarded the EU integration process as compatible with the Russian-guaranteed security umbrella, in 2013 Russia started increasing its pressure on the country to join the ECU – an option initially ruled out by Armenia.[22]

Russia has been Armenia's most important ally since its independence. Russian military bases are located in the country, and a Treaty on Friendship and Cooperation was signed in 1990s securing the military bond.[23] The defence cooperation securing Russia's future role was reaffirmed by a renewed agreement in 2010 securing the presence of the Russian military base in Armenia until 2044.[24] Armenia perceives Russia as its main security guarantor due to constant threats from Azerbaijan over the Nagorno-Karabakh conflict and the continuous economic isolation stemming from the close ties and cooperation between Georgia, Azerbaijan and Turkey.[25] Moreover, the country has a strong dependence on energy supplies from Russia.[26] In the area of energy cooperation Russia's leverage has been noted whereby it does not require resorting to hard power to achieve its objectives, but instead can do so by delivering energy for cheap prices.[27] Such strategies have been used regularly by Russia as a manipulative tool enabling it to acquire resources in the neighbouring states, but also to deliver certain policy results. Tolstrup notes the arbitrary differences in gas prices, whereby Georgia would be forced to pay twice the price of that paid by Armenia.[28] Moreover, Russia is traditionally the largest foreign investor in Armenia with stakes in sectors as important as banking, telecommunications and electricity, including the Hrazdan and Medzamor power plants.[29]

Russia's simultaneous use of different yet equally powerful leverages (massive arms sales to Azerbaijan in spring 2013, followed by Vladimir Putin's visit to Baku in August; and an increase of gas prices by 50 percent in July 2013) was perceived as a clear signal by Armenia,[30] a few weeks after DCFTA negotiations were completed and two months before the EaP summit in Vilnius. In essence, Armenia's decision not to initial the Association Agreement and the DCFTA was determined by the country's security situation. Ultimately, given the salience of the Nagorno-Karabakh conflict with Azerbaijan, Armenia's regional vulnerability in view of its closed border and lack of diplomatic relations with Turkey, and the latter's unequivocal support for Azerbaijan, the country had little choice but to accommodate Russian requirements and join the Eurasian project. Thus, Armenia was far from a willing candidate country for accession to the Eurasian integration project: it was 'more resigned to joining the EAEU than motivated by any genuine enthusiasm for the prospect'.[31] The decision was made public through a joint statement by Presidents Sargsyan and Putin, during the former's visit to Moscow, thereby giving a clear indication of Russia's role in Armenia's U-turn. This statement ran counter the principle of complementarity that had underpinned Armenian foreign policy thus far and established a clear connection between deeper political and security cooperation with Russia, on the one hand, and enhanced economic integration as part of the Eurasian project, on the other hand.[32]

While Armenia's backtracking from EU integration derives from its security concerns, the EAEU (in sharp contrast to the EU) has never been perceived as a vector of modernisation. Instead, for some Armenian businessmen, EAEU membership is a clear opportunity to maintain joint legacies from the Soviet period and avoid the costs of reforms.[33] In fact, the decision to join the EAEU was made despite the economic costs to be incurred by the country. The ECU's initial common external tariff was broadly aligned to Russia's tariff schedule and therefore much higher than Armenia's. Like Kazakhstan and Kyrgyzstan, the country should approximately double its average tariff to adopt the common tariff. Therefore, applying EAEU tariffs was expected to result in an increase in the price of imported goods while Armenia would gain only limited benefits from the redistribution of common customs duties. As stipulated in the Treaty on the Accession of the Republic of Armenia to the Eurasian Economic Union (2014), the country should receive 1.13% of the total custom duties, demonstrating the asymmetric nature of potential benefits for its members.[34] Besides, Armenia is still expected to incur significant costs as a result of trade diversion after joining the EAEU. According to a study commissioned by the EU, the implementation of the DCFTA would have implied a 2.3% increase in Armenia's GDP, while having no negative impact in Armenia's trade with third countries.[35] In particular, the DCFTA would have offered increased opportunities for foreign investment and it would also have enhanced the competitiveness of Armenia's economy based upon regulatory convergence with the EU's advanced technical standards.

In contrast, Armenia exports low-quality goods to Russia. In addition, accession to the EAEU has only strengthened the country's overreliance on Russia in strategic economic sectors, such as energy, communication and transports. For instance, the energy agreement signed on 16 January 2014 only tightens the Russian stranglehold over Armenia's energy sector, with the cession to Gazprom of the remaining shares in Armenia's gas distribution company (now called Gazprom Armenia) and a commitment to buy gas exclusively from Russia until 2043 in exchange for lower gas prices and repayment of only half of Armenian energy debt.[36] Other Russian investment projects, such as upgrading Armenia's railway system and plans to build a rubber plant, although they seem promising, threaten to increase further the country's dependence on Russia.[37] Moreover, the reversal can also have a negative effect on those emerging sectors, such as information technologies, that mostly depend on Western investment.[38]

In addition, as a consequence of its joining the EAEU and applying higher tariffs, Armenia faced possible renegotiations of tariffs with affected WTO members. However, the actual scope of these renegotiations remains to be ascertained. To entice Armenia and Kyrgyzstan (also a WTO member), Russia promised subsidies for possible claims by WTO members.[39] While the Treaty on Accession to the EAEU provides Armenia with a transition period (until 2022) for such renegotiations, no clear mechanism for compensation was envisaged by the Eurasian Economic Commission a few months after Armenia's accession.[40] This is also because the EAEU average common external tariff is decreasing (as a result of the gradual implementation by Russia of its WTO commitments) below Armenia's WTO bound average tariff.[41] The gradual reduction of the common external tariff in line with Russia's WTO commitments would see it fall below Armenia's average tariff in the course of 2016.

Overall, participation in the Eurasian integration process only perpetuates Armenia's paradoxical situation. The country regards Russia as the major ally to preserve its territory from threats in a very challenging regional environment and this perception has been decisive in the 2013 decision to join the EAEU. The upsurge of violence in Nagorno-Karabakh in April 2016[42] has only reignited the security and political concerns which prompted Armenia's 2013 U-turn.

However, Armenia's overreliance on Russia's energy resources and investments (stemming from Russia's leverage on security issues), as well as on remittances from migrants living in the Russian Federation, actually erodes the country's independence and increases its vulnerability.[43] In fact, despite closer links with Armenia since its turn-back, Russia continues to sell arms to Azerbaijan and thereby fuels the conflict as well as Armenia's security vulnerability.[44]

Furthermore, the economic impact of accession to the EAEU is still unclear. Shortly before Armenia's accession, economic experts expected very few short-term positive effects, while noting that in the long term they were uncertain.[45] Armenia's accession to the EAEU also came at a dire point. The economic crisis in Russia affected trade flows among EAEU members (that decreased significantly in the first six months of 2015)[46] and undermined the competitiveness of Armenian goods on the Russian market: Armenian exports decreased by 6.3% due to the ruble devaluation.[47]

Reversing the EU integration process or maintaining some degree of complementarity?

Despite their decision to join the Eurasian project, since 2013 Armenian authorities have attempted to maintain (and even to expand) the links with the EU. This is primarily because the reasons that prompted Armenia to embrace EU templates under the EaP have not vanished. As emphasised by President Sargsyan during the Vilnius EaP Summit, the EU is still regarded as a model for Armenia's modernisation:

> Building and strengthening Armenian nationhood upon a European model has been a conscious choice of ours, and that process is hence irreversible. Our major objective is to form such mechanisms with the EU that on the one hand would reflect the deep nature of our social, political and economic relationship, and on the other – would be compatible with other formats of co-operation.[48]

Therefore, since the decision to backtrack from the Association Agreement and the underlying DCFTA was announced, the Armenian bureaucracy has strived to preserve the substantial reforms conducted in 2010–2013 under the EaP. Prior to joining the EAEU, in 2013–2014, it completed the implementation of sectoral strategies and action plans adopted as part of the negotiations for a DCFTA.[49] Upon accession to the EAEU, a degree of autonomy has been preserved due to three factors. First, it is facilitated by the climate of uncertainty that followed the creation of the EAEU, as some key Eurasian common policies and standards are in the making. Second, Armenia managed to secure a high number of exemptions (approximately 800) during the accession negotiations to the EAEU. While most of these are temporary, the country will not have to comply fully with EAEU standards before 2022. Third, as both the DCFTA and the EAEU are (in principle) based upon WTO rules, some of their standards are compatible. Therefore, previous compliance with EU demands is broadly seen as an asset for Armenia in the Eurasian integration project. In fact, as a result of both its early WTO membership and especially its substantial adoption of EU templates in 2010–2013, Armenia is regarded as a frontrunner compared to other EAEU members.[50] Interestingly, the Eurasian Economic Commission refers to Armenia as an example to follow in a number of sectors.[51] The Armenian government intends to exploit this advanced status to 'act as a bridge' between the EU and the EAEU[52] and, more specifically, to promote EU standards (whenever possible) within the EAEU.[53] This narrative suggests that the EU integration process has not been fully reversed in the country. Instead, it is now subsumed within a broader narrative emphasising the role of the EU as a model for Eurasian integration and calling for a bloc-to-bloc dialogue.

Legal aspects of Eurasian integration and the status of EAEU legislation in the Armenian legal order

Unlike the EU integration process, which was incremental and covered reforms stretched over a number of years, the Eurasian integration efforts were hasty and rushed. This section considers some constitutional and legal issues concerning Armenia's accession to the EAEU.

The legal process of accession and its constitutional implications

Until the September 2013 U-turn, no prospect of accession to the ECU and the Common Economic Space were on the agenda of the government. Instead, a memorandum on cooperation between the Armenian Government and the Eurasian Economic Commission was adopted in April 2013 to hold consultations, organise seminars and conferences, conduct research activities etc.[54] However, after the September announcement and the December 2013 Decision of the Supreme Eurasian Economic Council on a roadmap for Armenia's membership, the Armenian Government was required to adopt swiftly 126 measures before its accession to the ECU and the Common Economic Space.[55] On 23 January 2014, the Government adopted a list of actions to implement the said roadmap.[56] The Decision established a set of measures to be implemented pre- and post-accession. Those measures which had been set for implementation prior to the accession appeared to be rather hasty. Despite their volume and number, most pre-accession measures were to be taken in the course of the two months following the adoption of the decision. The national measures were assigned to various ministries, state agencies and the Central Bank of Armenia with the leading roles of the Ministry of Finance and Ministry of Economy. Other measures, including those to be taken upon accession, were to be implemented jointly with the other Member States or with the Eurasian Economic Commission. Thus, the integration process hinged upon swift executive performance involving the Government at the expense of the national Parliament. While the measures were being implemented, the accession treaty to the EAEU was adopted in May 2014 and signed in October 2014.

According to Article 6 of the Armenian Constitution, once ratified, an international agreement becomes part of national legal order and prevails over national legislation. It is the task of the National Parliament to ratify international agreements upon a recommendation by the President. The Parliament should ratify among others agreements 'the implementation of which envisages amendments to laws or adoption of a new law or defines norms contradicting the laws'. The accession Treaty to the EAEU most certainly was of such nature and required parliamentary ratification. International agreements cannot be ratified if they contradict the national constitution.

Thus, before the ratification of the EAEU accession agreement in the Parliament, the Armenian President submitted an application to the Constitutional Court on the conformity of the agreement with the constitution. According to Article 100(2) of the Constitution, the Constitutional Court shall rule on the conformity of the international agreements with the Constitution. The approval of the Constitutional Court would ensure that there are no internal obstacles to the country's membership to the EAEU as the Government most certainly could count on the Parliament's approval. In a rather prompt decision the Constitutional Court affirmed the compatibility of the agreement with the fundamental principles of the Constitution, including the principles of sovereignty, rule of law and adherence to norms and principles of international law, as well as Armenia's international obligations, including in the WTO.[57] However, it should be noted that the decision of the Court offers only superficial analysis and fails to engage sufficiently with the issues it raised, for instance on Armenia's legal obligations stemming from its WTO membership. The Court also decided the case on the basis of a so-called 'written procedure' avoiding presentations by the Government and its opponents thus limiting opportunities for debate.[58]

Following the approval by the Constitutional Court, the agreement was ratified in the National Assembly with only a handful of votes against it. The fact that all major parties in the Parliament voted predominantly in favour of the EAEU accession does not necessarily indicate an overwhelming public support for this course. Rather, it can be explained by lack of genuine opposition capable of challenging the official course of the government, and the rubber-stamp role of the national Parliament. Thus, the lack of a substantive debate, including in the Parliament, was a notable feature of the Eurasian integration process, one from which the general public, as well as the civil society was excluded. Likewise, negotiations for an Association Agreement and a DCFTA in 2010–2013 were limited to officials and expert circles; yet these agreements did not involve a transfer of sovereignty to the same extent as the EAEU. Although the critics of the impending membership were rather vocal in warning about the consequences of EAEU accession in terms of Armenia's independence, they failed to mobilise mass support similar to Maidan protests in Ukraine.[59]

Another important issue related to Armenia's internal political situation and the rationale behind its accession to the EAEU is that of the application of the new trade regime to the Nagorno-Karabakh Republic. Despite its proclaimed independence status (albeit not recognised by the international community), Nagorno-Karabakh has a close association with Armenia, and the Karabakhi Armenians are citizens of the Republic of Armenia. Despite this arrangement, the EAEU rules will be restricted to the territory of the Republic of Armenia, hence excluding Nagorno-Karabakh from the arrangement. Kazakhstan was particularly firm on this restriction[60] to avoid possible complications under international law and probably in order to avoid Azerbaijan's discontentment. It is also in the Russian interest to avoid any complications as far as at the conflict is concerned: the status quo accords Russia with a certain leverage over Azerbaijan, as discussed further below. The exclusion of Karabakh from the arrangement is particularly noteworthy in view of applying the EAEU rules to Crimea following its annexation by Russia.[61] At the same time, it might be difficult to patrol in practice that the potential benefits of the EAEU are restricted to the territory of Armenia: for instance, Armenians from Karabakh hold Armenian passports and should therefore benefit from the rules on the free movement of labour.

The status of the EAEU legislation in the Armenian legal order

As noted above, the Armenian constitution regulates the status of international agreements which become part of national legal order upon their ratification and prevail upon any contradicting national law. The Constitution, however, does not contain any provisions on the status of the legislative acts made by an international organisation to which the country accedes.

The Constitutional Court in its decision on the constitutionality of the Treaty on the Accession of Armenia to the Treaty on the EAEU also ruled on the legality of the 'procedure of adoption of decisions by the bodies of the Union and their mandatory nature'. The Court derives a number of 'precise constitutional requirements' from the axiology and some concrete provisions of the Constitution which would be applicable to the decisions of supranational organisations to which Armenia choses to participate.[62] These include 'guaranteeing state, national and domestic sovereignty', 'legal equality and mutual expediency of international relations', 'prescription of such possible restrictions of human rights which are relevant to the norms and principles of international law', 'possibility of operation of the decisions of supranational bodies for Armenia, only in the scopes of concordance to the Constitution of the Republic of Armenia'.[63] The Court goes on to note that any decisions adopted by a supranational organisation breaching either of these requirements would not be applicable in the Republic of Armenia. The Court comes to a conclusion, therefore, that cooperation with any regional or international organisation which respects these requirements cannot *per se* raise any issue of constitutionality. In a way the Constitutional Court sets certain minimum requirements for the decisions of the EAEU to ensure compliance with the Armenian Constitution. The Court comes to a conclusion that the EAEU legal framework is compliant with these requirements rendering it *constitutionally valid* in Armenia. The next matter analysed by the Court is the relationship of the EAEU decisions and the national law, other than the Constitution.

The Court's analysis is premised on the provisions of the national Law on International Treaties of the Republic of Armenia.[64] Under Article 55 of the law, decisions and other acts of the institutions of an international organisation established under an international treaty signed by Armenia, should be implemented in accordance with the founding documents of the organisation. The legal force of these decisions depends on whether they have been accorded such by the founding documents of the relevant organisation. According to Article 6 of the Treaty on the EAEU, 'decisions of the Supreme Eurasian Economic Council and Eurasian Intergovernmental Council shall be enforceable by the Member States in the procedure provided for by the national law'[65] (decisions are acts of regulatory nature adopted by the EAEU institutions).[66] Two implications can be derived from this article. Firstly, the decisions of the EAEU institutions are 'enforceable' in the EAEU Member States, which would mean 'binding' for the purposes of Article 55 of the Armenian Law on International Treaties. This is also supported by Article 2 of the Treaty on Accession of the Republic of Armenia to the Treaty on the EAEU. The latter states that the acts of the EAEU institutions, which are in force at the time of the entry into force of the mentioned Accession Treaty, are applicable on the territory of Armenia. Secondly, the actual application of the EAEU decisions would depend on the procedure prescribed in the national law.

In Armenia, this procedure is set in Article 55(3) of the Law on International Treaties. In case a decision of the institutions of an international organisation is binding on Armenia, the responsible Armenian authority ensures their implementation by adopting appropriate normative, regulatory or other acts, or drafting acts of executive institutions.[67] The relevant provision notes 'if necessary', suggesting that the adoption of a new act will not always be required. It goes on to provide for the scenario whereby the subject matter of the decision of the international organisation is already adequately regulated in Armenia: in those circumstances the responsible authority is required to submit an explanatory note to the national government on the lack of necessity for the adoption of a new legal act.

Article 55 of the Law on International Treaties also regulates the issue of potential conflicts between the decision adopted by the international organisations and any internal Armenian law. In such a scenario, the decisions of the international organisation cannot be implemented until relevant amendments are made to the national law. On the one hand, the presence of the national conflicting law bars the application of the decisions of the international organisation. On the other hand, the application of the national law would also be put on hold. In a way, this suggests an inherent supremacy of the decisions of international organisations binding on Armenia whereby the law imposes an obligation on domestic authorities to amend the national law to pave the way for the implementation of the decisions of the international organisations. At the time of the accession to the EAEU, the Ministry of Justice established a list of more than twenty legislative acts which required amendments by the national parliament.[68] Thus, the issue of the conflict between the regulatory acts of the EAEU and the national law appears to be resolved at a national level in favour of the supranational rules.

It should also be noted that the EAEU inherited numerous regulatory acts from the preceding ECU. The status of these acts in the legal order of Armenia is regulated by Article 2 of the Treaty on Armenia's Accession to the Treaty on the EAEU noted above. It sets the same general rule that these acts are applicable on the territory of Armenia from the moment of the entry into force of the Accession Treaty. However, their application is mitigated by the provisions of Annex 2 on Conditions and Transitional Provisions which sets specific transition provision for various sectors which were part of the legal framework of the ECU.

Thus, while embarking on a new legal process of membership in the EAEU, Armenia at the same time seeks a new form of cooperation with the EU, which is discussed next.

The future of cooperation with the EU: bilateral or multilateral way forward?

Even after its accession to the EAEU, Armenia still endeavours to retain some degree of complementarity in terms of both domestic reforms and foreign policy. However, its membership in the new organisation has restricted the possibilities of EU-Armenia cooperation, particularly in the area of traditional EU strength, that is trade policy. After Armenia's accession to the EAEU, any bilateral engagement must accommodate the EAEU membership, and therefore is restricted in terms of trade and focus on other areas of EU competence. As to the future of trade relations, it can take place possibly through bloc-to-bloc cooperation. Here, albeit cautiously, Armenia attempts to posit itself as a 'bridge-builder' in relations with the EU.[69] Even though some consider that the revised ENP might allow for the possibility of developing inter-bloc cooperation (particularly the reference to the cooperation with neighbours of the neighbours),[70] the prospect of bloc-to-bloc cooperation, although invited by Russia, would not as yet appear to be either realistic or desired by the EU. A number of reasons for this supposition are discussed below.

In response to President Sargsyan's decision to join the Eurasian integration process, the EU initially reacted cautiously. While 'respecting Armenia's decision', the EU made it clear that no Association Agreement could be signed given the incompatibility between membership in the EAEU and the DCFTA, an integral part of the former.[71] While it seemed that Armenia was willing to sign the political chapters of the agreement, the EU was unwilling to divide the agreement in that manner.[72] However, the door was left open for a new type of agreement that would take into account Armenia's emerging international commitments. Accordingly, possible areas of cooperation were identified during a scoping exercise in 2014–2015, upon completion of Armenia's EAEU accession negotiations. Yet the exercise proved more difficult than expected, given the uncertainty of developments within the EAEU and hence the lack of clarity of commitments taken by Armenia.[73]

According to Armenian officials,[74] the new agreement is expected to cover a wide spectrum of policy areas, ranging from political dialogue to freedom, security and justice as well as sectoral cooperation.[75] Only some trade-related issues seem to be excluded after Armenia's accession to the EAEU, among which customs and tariffs. The EU's High Representative for Foreign and Security Policy confirmed that both sides aimed 'for a comprehensive framework agreement covering political, economic and sectoral cooperation and taking into account Armenia's more recent commitments'.[76] Based upon the negotiating mandate adopted by the Council in October 2015, the European Commission and the High Representative launched negotiations for a new legally binding agreement with Armenia in December 2015. The declared ambition of the two sides to establish a wide-ranging deal was an important political signal. It highlighted Armenia's determination to retain (as much as possible) a balanced foreign policy and the EU's readiness to depart from the EaP's initial Association Agreement/DCFTA package with the view to adjusting to partners' needs and specific circumstances. While differentiation among the neighbouring countries was one of the principles incorporated in the ENP, and later adopted also by the EaP initiative,[77] the revision of the ENP in 2015 puts a more pronounced emphasis on this notion.[78] This means that, as far as the EU is concerned, offering Armenia a tailored approach is well within the Union's current strategy in the region. In addition to the external factor of diversifying its foreign policy, an internal factor also contributed to Armenia's intention to establish new links. In the period preceding the April 2017 parliamentary elections, the ability to establish closer links with the EU was used by the authorities as a factor in favour of retaining the power.[79]

The newly initialled agreement appears to be of a framework nature. As to its possible legal basis, a few observations can be made. Article 217 TFEU can most certainly be ruled out, as an 'association' in terms of 'privileged' links is not an option.[80] Instead, Article 216 TFEU might be preferred as it allows for the conclusion of international agreements with third countries to achieve Treaty objectives. As the agreement would be of mixed nature due to inevitable inclusion of political dialogue and other CFSP matters, CFSP legal basis will also feature. It can also be suggested that a new agreement falling short of 'association' status can provide the EU with an opportunity to instil a new meaning into Article 8 TEU providing for 'specific agreements' to be concluded with neighbouring countries, which 'may contain reciprocal rights and obligations as well as the possibility of undertaking activities jointly' in order to develop 'special relationship' with them. The question to ask here is whether 'special relationship' can be interpreted here to denote anything less than an 'association' with the neighbours. However, it appears the EU has chosen to follow an already existing blueprint of the Enhanced Partnership and Cooperation Agreement adopted with Kazakhstan, a member of the EAEU.[81] If we are to judge by this example, then the EU will most probably opt out for a similar combined legal basis consisting of CFSP legal basis (Article 31 and 37 TEU) and a joint TFEU legal basis encompassing competence in transport, common commercial policy and development cooperation areas (Article 91, 100(2), 207 and 209 TFEU). If this assumption is correct, it might be seen as an emerging pattern of the legal framework to be offered to the EAEU Member States.

Notwithstanding Armenia's ability to conclude a new agreement envisaging relatively close cooperation with the EU, the success of the latter hinges crucially on two sets of factors involving external actors. Some of these are not specific to Armenia and are of a more general character.

First of all, the forthcoming deal is a test for Russia's readiness to accept other EAEU members' foreign policy choices.[82] In the case of Armenia, Russia officially indicated that a new agreement between Armenia and the EU would not contradict cooperation with the EAEU and Russia, provided that it is compatible with the commitments taken by Armenia as part of the EAEU.[83] In fact, as underlined by the Russian Ministry of Foreign Affairs, all EAEU members have developed bilateral ties with the EU over the past two decades and negotiated agreements (for instance, the PCA with Kazakhstan initialled in January 2015). However, in the Russian narrative this cobweb of agreements should eventually turn into a bloc-to-bloc dialogue involving the EU and the EAEU on an equal footing.

A 'conversion' of the EU cooperation into a triangle involving Russia, the EU and the neighbours, was long seen by political scientists as necessary for establishing the Union's presence in the region.[84] While the EU hitherto preferred dealing with individual countries,[85] the current context might appear to necessitate a departure from that approach entailing relations with the EAEU as a trading block on its own right.[86] Any such prospect seems distant at present due to a number of serious obstacles. First, the relations with Russia need to be stabilised prior to contemplating any closer cooperation. The armed conflict in Ukraine appears currently to have acquired a 'frozen' status, a scenario favoured by Russia as it creates a new leverage over Ukraine's political choices. Currently, the EU's policy of sanctions has not achieved desired effects, and it remains to be seen how the conflict will be resolved. The EU thus far has been reluctant to envisage a dialogue with the EAEU as it may eventually confer legitimacy on both Russia's foreign policy and developments within the EAEU, including the Russian annexation of Crimea and the destabilisation of Eastern Ukraine. The EU is also concerned about a deal that would *de facto* reinforce bipolarisation in Europe,[87] and thereby endorse Russia's preference for distinct zones of influence.

Other obstacles are linked to the uncertain process of Eurasian integration itself as any direct talks with the EAEU would depend on its success and viability. The latter has been doubted due to the lack of reliable integration criteria, as well as insignificant benefits to the founding states.[88] Disagreements among the founding states as to the finality of the union, including Belarus's and Kazakhstan's preference for economic integration only render the future of this venture unclear.[89] Scepticism has been expressed also regarding Russia's dominant position within the integration, and therefore its credibility in terms of being an equal partner.[90] The Eurasian Economic Community and its Customs Union were perceived to be a regional integration project centred on Russia's dominant role.[91] Concerns have also been raised about the state of the rule of law essential for a viable economic integration process based on common rules.[92] The main supranational authority, the Eurasian Economic Commission follows a one country, one vote approach (in difference with the previous Customs Union Commission with weighted votes largely in favour of Russia),[93] suggesting a certain concession on behalf of Russia in terms of its dominance within the integration project. Nevertheless, taking into account the coercive nature of the Armenian accession and its dependence on Russia one cannot exclude the possibility of coerced voting in the future despite the one country, one vote approach on paper. Furthermore, Russia's behaviour in Ukraine made its partner countries, including Kazakhstan, 'deeply unsettled' in the words of Dreyer and Popescu.[94] Dragneva and Wolczuk also note in this context the top-down nature of the integration closely linked to the national leaders and the quality of the regulation undermined by hastened integration efforts.[95]

In addition, Russia's willingness to establish a bloc-to-bloc trading stems more from the desire to validate the project, rather than a genuine desire to enhance trade relations.[96] If the trade cooperation between the emerging EAEU and the EU was, indeed, a genuine objective, theoretically such scenario could be envisaged. In principle, the EAEU is premised upon the WTO regime, which should also prevail for non-WTO members.[97] Thus, Belarus, a non-WTO member, has agreed to follow the WTO normative framework in their future obligations, and accept Russia's WTO tariff obligations.[98] However, the recent developments in the Eurasian project have only reinforced the EU's concerns about the EAEU's actual compatibility with WTO rules. Russia's reintroduction of customs checks with Belarus (in the context of retaliation for the sanctions adopted by the EU), as well as other non-tariff mutual restrictive measures cast doubt on the rule-based nature of the Eurasian project, as it is in clear breach of the Customs Union's rules.[99] This move also suggests that Russia is unlikely to tolerate other EAEU members' independent foreign policy actions, should these collide with its own political or economic interests.

Second, the future EU-Armenia cooperation may be affected by the broader regional security context. Southern Caucasus countries perhaps offer the best illustration of the discrepancy between the EU's long-term transformative power and the Eastern partners' pressing security needs. While the new agreement between Armenia and the EU is likely to be premised upon traditional EU policy instruments, such as the promotion of democracy and human rights as well as regulatory convergence, the flare up of the Nagorno-Karabakh conflict in April 2016 forcefully reminded the EU of the inherently fragile security situation in the South Caucasus. In fact, recent hostilities only highlighted the lack of direct EU involvement in the conflict and Russia's dominant role therein.[100] The EU cannot offer an alternative to the Russian presence, not only due to the inherent weaknesses of its foreign policy given its intergovernmental nature, but also due to the lack of military capacity. Although the ENP Action Plans for Armenia and Azerbaijan included a priority area on the peaceful resolution of the conflict, it was merely restricted to offering 'contribution' to the already existing framework of the OSCE Minsk Group.[101] The latter is the main forum for the resolution of the conflict co-chaired by the US, Russia and France. However the status quo in the conflict suits Russia as part of its 'controlled instability'[102] or 'managed instability'[103] approach, where the unresolved conflicts create a leverage for Russia over the parties to the conflict. The only mechanism through which the Union has maintained a certain presence in the conflict resolution process is the Special Representative for the South Caucasus and the crisis in Georgia.[104] His mandate is primarily focused on maintaining communication with the parties concerned and supporting the OSCE Minsk Group 'to contribute to the peaceful settlement of conflicts in accordance with the principles of international law and to facilitate the implementation of such settlement'.[105] Thus, no prospects can be envisaged in the EU's role in terms of the conflict resolution efforts: the EU would prefer to play a more active role once the parties find a solution to the conflict themselves.[106] The most recent episode of escalation in the conflict demonstrated Russia's continuous leading role. Any further deterioration of Armenia's security environment will most probably result in its enhanced dependence on Russia and push the country further away from economic and political reforms, thereby impeding possible cooperation with the EU.

At the same time, it should be noted that the EU retains a certain leverage over Armenia. Beyond offering a template for modernisation, it can offer much needed financial assistance, as well as the incentive of visa-free travel, even though the abolition of Schengen visas is not an immediate perspective for Armenia. The visa-free travel was particularly noted as a significant incentive to induce Armenia to undertake much needed reforms related to justice sector.[107]

Conclusion

The precarious political and economic situation of Armenia led to its coerced accession to the EAEU. Armenia's multifaceted dependence on Russia, most importantly in terms of the Nagorno-Karabakh conflict, ultimately paralysed its leadership and rendered years of EU integration reforms fruitless, sending the country into an uncertain future in an uncertain union. With less than obvious benefits, Armenia swiftly arranged its accession to the EAEU without much deliberation or public discussion and with acquiescence from its Constitutional Court and Parliament. The accession to the EAEU was judged to comply with the Armenian Constitution by the Constitutional Court, while any possible conflicts between the decisions of the EAEU and the secondary national law were prevented by making amendments to national legislation.

However, even in such entrapment, Armenia views the EU as an important partner with which new forms of cooperation ought to be sought. The future application of the Comprehensive and Enhanced Partnership Agreement will be an exercise in testing the parameters of engagement permitted not only by the EAEU membership *per se*, but also by Russia's political agenda. As far as trade is concerned, any future cooperation with the EU should accommodate Armenia's EAEU membership. As to the possibility of inter-bloc cooperation, the latter will depend on a number of external factors, including genuine trade integration, rule of law and adherence to the WTO rules, and other concerns with the current state of affairs within and around the EAEU.

Notes

1 L. Delcour and H. Kostanyan, 'Towards a Fragmented Neighbourhood: Policies of the EU and Russia and Their Consequences for the Area That Lies in Between', *CEPS Essay*, No 17/17, October 2014.
2 S. Vasilyan, 'The External Legitimacy of the EU in the South Caucasus', *European Foreign Affairs Review*, 16, 2011, 341–346; A. Iskandaryan, 'Armenia-Russia Relations: Geography Matters', in: A Hug (ed.), *Spotlight on Armenia*, London: Foreign Policy Centre, 2011, p. 54.
3 'Armenia Chooses Russia over EU', *European Voice*, 3 September 2013.
4 Russia, Belarus, Kazakhstan and Kyrgyzstan signed an agreement on 26 February 1999 on the Customs Union and Common Economic Area. A year later an agreement was signed on 10 October 2000 by the same countries plus Tajikistan on the creation of Eurasian Economic Community. On 19 September 2003 Russia, Belarus, Kazakhstan and Ukraine signed an agreement on the formation of

the Common Economic Area. On 6 October 2007 Russia, Belarus and Kazakhstan signed an agreement creating the customs territory and the customs union. On 28 November 2009 an agreement on the Common Customs Area was signed. From January 2012 the Customs Union was replaced by the Common Economic Area. In May 2014 the same three counties signed an agreement on the establishment of the Eurasian Economic Union, which was to come into existence in January 2015.
For the chronology of the integration projects, see Y. Vymyatnina and D. Antonova, *Creating a Eurasian Union: Economic Integration of the Former Soviet Republics*, Basingstoke: Palgrave, 2014, pp. 2–5; R. Dragneva, 'The Legal and Institutional Dimensions of the Eurasian Customs Union', in: R. Dragneva and K. Wolczuk (eds.), *Eurasian Economic Integration: Law, Policy and Politics*, Cheltenham: Edward Elgar, 2013, pp. 34–60.

5 Available at: www.eurasiancommission.org/en/nae/news/Pages/02-01-2015-1.aspx
6 Treaty on the Accession of the Republic of Armenia to the Treaty on Eurasian Economic Union, 29 May 2014. Available at: https://docs.eaeunion.org/docs/ru-ru/0047297/itia_11102014 (accessed 22 June 2016).
7 'Armenia Still Hopes for Association Agreement with EU', *Armenia Now*, 5 September 2013.
8 'EU and Armenia Launch Negotiations for a New Agreement', *EEAS Press Release*, Brussels, 7 December 2015.
9 'Joint Press Release by the European Union and Republic of Armenia on the Initialling of the EU-Armenia Comprehensive and Enhanced Partnership Agreement', *Yerevan*, 21 March 2017.
10 European Commission, *Wider Europe-Neighbourhood: A New Framework for Relations with our Eastern and Southern Neighbours*, COM (2003) 104 final, 11 April 2003; Commission Communication, Eastern Partnership COM (2008) 823 final, 3 December 2008.
11 N. Ghazaryan and A. Hakobyan, 'Legislative Approximation and Application of EU Law in Armenia', in: R. Petrov and P. Van Elsuwege (eds.), *Legislative Approximation and Application of EU Law in the Eastern Neighbourhood of the European Union*, London: Routledge, 2014, pp. 191–213.
12 L. Delcour, H. Kostanyan, B. Vandecasteele and P. Van Elsuwege, 'The Implications of Eurasian Integration for the EU's Relations with the Countries in the Post-Soviet Space', *Studia Diplomatica*, 68(1), 2015, 5–33; P. de Micco, 'When Choosing Means Losing: The Eastern Partners, the EU, and the Eurasian Economic Union', *European Parliament, Study*, 7–8, available at: www.europarl.europa.eu/RegData/etudes/STUD/2015/549026/EXPO_STUD(2015)549026_EN.pdf (accessed 22 June 2016).
13 N. Tocci, 'Can the EU Promote Democracy and Human Rights Through the ENP? The Case for Refocusing on the Rule of Law', in: M Cremona and G Meloni (eds.), *The European Neighbourhood Policy: A New Framework for Modernisation? EUI Working Papers*, LAW 2007/21, Fiesole: European University Institute, 2007, p. 27.
14 N. Ghazaryan, *The European Neighbourhood Policy and the Democratic Values of the EU: A Legal Analysis*, Oxford and Portland: Hart Publishing, 2014, p. 143.
15 E. Ademmer and T. Börzel, 'Migration, Energy and Good Governance in the EU's Eastern Neighbourhood', *Europe-Asia Studies*, 65(4), 2013, 591–608.
16 L. Delcour and K. Wolczuk, 'The EU's Unexpected "Ideal Neighbour"? The Perplexing Case of Armenia's Europeanisation', *Journal of European Integration*, 37(4), 2015, 491–507.
17 Slovenian Presidency of the EU 'EU Presidency Statement on the Situation in Armenia', 12 March 2008, available at : http://www.eu2008.si/en/

News_and_Documents/CFSP_Statements/March/0312MZZarmenia.html (accessed 22 September 2017).

18 Delcour and Wolczuk, *op. cit.*

19 President Sargsyan, speech before the plenary meeting of the 20th Congress of the European People's Party (EPP), Marseille, 7 December 2011, available at: www.president.am/en/foreign-visits/item/2011/12/07/news-344/ (accessed 22 June 2016).

20 L. Delcour, 'Faithful but Constrained? Armenia's Half-Hearted Support of Russia's Regional Integration Policies in the Post-Soviet Space', in: D Cadier (ed.), *The Geopolitics of Eurasian Economic Integration*, LSE, IDEAS Reports, p. 42, available at: www.lse.ac.uk/IDEAS/publications/reports/SR019.aspx (accessed 22 July 2016).

21 E. Ademmer, 'Interdependence and EU-Demanded Policy Change in a Shared Neighbourhood', *Journal of European Public Policy*, 22(5), 2015, 678–679.

22 This option was ruled out in particular by the then Prime Minister Tigran Sargsyan. Cf. G Arevian, 'Armenia Again Rules out Entry into Russian Customs Union', available at: www.accc.org.uk/armenia-again-rules-out-entry-into-russian-customs-union/ (accessed 22 June 2016).

23 According to Article 2 of the agreement the parties commit to close cooperation to guarantee 'the sovereignty, territorial integrity and security' of both countries. Armenia is also one of the founding members of the Collective Security Treaty Organisation established in 1992 whereby Russia guarantees its security.

24 'Russia, Armenia Sign Extended Defence Pact, *Radio Free Europe*, 20 August 2010.

25 The economic cooperation between Turkey, Armenia and Azerbaijan inter alia includes the transportation of oil via the Baku-Tbilisi-Ceyhan pipeline launched in May 2005 from the Caspian Sea to the Mediterranean port of Ceyhan, and of natural gas via the Baku-Tbilisi-Erzurum from Azeri Shah-Deniz gas field since 2006.

26 The opening of a gas pipeline from Iran on 19 March 2007 was expected to lessen the country's dependence on Russia. However, a large share in the project was sold to the Russian Gazprom; 'Shadow Dancing: Armenia's Courtship with Independence', *Armenian Diaspora*, 15 December 2006.

27 C. Nitoiu, 'Reconceptualizing "Cooperation" in EU-Russia Relations', *Perspectives on European Politics and Society*, 12, 2011, 462–466.

28 J. Tolstrup, 'Studying a Negative External Actor: Russia's Management of Stability and Instability in the "Near Abroad"', *Democratisation*, 16(5), 2009, 922–935.

29 'Armenia Selling More Infrastructure, Industry to Russia', *Eurasia Daily Monitor*, 7 November 2006; 'Russia Steps up Economic Presence in Armenia', *Armenian Diaspora*, 17 November 2006.

30 'Russia Starts Delivering $1 Billion Arms Package to Azerbaijan', *Reuters*, 18 June 2013; 'Gas Price Reduced as Armenia Joins Customs Union', *Asbarez*, 8 October 2013.

31 N. Popescu, 'Eurasian Union: The Real, the Imaginary and the Likely', *Chaillot Paper No 132*, September 2014, 22.

32 President of the Republic of Armenia, 'Joint Statement on the Results of the Visit of the President of the Republic of Armenia to the Russian Federation', 3 September 2013, available at: www.president.am/en/press-release/item/2013/09/03/President-Serzh-Sargsyan-and-President-Vladimir-Putin-joint-statement/ (accessed 22 June 2016).

33 A. Grigoryan, 'Armenia: Joining Under the Gun', in: S.F. Starr and S. Cornell (eds.), *Putin's Grand Strategy: The Eurasian Union and Its Discontents*, Washington: Central Asia-Caucasus Institute & Silk Road Studies Program, 2014, pp. 98–108.

34 R. Giragosyan, 'Armenia and the Eurasian Economic Union: A View from Yerevan', *ECFR Commentary*, 8 January 2015, available at: www.ecfr.eu/article/commentary_armenia_and_the_eurasian_economic_union_the_view_from_yerevan387 (accessed 22 June 2016).
35 ECORYS/CASE, *Trade Sustainability Impact Assessment in support of negotiations of a DCFTA between the EU and the Republic of Armenia*, ECORYS/CASE: Rotterdam, 2013, p. 13. However, it should be noted that the predicted benefits of the DCFTA did not take into account the possibility of Russian retaliation as seen in Ukraine and Moldova.
36 Delcour, *op. cit.*, p. 42.
37 De Micco, *op. cit.*, p. 54.
38 Giragosyan, *op. cit.*
39 De Micco, *op. cit.*, p. 54.
40 Authors' interview, Armenian Minister, Eurasian Economic Commission, Moscow, May 2015.
41 D. Tarr, 'The Eurasian Economic Union Among Russia, Belarus, Kazakhstan, Armenia and the Kyrgyz Republic: Can It Succeed Where Its Predecessor Failed?' *Eastern European Economics*, 54(1), 2016, 8.
42 'Armenia Warns Nagorno-Karabakh Clashes Could Turn into All-out War', *Reuters*, 4 April 2016.
43 Delcour, *op. cit.*, p. 42.
44 'More Russian Arms Deals with Azerbaijan Add Insult to Armenia's Injury', *EurasiaNet*, 27 May 2014.
45 'Armenia Economic Report 2014: Eurasian Integration and Trade', *Economic Development and Research Centre*, November 2014, 73–74, available at: www.edrc.am/images/Useful_Publications/aer_2014_eng.pdf (accessed 22 June 2016).
46 'Membership Benefits? Armenia's Exports to EEU Countries Plummet', *Hetq*, 7 August 2015.
47 De Micco, *op. cit.*, p. 55.
48 Statement by Serzh Sargsyan, President of the Republic of Armenia at the Third Eastern Partnership Summit, Vilnius, 29 November 2013, available at: www.president.am/en/statements-and-messages/item/2013/11/29/President-Serzh-Sargsyan-at-the-third-Eastern-Partnership-summit-speech/ (accessed 22 June 2016).
49 Authors' interviews, Ministry of Economy; Food Safety Service, Yerevan, March 2014.
50 This is particularly due to Armenia's accession to the WTO in early 2003, i.e. much earlier than the founding members of the Eurasian Customs Union. While Belarus is not a WTO member, Russia joined in 2012 and Kazakhstan in 2015. Among current EAEU members, only Kyrgyzstan acceded earlier than Armenia.
51 Authors' interview, Department of Integration, Eurasian Economic Commission, Moscow, May 2015.
52 Authors' interview, Ministry of Foreign Affairs, Yerevan, March 2015.
53 Authors' interview, Ministry of Economy, Yerevan, March 2015.
54 Available at: www.eurasiancommission.org/en/nae/news/Pages/02-01-2015-1.aspx (accessed 21 June 2017).
55 *Ibid.*
56 Decision No 61-N, 23 January 2014.
57 The Case on Conformity of the Obligations Stipulated in the Treaty on 'The Accession to the Treaty of May 20, 2014 on "The Eurasian Economic Union" signed by the Republic of Armenia' Signed on October 10, 2014 in Minsk with the Constitution of the Republic of Armenia, November 14, 2014 DCC – 1175, para 4.

58 'Constitutional Court OKs Armenian Entry to Eurasian Union', *Azatutyun*, 14 November 2014.
59 *Ibid.*
60 Popescu, *op. cit.*, p. 23.
61 *Ibid.*, p. 24.
62 Decision No 61-N, *op. cit.*, para. 7.
63 Official translation of the Constitutional Court Decision. Available at: http://concourt.am/english/decisions/common/pdf/1175.pdf (accessed 22 July 2016).
64 Decision No 61-N, *op. cit.*, para. 10; Law on International Treaties of the Republic of Armenia HO-123-N, 22 February 2007.
65 Courtesy translation of the Treaty on the EAEU, available at the website of the UN: Available at: www.un.org/en/ga/sixth/70/docs/treaty_on_eeu.pdf (accessed 21 July 2017).
66 See Art. 2 on definitions, Treaty on the EAEU.
67 These would include those of the President, Government or the Prime Minister.
68 Decision No 61-N, *op. cit.*, para 10.6.
69 Giragosyan, *op. cit.*
70 De Micco, *op. cit.*, pp. 73–74.
71 'Gunnar Wiegand: EU Respects Armenia's Decision to Join Eurasian Economic Union', *News.Am*, 4 November 2015.
72 H. Kostanyan, 'The Rocky Road to an EU-Armenia Agreement: From U-turn to Detour', *CEPS Commentary*, 3 February 2015.
73 *Ibid.*
74 Authors' interview, Ministry of Foreign Affairs, Yerevan, March 2015.
75 It should be noted that the text of the agreement is not publicly available at the time of writing. Therefore, we rely on interviews when it comes to the substance of this agreement.
76 European Union External Action Service, 'EU and Armenia Launch Negotiations for a New Agreement', Press Release 151207_04_en, 7/12/2015, available at: http://eeas.europa.eu/statements-eeas/2015/151207_04_en.htm (accessed 10 April 2016).
77 See P. Van Elsuwege, 'Variable Geometry in the European Neighbourhood Policy: The Principle of Differentiation and Its Consequences', in: E. Lannon (ed.), *The European Neighbourhood Policy's Challenges*, Brussels: Peter Lang, 2012, pp. 59–84; N. Ghazaryan, 'The Evolution of the European Neighbourhood Policy and the Consistent Evolvement of Its Inconsistencies', *Russian and European Affairs Review*, 7(1), 2013, 1–13.
78 European Commission/High Representative of the European Union for Foreign Affairs and Security Policy, Joint Communication, The Review of the European Neighbourhood Policy JOIN(2015) 50 final, Brussels, 18 November 2015.
79 H. Kostanyan and R. Giragosyan, 'EU-Armenia Relations: Seizing the Second Chance', *CEPS Commentary*, 31 October 2016. To avoid a constitutional restriction on a maximum of two terms in office, the Constitution was amended after a referendum in December 2015 to transform Armenia into a parliamentary republic to guarantee that President Sargsyan remained in power.
80 Case 12/86 *Demirel v City of Schwabisch Gmund*, EU:C:1987:400, para 9.
81 *EEAS* Press Release, 'EU and Kazakhstan Sign Enhanced Partnership and Cooperation Agreement', Brussels, 21 December 2015.
82 L. Delcour and K. Wolczuk, 'Armenia Is Becoming an Important Test-Case for Relations Between the EU and the Eurasian Economic Union', *London School of Economics EUROPP Blog*, 13 May 2015.
83 'MID: dogovor Armenii i ES ne protivorechit vzaimodejstviju s Rossiej' [MID: Armenia's agreement with the EU does not contradict cooperation with Russia],

RIA Novosti, 23 October 2015. Available at: http://ria.ru/world/20151023/1306967152.html (accessed 23 June 2016).

84 H. Haukkala and A. Moshes, 'Beyond "Bing Bang": The Challenges of the EU's Neighbourhood Policy in the East', *The Finnish Institute of International Affairs*, Report 9/2004, p. 50; J. Kulhanek, 'The Fundamentals of Russia's EU Policy', *Problems of Post-Communism*, 57, 2010, 56.

85 P. Kalinichenko, *The Clash and Cooperation of Integrative Trade Spaces: Anti-dumping Law and the Practice of the EU in Relations with Russia and Other Countries of EURASEC*, New Russian University, 2011, p. 35.

86 This intention was declared in the 'Concept on International Activities of the EURASEC', 344, 5 July 2007, available at: http://evrazes.com/docs/view/176 (accessed 23 June 2016).

87 Delcour, Kostanyan, Vandecasteele and Van Elsuwege, *op. cit.*, p. 14.

88 Vymyatnina and Antonova, *op. cit.*, p. 6, pp. 57, 59–61; N. Kassenova, 'Kazakhstan and Eurasian Economic Integration: Quick Start, Mixed Results and Uncertain Future', in: Dragneva and Wolczuk, *op. cit.*, p. 159.

89 Delcour, Kostanyan, Vandecasteele and Van Elsuwege, *op. cit.*, p. 12; J. Cooper, 'The Development of Eurasian Economic Integration', in Dragneva and Wolczuk, note 4 above pp. 15–33, 28–30.

90 J. Cooper, 'Russia and the Eurasian Customs Union', in Dragneva and Wolczuk, *op. cit.*, p. 97; H. Haukkala, 'The Impact of the Eurasian Customs Union on EU-Russia Relations', in Dragneva and Wolczuk, *op. cit.*, p. 177.

91 E. Vinokurov and A. Libman, *Eurasian Integration: Challenges of Transcontinental Regionalism*, Basingstoke: Palgrave, 2012, p. 54.

92 R. Dragneva and K. Wolczuk, 'The Eurasian Customs Union: Framing the Analysis', in Dragneva and Wolczuk, *op. cit.*, pp. 1–12.

93 Popescu, *op. cit.*, p. 11.

94 I. Dreyer and N. Popescu, 'The Eurasian Customs Union: The Economics and the Politics', *EU Institute for Security Studies, Brief Issue*, 11/2014, 2014, 4.

95 R. Dragneva and K. Wolczuk, 'Eurasian Economic Integration: Institutions, Promises and Faultlines', in D. Cadier (ed.), *op. cit.*, p. 13.

96 Popescu, *op. cit.*, p. 42.

97 Dragneva, *op. cit.*, p. 47.

98 The Treaty on the Functioning of the Customs Union in the Multilateral System which entered into force in November 2011.
Cooper, *op. cit.*, p. 23; R. Connolly, 'Russia, the Eurasian Customs Union and the WTO', in Dragneva and Wolczuk, *op. cit.*, pp. 61–77.

99 See Tarr, *op. cit.*

100 The EU is not involved in the OSCE Minsk Group which includes three co-chairs: France, Russia and the United States. When warfare erupted in early April 2016, the EU High Representative only reiterated her support for the efforts of the Minsk Group and called on both sides to stop the fighting, without mentioning any additional EU involvement in the conflict settlement. EEAS, 'Statement by High Representative/Vice-President Federica Mogherini on the escalation in the Nagorno-Karabakh conflict, 2 April 2016, http://eeas.europa.eu/statements-eeas/2016/160402_03_en.htm (accessed 23 June 2016).

101 See priority area 1 in EU-Azerbaijan ENP Action Plan; priority area 7 in EU-Armenia ENP Action Plan.

102 K. Barysch, 'The EU and Russia Strategic Partners or Squabbling Neighbours?' *Centre for European Reform*, 3 May 2004, pp. 41–42.

103 Tolstrup, *op. cit.*, pp. 929–932.

104 Herbert Salber is currently the Special Representative for the South Caucasus; Council Decision 2014/438/CFSP of 8 July 2014 amending and extending the

mandate of the European Union Special Representative for the South Caucasus and the crisis in Georgia, 2014, L 200.

105 Art. 3, Council Decision 2013/353/CFSP of 2 July 2013 amending and extending the mandate of the European Union Special Representative for the South Caucasus and the crisis in Georgia, *OJ*, 2013, L 185.

106 See further N. Ghazaryan, '"Good Neighbourliness" and Conflict Resolution in Nagorno-Karabakh: A Rhetoric or Part of the Legal Method of the European Neighbourhood Policy?' in: D. Kochenov and E. Basheska (eds.), *The Principle of Good Neighbourly Relations in the European Legal Context*, Leiden: Martinus Nijhoff, 2015, pp. 306–333.

107 Kostanyan and Giragosian, *op. cit.*

9 The constitutional order of Belarus and its adaptability to the Eurasian Economic Union

A 'living constitution' workaround

Maksim Karliuk

. . . we must never forget that it is a constitution we are expounding.
—Chief Justice John Marshall[1]

Introduction

Belarus is a founding member of the Eurasian Economic Union (EAEU) and is deeply entrenched into Eurasian integration. The legal framework of Eurasian integration by which Belarus is bound is enormous.[2] In comparison, EU-Belarus relations are governed by such a scarce legal framework that the central international agreement within it is still the one concluded by the Soviet Union.[3] Even though there are plans to change the situation and to conclude a new international framework agreement with the EU,[4] it does not come close to what has been achieved within Eurasian integration.

As a founding member of the EAEU, Belarus took an active part in drafting the EAEU Treaty. The drafting in general was supposed to take place, among others, in line with the generally recognised principles of international law and the national legislation of Member States, taking into account international experience, but *first and foremost in line with the national constitutions.*[5] As will be shown below, this concern for national constitutions was not fully reflected in the final version of the EAEU, as there are a number of issues with regard to the effect of EAEU law in the national legal order of Belarus as a result of national constitutional restrictions.

Belarusian constitutionalism, international law and the EAEU Treaty

The Constitution of the Republic of Belarus[6] possesses the highest legal force on the territory of Belarus. It is believed that, according to Napoleon, constitutions should be *court et obscure* and, similarly, according to some of the American founding fathers, 'short and dark'.[7] The Belarusian Constitution, as well as the constitutions of the other EAEU Member States, is almost twice as long as the American one.[8] It is, arguably, not as 'dark' either.[9] However, there is an exception. A 'dark' spot of the Belarusian Constitution, which interests us the most in this contribution, concerns the relation of international law and national law, in general, and the acts of international institutions, specifically.

The Belarusian Constitution is strikingly different from those of all other EAEU Member States as far as relations with the international legal order are concerned. It does not have provisions on the priority of international agreements and only stipulates that the state shall recognise the supremacy of the universally acknowledged principles of international law and ensure that its laws comply with such principles.[10] Some of these principles are listed in Article 18 of the Constitution:

> In its foreign policy the Republic of Belarus shall proceed from the principles of equality of states, non-use of force or threat of force, inviolability of frontiers, peaceful settlement of disputes, non-interference in internal affairs and other generally recognised principles and norms of international law.

The former head of the Constitutional Court believes that the universally acknowledged principles of international law are, in fact, higher than the national Constitution, and the latter must be interpreted in light of the former.[11]

At least as compared to the previous 1978 Constitution of the Byelorussian Soviet Socialist Republic, which referred to international treaties only with regard to their conclusion and ratification, the current Constitution recognises them as a source of law and refers to them six times in the text.[12] One of the provisions precludes conclusion of international agreements that contradict the Constitution.[13]

Another notion used alongside 'international treaties' is 'international legal acts'. The latter are used in the Constitution in the context of ratification,[14] but can be understood as including such acts as international agreements and acts of international organisations, as well as international individual legal acts.[15]

The status of international agreements (and here we have in mind the EAEU Treaty) is not clearly defined in other national legislative acts either. In principle, it depends on the status of national legal acts, by which such agreements are adopted as binding. According to the Law on International Treaties, legal norms of international agreements concluded by Belarus form part of national legislation and are subject to direct applicability, apart from situations where it follows from the agreement itself that a national legal act should be adopted. In this case, international agreements essentially have the force of the ratifying act.[16] A similar provision is part of the Law on Normative Legal Acts.[17] This means that the legal force of Belarusian international agreements is equated to that of national legal acts, by which such agreements are adopted as binding. As a general rule, in case of a collision between legal acts, the act with higher legal force is applicable. However, in case such acts are of equal legal force, the act adopted later takes precedence. Following this rule, as noted by L. Pavlova[18] and A. Zybailo,[19] the force of norms of an international agreement on the territory of Belarus can be annulled through adoption of a new law, decree or edict. Similar provisions are part of the civil code, bank code and a number of other legal acts.[20] Only the civil procedure code, criminal code and labour code as well as a number of other laws give prevalence to international agreements in case of conflict with national legislation.[21]

Therefore, according to these rules, the EAEU Treaty, which was ratified by a national law, could in principle become lower in status than a future new act of national legislation. Hence, there is nothing to prevent the rule *lex posterior derogat legi priori*. However, Vasilevich believes that this principle does not apply, but the principle *lex specialis derogat legi generali* applies instead.[22] In this case, international agreements enjoy priority over any kind of laws, while still remaining lower than the Constitution, essentially claiming that the legislative provisions mentioned above are unconstitutional.[23] At any rate, it is plausible that an international law–friendly interpretation would give prevalence to the EAEU Treaty over national legislation.

In terms of direct applicability of international agreements, the Constitution does not provide any relevant formulation. However, article 116 can be interpreted in such a manner, since the Constitutional Court can recognise laws, decrees and edicts of the President unconstitutional, if they do not conform to ratified international legal acts.[24]

In any event, the overview above shows regulatory deficiencies regarding the status of international agreements in the national law of Belarus. The situation is even more complicated in the case of acts of international institutions. This is especially relevant in case of the EAEU, where the EAEU Treaty provides that Commission decisions are directly applicable on the territory of Member States.[25] It does not help that the Treaty does not specify the relation of legal force between such Commission acts and national legislation of the Member States.

Belarusian constitutionalism and EAEU legal acts

There are very few provisions available in national law of the Member States regarding the effect of legal acts of international organisations and their bodies. Back in 2006, the CIS Economic Court, performing the duties of the Court of the Eurasian Economic Community (EurAsEC),[26] the predecessor of the EAEU Court, analysed the legislation of EurAsEC Member States and came to the conclusion that there was no national constitutional basis for direct applicability of EurAsEC acts.[27] Not much has changed in this respect since then.

The Constitutional Court has pronounced itself on the priority of EAEU acts. When reviewing the constitutionality of the new technical standards legislation, which was adopted to align national law with EAEU law, it recognised the priority of EAEU law in the respective field.[28] However, it stated that such priority cannot result in violation of rights and freedoms guaranteed by the Constitution. Essentially, the Constitutional Court claimed the right to review EAEU acts and EAEU law in general on human rights grounds. The court based this conclusion on the supremacy of the Constitution and the provision of the EAEU Treaty preamble, stipulating the necessity for unconditional respect for the supremacy of constitutional human rights and freedoms.

The discussion of the place of acts of international organisations in the Belarusian legal system starts with a provision on the Constitutional Court. While the President is the guarantor of the Constitution,[29] the Constitutional Court has been set up to review the constitutionality of legal acts.[30] The legal force of acts of international organisations can be deduced from the competence of the Constitutional Court. The Constitutional Court has powers to deliver opinions on the conformity of acts adopted by international institutions to the Constitution, international agreements ratified by Belarus, and to laws and decrees of the President.[31] The Constitutional Court cannot do this on its own, but only on the proposal of the president, the parliament chambers, the supreme courts, and the government.[32] In any event, acts of international institutions are therefore hierarchically lower than national legal acts. Until recently, it even followed from Article 9 of the Law on the Constitutional Court[33] that acts of international institutions (as well as international agreements of Belarus) could be unilaterally found inapplicable by the Constitutional Court:

> laws, decrees and edicts of the President of the Republic of Belarus, international treaty and other obligations of the Republic of Belarus, acts of intergovernmental entities, in which Republic of Belarus participates, . . ., acts of other state bodies, which are found by the Constitutional Court inconsistent with the Constitution or acts, which have higher legal force, are considered void . . . as of the moment determined by the Constitutional Court.

However, the new Law on Constitutional Legal Procedure[34] no longer has this provision and foresees that when an international obligation or an act of an international entity contradicts certain legal acts, the relevant state authorities take measures to terminate the participation of Belarus in such an international agreement, terminate the obligatory nature of such an act, or introduce changes therein.[35] In our view, one of the reasons to introduce such a change is to avoid the international legal responsibility of Belarus, which could have followed if the original provision was applied in practice. The new law has found a compromise between national constitutional rules and rules of international law with a view to ensure that the Constitution is respected while avoiding international legal responsibility. Arguably, these new provisions are also aimed at ameliorating the constitutional rules with a view to taking a more favourable stance towards Belarus's participation in the EAEU. However, these changes fall short of changing the dependency direction – according to domestic law, the decisions of EAEU institutions remain dependent on national legislation.

Belarusian legal scholars are of the opinion that acts of international institutions are of lower force than national legislation. For instance, A. Zybailo states that acts of international institutions rank below the Constitution, ratified international agreements, laws and decrees of the president.[36] G. Vasilevich agrees: the wording of Article 116(4) of the Constitution, discussed above, gives him reason to believe that acts of international institutions are of sublegislative character.[37] However, he has also proposed a solution to the issue of supremacy of acts of international institutions in Belarus.[38]

It has been mentioned before that Belarus acknowledges the generally recognised principles of international law. Among such principles is *pacta sunt servanda*. Vasilevich claims that without fulfilment of decisions of an interstate entity and its bodies it is not possible to talk about fulfilment of this principle.[39] He further claims that this conclusion does not contradict Article 116 of the constitution as "a constitutional norm lives in time and its perception can change (if its formulation allows it)."[40] This resonates with the epigraph to this chapter and the statement by the Chief Justice of the U.S. Supreme Court made in the case *McCulloch v. Maryland*.[41] This statement showed the understanding of a constitution as a 'living document', which should be distinguished from a legislative act and should be interpreted in a different way, changing over time.

Based on the provision of the Law on Normative Legal Acts[42] that a new law enjoys priority over an older law (*lex posterior derogat legi priori*) and based on the principle *lex specialis derogat legi generali*, Vasilevich proposes to specify the status of acts of interstate entities in a special law (and even better in a programme law). The same should be done with regard to decrees. This will comply with the requirement of Article 116 of the Constitution regarding the compliance of acts of interstate entities with laws and decrees, and other constitutional provisions, and will comply with international agreements.

This proposal is, of course, an important contribution to the issue of collision of international legal obligations and national legal rules and could be valid for other EAEU Member States as well. At the same time, some remarks should be made. It is evident from the article that Vasilevich does not make a clear distinction between direct applicability and supremacy. Even though these two notions are intrinsically linked, they are separate notions of a different nature. They are linked in terms of effectiveness – both acquire higher effectiveness when applied together in order for a directly applicable provision not to be overruled by national law in accordance with the rule *lex posterior derogat legi priori*. However, they can also exist separately, albeit with ensuing limitations. Moreover, even though there is no single view on the issue,[43] a distinction is sometimes also made between *direct effect* and *direct applicability*. Direct effect, in this case, is understood as an ability of an individual to acquire rights and obligations from corresponding legal rules, while direct applicability is operation of an act on the territory on its own, without the need for national legislative intervention (effectively self-executing norms as they are known in international law[44]). In fact, the EAEU Treaty uses the term *direct applicability*.[45] Therefore, there is quite some terminological confusion. The author uses the term *direct effect*, while it should be *direct applicability*, but in any event he means *supremacy*.

Further, the Regulation on the Eurasian Economic Commission provides that decisions of the Commission are *binding* on the Member States.[46] However, supremacy and binding nature of legal norms are not identical notions. There is nothing on supremacy of Commission decisions over national law in the Treaty.[47] To compare, one of the drafts of the EAEU Treaty had the following provision:

> Legal acts of the Union shall be *binding*, shall have *direct applicability* on the territories of Member States, and shall have *priority* over the legislation of Member States.[48]

Therefore, the drafters of the final version of the EAEU Treaty did not only decide to limit themselves to the binding nature of the Commission decisions instead of all EAEU legal acts, but also have decided to exclude the notion of *priority* over national law. This means that the final EAEU provisions are limited to the binding character and direct applicability of certain acts, but their legal consequences are not described. This means that priority (which, in our view, equals supremacy) is not regulated by the Treaty. Therefore, formally, there are no contradictions with the provisions of Article 116 of the Constitution, as the Commission decisions can be binding and directly applicable, while they also can be checked for consistency with the Constitution, laws and decrees. There would be a contradiction in case supremacy is introduced into the Treaty or identified by the EAEU Court or by a joint interpretation of the Member States.[49] Here it is important to look at EU law, where supremacy, as well as direct effect and direct applicability (in the latter case excluding regulations), were not defined by the founding treaties but identified by the CJEU teleologically.[50] However, the ability of the EAEU Court to do a similar job has been diminished as compared to its predecessor: it has lost a number of powers, the biggest being the preliminary ruling procedure.[51] The main difficulty that arises is that of effectiveness of the binding nature of Commission decisions without supremacy and viability of the EAEU legal order as such.

The way to resolve the collision, proposed by Vasilevich, can help in avoiding international responsibility while respecting the Constitution. However, a special act determining the force of acts of international entities can be overruled by a new special law. This will mean that the functioning of the EAEU legal order will still be dependent on national legislation. This will not favour the effective functioning of the former and a collision can still take place.

Interpreting the Constitution

In our view, the best way, even though not the easiest one, to deal with the issue is to amend Article 116 of the Constitution by removing the ability of the Constitutional Court to rule on conformity of acts of international institutions with laws and decrees. This practice is common, e.g. many countries amended their constitution in this or that manner when joining the EU.[52] The window of opportunity to amend this provision might indeed exist, since the President of Belarus has mentioned a possibility of amending the Constitution:

> New problems and challenges have emerged. And time may require something new. It is necessary to start with important things if we dare to do it. We should create a group of wise people, lawyers to analyze the Constitution. If necessary, we will [amend the Constitution].[53]

Amendment of the Constitution is indeed the best option. However, it is not clear how soon this will happen, whether the relevant provision will be amended, and whether the Constitution will be amended at all at the end of the day. Moreover, this part of the Constitution can be amended only by a referendum.[54]

In these circumstances, there is another way to deal with the issue: by reading the Constitution further as a 'living document'. To do so, at the very start we must clarify what an 'interstate formation' is. When analysing the notion of an 'interstate formation', the constitutional commentator Pliakhimovich refers to Article 8(2), which goes as follows:

> The Republic of Belarus in conformity with the rules of international law may on a voluntary basis enter interstate formations and withdraw from them.

This provision was added to the Constitution following the 1996 referendum. Pliakhimovich attributes it to the integration processes that were taking place in the post-Soviet space, in particular the rapprochement of Belarus and Russia.[55] Given that, and since the Constitution uses the standard notion of 'international organisations' as well,[56] Pliakhimovich understands 'interstate formations' as a special type of 'international organisations', which, among others, possess features of supranationality and closer cooperation of Member States.[57] This is, however, hard to sustain. There are a number of reasons for that. First, making this differentiation will mean that Article 116 does not empower the Constitutional Court to check the compatibility of acts of other international organisations. There are, however, no compelling reasons why acts of international organisations, which do not possess supranationality, would be excluded from constitutional control. The argument could be that acts of such other international organisations are not directly applicable on the territory of Belarus. However, this does not deny the possibility of implementing such acts on the territory of Belarus, which would mean that it could give rise to implementation of an unconstitutional act. Second, the notion of an 'interstate formation' was not introduced with the amendment of the Constitution in 1996, but existed in the original Constitution of 1994 with regard to the powers of the Constitutional Court on checking constitutionality of acts adopted by interstate formations.[58] Moreover, when interpreting Article 116, Pliakhimovich himself abandons his own theory by proposing to interpret 'interstate formations' as encompassing international organisations.[59]

Vasilevich suggests that the provision of Article 116 was formulated in that manner due to the discourse in which the drafting took place: the fall of the Soviet Union and belief that Belarus and other post-Soviet states would not join interstate entities, and, in case they do, national legislation would always prevail.[60] Either way, for a 'living constitution', interpreting the original meaning is not paramount.

This leads to either understanding the notions of 'interstate formations' and 'international organisations' as interchangeable, or to making 'interstate formations' a broader term encompassing all kinds of international organisations and institutions, e.g. those which are not considered international organisations. The latter interpretation is less plausible, since it would deny individuals the ability to defend their rights and freedoms in such other international organisations and institutions (such a right is provided by Article 61, which refers to 'international organisations'), deny the President the right to represent Belarus in relations with such other international organisations and institutions (Article 79 provides for representation in relations with 'international organisations'), including conducting negotiations and signing treaties, appointing and recalling diplomatic representatives to/from them (Article 84 (20) provides for that vis-à-vis 'international organisations'). Therefore, it seems to be more plausible to use the notions of 'international organisations' and 'interstate formations' interchangeably.

Having established that, we turn to the interpretation of Article 116, which empowers the Constitutional Court to check the compatibility of *acts of interstate formations*. The 'living constitution' reading of this provision we propose would suggest that the provision is devoted to intergovernmental entities and institutions, while leaving *supranational* ones outside of its scope. Effectively, this provision would not be applicable to supranational institutions and organisations. Taking into account certain supranational features of the Eurasian Economic Commission (or at least the Commission Board[61]), with powers conferred from the intergovernmental to supranational level, it is conceivable to recognise it as a supranational body of the EAEU. In this case, the aforementioned constitutional provision can be interpreted as not applicable to the Commission because of its supranational, rather than interstate character.

This proposal is unorthodox for the interpretation practices in the country; therefore, several objections could be raised. First, the 'living document' interpretation should not limit interstate formations to intergovernmental institutions only, but should be expanded to include supranational institutions in its scope. Therefore, following this counterargument, there is a deadlock, which seemingly can be overcome only by a constitutional amendment. However, this is precisely the point of this 'living constitution' interpretation: the discourse has changed dramatically since the days of drafting the Constitution. And although either interpretation is plausible, the one removing supranational institutions from the scope of interstate formation is more consistent with the current discourse and practice.

Second, the logic of the interpretative proposal seemingly contradicts Article 8(2) discussed above: that Belarus can join and withdraw from interstate formations. If the distinction between intergovernmental and supranational institutions is made, the notion that Belarus can join interstate formations can be interpreted by some as only allowing Belarus to be part of intergovernmental institutions, barring it from (or not explicitly allowing) joining supranational ones. Therefore, according to this counterargument, Belarus might well not be able to become part of such an institution or organisation in the first place. A reply to this lies mainly in the fact that there is no express prohibition against participation in such entities. In fact, Article 8 is not a permission to join or withdraw from interstate formations. Indeed, this provision is fundamentally different in comparison to clauses regarding the transfer of powers which were used by some countries that joined the EU. For instance, the Danish constitution specifically required that the powers vested in the constitution might be transferred only to a specific extent.[62] In fact, the limited character of this transfer was a pre-requisite in the majority of the European countries.[63] In comparison, Belarus does not have a constitutional clause for the transfer of sovereign powers. Article 8 is not about that. This article starts with the observation that Belarus respects the priority of generally recognised principles of international law, and then continues that 'in accordance to the norms of international law [Belarus] may on a voluntary basis enter interstate formations and withdraw from them'. It is important to note the wording of this passage, which underlines the sovereignty and independence of the country, by mentioning that joining is voluntarily and it is free to withdraw from such entities. Indeed, it is hard to imagine a sovereign country not being able to join an international organisation without an explicit provision for such a right in its constitution, especially that not all countries have such a provision. At the same time, the provision shows respect to international law. Therefore, this provision's focus is other than permission or drawing a limit.

Third, the question arises regarding the effect of acts of other institutions, which under the majority of criteria are not supranational.[64] At this stage of development of Eurasian integration, this issue should not cause difficulties as only the Commission is defined as a body adopting decisions 'with regulatory and binding effect for the Member State" which form "part of the Union law and shall be directly applicable on [their] territories'.[65]

Fourth, this would mean that the Constitutional Court will not have powers to check the constitutionality of acts of interstate formations. One possible answer is that the Constitution hierarchically still remains the highest law of the land, which *ipso facto* means that any other legal norm operating on the territory has to be in compliance with the Constitution. Therefore, the proposed interpretation will *de facto* exclude only the compatibility check with laws and decrees, but not the Constitution.

Finally, the entire division into intergovernmental and supranational institutions is doubtful. The issue of supranationality is complex indeed, and there is no single definition thereof, but rather a number of fundamental characteristics.[66] However, it is clear that some organisations and institutions are more dependent on respective Member States, while others are less so and possess more powers. In some cases, there is recognition of such distinctions between organisations in national constitutional law of other states.[67] Even though Belarus's constitutional law does not make such a distinction, this can be made using the power of interpretation, which is being proposed here.

How this is to work in practice in the current national legal framework is yet to be seen. The Constitutional Court has never discussed any issues arising from the new legal order Belarus has become part of. So far, no challenges were made regarding this issue. The Commission decisions are being implemented, and the government works closely with the EAEU institutions. However, it is not so in the case of the judicial branch. There was an attempt for formal cooperation between a national court of Belarus and the EurAsEC Court – the predecessor of the EAEU Court. The EurAsEC Court possessed the powers of preliminary ruling. It was used only once – by the Supreme Economic Court of Belarus.[68] The Supreme Economic Court asked the EurAsEC Court about the application of an international treaty and two Commission decisions. Interestingly enough, the Belarusian court almost immediately withdrew the request (even asked for it twice),[69] while the Grand Chamber of the EurAsEC Court, having a right to reject the withdrawal, continued with the examination of the case explaining it, somewhat strangely, by procedural economy.[70] There can be many reasons why the EurAsEC Court continued with the case, e.g. it was the first preliminary ruling application, and the court, not overwhelmed with a heavy workload, and having an activist stance, was happy to rule on the case for the sake of it and to enforce its jurisdiction. It could have also been done to protect the rights of the legal entity, that asked the Belarusian court to refer to the EurAsEC Court in the first place.[71] In any event, the communication between the national and supranational institutions did not work out. The EurAsEC Court delivered a ruling the referring court did not want, an unsolicited advice of sorts. Moreover, the supranational court suffered in the end: the successor – the EAEU Court – was deprived of the preliminary ruling procedure altogether.[72]

Conclusion

The analysis above shows that the Belarusian legal order is not entirely compatible with the EAEU legal framework. Such compatibility is relevant for the full effect of EAEU law. In order to ensure its effectiveness, it would certainly help to change certain national constitutional norms as well as interpret the EAEU Treaty with doctrines to effectuate the Union law in the Belarusian legal order.

The main problematic provision is, according to one interpretation, the ability of the Constitutional Court to check the compatibility of decisions of the Commission with national laws and decrees. As long as changing constitutional norms does not seem to be easy, and the one in hand requires a referendum, we propose a different, albeit temporary, interpretation based on the 'living document' doctrine and using the concept of supranationality. The 'living constitution' reading of this provision suggests that supranational institutions fall outside the Constitutional Court's right to check compatibility of decisions of the Commission with national laws and decrees, while leaving its right to rule on the constitutionality of such decisions. This solution makes the Belarusian legal order fully compatible with the current EAEU law and allows it to function and develop more effectively.

Notes

1 McCulloch v. Maryland, 17 U.S. (4 Wheat.) 316 (1819) at 407.

2 The EAEU Treaty has codified almost 100 international agreements concluded within the Eurasian integration process, most of them codified into the EAEU Treaty. See 'Codification', available at: www.eurasiancommission.org/ru/act/integr_i_makroec/dep_razv_integr/Pages/codification.aspx (accessed 1 March 2016).

3 Agreement between the European Community and the European Atomic Energy Community and the Union of Soviet Socialist Republics on Trade and Commercial and Economic Cooperation, *OJ*, 1990, L 68/3. For further information on the legal framework of the EU-Belarus relations see M. Karliuk, 'Legislative Approximation and Application Of EU Law in Belarus', in: P. Van Elsuwege and R. Petrov (eds.), *Legislative Approximation and Application of EU Law in the Eastern Neighbourhood of the European Union: Towards a Common Regulatory Space?* London: Routledge, 2014, pp. 228–245.

4 See 'Makei: Belarus Ready for New Framework Agreement with EU', available at: www.belta.by/politics/view/belarus-hochet-zakljuchit-s-es-novoe-soglashenie-dlja-razvitija-otnoshenij-176293-2016/ (accessed 26 December 2016).

5 Reshenie Komissii tamozhennogo soiuza, 'O Rabochei gruppe po kodifikatsii mezhdunarodnykh dogovorv, sostavliaiushchikh dogovorno-pravovuiu bazu Tamozhennogo soiuza i Edinogo ekonomicheskogo prostranstva' (Decision of the Customs Union Commission on the working group on codification of international agreements, forming the legal basis of the Customs Union and Single Economic Space), adopted on 22 June 2011, No 902.

6 The Constitution of the Republic of Belarus, adopted on 15 May 1994, No 2878-XII (as amended by the republican referendums on 24 November 1996, 17 October 2004). The full text of the Constitution in English is available at: http://law.by/main.aspx?guid=3871&p0=V19402875e (accessed 26 December 2016).

7 G. Frankenberg, 'Comparing Constitutions: Ideas, Ideals, and Ideology – Toward a Layered Narrative', *Int'l Journal of Constitutional Law*, 3(4), 2006, 439–459, fn. 2.

8 See the Constitute Project for the English versions of constitutions at: www.constituteproject.org

9 Thus, there are no such debatable provisions as "proper and necessary" clause.

10 Article 8(1) Constitution of Belarus.

11 G. A. Vasilevich, *Konstitutsionnye osnovy implementatsii mezhdunarodnykh dogovorov Respubliki Belarus' i norm, integratsionnogo prava* (Constitutional Basics of Implementation of International Treaties of the Republic of Belarus and Norms of Integration Law), Minsk: Pravo i ekonomika, 2015, p. 104.

12 I. I. Pliakhimovich, *Kommentarii k Konstitutsii Respubliki Belarus': Tom 1* (Commentary to the Constitution of the Republic of Belarus), Minsk: Amalfeia, p. 209.

13 Art. 8(3) Constitution.

14 Art. 61, Art. 116 (part 4) Constitution of Belarus.

15 Pliakhimovich, *op. cit.*, p. 248.

16 Zakon Respubliki Belarus, 'O mezhdunarodnykh dogovorakh Respubliki Belarus' (Law on International Treaties of the Republic of Belarus), adopted on 23 July 2008, No 4213, *Natsionalnyi reestr pravovykh aktov Respubliki Belarus'* (4 August 2008) No 184, 2/1518, Art. 33(2).

17 Zakon Respubliki Belarus, 'O normativnykh pravovykh aktakh Respubliki Belarus' (Law on Normative Legal Acts of the Republic of Belarus), adopted on 10 January 2000, No 361-Z, *Natsionalnyi reestr pravovykh aktov Respubliki Belarus'* (13 January 2000) No 2/136, Art. 20.

18 L. V. Pavlova, 'Osobennosti zakonotvorchestva Respubliki Belarus' v oblasti zakliucheniia mezhdunarodnykh dogovorov' (Features of the Republic of Belarus' Law-making in the Field of Conclusion of International Treaties), in: E.V. Babkina et al. (eds.), *Aktualnyie problemy mezhdunarodnogo publichnogo i mezhdunarodnogo chastnogo prava: sbornik nauchnykh trudov*, No 1, Minsk: BSU, 2011, p. 109.

19 A. I. Zybailo, 'Mesto istochnikov prava EvrAzES v pravovykh sistemakh gosudarstv-chlenov' (Place of EURASEC sources of law in legal systems of Member States), *Evraziiskii iuridicheskii zhurnal*, No 7, 2013, 14–18.

20 Civil Code of the Republic of Belarus, adopted on 7 December 1998, No 2183, Art. 6; Bank Code of the Republic of Belarus, adopted on 25 October 2000, No 4413, Art. 3; L.V. Pavlova, 'Rol' mezhdunarodnogo prava kak reguliatora mezhdunarodnykh otnoshenii v usloviiakh globalizatsii'(Role of international law as regulator of international relations in the context of globalization') in: E. V. Babkina et al. (eds.), *Aktualnye problemy mezhdunarodnogo publichnogo i mezhdunarodnogo chastnogo prava: sbornik nauchnykh trudov*, No. 3, Minsk: BSU, 2011, pp. 76–85.

21 Code of Civil Procedure, adopted on 11 January 1999, No 2383, Art. 543; Criminal Code, adopted on 9 July 1999, No 2753, Art. 7 (regarding extradition); Labour Code, adopted on 26 July 1999, No 2963, Art. 8 (regarding agreements that are ratified and entered into force); Criminal Enforcement Code, adopted on 11 January 2000, No 3653, Art. 3 (prioritises self-executive norms of international agreements). See also the Investment Code, adopted on 22June 2001, No 373, Art.6(3); Marriage and Family Code, adopted on 9 July 1999, No 2783, Art. 237; Tax Code, adopted on 19 December 2002, No 1663, Art. 5; Air Code, adopted on 16 May 2006, No 1173, Art. 4; and others.

22 Vasilevich, *Konstitutsionnye osnovy*, *op. cit.*, 124.

23 See also G. A. Vasilevich, *Kostitutsionnoe parvo* (Constitutional law), Minsk: Registr, 2012, p. 37; Pliakhimovich, *op. cit.*, p. 244.

24 Art. 116(5).

25 Regulation on the Eurasian Economic Commission (Annex 1 to the Treaty on the Eurasian Economic Union), pt.13.

26 Reshenie Mezhgosudarstvennogo soveta EvrAzES 'Ob organizatsii funktsionirovaniia Suda Evrasiiskogo ekonomicheskogo soobshchestva' (Decision of the EurAsEC Interstate Council 'On organization of functioning of the Court of the Eurasian Economic Community'), adopted on 27 April 2003, No 123; Reshenie Soveta glav gosudarstv SNG o vozlozhenii na Ekonomicheskii Sud Sodruzhestva Nezavisimykh Gosudarstv funkcii Suda Evraziiskogo ekonomicheskogo soobschestva (Decision of the CIS Council of Heads of States on assigning the Economic Court of the Commonwealth of Independent States with the functions of the Court of the Eurasian Economic Union), adopted on 19 September 2003; Soglashenie mezhdu Sodruzhestvom Nezavisimykh Gosudarstv i Evraziiskim ekonomicheskim soobschestvom o vypolnenii Ekonomicheskim Sudom SNG funktsii Suda Evraziiskogo ekonomicheskogo soobschestva o vypolnenii Ekonomicheskim Sudom SNG funkcii Suda Evraziiskogo ekonomicheskogo soobshchestva (Agreement between the Commonwealth of Independent States and the Eurasian Economic Community on the functions of the Court of the Eurasian Economic Community carried out by the Economic Court of the Commonwealth of Independent States), signed on 3 March 2004.

27 'Konsultativnoe zakliuchenie Ekonomicheskogo Suda SNG No. 01–1/3–05 (10 March 2006) po zaprosu Integratsionnogo Komiteta Evraziiskogo ekonomicheskogo soobschestva o tolkovanii chasti vtoroi stat'i 1, chasti pervoi stat'i 14 Dogovora ob uchrezhdenii Evraziiskogo ekonomicheskogo soobschestva ot 10 oktiabria 2000 goda' (Consultative Opinion of the CIS Economic Court on the request of the Integration Committee of the Eurasian Economic Community about interpretation of Articles 1(2) and 14(2) of the Treaty on the establishment of the Eurasian Economic Community of 10 October 2000), in *Resheniia Ekonomicheskogo Suda Sodruzhestva Niezavisimykh Gosudarstv, 1992–2006*, Minsk: Kovcheg, 2007, p. 540.

28 Reshenie Konstitutsionnogo Suda Respubliki Belarus' 'O sootvetstvii Konstitutsii Respubliki Belarus' Zakona Respubliki Belarus "Ob otsenke sootvetstviia tekhnicheskim trebovaniiam i akkreditatsii organov po otsenke sootvetstviia" (Decision of the Constitutional Court of the Republic of Belarus 'On conformity of the Law of the Republic of Belarus 'On technical requirements conformity assessment and accreditation of conformity assessment bodies' to the Constitution of the Republic of Belarus), adopted on 13 October 2016, No R-1069/2016, available at: www.kc.gov.by/main.aspx?guid=44693

29 Art. 79 Constitution.

30 Art. 116 Constitution.

31 Article 116(4) Constitution.

32 The Constitutional Court possessed the powers of its own initiative prior to the amendments to the Constitution. See Pliakhimovich, *op. cit.*, p. 530.

33 Zakon Respubliki Belarus, 'O Kostitutsionnom Sude Respubliki Belarus' (Law on the Constitutional Court), adopted on 30 March 1994, No 2914-XII, *Viedamaści Viarchoŭnaha Savieta Respubliki Bielaruś*, 1994, No.15, p. 220.

34 Zakon Respubliki Belarus, 'O konstitutsionnom sudoproizvodstve' (Law on Constitutional Legal Procedure), adopted on 8 January 2014, No 124-Z, *Natsionalnyi pravovoi Internet-portal Respubliki Belarus'*, 16 January 2014, 2/2122.

35 Paras 7 and 8 of Art. 85 Law on Constitutional Legal Procedure.

36 Zybailo, *op. cit.*

37 G. A. Vasilevich and S. G. Vasilevich, 'O neposredstvennom deistvii aktov Evraziiskoi ekonomicheskoi komissii' (On direct applicability of acts of the Eurasian Economic Commission), *Evraziiskii iuridicheskii zhurnal*, No 10(77), 2014, 35.

38 *Ibid.*

39 *Ibid.*

40 *Ibid.*, p. 36.

41 McCulloch v. Maryland, 17 U.S. (4 Wheat.) 316 (1819). Overview of other cases is available in Ch. Warren, *The Supreme Court in United States History in Three Volumes: Volume One 1789–1821*, Boston: Little, Brown, and Company, 1922.

42 Zakon Respubliki Belarus, 'O normativnykh pravovykh aktakh Respubliki Belarus', *op. cit.*

43 Th. Eilmansberger, 'The Relationship Between Rights and Remedies in EC Law: In Search of the Missing Link', *Common Market Law Review*, 41(5), 2004, 1199–1246; J.A. Winter, 'Direct Applicability and Direct Effect: Two Distinct and Different Concepts in Community Law', *Common Market Law Review*, 9(4), 1972, 425–438; P. Craig and G. de Búrca, *EU Law: Text, Cases, and Materials*, 5th ed., Oxford: Oxford University Press, 2011, p. 105.

44 M. N. Shaw, *International Law*, 6th ed., Cambridge: Cambridge University Press, 2008, pp. 164–177.

45 See, e.g., point 13, para 2 of the Regulation on the Eurasian Economic Commission (Annex 1 to the Treaty on the Eurasian Economic Union): 'Decisions of the

Commission shall form part of the Union law and shall be directly applicable on the territories of the Member States.'

46 Point 13, para 1 Regulation on the Eurasian Economic Commission.

47 See R. Dragneva, 'The Eurasian Economic Union: Balancing Sovereignty and Integration' in this volume.

48 'Draft Treaty on the Eurasian Economic Union', available at: http://kazenergy.com/ru/2012-09-05-04-11-04/2011-05-13-18-20-44/10777-2013-09-10–07–03–15.html (accessed 27 December 2016).

49 The Statute of the EAEU Court (Annex 2 to the Treaty on the Eurasian Economic Union) provides that the Court's "clarifications of provisions of the Treaty" do not deprive the Member States of the right for joint interpretation.

50 See e.g. B. de Witte, 'Direct Effect, Primacy, and the Nature of the Legal Order', in P. Craig and G. de Búrca (eds.), *The Evolution of EU Law*, Oxford: Oxford University Press, 2011, pp. 323–362.

51 M. Karliuk, 'The Limits of the Judiciary Within the Eurasian Integration Process', in: A. Di Gregorio and A. Angeli (eds.), *The European Union and the Eurasian Economic Union: Moving Toward a Greater Understanding*, The Hague: Eleven International Publishing, 2016, pp. 171–183.

52 See e.g. 'The Constitution of the Republic of Estonia Amendment Act', available at: www.president.ee/en/republic-of-estonia/the-constitution/ (accessed 27 December 2016). The main provisions are: § 1. Estonia may belong to the European Union, provided the fundamental principles of the Constitution of the Republic of Estonia are respected. § 2. When Estonia has acceded to the European Union, the Constitution of the Republic of Estonia is applied without prejudice to the rights and obligations arising from the Accession Treaty; See also 'Constitutional Act of the Republic of Lithuania on Membership of the Republic of Lithuania in the European Union', available at: <www.lrs.lt/upl_files/Lietuvos_pirmininkavimas_ES/dokumentai/CONSTITUTIONAL_ACT.pdf>(accessed 27 December 2016); Additionally see A.E. Kellermann et al. (eds.), *The Impact of EU Accession on the Legal Orders of New EU Member States and (Pre-) Candidate Countries: Hopes and Fears*, The Hague: TMC Asser Press, 2006. See also Art. 23 of the 'Basic Law for the Republic of Germany of 1949 (rev. 2012)', available at: www.constituteproject.org/constitution/German_Federal_Republic_2012?lang=en (accessed 27 December 2016) and Art. 88 of the 'Constitution of France of 1958 (rev. 2008)', available at: www.constituteproject.org/constitution/France_2008?lang=en (accessed 27 December 2016).

53 'Lukashenko Contemplates Adjusting Belarus' Constitution to Meet Present-day Challenges', *Belarusian Telegraph Agency*, available at: http://eng.belta.by/president/view/lukashenko-contemplates-adjusting-belarus-constitution-to-meet-present-day-challenges-95196–2016/ (accessed 27 December 2016).

54 Art. 140 Constitution.

55 Pliakhimovich, *op. cit.*, p. 221.

56 Art. 61, 79, 84(point 20) Constitution.

57 Pliakhimovich, *op. cit.*, p. 223.

58 Art. 127 Constitution 1994.

59 Pliakhimovich, *op. cit.*, p. 233.

60 Vasilevich, *Konstitutsionnye osnovy*, *op. cit.*, p. 113.

61 M. Karliuk, 'The Eurasian Economic Union: An EU-Inspired Legal Order and Its Limits', *Review of Central and East European Law*, 42(1), 2017, 50; R. Dragneva, 'The Eurasian Economic Union: Balancing Sovereignty and Integration', in this volume.

62 M.M. Martin Martinez, *National Sovereignty and International Organizations*, The Hague: Kluwer Law International, 1996, p. 122.

63 *Ibid.*
64 M. Karliuk, 'Eurasian Economic Union', *op. cit.*
65 Para 13 Regulation on the Eurasian Economic Commission.
66 Arguably, the most comprehensive list of fundamental characteristics of a fully supranational organisation was developed by Schermers and Blokker. See H.G. Schermers and N.M. Blokker, *International Institutional Law: Unity Within Diversity*, 5th ed., Leiden: Martinus Nijhoff Publishers, 2003, pp. 46–47.
67 See e.g. BVerfG, Judgment of the Second Senate of 30 June 2009–2 BvE 2/08 (Lisbon judgment), available at: www.bundesverfassungsgericht.de/SharedDocs/Entscheidungen/EN/2009/06/es20090630_2bve000208en.html (accessed 28 December 2016).
68 'Reshenie Bolshoi kollegii Suda EvrAzES (10 July 2013)', *Biulleten' Suda Evraziiskogo ekonomicheskogo soobshchestva* (2013) No.2, 7–17. For analysis, see A.S. Ispolinov, 'Naviazannyi monolog: pervoe preiuditsial'noe zakliuchenie Suda EvrAzES' (An imposed monologue: the first preliminary ruling of the EurAsEC Court), *Evraziiskii juridicheskii zhurnal*, 63(8), (2013), 21–30.
69 'Osoboe mnenie (delo No 1–6/1–2013)' (Dissenting opinion of Judge Smirnov in Case No 1–6/1–2013), available at: http://courteurasian.org/page-20991 (accessed 30 November 2015).
70 'Postanovlenie' (Decision of the EAEU Court of 20 May 2013), available at: http://courteurasian.org/page-20991 (accessed 30 November 2015).
71 'Osoboe mnenie po resheniiu o preiuditsial'nom zaprose (delo No 1–6/1–2013)' (Dissenting opinion of Judge Neshataeva on the preliminary request in Case No 1–6/1–2013), available at: http://courteurasian.org/page-20991 (accessed 30 November 2015).
72 M. Karliuk, 'Eurasian Economic Union', *op. cit.*

10 The constitutional order of the Russian Federation and its adaptability to European and Eurasian integration projects

*Paul Kalinichenko**

Introduction

Immediately after the collapse of the Soviet Union in 1991, the Russian Federation (Russia) showed an interest in European integration. Russia was one of the first post-Soviet countries to sign a Partnership and Cooperation Agreement (PCA)[1] with the EU and to join the Council of Europe.[2] In the beginning of the 21st century, the Russian political establishment was captivated by the concept of the Four Common Spaces that provided a new agenda for legal approximation and economic convergence between the EU and Russia.[3] Russia was seriously committed to getting involved in the European integration process as an equal and reliable strategic partner.[4] However, following the Ukrainian crisis, the evolution of close EU-Russia relations has come to a halt.[5] In the meantime, the EU-Russia bilateral relations have been effectively frozen. As a result of the EU's restrictive measures (sanctions),[6] the negotiations on a new bilateral framework agreement replacing the PCA have been stopped. Moreover, the effective application of the PCA has been significantly limited due to public security reasons (application of diplomatic, political and economic restrictive measures against Russian companies and nationals).[7]

Despite seeking closer rapprochement with the EU, Russia never dropped its ambitions as a spearhead of political, economic and legal integration within the post-Soviet area. Since the fall of the Soviet Union, Russia led the evolution of regional integration within the post-Soviet area: from the CIS, the Eurasian Economic Community, the Single Economic Area and the Custom Union, the Russia-Belarus Union State to the contemporary Eurasian Economic Union (EAEU).[8]

Against this backdrop, this chapter aims to study the constitutional dimension of Russia's participation in various regional integration projects. First, a short description of the constitutional foundations of the Russian political system and concepts of sovereignty in the Russian Constitution of 1993 will be discussed. Special emphasis will be placed on the application of international law in the Russian legal order. Second, this chapter will focus on the impact of the EAEU *acquis* on the constitutional system of Russia. It will be argued that the

EAEU project is more likely to become a political imitation of integration than an attempt to establish a genuine supranational economic union within the territory of the former Soviet Union. Finally, this chapter addresses the issue of Russia's participation in the European Convention on Human Rights (ECHR) and its new approaches to implementation of the European Court of Human Rights (ECtHR) judgments in the Russian legal order on the ground of the latest decisions of the Constitutional Court of the Russian Federation.

The constitutional system and the concept of sovereignty in Russia

The Russian Constitution was adopted by a nationwide referendum on 12 December 1993 as the basic law of Russia. It was inspired by Western constitutional traditions and internationally recognised democratic and human rights values.[9] Undoubtedly, this document laid down a firm foundation stone for the Europeanization of contemporary Russian law.[10]

The constitutional order of Russia is characterised by three features. First of all, some provisions of the Russian Constitution are immune from further amendments. It concerns the provisions on fundamentals of the constitutional system, on human rights and on constitutional review. If these provisions are to be amended, the Constitution requires the summoning of a Constitutional Assembly or a referendum.[11] Secondly, the Constitution of Russia integrates international law acts into its national legal order and recognises the priority of duly ratified international agreements above conflicting domestic laws.[12] Thirdly, the Constitutional Court possesses the exclusive competence to interpret the Constitution. Its legal positions are binding[13] and are considered as judicial precedents within the Russian legal system.[14]

Notwithstanding the ongoing academic debate on the Russian approach of sharing European common values,[15] it must be acknowledged that the Russian Constitution laid down the basis for a principally new Western-style legal system in post-Soviet Russia. The major breakthrough of the Constitution of 1993 is the decisive departure from the Soviet legal heritage, in particular, with regard to the implementation and application of international law within the national legal order.[16] It is noteworthy that, at the time of its adoption, the Russian Constitution had the most liberal provision regarding the application of international law within a national legal system among all former Soviet countries. Consequently, the provisions of the Russian Constitution on application of international law gave greater opportunities for Russian judges to apply and interpret international law in accordance with their constitutional acts than any other judges from the former USSR.[17]

Moreover, the Russian Constitution is the only in the post-Soviet area which contains a so-called 'integration clause', authorising the transfer of sovereign powers in order to participate in the functioning of international organisations.[18] According to the Federal Law 'On International Treaties of Russian Federation' of 15 July 1995, Russia can join any international organisation on the ground of a ratified international agreement.[19] The provisions of such an international agreement should be in conformity with the fundamentals of the Russian constitutional order and must respect the protection of human rights. Hence, it is obvious that Russia as a sovereign country may join any international organisation taking into account the limits described in its national legislation and pursuant to the terms and conditions of the concrete international organisation.

Significantly, the Russian Constitution of 1993 completely changed the previous perspective on sovereignty. The core of the Soviet legal doctrine was to preserve the concept of 'sovereignty' in order to protect the country's own system of socialistic government and the supremacy of Soviet law and, in particular, the supremacy of the fundamental principles of the socialist state order (nationalization of property without compensation, wars against colonialism, no protection of private property). Even during *perestroika*, the formal theory of international law in the USSR stated that no international treaty could automatically take precedence over conflicting provisions of Soviet domestic law. International agreements were supposed to be considered as self-executing if their provisions either fully corresponded to existing national laws or regulated gaps in national legislation. International human rights conventions were deprived supremacy over national law due to their 'vagueness and generality', and, therefore, were not directly applicable. It should be emphasised that the Soviet legal doctrine did not recognise the primacy of international law over national law as a matter of principle.[20]

The political and legal origin of sovereignty in contemporary Russia comes from the Declaration on the State Sovereignty of the Russian Soviet Federative Socialists Republic on 12 July 1990[21] that proclaimed the priority of the Constitution of the Russian Soviet Federative Socialists Republic (RSFSR) and its legislation over the legislation of the USSR. The sovereignty of Russia covers its entire territory and the state ensures the integrity and inviolability of its territory.

It is noteworthy that the Constitution of Russia is strongly influenced by the Federation Treaty between Russia's regions and the central government of 1992.[22] This document was based on the populist slogan of Boris Yeltsin: 'you may take as much of sovereignty as you can swallow'.[23] Consequently, the Constitution identifies the subjects of the Russian Federation as 'States'.[24] Nevertheless, the Constitutional Court had unequivocally rejected all claims of sovereignty for the subjects of the Russian Federation in 2000.[25]

Application of international law in the Russian legal order

The adoption of the new Constitution of the Russian Federation in 1993 ensured the previously impossible direct applicability of international law within the Russian legal system. In accordance with Article 15 (4) of the Russian Constitution:

> Universally recognised principles and norms of international law as well as international agreements of the Russian Federation should be an integral

> part of its legal system. If an international agreement of the Russian Federation establishes rules, which differ from those stipulated by law, then the rules of the international agreement shall be applied.

These provisions go further than the 1992 Soviet Constitution Amendments, which only established supremacy of the internationally recognised human rights over domestic legislation. Arguably, it is the most stringent rule concerning primacy of international law in a national constitution within the post-Soviet area.[26] Hence, the Russian Constitution unequivocally established that provisions of ratified international agreements prevail over rules of the Russian domestic legislation.

In 1997, the Constitutional Court of the Russian Federation interpreted in this context that 'law' means laws and all other rules.[27] However, it does not concern the Constitution. On the one hand, the Constitutional Court ruled that 'international treaties of the Russian Federation that do not correspond to the Constitution of the Russian Federation, shall not be implemented or used'.[28] On the other hand, if an international treaty contradicts the Constitution, Russia cannot sign it without the necessary constitutional amendments.[29] Moreover, the range of international agreements possessing primacy over domestic legislation is limited by the requirement of ratification.

Duly ratified international treaties are part of the Russian legal system. However, it is impossible to interpret this rule in light of the *lex posteriori derogat legi priori* principle in the case of contradiction between the provisions of international treaties and future domestic acts. The Supreme Court of the Russian Federation has clarified that national courts should not apply national legal provisions that are different from the provisions contained in ratified international agreements.[30]

It is important to emphasise that the Constitution offered greater opportunities for Russian judges to apply and interpret various sources of international law in their judgments. As commentators acknowledge, 'international law is no longer "alien" for [Russian] courts. They widely refer to it and apply it as well as domestic norms.'[31]

The practice of the Russian judiciary is significant for understanding the application of international law in Russia. Though there is no rule of precedent of case law in the Russian legal order, the resolutions (explanatory notes) of higher Russian courts[32] are extremely important for comprehending the legal force of a particular international agreement within the Russian legal system. These explanatory notes constitute a source of interpretation of primary and secondary Russian law for lower courts that *de facto* always follow them. For instance, the explanatory notes of the Supreme Court of Russia[33] specified precise criteria of various sources of international law to be applied by Russian courts in their judgments: 1) when Russia is a party to an international agreement; 2) when an international agreement has been duly ratified by the Russian Parliament; 3) when an international agreement has been published in a designated governmental official journal; 4) when an international agreement is self-executive by its nature.

Therefore, it can be stated that Russian judges widely refer to and apply sources of international law in their judgments.[34] The interpretation and application of the ECHR is of particular significance for the Russian judiciary. However, as explained further in this contribution, Russia's Constitutional Court has adopted a more cautious approach with respect to the ECHR in recent years. This is also relevant for the application of the EU-Russia PCA and other bilateral agreements between the EU and Russia.[35]

The impact of Eurasian integration on the Russian constitutional system

In 2010, Russia, Belarus and Kazakhstan established a Custom Union with common customs rules and supranational institutions. Consequently, since 2010, Russia has transferred its competence in the field of technical regulation and customs matters to the Eurasian Economic Commission. The next level of political and economic integration in the post-Soviet area took place in Astana (Kazakhstan) on 28 May 2014 when Russia, Belarus and Kazakhstan signed the EAEU Treaty (Astana Treaty), which was later also joined by Armenia and Kyrgystan.

Since the entry into force of this treaty on 1 January 2015, the Russian legal order has faced new challenges regarding the influence of international law. The EAEU Treaty established a new international organisation of regional economic integration with its own legal order.

The legal framework of Eurasian integration by which Russia is bound is enormous.[36] It includes the EAEU Treaty and international treaties that had been concluded in the framework of the Eurasian Economic Community (EurAsEC), and of the Customs Union and the Single Economic Space, decisions of the Eurasian Economic Commission and the case law of the EAEU Court.

The EAEU Court possesses the full competence of interpretation of the Astana Treaty, other founding treaties and other sources of the 'Eurasian *acquis*'.[37] However, the competences of the EAEU Court are significantly curtailed compared to the powers of its predecessor – the EurAsEC Court – which had powers similar to those of the Court of Justice of the EU (CJEU).[38] Nevertheless, the EAEU Court may rely on the jurisprudence of the EurAsEC Court on the ground of *stare decisis*.[39]

On 4 April 2017, the EAEU Court decided one of the most important cases in its history. In an Advisory Opinion on request of the Belarusian Ministry of Justice concerning the interpretation of the Astana Treaty provisions in the field of competition, the EAEU Court formulated the principle of 'direct effect'.[40] The question before the EAEU Court concerned the interpretation of the EAEU Treaty provisions regarding the *de minimis* rules (cannot exceed 20 percent) for vertical agreements between the EAEU companies (Articles 74–76 of the Astana Treaty). The Belarusian draft law allowed the reduction of the EAEU's *de minimis* rules to 15 percent for the domestic market (being comparable with the EU rules).

In this context, the EAEU Court particularly stressed that the Eurasian Economic Commission had a supranational competence in the field of competition.[41] Further, the EAEU Court examined the EAEU competence in the field of competition under the Astana Treaty and stated that the competition rules for the EAEU market are covered by common policy or, in other words, by supranational regulation.[42] In regard to domestic markets, the EAEU Court decided that the EAEU and its Member States implement the coordinated policy, wherein the EAEU institutions define common approaches to achieve the objectives of the EAEU Treaty.

Therefore, the EAEU Court rejected the possibility for the Member States to revise the EAEU common rules, in particular the Astana Treaty provisions concerning *de minimis* criteria for vertical agreements. Moreover, for the very first time, the EAEU Court applied the 'direct effect' doctrine for the EAEU 'common rules'. It concluded that 'common rules of competition have a direct effect and should be applied by the Member States directly as international treaty provisions'.[43]

Recognition of the 'direct effect' principle in the *Vertical agreements* case can be considered as a breakthrough in considering the supranational nature of the EAEU legal order. It is obvious to draw a parallel with the *Van Gend en Loos* judgment of the CJEU in 1963.[44] Nevertheless, the EAEU Court in the *Vertical agreements* case avoided any quotes and references to the relevant CJEU case law. There is no doubt that the *Vertical agreements* case appears to be less ambitious in its conclusions and impact on the EAEU legal order than the *Van Gend en Loos* case on its impact on the EU legal order.

Furthermore, it is questionable whether the EAEU Court will be able and keen to develop and promote the 'direct effect' principle as a fundamental part of the EAEU legal order. First of all, it is uncertain whether the EAEU Member States consider themselves bound by the EAEU Court case law, especially by its Advisory Opinions. Secondly, the position of the EAEU Court judges in the *Vertical agreements* case was not unanimous.[45] Thirdly, in recent years the Constitutional Court has adopted a strict approach regarding the influence of decisions of international bodies on the Russian legal order. For instance, in the *Avangard Agro Orel* case of 2015, the Constitutional Court re-affirmed its jurisdiction to verify the compliance of decisions of EAEU bodies with respect to human rights protected in the Constitution.[46]

Nonetheless, the importance of the EAEU Court case law concerning the recognition of the principle of 'direct effect' of the Astana Treaty cannot be underestimated. On one hand, the EAEU Court was definitely inspired by the 'integration-motivated' case law of the EU courts. On the other hand, the EAEU Court was pushed to formalise the principle of 'direct effect' due to the pending demands of economic integration within the EAEU. Hence, the EAEU law may evolve dynamically together with further economic integration within the former Soviet space.

Enforcement of case law of the ECtHR within the Russian legal order

Enforcement of judgments of the ECtHR has become an extremely politicised and notorious issue in Russia since 2013. The enforcement of the ECtHR case law was questioned for the first time in relation to ECtHR judgments *Hirst v. the United Kingdom*[47] of 6 October 2005 and *Anchugov and Gladkov v. Russia* of 4 July 2013[48] and. In these cases, the ECtHR found a contradiction between the ECHR and Article 32(3) of the Russian Constitution on disenfranchisement of prisoners.[49] Further difficulties in enforcing the ECtHR judgments were caused by the decision of the Constitutional Court on 14 July 2015.[50] The decision was adopted after a group of members of the Russian Parliament (*State Duma*) asked the Constitutional Court to verify the constitutionality of the provisions of six Russian laws, which, in their opinion, contradicted Articles 15 and 79 of the Constitution. In their opinion, these laws allowed the enforcement of the ECtHR judgments in Russia even if they conflicted with the Russian Constitution and the Constitutional Court judgments.[51] Furthermore, Members of the *State Duma* considered the enforcement of the ECtHR judgments as a potential threat to the state sovereignty.

The Russian mass media immediately linked this situation to the judgment of the ECtHR in the case *OAO Neftyanayakompaniya Yukos v. Russia*.[52] Therein, the Russian government was obliged to pay almost 2 billion Euro compensation to the former owners of Yukos, the once largest oil company in Russia.[53] Arguably, the statement of the Members of the *State Duma* was an attempt to prevent enforcement of further ECtHR judgments against Russia, in particular, in the cases on compensation for acts caused and linked to the Ukrainian crisis.[54]

The Constitutional Court bluntly rejected the claims of the Members of the *State Duma* in its judgment of 14 July 2015. Therein, the impugned provisions of six Russian laws were declared as in line with the Russian Constitution. In the opinion of the Constitutional Court, the recognition of certain provisions of the Russian law as unconstitutional, due to the necessity of implementation of the ECtHR case law, could only deteriorate the balance in the Russian system of protection of human rights and create a disharmony between the ECHR's and Russian legal systems.

The Constitutional Court argued that Russia's participation in international agreements does not imply any transfer of national sovereignty. Therefore, no international treaty, including the ECHR and relevant ECtHR case law, can question the primacy of the Constitution within the Russian legal order. The Constitutional Court stressed that the Constitution and the ECHR were based on the same democratic values and, therefore, any conflict between these documents is exceptional. If it happens, Russia should abandon enforcement of respective ECtHR judgments in favour of the primacy of the Constitution. According to the Constitutional Court, this approach complies with the practice of other countries and must be based on the ideas of non-self-isolation, mutual respect and the dialogue between different human rights protection systems. However, only the Constitutional Court possesses the exclusive competence to question the constitutionality of the execution and enforcement of ECtHR judgments within the Russian legal system.

Following this judgment of the Constitutional Court, the *State Duma* amended the Russian Federal Constitutional Law 'On the Constitutional Court of the Russian Federation.'[55] These amendments empowered the Constitutional Court to verify the compliance of decisions of international organisations and institutions with the standards of protection of human rights in the Constitution, and to consider the enforceability of such decisions in the Russian legal order. It is obvious that these legal amendments pursue the objective of narrowing if not making impossible the application and enforcement of the ECtHR case law in the Russian legal system.

On 11 March 2016, the European Commission for Democracy through Law of the Council of Europe (Venice Commission) adopted an Interim report,[56] wherein it indicated that amendments to the Federal Constitutional Law 'On the Constitutional Court of the Russian Federation' are not compatible with Russia's international obligations for several reasons. First, the new powers of the Constitutional Court may prevent the effective implementation of international decisions within the Russian legal order. Second, the amendments imply a revision the Constitution. The Venice Commission experts supported the idea of dialogue between the Russian and the Strasbourg human rights protection systems, and asked Russia to refrain from taking unilateral measures on the basis of the amendments.[57] On 19 April 2016, the Constitutional Court issued judgment No 12-P on the request of the Russian Ministry of Justice.[58] Therein the Constitutional Court echoed the comments of the Venice Commission and ruled that the interaction of the ECHR and the Russian constitutional order is impossible under the conditions of subordination 'because only dialogue between different legal systems is the basis of their proper balance.'[59]

Subsequently, the Constitutional Court declared that it was impossible to enforce the ECtHR judgment *Anchugov and Gladkov v. Russia*. In the opinion of the Constitutional Court, the enforcement of the ECtHR judgment would require a revision of the conflicting Russian laws in order to grant voting rights to all convicted people in Russia. The Constitutional Court emphasised that the ECtHR judgment allows Russia to achieve this objective by alternative means.

On 12 October 2016, the Russian Ministry of Justice sent to the Constitutional Court a new request on the constitutionality of the enforcement of the ECtHR judgment of 31 July 2014 *OAO Neftyanaya Kompaniya Yukos v. Russia*.[60] Already on 19 January 2017, the Constitutional Court issued its decision. In essence, the Constitutional Court recognised the impossibility of enforcement of the relevant ECtHR judgment within the Russian legal order due to the fact that the ECtHR as an 'intergovernmental subsidiary body on human rights protection' failed in its interpretation of the Convention and the Russian constitutional provisions.[61] Nevertheless, the Constitutional Court proposed a quite original way of enforcing the *Yukos* judgment. In particular, it suggested the selling of 'identified property of the Yukos company and its management' in order ensure the payment of the compensation and legal costs.[62]

Hence, the recent case law of the Constitutional Court reveals how it is gradually turning the international-friendly provisions of the Constitution to a defensive shield against supranational decisions of international institutions and organisations and judgments of international courts.

Concluding remarks

Our study indicates that, arguably, the Russian Constitution of 1993 is the most international law–friendly constitution among the countries of the post-Soviet area. It is the only Constitution with an explicit 'integration clause' (Article 79). Nevertheless, despite the initial openness to international law and a favourable attitude towards the Europeanisation of the Russian legal order, recent constitutional developments in Russia shifted towards a completely different direction. In particular, the case law of the Russian Constitutional Court regarding the enforcement of decisions of the ECtHR reveals an increasingly defensive and isolationist position justified by the objective of guarding the national sovereignty and protection of the domestic constitutional principles against the influence of international law. Obviously, this trend creates increasing and worrying tensions with regard to Russia's participation in the Council of Europe and the ECHR and its commitment to common European values. In this respect, the recommendations of the Venice Commission are of crucial importance to restore the fragile balance between the ECHR and the Russian constitutional order and to ensure the effective protection of fundamental rights in Russia.

Simultaneously, the process of the Eurasian integration creates new challenges for the Russian constitutional order. In particular, the recent case law of the EAEU Court introducing the direct effect of the Astana Treaty within the legal orders of the EAEU Member States may potentially conflict with the Constitutional Court's attempts to restore the full and unquestionable supremacy of the Constitution over decisions of international institutions and organisations and judgments of international courts. In the end, this strategy may endanger the effectiveness of the Eurasian integration project within the post-Soviet area and beyond.

Notes

* This contribution is based on results obtained within the framework of the state assignment of the Ministry of Education and Science of Russia 29.6607.2017/8.9 ('Science of the Future', Kutafin Moscow State Law University) on the topic 'Legal Aspects of Development of the Relations between Russia and the European Union in the Context of Russia's Priorities for Participation in Global and Regional Integration Taking into Account the Current International

Situation'. The author wishes to thank Maksim Karliuk for research support and valuable comments. The text is prepared with the support of the Erasmus+ programme of the European Union, Jean Monnet Chair, Project number 575077-EPP-1-2016-1-RU-EPPJMO-CHAIR

1 Sobraniye Zakonodatelstva Rosiyskoy Federatsii (Compilation of legislation of the Russian Federation – SZ RF), 1998, No 16, st. 1802; *OJ*, 1997, L 327/1.

2 Federal Law of 23.02.1996 Nj 19-FZ "On the Russian Federation accession to the Statute of the Council of Europe", SZ RF, 1996, No 9, art. 774.

3 P. Van Elsuwege, 'The Four Common Spaces: New Impetus to the EU-Russia Strategic Partnership?' in: A. Dashwood and M. Maresceau (eds.), *Law and Practice of EU External Relations*, Cambridge: Cambridge University Press, 2008, pp. 334–359.

4 The concept 'Strategic Partnership' appeared for the first time in the Joint Statements of the EU-Russia Summits in 1999–2001. In 2010, the EU-Russia Strategic Partnership was supplemented by another initiative – the 'Partnership for Modernisation', which included a work plan with cooperation activities and common projects (Joint Statement of the EU-Russia Summit of 31 May 2010 and Work Plan on Partnership for Modernisation of December 2010). However, after the Ukrainian crisis of 2014, the concept of Strategic Partnership regarding Russia is no longer used by the EU institutions. The European Parliament in its Resolution of 10 June 2015 stressed that the EU cannot envisage a return to 'business as usual' and has no choice but to conduct a critical re-assessment of its relations with Russia. It highlighted that due to its actions in Crimea and in Eastern Ukraine, Russia can no longer be treated or considered as a 'Strategic Partner' (European Parliament resolution of 10 June 2015 on the state of the EU-Russia relations (2015/2001 /INI)), point 2).

5 P. Kalinichenko, 'Some Legal Issues of the EU-Russia Relations in the Post-Crimea Era: From Good Neighbourliness to Crisis and Back?' in: D. Kochenov and E. Basheska (eds.), *Good Neighbourliness in the European Legal Context*, Leiden: Brill Nijhoff, 2015, pp. 334–353.

6 The EU restrictive measures in accordance with Article 215 TFEU against Russia were introduced in accordance with the Council Conclusions on Ukraine of 3–4 March 2014 (see: Council of the European Union Conclusions of 4 March 2014 "Relations with Ukraine", COEST 62, 7208/14). These measures include *inter alia* suspending negotiations on the EU-Russia New Basic Agreement, suspending visa-free dialog, cancelling EU-Russia summits, and other restrictive measures of political and economic nature.

7 See: Case C-72/15, *Rosneft*, EU:C:2017:236, paras 108–116 and Case T-262/15, *Dmitrii Kyselov v. Council*, EU:T:2017:392, paras 28–35. For comments, see: P. Van Elsuwege, 'Judicial Review of the EU's Common Foreign and Security Policy: Lessons from the Rosneft Case', *VerfBlog*, 6 April 2017, available at: http://verfassungsblog.de/judicial-review-of-the-eus-commonforeign-and-security-policy-lessons-from-the-rosneft-case (accessed 7 July 2017).

8 Z. Kembayev, 'Regional Integration in Eurasia: The Legal and Political Framework', *Review of Central and East European Law*, 41, 2016, 157–194.

9 J. J. Hesse and V. Wright (eds.), *Federalizing Europe? The Costs, Benefits, and Preconditions of Federal Political Systems*, Oxford: Oxford University Press, 1996, p. 353; S.E. Finner, V. Bogdanor and B. Rudden (eds.), *Comparing Constitutions*, Oxford: Clarendon Press, 1995, p. 17.

10 In fact, the adoption of the Russian Constitution coincided with the entry into force of the Treaty on European Union on November 1, 1993 (TEU).

11 Article 135 of the Constitution of Russia, available at: www.constitution.ru/en/10003000-01.htm (accessed 7 July 2017).

12 Article 15(4) of the Constitution of Russia available at: www.constitution.ru/en/10003000-01.htm (accessed 7 July 2017).

13 "The decisions of the Constitutional Court of the Russian Federation shall be obligatory throughout the territory of the Russian Federation for all representative, executive, and judicial bodies of State Power, bodies of local government, enterprises, agencies, organisations, officials, citizens and their associations" (The Article 6 of the Federal Constitutional Law no. 1-FKZ of 21 July 1994 "On the Constitutional Court of the Russian Federation", SZ RF, 1994, No 13, art. 1447).

14 V. Zorkin, 'Precedent Character of the Decisions of the Constitutional Court of the Russian Federation', *Journal of Russian Law*, 12, 2004, 3–9. (in Russian).

15 P. Leino and R. Petrov, 'Between "Common Values" and Competing Universals – The Promotion of the EU's Common Values Though the European Neighbourhood Policy', *European Law Journal*, 5(15), 2009, 669–670.

16 G. Danilenko, 'Implementation of International Law in the CIS States: Theory and Practice', *European Journal of International Law*, 10, 1999, 51–69.

17 R. Petrov and P. Kalinichenko, 'The Europeanization of Third Country Judiciaries Through the Application of the EU Acquis: The Cases of Russia and Ukraine', *International and Comparative Law Quarterly*, 60, 2011, 336.

18 Article 79 of the Constitution of Russia reads: 'The Russian Federation may participate in interstate associations and transfer to them part of its powers according to international treaties and agreements, if this does not involve the limitation of the rights and freedoms of man and citizen and does not contradict the principles of the constitutional system of the Russian Federation', available at: www.constitution.ru/en/10003000-01.htm (accessed 7 July 2017).

19 Federal law No. 101-FZ 'On International Treaties of Russian Federation' of 15 July 1995, SZ RF, 1995, No 29, art. 2757.

20 J. Hazard, 'Soviet Yearbook on International Law 1987', *The American Journal of International Law*, 84(1), 1990, 303–305. See also F.J.M. Feldbrugge, *Encyclopedia of Soviet Law*, New York: Oceana Publications, 1973. The official Soviet doctrine of the application of international law explicitly stated that the Soviet Constitution of 1977 'possessed prior legal power upon the territory of the country and had priority over the international obligations of the country', in N. Blatova (ed.), Mezhdunarodnoe Publichnoe Pravo, Moscow, 1987, p. 64.

21 Declaration on the State Sovereignty of the Russian Soviet Federative Socialists Republic on 12 July 1990, Vedomosti Syezda narodnikh deputatov RSFSR I Verkhovnogo Sovieta RSFSR (Bulletin of the Congress of People's Deputies and of the Supreme Council the Russian Soviet Federative Socialists Republic) of 14 July 1990, N 2, art. 22.

22 Bulletin of the Congress of People's Deputies and of the Supreme Council the Russian Soviet Federative Socialists Republic of 23 April 1992, No 17, art. 898.

23 See B. Yeltsin's speech in Kazan of 6 August 1990, materials is available at: http://yeltsin.ru/news/boris-elcin-berite-stolko-suverineteta-skolko-smozhete-proglotit (accessed 26 June 2017).

24 Article 5(2) of the Constitution of Russia, available at: www.constitution.ru/en/10003000-01.htm (accessed 7 July 2017).

25 Order of the Constitutional Court of the Russian Federation of 27 June 2000, No 92-O, SZ RF of 17 July 2000. No 29 art. 311; Judgment of the Constitutional Court of the Russian Federation of 7 June 2000, No 10-P, SZ RF of 19 June 2000 г. No 25 art. 2728.

26 M. Karliuk, 'Russian Legal Order and the Legal Order of the Eurasian Economic Union: An Uneasy Relationship', *Russian Law Journal*, 5(2), 2017, 38–39.

27 P. 3 of the Order of the Constitutional Court of the Rusian Federation of 3 July 1997 No. 87-O, Bulletin of the Constitutional Court of the Russian Federation, 1997, No. 5.
28 Art. 125(6) of the Constitution of Russia, available at: www.constitution.ru/en/10003000-01.htm (accessed 7 July 2017).
29 Article 22 of the Federal law No. 101-FZ "On International Treaties of Russian Federation" of 15 July 1995, SZ RF, 1995, No 29, art. 2757.
30 Resolution of the Supreme Court of the Russian Federation of 10 October 2003 "On application by courts of general jurisdiction of the commonly recognised principles and norms of the international law and the international treaties of the Russian Federation, Bulleten Verkhovnogo Suda Rossiyskoy Federatsii (Bulletin of the Supreme Court of the Russian Federation), No 12, 2003.
31 R. Petrov and P. Kalinichenko, 'The Europeanization of Third Country Judiciaries Through the Application of the EU Acquis: The Cases of Russia and Ukraine', *International and Comparative Law Quarterly*, 60, 2011, 337–339.
32 The high level of the Russian judicial system consists in the Constitutional Court of the Russian Federation and the Supreme Court of Russia.
33 It was issued by the Plenum of the Supreme Court of Russia that is the highest body of the Supreme Court. It is empowered to issue unified interpretation of secondary laws and their application by lower national courts. For instance, Plenum's Resolution of 10 October 2003: "On application by courts of general jurisdiction of the commonly recognised principles and norms of the international law and the international treaties of the Russian Federation", BulletenVerkhovnogo Suda Rossiyskoy Federatsii (Bulletin of the Supreme Court of the Russian Federation) No 12, 2003. Resolution and of 11 June 1999 No 8: "On implementation of the international agreements of the Russian Federation referred to the questions of the arbitration procedures", Vestnik Vysshego Arbitrazhnogo Suda Rossiyskoy Federatsii (Herald of the Supreme Arbitration Court of the Russian Federation) No 6, 1999.
34 S. Marochkin, 'International Law in the Courts of the Russian Federation: Practice of Application', *Chinese Journal of International Law*, 2, 2007, 333.
35 A. E. Kellermann, 'The Impact of EU Enlargement on the Russian Federation', *Azerbaijani-Russian Journal of International and Comparative Law*, 2(1), 2005, 172.
36 M. Karliuk, "Russian Legal Order and the Legal Order of the Eurasian Economic Union: An Uneasy Relationship', *Russian Law Journal*, 5(2), 2017, 35.
37 E. Diyachenko and K. Entin, 'The Court of the Eurasian Economic Union: Challenges and Perspectives', *Russian Law Journal*, 5(2), 2017, 53–74.
38 R. Petrov and P. Kalinichenko, 'On Similarities and Differences of the European Union and Eurasian Economic Union Legal Orders: Is There the "Eurasian Economic Union *Acquis*"?' *Legal Issues of Economic Integration*, 43(3), 2016, 295–308.
39 Indent 10 of the Section 'Applicable law' in the EAEU Court Judgment of 4 April 2016 in the Case No CE-1–2/2–16-KC '*ZAO General Fright*', available at: http://courteurasian.org/doc-15423 (accessed 26 June 2017).
40 Advisory Opinion of the EAEU Court on 4 April 2017 in the Case No SE-2–1/1–17-BK, 'Vertical Agreements', available at: http://courteurasian.org/doc-18093 (accessed 26 June 2017). For comments, see: P. Kalinichenko, 'A Principle of Direct Effect: The Eurasian Economic Union's Court pushes for more Integration', *VerfBlog*, 16 May 2017, available at: http://verfassungsblog.de/the-principle-of-direct-effect-the-eurasian-economic-unions-court-pushes-for-more-integration (accessed 26 June 2017).

41 Indent 10 par. 1 section IV of the Advisory Opinion.
42 Indent 11 par. 1 section IV of the Advisory Opinion.
43 Indent 1 par. 2 section IV of the Advisory Opinion.
44 Case 26/62, *Van Gend en Loos v. Nederlandse Asministratie der Berlastingen*, EU:C:1963:1.
45 Par. 1.2 of the Dissent of Judge Ayriyan to the Advisory Opinion of the EAEU Court on 4 April 2017 in the Case No SE-2–1/1–17-BK, 'Vertical Agreements', available at: http://courteurasian.org/doc-18153 (accessed 26 June 2017).
46 Order of 03.03.2015 N 417-O *Avangard-Agro-Orel*, Report of the Constitutional Court of the Russian Federation, 2015, No 3.
47 *Hirst v. the United Kingdom*, application N 74025/01, Judgment of 6 October 2005.
48 *Anchugov and Gladkov v. Russia*, applications nos. 11157/04 and 15162/05, Judgment of 4 July 2013.
49 The Article 32(3) of the Constitution states: 'Deprived of the right to elect and be elected shall be citizens recognised by court as legally unfit, as well as citizens kept in places of confinement by a court sentence' available at: www.constitution.ru/en/10003000-01.htm (accessed 7 July 2017).
50 Judgment of the Constitutional Court of the Russian Federation of 14 July 2015 No 21-P, on the case concerning the review of constitutionality of the provisions of Federal Law, 'On Ratification of the Convention for the Protection of Human Rights and Fundamental Freedoms and Protocols thereto', Federal Law 'On International Treaties of the Russian Federation', Sections the Civil Procedure Code of the Russian Federation, the Arbitration Procedure Code of the Russian Federation, the Administrative Judicial Proceedings Code of the Russian Federation and Criminal Procedure Code of the Russian Federation in connection with the request of a group of deputies of the State Duma. SZ RF 27 July 2015, N 30.
51 Previously, the Constitutional Court of Russia had already dealt with these issues in its Judgment of 6 December 2013 N 27-P *Marki* concerning to the ECtHR decisions and in its Order of 03.03.2015 N 417-O *Avangard-Agro-Ore* concerning to decisions of the EAEU institutions.
52 *OAO Neftyanayakompaniya Yukos v. Russia*, application N 14902/04, Judgment of 24 June 2014
53 Russian Constitutional Court Determines Moscow Not Bound to All Human Rights Court Rulings, *The Moscow Times* of 14 July 2015, available at: https://themoscowtimes.com/news/russian-constitutional-court-determines-moscow-not-bound-to-all-human-rights-court-rulings-48135 (accessed 26 July 2016).
54 *Ukraine v. Russia* (I), application no. 20958/14; *Ukraine v. Russia* (II), application no. 43800/14; *Ukraine v. Russia* (III), application no. 49537/14; *Ukraine v. Russia* (IV), application no. 42410/15; apart from the interstate applications, there are currently more than 1,400 individual applications related to the events in Crimea or the hostilities in Eastern Ukraine pending before the ECtHR.
55 Federal Law of the Russian Federation No. 7-KFZ introducing amendments to the Federal Constitutional Law No. 1-FKZ of 21 July 1994 on the Constitutional Court of the Russian Federation was passed by the State Duma on 4 December 2015, ratified by the Federation Council on 9 December, signed by the President on 14 December and published the following day. The law entered into force on 15 December 2015. SZ RF, 21 December 2015.
56 Interim Opinion on the Amendments to the Federal Constitutional Law On the Constitutional Court of Russian Federation, Adopted by the Venice Commission at its 106th Plenary Session (Venice, 11–12 March 2016), Opinion No. 832/2015, CDL-AD(2016)005.
57 *Ibid.*

58 Judgment of the Constitutional Court of 19 April 2016 No 12-P, SZ RF, 25 April 2016, N 17, art. 2480.
59 Indent 3, par. 2 of the judgment of the Constitutional Court of 19 April 2016 No 12-P, SZ RF, 25 April 2016.
60 On 15 December 2016 the Constitutional Court of the Russian Federation considered the Request of the Ministry of Justice of the Russian Federation on enforcement of the decision of the ECtHR, available at: www.ksrf.ru/en/News/Pages/ViewItem.aspx?ParamId=1967 (accessed 26 June 2017).
61 Indent 6 par. 2 of the Constitutional Court Judgment on 19 January 2017.
62 Indent 2 par. 7 of the Constitutional Court Judgment on 19 January 2017. Two judges of the Constitutional Court – judge Yaroslavtsev and judge Aranovsky – delivered their dissenting opinions to this case and criticized the controversial conclusions of the Constitutional Court. In their opinion, the Constitutional Court had to reject the request of the Ministry of Justice as inadmissible, because this request by its nature was aimed to justify the incompetence and failure to use the Ministry's authority in the field of the ECtHR judgments enforcement.

11 The constitutional order of Kazakhstan and its adaptability to the Eurasian Economic Union

Zhenis Kembayev

Introduction

The Republic of Kazakhstan has been an active participant and one of the major driving forces of the regional integration processes that have taken place in Eurasia since the collapse of the Soviet Union and that culminated in the signing of the Treaty on the Eurasian Economic Union (TEAEU) between Kazakhstan, Belarus and Russia on 29 May 2014. The purpose of this chapter is to examine the adaptability of the constitutional order of Kazakhstan to the operation of the Eurasian Economic Union (EAEU). Foremost, the chapter demonstrates the major characteristics of Kazakhstan's constitutional order and its foreign policy. Subsequently, it distinguishes and explores the major characteristics of the Eurasian integration processes, in particular paying attention to the development of the EAEU's institutional framework that has some rudimentary characteristics of a supranational organisation.[1] Also, it analyses the application of international treaties in the Republic of Kazakhstan as well as major provisions stipulated by the Constitutional Council as related to the participation of the Republic of Kazakhstan in international organisations. Finally, the chapter purports to provide an answer whether the constitutional order of the Republic of Kazakhstan is compatible with integration processes in the framework of the EAEU.

Major characteristics of the constitutional order of Kazakhstan

The Republic of Kazakhstan is situated in the heart of Eurasia, lying mainly in Central Asia, but also partly in Europe. Vast in size (being the ninth largest country in the world), Kazakhstan has a population of about 17 million which is very diverse in its composition, consisting of more than 100 ethnic groups and a number of religions, the two most important ones being Islam and Orthodox Christianity.

Having emerged as an independent state after the collapse of the USSR, Kazakhstan, like many other post-Soviet countries, has been in a process of unprecedented fundamental transformation. This process included, on the one hand, the transition from a communist political system and a state-managed economy to an – at least theoretically – democratic and market-oriented state, and, on the other hand, the restoration and development of national statehood. These dramatic changes could easily have caused the division of the population into antagonistic ethnic, religious but also social groups, as the removal of the socialist planned economy resulted in a catastrophic economic recession and massive inequalities in income. But despite many assumptions that Kazakhstan would necessarily slide toward political and economic chaos and even military conflicts comparable to those in Bosnia,[2] the country established a solid constitutional order, remained united and started developing a cohesive multinational identity and ideology.

The constitutional order of Kazakhstan fully reflects the vision of the major architect of the country's state-building process, its first (and so far the only) President Nursultan Nazarbayev, on how to address numerous acute challenges and problems faced by the newly established state. As the first Constitution of the Republic of Kazakhstan of 28 January 1993, which was adopted in the spirit of democratic euphoria of the early 1990s and allowed the legislature to effectively control the executive branch headed by the President,[3] was not able to ensure the smooth progress of large-scale privatization and the consolidation of various and diverse parts of the country, President Nazarbayev set a course for the adoption of a new Constitution that significantly increased his powers.[4]

The new Constitution, which currently serves as the supreme law of the country, was approved by a popular referendum on 30 August 1995 by a majority of nearly 90 percent of voters. Arguably, this demonstrates that the overwhelming majority of Kazakhstan's population supported the policy of stability and public concord, which they associated with the personality of the President. Accordingly, the 1995 Constitution was very aptly characterised as

> Nazarbayev's Constitution, as it reflects a firm conviction of a politician, who, under the complicated circumstances of the transition of his state . . . sees himself as the only guarantor for [Kazakhstan's] success . . . [and] pursues an authoritarian mode of government with the aim of economic and administrative modernisation under unconditional safeguarding of political stability.[5]

President Nazarbayev's policy is based on the mantra 'economy first, then politics' and 'democracy is not the beginning of [Kazakhstan's] path, it is the end'.[6] In line with this approach, the Constitution stipulates the following main values of Kazakhstan's constitutional order (officially called 'fundamental principles of the state's activity'): (a) public concord; (b) political stability; (c) economic development for the benefit of the entire nation; (d) Kazakhstani patriotism; and only then (e) 'resolution of important issues of the state affairs by democratic methods'.[7] All other basic tenets of Kazakhstan's constitutional structure, which include: (a) a strong presidential form of governance, (b) a centralised unitary state, (c) a social state, and (d) a secular state, are basically designed to serve the 'fundamental principles of the state's activity' exactly in the order of priority indicated above. The major aim of this combination of a strong presidency, a centralised government and a social and secular state is obviously to ensure public harmony and political stability in a multi-ethnic and multi-confessional country that had no tradition of modern democracy and is still in the process of consolidation.

The 1995 Constitution explicitly provides that Kazakhstan is a 'state with a presidential form of governance'.[8] However, in contrast to its American and French counterparts, Kazakhstan's presidency may be described as a super-presidential one, a fact that can easily be seen by looking at the Kazakh leader's diverse roles as: 1) the head of state representing Kazakhstan both within the country and in international relations; 2) the highest official determining the primary course of domestic and foreign policy in the Republic of Kazakhstan; 3) the arbiter ensuring concerted functioning of all branches of state power; 4) 'the guarantor of rights and freedoms of individuals' and the 'symbol and guarantor of the unity of the people and the state power' ensuring responsibility of the state institutions before the people; and 5) the guarantor of the inviolability of the constitution, virtually exclusively entitled to approve any amendments or additions to the Constitution.[9]

Also, the Constitution guarantees the President full immunity from prosecution for all potential criminal acts, except high treason.[10] Additionally, on 20 July 2000, the Parliament adopted a Constitutional Law that bestowed on Nazarbayev the status of 'the First President' and on 13 May 2010, another Constitutional Law granting the incumbent President the title of the *Elbasy* (the Leader of the Nation). Those laws assured his full life-long inviolability and provided him significant privileges and authority even after he retires from the presidential office (in particular, he will remain Chairperson of the Assembly of Peoples of Kazakhstan and will become a member of the Constitutional Council and of the Security Council). Furthermore, of particular note is that the constitutional amendments of 10 March 2017 made the inviolability of the status of President Nazarbayev as 'the Founder of independent Kazakhstan, the First President and the Leader of Nation' a part of the Constitution's eternity clause, which includes also the Republic's independence and territorial integrity, a presidential form of government, a centralised unitary state as well as the fundamental principles of the state's activity.[11]

Although the Constitution does not formally define the presidency as an executive power, it creates a *de facto* dual executive that includes, along with the President, the Government as a separate organ 'implementing the executive power of the Republic of Kazakhstan'.[12] However, the President is the dominant figure and fully controls the executive branch. The Government 'in its entire activity' is responsible to the President and thus has a purely administrative character. Further, the Constitution defines the Government as a 'corporate organ', which means that those members who do not agree with the policy pursued by the Government, as actually determined by the President, must resign or face removal from office.[13] It is also very telling that the members of the Government must take an oath not only to the people but also to the President.[14] The President appoints the Prime Minister (with the consent of the Parliament's lower chamber, the Mazhilis) and other members of Government, as well as the chairperson of the National Bank, the chairperson of the National Security Committee, the Prosecutor General, the heads of the local government entities and many other high-ranking officials, and may, at any time, and at his own discretion, remove them from office.[15] The President has broad authority to issue decrees and overrule actions taken by the executive and other bodies.[16]

Also, the Constitution puts the President in a superior position *vis-à-vis* the legislature. Even though the recent constitutional amendments repealed provisions allowing the President to issue decrees having the force of law and even to exercise legislative powers for a term of one year, the President still has enormous powers with regard to both the formation of Parliament and the legislative process. Of particular note is that Nazarbayev is the chairperson of Kazakhstan's ruling party of power, Nur Otan, which consistently has the overwhelming majority of seats in the Parliament. Moreover, the President has the right to dissolve either the entire Parliament or only its lower chamber, the Mazhilis.[17]

The President also appoints judges of all local courts in Kazakhstan at the recommendation of the Highest Judicial Council, whose chairperson and members are appointed by the President. Finally, based on the recommendation of the Highest Judicial Council, the President may propose candidacies of judges of the Supreme Court, who are subsequently elected by the Parliament's upper chamber, the Senate.[18] Although judges may serve until the age of retirement (which is 65 years and may be prolonged in exceptional cases for five years),[19] their powers may be terminated for a variety of reasons, which seriously undermines their judicial independence and thus moves them to decide in line with the official state doctrine as determined by the President.[20]

Major characteristics of Kazakhstan's foreign policy

Completely dominating in domestic affairs, the President also represents Kazakhstan in international relations and directs, essentially at his own discretion, Kazakhstan's foreign policy.[21] The President is bound only by the Constitution, which stipulates that 'the Republic of Kazakhstan shall respect principles and norms of international law, pursue the policy of cooperation and good-neighbourly relations between states, their equality and non-interference in each other's domestic affairs, peaceful settlement of international disputes and renounce the first use of the military force'.[22]

The President signs international treaties on behalf of the Republic of Kazakhstan[23] and he takes decisions on their suspension or denunciation.[24] The adoption of international treaties and their denunciation requires the approval of the Parliament.[25] However, given the peculiarities of Kazakhstan's constitutional order (cf. *supra*), it is obviously the President who dominates the decision-making.

Emphasising political stability within Kazakhstan and realising that it depends on the balance of interests of the major world powers, Nazarbayev sets promoting and maintaining international peace and security in Kazakhstan's neighbourhood and in the wider region as the major goal of Kazakh foreign policy. Therefore, according to the President's vision, Kazakhstan's relations with other members of the international community are predicated on a so-called balanced or multi-vectored approach, which is defined as 'developing friendly and predictable relations with all countries that are of practical interest to Kazakhstan'.[26]

In actual practice, this approach means that Kazakhstan seeks peaceful and mutually beneficial relations with all major international actors. Consequently, Kazakhstan has developed a strong and wide-ranging partnership with the European Union (EU), which is Kazakhstan's leading trading partner and largest investor. On 21 December 2015, Kazakhstan and the EU signed an Enhanced Partnership and Cooperation Agreement (EPCA) that aims at further strengthening the bilateral political and economic relationship.[27] Besides, Kazakhstan plays an important role in the Organisation for Security and Cooperation in Europe (OSCE). It held the chairmanship of this organisation in 2010 and hosted an OSCE summit in Astana in December 2010. In 2004, the Parliament of Kazakhstan concluded an agreement on cooperation with the Parliamentary Assembly of the Council of Europe, and in 2012, Kazakhstan became a member of the European Commission for Democracy through Law (Venice Commission). Kazakhstan has also developed a broad-based relationship with the United States, cooperating in such areas as border and regional security programmes, economic relations, political and civil society issues. Furthermore, in 1994, Kazakhstan signed the Partnership for Peace Framework Document, it is a member of the Euro-Atlantic Partnership Council and an active participant in the Partnership for Peace programme. In 2006, Kazakhstan chose to deepen its cooperation with NATO by developing an Individual Partnership Action Plan.

At the same time, Kazakhstan, as a truly Eurasian country, desires to build positive and cooperative relations with Asian countries. Kazakhstan engages in a regional security dialogue with the Association of Southeast Asian Nations (ASEAN). In June 2011, Kazakhstan became the chairman of the Foreign Ministers' Council of the Organisation of Islamic Cooperation. Besides, Kazakhstan is the founder of the Conference on Interaction and Confidence Building Measures in Asia and hosted its ministerial meeting in September 2012. Of particular note is that Kazakhstan is one of the founders of the China-led Shanghai Cooperation Organisation (SCO), which may potentially transform from a hitherto primarily security-oriented alliance to an organisation pursuing also deep economic cooperation along the new Silk Road.[28]

Despite Kazakhstan's commitment to a balanced or multi-vectored approach in international relations and its willingness to cooperate with all its partners for the purpose of ensuring security, stability and economic growth, one vector of its foreign policy is obviously of greater importance than others. Specifically, Kazakhstan pays particular attention to maintaining and strengthening close links with Russia, as those links are crucially important to achieve the main objectives of Kazakhstan's constitutional order, in particular maintaining public concord, safeguarding political stability, and ensuring economic development. Having a 7,500 km border with Russia (the longest continuous border in the world)[29] and a significant Russian-speaking population,[30] Kazakhstan is vitally interested in a stable, predictable, and comprehensive partnership with its northern neighbour. Accordingly, Kazakhstan, from the very beginning of its independence, has been in favour of and actively supported the regional integration processes in the post-Soviet area (or Eurasia).

Major characteristics of regional integration processes in Eurasia

The starting point of the regional integration processes in Eurasia is the conclusion of the Minsk Agreement by Belarus, Russia, and Ukraine on 8 December 1991, that put an end to the Soviet Union, while, at the same time, proclaiming the establishment of the Commonwealth of Independent States (CIS),[31] a regional organisation that was also joined by Armenia, Azerbaijan, Kazakhstan, Kyrgyzstan, Moldova, Tajikistan, Turkmenistan, and Uzbekistan later that same month.[32] Accordingly, the regional integration processes in Eurasia have been developing already more than a quarter of a century and assumed a number of important characteristics.[33]

First, the regional integration processes in Eurasia are driven and inspired by Russia that, despite significant loss of power in the early 1990s, remained the major Eurasian continental power and had a vital interest in reconfiguring its relations with the former Soviet republics in order to maintain its influence in the post-Soviet area and enhance its bargaining position in international relations. Therefore, Moscow had from the very beginning both political and economic objectives in pursuing regional integration processes in Eurasia. Already in December 1991, Russia wanted the CIS to become a strong decision-making entity capable of preserving and maintaining 'a common military-strategic space under united command'[34] and 'a common Eurasian market'.[35] These objectives were reiterated in the CIS Charter of 22 January 1993[36] and found their expression in the adoption of the following two major instruments: the Treaty on Collective Security (TCS) of 15 May 1992,[37] and the Treaty on Economic Union of 24 September 1993.[38]

Second, Russia's geopolitical ambitions have not been the only driving and consolidating reason of the Eurasian integration. Although Russia failed to get all CIS countries into one geopolitical and economic bloc due to the resistance of a number of post-Soviet countries (in particular Azerbaijan, Georgia, Moldova, and Ukraine) that envisaged the CIS merely as a transitional association intended to prepare the individual republics for complete independence and categorically rejected any plans to join advanced integration schemes, a group of other CIS members (in particular, Armenia, Belarus, Kazakhstan, Kyrgyzstan and Tajikistan) was willing to preserve a common military-political and economic space along the lines of the former USSR for a variety of different reasons.

All pro-integration countries, just as Russia, have similar centralised (semi-) authoritarian political regimes based on managed national elections. Power is concentrated in the hands of the respective presidents and political freedoms are limited to a substantial extent.[39] The leaders of these countries, just as President Nazarbayev, consider the process of Eurasian integration as a convenient and useful tool for achieving their objectives of political stability and economic growth. A major threat many of them have in common is the fear of so-called colour revolutions of the sort that rocked Georgia, Kyrgyzstan and Ukraine in the 2000s. Furthermore, they are also interested in the restoration and maintenance of traditional economic links in the framework of the former Soviet Union. It was Kazakhstan's President Nursultan Nazarbayev who first proposed the creation of a Eurasian Union in March 1994. He envisioned the Eurasian Union as a confederation of 'integration-willing states' ensuring close cooperation in security matters and integration of national economies and as 'a form of integration of sovereign states aimed at strengthening stability and security and achieving socio-economic modernisation in the post-Soviet space'.[40]

Third, the regional integration processes in Eurasia have both political and economic motivations and dimensions, which is confirmed by the culmination of those processes in the establishment of the Collective Security Treaty Organisation (CSTO)[41] and the Eurasian Economic Community (EurAsEC),[42] that was replaced by the Eurasian Economic Union (EAEU) in 2015.[43] The CSTO and the EAEU have (almost) identical memberships uniting Armenia, Belarus, Kazakhstan, Kyrgyzstan, Russia and Tajikistan (the latter did not yet join the EAEU but is expected to become a member state in the near future). Taken together, these two organisations constitute a single *de facto* structure that, for discussion purposes, may be referred to as 'the Eurasian alliance'.[44] The establishment of this alliance is the result of its members' commitment to the idea of a multi-polar world and their desire to make their association one of the world's geopolitical centres along with China, the EU, India, and the USA.

Fourth, having created an independent geopolitical bloc, most EAEU members (including Kazakhstan) have formally never even considered the possibility of entering into Association Agreements (AA) with or potential membership in the EU.[45] Instead, the EAEU members aspire for the establishment of formal relations between the EAEU and the EU, in particular by concluding a free trade agreement (FTA).[46] In fact, constituting a customs union and moving towards a common market, the EAEU members are technically not able to conclude an FTA with the EU on an individual basis. Revealingly, the EPCA signed between Kazakhstan and the EU, which is the first updated PCA concluded with those CIS countries that do not enter into an association with the EU, does not contain any clause on an FTA, as Kazakhstan, in its capacity of EAEU Member States, has no independent authority over its customs tariffs and is currently unable to independently commit itself to such an undertaking.[47] Consequently, free trade between Kazakhstan and the EU is possible only on the basis of a free trade agreement between the EU and the EAEU.[48]

Fifth, the EAEU (just as the CSTO and the CIS) fulfils the criteria required for the attribution of the status of a regional intergovernmental organisation under the UN Charter. It is an organisation based on the principles of public international law, most notably sovereign equality, territorial integrity of the Member

States and non-interference into their internal affairs.[49] In particular, the EAEU emphasises that it is a multilateral framework respecting 'specific qualities' of the constitutional order of each Member State.[50] In addition, it is noteworthy that the Member States may freely withdraw from the EAEU[51] (the same applies for the CSTO[52]).

Sixth, while approving the creation of an advanced economic integration scheme, the presidents of the Member States continue to keep a tight rein on the regional integration processes in Eurasia.[53] The EAEU is a very hierarchical, top-down structure and its institutional framework is completely dominated by its supreme body, the Supreme Eurasian Economic Council (SEAEC),[54] which consists of the Heads of the Member States and meets at least once a year to adopt decisions, by consensus, on all important issues.[55] The SEAEC is supported by the Eurasian Intergovernmental Council, which is comprised of the Heads of Government of the Member States and takes decisions, by consensus, that are aimed at achieving the EAEU's objectives in accordance with directions provided by the Heads of State.[56] Of particular note is that the EAEU's executive body, Eurasian Economic Commission (EEC), was endowed with some rudimentary characteristics of a supranational organisation.[57] Yet, with respect to the Commissions' status, Nazarbayev's following words are very telling:

> We [the Heads of States] appoint members of the Commission, define strategy, give instructions to the Commission, approve its actions, and adopt agreements to be implemented by the Commission. This structure must be maintained.[58]

Obviously, the EEC is designed to implement and enforce Eurasian integration law under the guidance and strict supervision of the SEAEC. Furthermore, even though the EAEU institutional framework includes a judicial body, the EAEU Court, its decisions may not change or revoke the law of the Union or the legislation of the Member States.[59] Moreover, the EAEU Court is not the final arbiter of Eurasian integration law, as this function is performed by the SEAEC.[60] Although the EAEU Court's predecessor, the EurAsEC Court attempted in the spirit of judicial activism to establish itself as a genuine law-making body,[61] its endeavours led only to a substantial reduction of the judicial body's competences after the transformation from the EurAsEC to the EAEU.[62] The full domination of the SEAEC is confirmed by the fact that the EAEU institutional framework does not include any parliamentary body.[63]

International treaties in the Republic of Kazakhstan

The country's dynamic foreign policy and, in particular, active participation in the regional integration processes in Eurasia necessarily raise a number of issues related to the status of international treaties, judicial review and application of international treaties in the Republic of Kazakhstan.

Status of international treaties in the legal hierarchy of the Republic of Kazakhstan

According to the Constitution, international treaties are considered 'the functioning law in the Republic of Kazakhstan' along with 'the Constitution, the laws corresponding to it, other regulatory legal acts, as well as regulatory resolutions of Constitutional Council and the Supreme Court of the Republic'.[64]

Kazakhstan's international treaties may be divided into: (a) bilateral or multilateral;[65] and (b) those concluded on behalf of the Republic, those concluded on behalf of the Government, and those concluded on behalf of the state bodies directly subordinated or responsible to the President and the central executive bodies within the limits of their competences.[66] However, from the legal point of view, the most important differentiation of international treaties is their division into those subject to ratification and those capable of entering into force without ratification.

The Constitution provides that 'ratified international treaties shall have priority over the laws of the Republic and may be directly applied except in cases when the application of an international treaty requires the promulgation of a law'.[67] However, international treaties that entered into force without ratification do not have priority over the laws of the Republic and may be implemented only if they do not contradict the national legislation.[68]

(Quasi-)Judicial review of international treaties in the Republic of Kazakhstan

As discussed above, Kazakhstan's legislation allows for the conclusion of international treaties enabling the participation of the Republic in supranational organisations provided those treaties are ratified by the Parliament.

Yet before any international treaty is ratified, the Constitutional Council may review its compliance with the Constitution.[69] Should the Constitutional Council consider an international treaty before its ratification and recognise it as contradictory to the Constitution, this international treaty may not be ratified.[70] The Constitutional Council may also review any international treaty that has already entered into force. Should an already ratified (or enacted without ratification) international treaty (or a part of it) be recognised as contradicting the Constitution, it (or its particular part) may not be implemented.[71]

In the hierarchy of norms, resolutions of the Constitutional Council occupy a rank directly after the Constitution and no other regulatory acts of Kazakhstan may be in conflict with them.[72] Apart from considering whether international treaties of the Republic comply with the Constitution, the Constitutional Council decides on the validity of presidential and parliamentary elections as well as nationwide referenda; it considers whether laws adopted by Parliament comply with the Constitution before they are signed by the President; and it provides an official interpretation of constitutional rules.[73]

Significantly, the President may strongly influence the activities of the Constitutional Council. The President appoints the Chairperson and two of its members.[74] Only the President (along with a limited number of other political actors, who are fully under his control) may petition the Constitutional Council.[75] This rule, which allows the Constitutional Council to hold formal hearings only if mandated to do so by few officials, differentiates the Council from a truly judicial body and qualifies it as a quasi-judicial one.

Application of international treaties in the Republic of Kazakhstan

On 11 October 2000, upon a petition of the Prime Minister, who requested an official interpretation of Article 4(3) of the Constitution providing that 'ratified international treaties shall have priority over the laws of the Republic', the Constitutional Council ruled that ratified international treaties have *ad hoc* superiority over national legislation in the case of conflict of their provisions.[76] This practically means that the international treaty provisions prevail over contradictory provisions of national law in a particular case without implying the invalidation or abolition of the latter. Even though the ruling of the Constitutional Council does not contain any information as to the context of its adoption, it is interesting to note that it was issued the next day after the Treaty establishing the EurAsEC was signed.

The issue of application of ratified international treaties was also dealt with by the Supreme Court of the Republic of Kazakhstan that may issue regulatory resolutions, which contain 'explanations on the issues of how to apply legislation' in judicial practice and are mandatory to all lower courts of the Republic. Thus, the Supreme Court ruled that 'Kazakhstan's courts are obliged, where necessary, to be guided by the norms of international law' and that 'ratified international treaties, which are directly applicable and do not require the promulgation of a law, may be used as material (except for criminal and administrative matters) or procedural law in adjudication in Kazakhstan'.[77]

However, as international treaties have solely *ad hoc* superiority over national legislation and do not invalidate the conflicting national rules, Kazakhstan's courts apply international treaties only in very rare cases, usually related to disputes arising from bilateral agreements on avoidance of double taxation or protection of foreign direct investment.[78]

Legal implications of the EEC's decisions for the Republic of Kazakhstan

The EEC (like its predecessor, the Commission of the Customs Union) may adopt binding and directly applicable decisions. In this regard, it is important to note that, in October 2009, on the eve of launching a trilateral Customs Union of Belarus, Kazakhstan and Russia, the Prime Minister of Kazakhstan requested that the Constitutional Council clarify the legal nature of the decisions of the Commission of the Customs Union.

The Constitutional Council first referred to the fact that the Constitution does not include any norm 'foreseeing the possibility of transferring competences of the state organs to international organisations or their organs'.[79] At the same time, however, it emphasised that the Republic of Kazakhstan is a sovereign state that may independently formulate and realise its domestic and foreign policy on the basis of its Constitution. Further, the Council noted that the Parliament, representing the sovereign will of the people of Kazakhstan, adopted in due procedure the 'Law on International Treaties', which provides, *inter alia*, that Kazakhstan may ratify international treaties enabling the participation of the Republic in international organisations that feature the transfer of a part of the sovereign powers of the Member States to those international organisations.[80] Accordingly, Kazakhstan may be a member of even those international organisations whose organs are able to adopt mandatory decisions by majority voting.[81]

Since the Agreement on the Commission of the Customs Union of 6 October 2007 was properly ratified by the Republic of Kazakhstan, the Constitutional Council stated that its provisions have priority over the laws of the Republic and may be directly applied. In view of the Agreement's provision that the Commission may take binding decisions, the Council noted that Kazakhstan 'must carry out all necessary organisational and legal measures for the implementation of this provision, including the adjustment of the national legislation'. Furthermore, the Constitutional Council referred to Article 4(1) of the Constitution stipulating that 'the functioning law in the Republic of Kazakhstan' consists of 'international treaties and other commitments of the Republic'. Stipulating that the execution of the decisions of the Commission 'should be considered as the implementation of other commitments of the Republic', the Constitutional Council provided that the decisions of the Commission have priority over the laws of the Republic.[82]

At the same time, the Constitutional Council resolved that decisions of the Commission of the Customs Union (like organs of any other international organisation) may not have priority over the laws of the Republic in the event that they infringe upon the constitutional rights and freedoms of individuals in Kazakhstan. Also, the Constitutional Council stipulated that the decisions of the Commission (like organs of any other international organisations) may not contradict the Constitution. In particular, it was emphasised that the decisions of any international organisations may not violate the sovereignty of the Republic, its territorial integrity or its form of governance.[83]

Conclusions

The constitutional order of the Republic of Kazakhstan is characterised by a very high degree of concentration of political power in the personality of the first Kazakh President Nursultan Nazarbayev. It reflects the President's vision of the development of Kazakhstan emphasising political stability and public concord for the sake of the country's consolidation and sustainable progress. Giving a top-priority importance to the steadiness and solidity of the political regime inside Kazakhstan, Nazarbayev is strongly committed to conducting a so-called balanced or multi-vectored foreign policy with the purpose of promoting and maintaining international peace and security in Kazakhstan's neighbourhood and in the wider region.

As Kazakhstan's stability and sustainable development crucially depends on strategic partnership with Russia, Nazarbayev actively supports regional integration processes in Eurasia, which have both political and economic dimensions implemented in the framework of the CSTO and the EAEU. Kazakhstan considers its participation in Eurasian integration a vital factor for safeguarding its existing constitutional order, as it envisages the CSTO's activities to prevent 'colour revolutions' and other threats to the current political regime while the EAEU's operation is expected to help promoting economic growth and thus contributing to political stability.

The institutional framework of the EAEU and the CSTO reflects the constitutional structures of their Member States, which are all republics with strong presidential authorities. Despite conducting institutional experiments and acquiring some rudimentary characteristics of a supranational organisation, the EAEU's structure replicates the lack of democratic traditions and an effective separation of powers in Eurasian countries clearly demonstrating the pre-eminence of its supreme body and thus the complete domination of the presidents of its Member States, who make virtually all important decisions.

Furthermore, even though the Constitution of Kazakhstan stipulates that ratified international treaties have priority over national laws and may be directly implemented, according to the official interpretation of the Constitutional Council, ratified international treaties have only *ad hoc* superiority. In the case of conflict the direct application of international treaties does not imply invalidation and abolition of the respective national laws. Also, notwithstanding that Kazakhstan's legislation allows for the conclusion of international treaties enabling participation of the Republic of Kazakhstan in supranational organisations, any international treaty may be invalidated by the Constitutional Council, the activities of which may be strongly influenced by the President. In addition, in spite of the fact that the Constitutional Council ruled that the decisions of the Commission have priority over the laws of the Republic, it has also indicated a broad range of reasons (in particular, infringement upon the constitutional rights and freedoms of individuals) that may potentially lead to the invalidation of any of the Commission's decision.

Summing up the aforementioned points, it may be argued that the constitutional order of the Republic of Kazakhstan, which establishes a highly centralised presidential form of governance and gives prominence to political stability is fully compatible with integration processes in the framework of the EAEU/CSTO, creating an alliance of (semi-) authoritarian political regimes aimed at preserving the political status quo in Eurasia.

Notes

1 See also the contribution of R. Dragneva, 'The Eurasian Economic Union: Balancing Sovereignty and Integration', in this volume.
2 See numerous proofs in B. Eschment, *Hat Kasachstan ein russisches Problem?* Cologne: BIOst, 1998.
3 See the text in R. Ludwikowski, *Constitution-making in the Region of Former Soviet Dominance*, Durham: Duke University Press, 1996, p. 443 ff.
4 See, *e.g.*, Z. Kembayev, 'The Rise of Presidentialism in Post-Soviet Central Asia: The Example of Kazakhstan', in: R. Grote and T. Röder (eds.), *Constitutionalism in Islamic Countries: Between Upheaval and Continuity*, Oxford and New York: Oxford University Press, 2011, pp. 415–430.
5 O. Luchterhandt, 'Die Verfassung der Republik Kasachstan von 1995', *Jahrbuch des Öffentlichen Rechts der Gegenwart*, 47, 1999, 633. [Translation by the author].
6 N. Nazarbayev, 'Economy First, Then Politics', available at: www.euronews.com/2010/01/15/nazarbayev-economy-first-then-politics (accessed 1 September 2016).
7 Constitution of the Republic of Kazakhstan, 30 August 1995, Art. 1(2). The text in English is available at: www.akorda.kz/en/official_documents/constitution (accessed 1 September 2016).
8 *Ibid.*, Art. 2(1).
9 *Ibid.*, Art. 40.
10 *Ibid.*, Art. 46.
11 *Ibid.*, Art. 91(2).
12 *Ibid.*, Art. 64(1).
13 *Ibid.*, Art. 68(1).
14 *Ibid.*, Art. 65(3).
15 *Ibid.*, Art. 44.
16 *Ibid.*, Arts 44–45.
17 *Ibid.*, Art. 63(1). In doing so, the President is merely required to conduct consultations with the Chairpersons of the Parliament's chambers and the Prime Minister. The Parliament or its lower chamber may not be dissolved only in the period of a state of emergency or martial law, during the last six months of the President's term, as well as within a year after a previous dissolution. *Ibid.*, Art. 63(2).
18 *Ibid.*, Art. 82.
19 See Constitutional Law of RK, 25 December 2000, No. 132-II, 'On Judicial System and Status of Judges', Art. 34–1(2).
20 See, *e.g.*, Z. Kembayev, 'Probleme der richterlichen Unabhängigkeit in Kasachstan', *Osteuropa-Recht*, 63, 2017, 45 ff.
21 *Ibid.*, Art. 40.
22 *Ibid.*, Art. 8.
23 *Ibid.*, Art. 44(11). Along with the President, international treaties of Kazakhstan may be concluded by the Government of Kazakhstan, state organs that are directly subordinated to the President, as well as central executive bodies within the limits of their competences. See Law of RK, 30 May 2005, No. 54-III, 'On International Treaties of the Republic of Kazakhstan', Art. 2.
24 Law of RK, 'On International Treaties of the Republic of Kazakhstan', *op. cit.* note 23, Art. 30(2).
25 Constitution of the Republic of Kazakhstan, *op. cit.* note 7, Art. 54(1).
26 See 'Kazakhstan 2050 Strategy' announced by the President of Kazakhstan on 14 December 2012, available in Kazakh and Russian at: www.akorda.kz/ru/addresses/addresses_of_president (accessed 1 September 2016).

27 On the EU-Kazakhstan partnership see e.g. Z. Kembayev, 'Partnership Between the European Union and the Republic of Kazakhstan: Problems and Perspectives', *European Foreign Affairs Review*, 21(2), 2016, 185–203.
28 See e.g. Z. Kembayev, 'Towards a Silk Road Union?' *Chinese Journal of International Law*, 15(3), 2016, 691–699.
29 See 'Kazakhstan', available at: www.rosgranitsa.ru/ru/activity/international/countries/ kazakhstan (accessed 1 September 2016). On 18 January 2005, a Treaty on the Russian-Kazakh State Border was signed by the presidents of both countries and on 12 January 2006, it entered into force. As of the present, about 5200 km of the Russian-Kazakh border (69% of the entire length) is demarcated. See 'Delimitation and Demarcation of State Border', available at: http://mfa.gov.kz/index.php/ru/vneshnyaya-politika/aktualnye-voprosy-vneshnej-politiki-kazakhstana/ delimitatsiya-i-demarkatsiya-gosudarstvennoj-granitsy (accessed 1 September 2016). The completion of the demarcation is due by 2020. See 'Rossiya-Kazakhstan', available at: www.rfembassy.kz/lm/ dvustoronnie_otnosheniya/rossiya-kazakhstan (accessed 1 September 2016).
30 Even though the number of ethnic Russians is continuously declining due to low birth rates and emigration, they still made up 23.7 percent of the Kazakhstan population in 2009 and constitute currently the majority of inhabitants in a number of northern regions of Kazakhstan.
31 See Agreement establishing the CIS, 8 December 1991, 31 ILM 138 (1992).
32 See Protocol to the Agreement establishing the CIS, 21 December 1991, 31 ILM 147 (1992).
33 On the development of the Eurasian integration see e.g. Z. Kembayev, *Legal Aspects of the Regional Integration Processes in the Post-Soviet Area*, Berlin and Heidelberg: Springer Verlag, 2009.
34 Agreement establishing the CIS, *op. cit.* note 31, Art.6.
35 *Ibid.*, Art.7.
36 Charter of the CIS, 22 January 1993, 34 ILM 1279 (1995).
37 CIS Treaty on Collective Security, 15 May 1992, 1894 UNTS 309.
38 CIS Treaty on Establishment of the Economic Union, 24 September 1993, 34 ILM 1298 (1995).
39 Belarus, Kazakhstan, Russia, and Tajikistan are considered as authoritarian countries, while Armenia and Kyrgyzstan as hybrid states. See 'Democracy Index 2015', www.eiu.com/public/topical_report.aspx?campaignid=DemocracyIndex2015 (accessed 1 September 2016).
40 See N. Nazarbaev, *Evraziiskii Soyuz Idei, Praktika, Perspektivy: 1994–1997*, Moscow: FSRSPN, 1997, p. 44.
41 See Charter of the Collective Security Treaty Organisation, 7 October 2002, 2235 UNTS 79.
42 See Treaty on the Establishment of the Eurasian Economic Community, 10 October 2000, 2212 UNTS 309.
43 See Treaty on the Eurasian Economic Union, (hereinafter TEAEU), 29 May 2014, available at: www.un.org/en/ga/sixth/70/docs/treaty_on_eeu.pdf (accessed 16 June 2017). The Treaty entered into force on 1 January 2015.
44 On the concept of the Eurasian Alliance see Z. Kembayev, 'Regional Integration in Eurasia: The Legal and Political Framework', *Review of Central and East European Law*, 41(2), 2016, 117–154.
45 The only exception is Armenia, which began negotiating an AA with the EU in July 2010. However, ultimately Armenia decided not to initial the negotiated AA with the EU in September 2013, deciding to join the EAEU instead. This decision was motivated not only by potential economic benefits but, primarily, by the fact that Armenia's security fundamentally depends on the CSTO. By contrast,

the conclusion of the AA would have provided no security guarantees and would have risked alienating the country's major security guarantor, Russia.

46 Russian President Putin called for concluding a free trade agreement between the (at that time still emerging) EAEU and the EU on 28 January 2014. See 'Sammit Rossiya-Evropeiskii Soyuz', available at: http://kremlin.ru/events/president/news/20113 (accessed 1 September 2016). Putin's call was almost immediately supported by Nazarbayev on 5 February 2014. See 'Vystuplenie Prezidenta Kazakhstana N.Nazarbaeva na vstreche s glavami zarubezhnykh dipmissij, akkreditovannykh v Kazakhstane', available at: www.akorda.kz/ru/speeches/internal_political_affairs/in_speeches_and_addresses/page_215891_vystuplenie-prezidenta-kazakhstana-n-nazarbaeva-na-vstreche-s-glavami-zarubezhnykh-dipmissii-akkredit (accessed 1 September 2016).

47 Agreeing to deep economic integration within the EAEU, Kazakhstan was, however, asserting that any type of political cooperation should be entirely intergovernmental in nature. According to Kazakh President Nazarbayev: "areas such as defense and security, border safety, migration policy, as well as health, education, science, culture, legal cooperation in civil and criminal matters are not relevant for economic integration and . . . are to be dealt with by the CSTO and the CIS [organisations based on purely intergovernmental principles] as well as on the basis of bilateral agreements. Political sovereignty of Member States is to be unshakable and economic integration is to strengthen national sovereignty of the Member States and to make it more sustainable". See 'Nazarbaev vystupil protiv politizatsii Evraziiskogo soiuza', available at: http://lenta.ru/news/2013/12/24/union (accessed 1 September 2016). This reflects Kazakhstan's resolve to continue conducting a balanced, or multi-vector, foreign policy that assumes the preservation of independence in international relations and cooperation with a wide range of partners.

48 See Kembayev, *op. cit.* note 27, 199.

49 TEAEU, *op. cit.* note 43, Art. 3.

50 *Ibid.*, Art. 3.

51 *Ibid.*, Art. 118.

52 CSTO Charter, *op. cit.* note 41, Art. 19.

53 See R. Dragneva, 'The Eurasian Economic Union: Balancing Sovereignty and Integration', in this volume.

54 As these bodies are almost identical with respect to their composition, their meetings may coincide with respect to time and place (or follow one another). For example, on 19 December 2012, meetings of both the Collective Security Council and the Supreme Eurasian Economic Council took place in Moscow.

55 CSTO Charter, *op. cit.* note 41, Arts 12–13; TEAEU, op. cit. note 43, Arts 10–11, 13.

56 TEAEU, *op. cit.* note 43, Art.16.

57 See Dragneva, *op. cit.* note 53.

58 See 'Nachalo zasedaniia Vysshego Evraziiskogo ekonomicheskogo soveta v uzkom sostave (24 December 2013)', available at: http://kremlin.ru/events/president/transcripts/19913 (accessed 1 September 2016).

59 See Prilozhenie No.2 k Dogovoru o Evraziiskom ekonomicheskom soiuze: Statut Suda Evraziiskogo ekonomicheskogo soiuza (Statute of the EAEU Court), 29 May 2014, available in Russian at: www.consultant.ru/document/cons_doc_LAW_163855, para. 102 (accessed 1 September 2016).

60 In case of non-implementation of a decision of the Court, a Member State may ask the SEAEC to adopt necessary measures for the implementation of the decision. *Ibid.*, para. 114.

61 See A. Ispolinov, 'First Judgments of the Court of the Eurasian Economic Community: Reviewing Private Rights in a New Regional Agreement', *Legal Issues of Economic Integration*, 40(3), 2013, 225–246.

62 See Z. Kembayev, 'The Court of the Eurasian Economic Union: An Adequate Body for Facilitating Eurasian Integration?' *Review of Central and East European Law*, 41(3–4), 2016, 342–367.
63 See Kembayev, *op. cit.* note 44, p. 191.
64 Constitution of the Republic of Kazakhstan, *op. cit.* note 7, Art. 4(1).
65 Law of the Republic of Kazakhstan 'On International Treaties of the Republic of Kazakhstan', *op. cit.* note 23, Art. 7.
66 *Ibid.*, Art. 2.
67 Constitution of the Republic of Kazakhstan, *op. cit.* note 7, Art. 4(2).
68 See Resolution of the Constitutional Council of the Republic of Kazakhstan, 11 October 2000, No.18/2, available in Russian at: http://egov.kz/wps/poc?uri=mjnpa:document&language=ru&documentId= S000000018_ (accessed 1 September 2016).
69 Constitution of the Republic of Kazakhstan, op. cit. note 7, Art. 72(1).
70 Law of the Republic of Kazakhstan, 'On International Treaties of the Republic of Kazakhstan', *op. cit.* note 23, Art. 12(3).
71 See Resolution of the Constitutional Council of the Republic of Kazakhstan, 18 May 2006, No.2, available in Russian at: https://egov.kz/cms/ru/law/list/S060000002_ (accessed 1 September 2016).
72 See Law of RK of 6 April 2016, No. 480-V, 'On Legal Acts', Art. 2, available in Russian at: http://online.zakon.kz/Document/?doc_id=37312788 (accessed 1 September 2016).
73 Constitution of the Republic of Kazakhstan, *op. cit.* note 7, Art. 72(1).
74 *Ibid.*, Art. 71(2,3). The Council also consists of four other members, who are appointed by the Senate and the Mazhilis, each selecting two members. *Ibid.*, Art. 71(3).
75 The sessions of the Constitutional Council are also organized only when it is petitioned by the following political actors: a) the Chairperson of the Senate; b) the Chairperson of the Mazhilis; c) a group of deputies of not less than one-fifth of the total number of parliamentarians; or d) the Prime Minister. *Ibid.*
76 See Resolution of the Constitutional Council of the Republic of Kazakhstan, 11 October 2000, *op. cit.* note 68.
77 See Resolution of the Supreme Court of the Republic of Kazakhstan, 10 July 2008, No.1, available in Russian at: https://egov.kz/cms/ru/law/list/P08000001S_ (accessed 1 September 2016).
78 See Z. Kembayev, 'Deistvie mezhdunarodnykh dogovorov v Respublike Kazakhstan', *Pravo i Gosudarstvo*, 4, 2013, 88–93.
79 See Resolution of the Constitutional Council of the Republic of Kazakhstan, 5 November 2009, No.6, available in Russian at: www.ksrk.gov.kz/rus/resheniya?cid=11&rid=533 (accessed 1 September 2016).
80 Law of the Republic of Kazakhstan, 'On International Treaties of the Republic of Kazakhstan', *op. cit.* note 23, Art. 11(5).
81 See Resolution of the Constitutional Council of the Republic of Kazakhstan, 5 November 2009, *op. cit.* note 80.
82 *Ibid.*
83 *Ibid.*

Concluding remarks

Roman Petrov and Peter Van Elsuwege

The notion of 'transitional constitutionalism', developed by Prof. Sadurski in relation to the post-1989 constitutional reforms in Central and Eastern Europe,[1] is equally relevant for the countries of the former Soviet Union. Several observations support this statement. First, the post-Soviet countries share the same (Soviet) legal heritage and common constitutional traditions based on almost identical Soviet constitutions adopted at the end of the 1970-ies. Second, the countries analysed in this volume (Armenia, Belarus, Georgia, Kazakhstan, Moldova, Russia and Ukraine) almost simultaneously embarked upon ambitious constitutional reforms after the demise of the Soviet Union in 1991. Third, the post-Soviet constitutions share a number of common features. For instance, they are all inspired by theories and concepts of Western constitutionalism and recognise the significance of international treaties, principles of international law and the protection of fundamental human rights as part of their national legal orders. In other words, they all established a Western-type system of constitutional justice.

However, as observed by Paul Blokker in his contribution, 'the processes of constitutionalisation, democratisation, and rule of law development in post-Soviet countries [. . .] are bound to suffer from similar drawbacks as those that have become evident from the discussion of the Central and East European experiences.'[2] Transitional constitutionalism is not a linear process and largely depends upon divergent domestic contexts and external influences. As evidenced in the contribution of Olga Burlyuk and Vera Axyonova, the processes of European and Eurasian integration affect the development of rule of law protection mechanisms in different respects leading to an increased differentiation in the post-Soviet space. Both the establishment of the EAEU and the conclusion of a new generation of Association Agreements created new constitutional challenges, requiring a (re-)definition of the balance between sovereignty and integration. As argued by Rilka Dragneva, this evolution cannot be disconnected from the broader (geo-)political developments in the region. The constitutional orders of the post-Soviet countries have to adapt to the volatile political and security challenges within the post-Soviet area and beyond in order to preserve their newly acquired sovereignty.

Two kinds of constitutional challenges are common to the countries of our study. The first challenge is the issue of *centralisation versus parliamentarism*. Indeed, all the post-Soviet countries had to solve the dilemma of a vertical and horizontal state power building. While Russia has been consistently cementing strong presidential powers while avoiding the legalisation of the institution of the 'eternal presidency', Kazakhstan and Belarus quickly legalised the latter and granted their presidents extremely wide constitutional powers and a *de facto* eternal status. Ukraine experienced with different constitutional systems (mixed and presidential) caused by major domestic and external upheavals. Moldova remained open and receptive to the influence of international law and the EU until the emergence of the EAEU and President Dodon's ambitions to develop close relations with the latter. In the meantime, the Moldovan Constitution remains a main obstacle for President Dodon to explore two different and conflicting paths of regional integration.

The second challenge is the constitutionality of participation in supranational organisations. Every country of our study had to choose the vector of its regional integration either voluntary or under inevitable external pressures. Belarus, Kazakhstan and Armenia made their geopolitical decision to join the Russia-led EAEU and to transfer some of their sovereign competences to the EAEU institutions. Ukraine, Georgia and Moldova embarked upon the long and enduring path of EU integration and concluded ambitious Association Agreements with the EU, including a commitment to the common values of the EU and far-reaching approximation with the EU *acquis*. Nevertheless, either of these choices implied that national constitutions had to adjust to the objectives and specifics of these integration projects.

The country reports highlight three crucial constitutional issues. The first issue is the direct applicability and direct effect of international agreements ratified by the countries concerned (either the Astana Treaty for Armenia, Belarus, Kazakhstan and Russia or the AAs for Ukraine, Moldova and Georgia). The second issue is the recognition of the binding force of decisions of common institutions established under the respective agreements and the application of case law of either the Court of the EAEU or the CJEU by the national judiciaries. The third issue is the introduction of a so-called 'integration clause' in the constitutions of the post-Soviet countries, which can formalise the primacy of the *acquis* of the regional integration organisations (EU and EAEU) within their domestic legal orders.

The individual country reports in this volume reveal that not all these issues have been successfully solved. The example of Ukraine showed that the political commitment towards closer integration with the EU and the objective of effective implementation of the long-awaited AA caused a significant rise of judicial activism via voluntary references to the case law of the CJEU and references to the EU *acquis*. Constitutional amendments and new laws were adopted in order to allow Ukraine to join the Rome Statute, to launch ambitious judicial reforms and to eliminate discrimination of sexual minorities in work and employment.

Nevertheless, the Ukrainian Parliament still has to consider further constitutional amendments related to the effective implementation of the AA, for instance as far as the status of decisions of the Association Council is concerned.[3] The study on Georgia shows how a national consensus on European and Euro-Atlantic (NATO) integration affects the development of the domestic constitutional order.[4] In this respect, the introduction of a far-reaching 'integration clause' allowing Georgia's full integration into the EU and NATO is remarkable. Such a step is unprecedented in the post-Soviet space and clearly illustrates how the ambitions of the political elite determine the constitutional framework. A similar trend may be discerned in Moldova, even though this case represents a high degree of complexity due to the decision of President Dodon to acquire closer integration with the EAEU while at the same time being formally committed to the implementation of the AA. In order to reach such a complicated geopolitical balance, President Dodon seeks the possibility of amending the international law–friendly Moldovan Constitution and to enhance his own constitutional powers. Undoubtedly, this may lead to new challenges before the Constitutional Court, not least because Moldova's commitments under the AA with the EU may conflict with its obligations within the EAEU.[5]

Even though the alleged supranational features of the EAEU should be put in perspective, as convincingly argued by Rilka Dragneva in the first part of this book, the country reports reveal that the constitutional implications of the process of Eurasian integration cannot be underestimated. In particular, the issue of direct applicability of decisions adopted by the EAEU institutions remains controversial. In this respect, it is noteworthy that all EAEU Member States adopt a rather cautious approach towards the implications of acts adopted in the context of international organisations. A case in point is the evolution in Russia. The Russian Constitution was adopted in 1993 as the most international law-friendly constitution within the post-Soviet area. For instance, it was the only Constitution with an explicit integration clause providing for the country's participation in interstate associations involving the partial transfer of sovereign powers.[6] However, despite this basic openness towards international law, recent constitutional developments in Russia shifted towards a completely different direction. In particular, the case law of the Russian Constitutional Court regarding the enforcement of decisions of the ECtHR reveals 'an increasingly defensive and isolationist position justified by the objective of guarding the national sovereignty and protection of the domestic constitutional principles against the influence of international law.'[7] A similar trend can be observed in other EAEU Member States. Despite constitutional provisions on respect for the supremacy of principles of international law in the Belarusian Constitution, the Belarusian Constitutional Court confirmed its right to check the compatibility of decisions of the EAEU Commission with national laws and decrees. As argued by Maksim Karliuk, this may undermine the effective implementation of the Astana Treaty in the Belarusian legal order.[8] The case of Armenia also shows that the objective of 'guaranteeing state, national and domestic sovereignty' remains the priority of the national constitutional system. The Constitutional Court is unequivocal that the application of the decisions of supranational bodies in Armenia is only possible within certain constitutional limits.[9] Finally, the Kazakh constitutional system has shifted towards a full presidential republic, granting the President the constitutional title of 'Leader of the Nation'. Furthermore, following the official interpretation of the Constitutional Council, ratified international treaties have only *ad hoc* superiority within the Kazakh legal system. In the case of conflict, the direct application of international treaties does not imply invalidation and abolition of the respective national laws. Accordingly, the Constitutional Council, which is strongly influenced by the President, may block the implementation of any international treaty and decisions of international organisations.[10]

Hence, it is obvious that the post-Soviet constitutions have been subjected to domestic and external pressures. In the latter case, the regional integration initiatives lead to new challenges related to the recognition of decisions and acts adopted at the supranational level. Constitutional Courts play a crucial role, either as guardians of the constitution or as obedient tools of the ruling political elite. However, in all these cases the shadow of the EU is always behind. This is most visible in relation to the associated countries (Ukraine, Moldova and Georgia) where the integration-oriented agenda of the AAs influences national judges to pursue judicial activism via voluntary application of the EU *acquis* as a 'persuasive source of reference'. Whereas the influence of the EU is obviously less evident in relation to the EAEU Member States, it may well be argued that the EU integration experience, especially the far-reaching teleological interpretation of the EU *acquis* by the CJEU, pushed Russia, Belarus, Armenia and Kazakhstan towards protective constitutional policies and encouraged them to abandon ambitious integration objectives for the EAEU in favour of preserving national sovereignty at any cost. In any event, the constitutional developments identified in this volume reveal that the process of transitional constitutionalism in the post-Soviet space is still a work in progress, which is to a large extent determined by the processes of European and Eurasian regional integration.

Notes

1 W. Sadurski, 'Transitional Constitutionalism: Simplistic and Fancy Theories', in: A. Czarnota, M. Krygier and W. Sadurski (eds.), *Rethinking the Rule of Law After Communism*, Budapest and New York: CEU Press, 2005, pp. 9–24; R. Teitel, 'Post-Communist Constitutionalism: A Transitional Perspective', *Columbia Human Rights Law Review*, 1994, 167–190.
2 See the contribution of Paul Blokker in this volume.
3 See the contribution of Roman Petrov in this volume.
4 See the contribution of Gaga Gabrichize in this volume.
5 See the contribution of Mihaela Tofan in this volume.
6 Article 79 of the Russian Constitution.
7 See the contribution of Paul Kalinichenko in this volume.
8 See the contribution of Maksim Karliuk in this volume.
9 See the contribution of Laure Delcour and Narine Ghazaryan in this volume.
10 See the contribution of Zhenis Kembayev in this volume.

Annex 1

Rule of law provisions in the Constitutions of post-Soviet states[1]

Country	*Rule of law provision with direct mentioning of the term*	*Supremacy of the law/ the constitution*	*Separation of powers*	*Independence of the judiciary/courts*	*Respect for fundamental rights*	*Equal rights/equality before the law*
Armenia	'The Republic of Armenia is a sovereign, democratic state, based on social justice and the rule of law'. (Article 1)	'The Constitution has supreme legal force and the norms thereof shall apply directly'. (Article 6)	'State power shall be exercised in accordance with the Constitution and the laws based on the principle of the separation and balance of the legislative, executive and judicial powers'. (Article 5)	'The independence of courts shall be guaranteed by the Constitution and laws'. (Article 94) 'The President may, on the basis of a conclusion of the Constitutional Court terminate the powers of any of his appointees in the Constitutional Court or give his consent to name the member as an accused, detain, authorise the institution of a court proceeding to subject the member to administrative responsibility'. (Article 55.10) 'The President upon the recommendation of the Council of Justice:	'A human being, his/her dignity, fundamental rights and freedoms are an inalienable and ultimate value'. (Article 3) 'Human dignity shall be respected and protected by the State as an inviolable foundation of human rights and freedoms'. (Article 14) 'No one shall be subjected to torture, inhuman or degrading treatment or punishment. Arrested, detained or incarcerated persons shall be entitled to humane treatment and the respect of their dignity'. (Article 17) 'The fundamental human and civil rights and freedoms set forth in Articles 23–25, 27, 28–30, 30.1, paragraph 3 of Article 32 can only be temporarily restricted by law if it is necessary in a	'All people are equal before the law. Discrimination based on sex, race, colour of the skin, ethnic or social origin, genetic circumstances, language, religion, viewpoints, political or other opinions, belonging to a national minority, property status, birth, disability, age or other conditions of personal or social character shall be prohibited'. (Article 14.1)

(*Continued*)

Annex 1 (Continued)

Country	*Rule of law provision with direct mentioning of the term*	*Supremacy of the law/ the constitution*	*Separation of powers*	*Independence of the judiciary/courts*	*Respect for fundamental rights*	*Equal rights/equality before the law*
				a. shall appoint the presidents and the judges of the Court of Cassation and its chambers, the Courts of Appeals, the courts of first instance and specialised courts; **b.** may terminate their powers; **c.** give agreement to include as a defendant, detain or authorise administrative proceedings through the judicial process; upon the conclusion of the Council of Justice, appoint judges of the appellate, first instance and professional courts'. (Article 55.11)	democratic society in the interests of national security, public order, crime prevention, protection of public health and morality, constitutional rights and freedoms, as well as the honour and reputation of others'. (Article 43) 'Special categories of human and civil rights, except for those stipulated in Articles 15, 17–22, and 42 of the Constitution, can be temporarily restricted as prescribed by law in case of martial law or a state of emergency within the scope of international commitments on deviating from commitments in cases of emergency'. (Article 44) 'Everyone shall be obliged to honour the Constitutions and the laws, to respect the rights, freedoms and dignity of others'. (Article 47)	

Azerbaijan	–	'The Azerbaijan people. . . [declare] the following goals . . . to establish a law-governed, secular state which assures the supremacy of the law as an expression of the will of the people'; (Preamble) 'The Azerbaijan State is a democratic, law-governed, secular, unitary republic'. (Article 7)	'State power in the Republic of Azerbaijan is based on the principle of separation of powers: Legislative power is exercised by the Milli Majlis of the Republic of Azerbaijan. Executive power is vested in a President of the Republic of Azerbaijan. Judicial power is administered by courts'. (Article 7.III)	'According to the constitutional provisions, executive, legislative and judicial powers cooperate and are independent within the framework of their authority'. (Article 7.IV) 'The President of the Republic of Azerbaijan ensures the independence of the judicial power'. (Article 8, IV) [More info in Article 109.9] 'Judges are autonomous, they are subordinate only to the Constitution and the laws of the Republic of Azerbaijan and are irremovable during their term of office'. 'Judges decide the cases in an unbiased, fair way, following the legal equality of the sides, on the basis of facts and in accordance with the law'. (Article 127.I-II)	'The supreme objective of the State shall be to ensure human rights and civil liberties and an adequate standard of living for the citizens of Azerbaijan'. (Article 12.I) 'Every citizen from birth enjoys inviolable, undeniable and inalienable rights and freedoms'. (Article 24.I) 'No one can curtail the implementation of the rights and freedoms of man and citizen. Everyone's rights and freedoms are subject to the restrictions provided for in the Constitution and the laws as well as to the limits resulting from the rights and freedoms of others'. (Article 24.II) 'Upon declaration of war, martial law and exceptional situation, as well as mobilisation that the implementation of human rights and freedoms can be partially and temporarily curtailed taking into	'Everyone is equal before the law and the court'. 'Men and women have equal rights and freedoms'. 'Everyone has equal rights and freedoms irrespective of race, nationality, religion, sex, origin, property status, social position, convictions, political party, trade union organisation and social unity affiliation. Limitations or recognition of rights and freedoms because of race, nationality, social status, language, origin, convictions and religion are prohibited'. (Article 25.I-III)

(*Continued*)

Annex 1 (Continued)

Country	*Rule of law provision with direct mentioning of the term*	*Supremacy of the law/ the constitution*	*Separation of powers*	*Independence of the judiciary/courts*	*Respect for fundamental rights*	*Equal rights/equality before the law*
				'Decisions on the removal of members of the Constitutional Court of the Republic of Azerbaijan, the Supreme Court of the Republic of Azerbaijan and the Economic Court of the Republic of Azerbaijan shall be taken by a majority of 83 votes, decisions on the removal of other judges by a majority of 63 votes in the Milli Majlis of the Republic of Azerbaijan'. (Article 128.V)	'into consideration international obligations of the Republic of Azerbaijan. The population shall be notified in advance of the temporary suspension of human rights and freedoms'. (Article 71.I-II) 'None of the provisions of the Constitution may be used to abolish human rights and civil liberties'. (Article 71.V)	'Upon declaration of war, martial law and exceptional situation, as well as mobilization that the implementation of human rights and freedoms can be partially and temporarily curtailed taking into consideration international obligations of the Republic of Azerbaijan. The population shall be notified in advance of the temporary suspension of human rights and freedoms'. (Article 71.III)

Belarus	'The Republic of Belarus is a unitary, democratic, social state based on the rule of law'. (Article 1)	'The Republic of Belarus shall be bound by the principle of supremacy of law'. (Article 7)	'State power in the Republic of Belarus is exercised on the principle of division of powers between the legislature, executive and judiciary. State bodies within the confines of their powers, shall be independent: they shall co-operate among themselves acting on the principle of checks and balances'. (Article 6)	'In administering justice judges shall be independent and subordinate to law alone'. (Article 110) 'The President of the Republic of Belarus shall: . . . 9. appoint with the consent of the Council of the Republic the judges of the Supreme and Economic Courts, Chairperson of the Central Commission of the Republic of Belarus on Elections and National Referenda, the Procurator-General, the Chairperson and members of the Governing Board of the National Bank; 10. appoint six members of the Constitutional Court, and other judges of the Republic of Belarus;	'The individual, his rights, freedoms and guarantees for their attainment manifest the supreme goal and value of society and the State'. (Article 2) 'The State shall safeguard personal liberty, inviolability and dignity. The restriction or denial of personal liberty is possible in the instances and under the procedure specified in law'. (Article 25) 'Everyone shall respect the dignity, rights, liberties and legitimate interests of others'. (Article 53) 'The exercise of the personal rights and liberties specified in this Constitution may be suspended only during a state of emergency or martial law under the procedure and within the limits specified in the Constitution and the law In carrying out special measures during a state of emergency, the rights	'The State shall regulate relations among social, ethnic and other communities on the basis of the principles of equality before the law and respect of their rights and interests'. (Article 14) 'All shall be equal before the law and entitled without discrimination to equal protection of their rights and legitimate interests'. (Article 22)

(*Continued*)

Annex 1 (Continued)

Country	*Rule of law provision with direct mentioning of the term*	*Supremacy of the law/ the constitution*	*Separation of powers*	*Independence of the judiciary/courts*	*Respect for fundamental rights*	*Equal rights/equality before the law*
				11. dismiss the Chairperson and judges of the Constitutional, Supreme and Economic Courts, the Chairperson of the Central Commission of the Republic of Belarus on Elections and National Referenda, the Procurator-General, the Chair-person and members of the Board of the National Bank to the order and instances determined by the law and to the notification of the Council of the Republic'. (Article 84.9–11)	specified in Article 24, part three of Article 25 and Articles 26 and 31 of the Constitution may not be restricted'. (Article 63)	

Georgia	'We, the citizens of Georgia, whose firm will is to establish a democratic social order, economic freedom, a rule of-law and a social state. . .' (Preamble)	'The Constitution of Georgia shall be the supreme law of the State. All other legal acts shall comply with the Constitution'. (Article 6)	'State authority shall be exercised under the principle of separation of powers'. (Article 5.4)	'Judicial authority shall be independent and be exercised exclusively by the courts'. (Article 82.3) 'The President of Georgia shall nominate before Parliament, appoint, release, and dismiss officials in accordance with the Constitution, appoint a member of the High Council of Justice as determined by law, participate in the appointment of the Chairperson and members of the Central Election Commission under the procedure and in the cases defined by organic law, nominate candidates for the members of the National Regulatory Authorities to Parliament in agreement with the Government'. (Article 73.e)	'The State shall recognise and protect universally recognised human rights and freedoms as eternal and supreme human values. While exercising authority, the people and the State shall be bound by these rights and freedoms as directly applicable law'. (Article 7) 'Human honour and dignity shall be inviolable'. (Article 17) 'The President of Georgia shall have the right to restrict the rights and freedoms listed in Articles 18, 20, 21, 22, 24, 25, 30, 33, and 41 of the Constitution either throughout the territory of Georgia or in any part thereof during a state of emergency or martial law. The President of Georgia shall be obliged to submit the decision to Parliament for approval not later than 48 hours'. (Article 46.1)	'Everyone is born free and is equal before the law regardless of race, colour of skin, language, sex, religion, political or other opinions, national, ethnic and social affiliation, origin, property or social status, place of residence'. (Article 14)

(*Continued*)

Annex 1 (Continued)

Country	*Rule of law provision with direct mentioning of the term*	*Supremacy of the law/ the constitution*	*Separation of powers*	*Independence of the judiciary/courts*	*Respect for fundamental rights*	*Equal rights/equality before the law*
Kazakhstan	–	'The provisions of the Constitution, the laws corresponding to it, other regulatory legal acts, international treaty and other commitments of the Republic as well as regulatory resolutions of Constitutional Council and the Supreme Court of the Republic shall be the functioning law in the Republic of Kazakhstan'. 'The Constitution shall have the highest juridical force and direct effect on the entire territory of the Republic'. (Article 4.1–2)	"The state power in the Republic of Kazakhstan is unified and executed on the basis of the Constitution and laws in accordance with the principle of its division into the legislative, executive and judicial branches and system of checks and balances that governs their interaction'. (Article 3.4)	'Courts shall consist of permanent judges whose independence shall be protected by the Constitution and law. judge's powers may be terminated or suspended exclusively on the grounds established by law'. (Article 79.1) 'The following shall belong to exclusive jurisdiction of the Senate: 'approval of the appointment of the Chairperson of National Bank, the Procurator General and the Chairperson of the Committee of National Security by the President of the Republic of Kazakhstan'. (Article 55.2)	'Human rights and freedoms in the Republic of Kazakhstan shall be recognised and guaranteed in accordance with this Constitution'. 'Human rights and freedoms shall belong to everyone by virtue of birth, be recognised as absolute and inalienable, and define the contents and implementation of laws and other regulatory legal acts'. (Article 12.1–2) 'A person's dignity shall be inviolable'. (Article 17) 'Everyone must observe the Constitution, legislation of the Republic of Kazakhstan and respect the rights, freedoms, honour and dignity of other persons'. (Article 34)	'Everyone shall be equal before the law and court'. 'No one shall be subject to any discrimination for reasons of origin, social, property status, occupation, sex, race, nationality, language, attitude towards religion, convictions, place of residence or any other circumstances'. (Article 14.1–2)

		'Everyone must observe the Constitution, legislation of the Republic of Kazakhstan and respect the rights, freedoms, honour and dignity of other persons'. (Article 34)			'Any form of restrictions to the rights and freedoms of the citizens on political grounds shall not be permitted. Rights and freedoms stipulated by articles 10–11; 13–15 paragraph of article 16; article 17; article 19; article 22; paragraph of article 26 of the Constitution shall not be restricted in any event'. (Article 39.3)	
Kyrgyzstan	'Aspiring to strengthen the rule of law as well as ensure social justice, economic welfare and spiritual development of the people'; (Preamble) 'The Kyrgyz Republic (Kyrgyzstan) is a sovereign, democratic,	'The Constitution shall have supreme legal force and direct application in the Kyrgyz Republic'. (Article 6.1)	'The state power in the Kyrgyz Republic shall be based on the following principles: . . . Separation of state power . . . Separation of functions of state authorities and local government bodies'. (Article 3.2, 3.4)	'Judges shall be independent and subordinate only to the Constitution and laws'. (Article 94.1) 'The President: 1. at the proposal of the Judicial Appointments Committee, shall submit to the Jogorku Kenesh candidates for election as judges of the Supreme Court; 2. at the proposal of the Council of the Judiciary shall submit to the Jogorku	'Fundamental human rights and freedoms are inalienable and belong to each person from birth. Human rights and freedoms are of superior value. They act directly and define the meaning and the content of the activity of legislative, executive power and government bodies'. (Article 16.1) 'Human and civil rights and freedoms may be limited by the Constitution and Acts of Parliament for the purposes of protecting national security, public order, health and morale	'The Kyrgyz Republic shall respect and ensure human rights and freedoms to all persons on its territory and under its jurisdiction. No one may be subject to discrimination on the basis of sex, race, language, disability, ethnicity, belief, age, political and other convictions, education, background, proprietary and

(*Continued*)

Annex 1 (Continued)

Country	*Rule of law provision with direct mentioning of the term*	*Supremacy of the law/ the constitution*	*Separation of powers*	*Independence of the judiciary/courts*	*Respect for fundamental rights*	*Equal rights/equality before the law*
	secular, unitary and social state governed by the rule of law'. (Article 1.1)			Kenesh the judges to be dismissed from the membership in the Supreme Court; 3. shall appoint local court judges at the proposal of the Judicial Appointments Committee; 4. shall dismiss local court judges at the proposal of the Council of the Judiciary in cases envisaged in the constitutional law'. (Article 64.3.1–4) 'In the event of death of a judge or him being declared dead or missing, legally incapable, loss of citizenship, withdrawal from	of the population as well as rights and freedoms of other persons. The introduced limitations should be commensurate to the declared objectives'. (Article 20.2) [More detailed list of which cannot rights can be limited in Article 20.4–5)	other status as well as other circumstances. Special measures defined by law and aimed at ensuring equal opportunities for various social groups in accordance with international commitments shall not be considered as discrimination.' 'In the Kyrgyz Republic everyone shall be equal before the law and the courts'. 'In the Kyrgyz Republic men and women shall have equal rights and freedoms and equal opportunities for their realisation'. (Article 16.2–4)

				citizenship or acquisition of another citizenship, the powers of the judge shall be terminated by the body which elected or appointed him, from the date of emergence of grounds in accordance with the constitutional law'. (Article 95.3)		'The following rights established in the present Constitution, shall not be subject to an limitation whatsoever: 1. That of each detained person to human treatment and respect of human dignity; . . . ' (Article 20.5.2)
Moldova	'Considering the rule of law, civic peace, democracy, human dignity, fundamental human rights and freedoms, the free development of human personality, justice and political	'The Constitution of the Republic of Moldova shall be the Supreme Law of the State. No law or any other legal act, which contravenes the provisions of the Constitution, shall have legal force'. (Article 7.19	'In the Republic of Moldova the legislature, the executive and the judiciary shall be separate and cooperate in the exercise of the assigned prerogatives pursuant to the provisions of the Constitution'. (Article 6)	'Judges sitting in the courts of law shall be independent, impartial and irremovable under the law'. (Article 116) 'Constitutional Court shall be independent of any other public authority and shall obey only the Constitution'. (Article 134.2)	'Constitutional provisions on human rights and freedoms shall be interpreted and enforced in accordance with the Universal Declaration of Human Rights, other conventions and treaties to which the Republic of Moldova is a party'. (Article 4.1) 'The foremost duty of the State shall be the respect and protection of human Person'. (Article 16.1)	'All citizens of the Republic of Moldova shall be equal before the law and public authorities, regardless of the race, nationality, ethnic origin, language, religion, sex, opinion, political affiliation, property or social origin'. (Article 16.2)

(*Continued*)

Annex 1 (Continued)

Country	*Rule of law provision with direct mentioning of the term*	*Supremacy of the law/ the constitution*	*Separation of powers*	*Independence of the judiciary/courts*	*Respect for fundamental rights*	*Equal rights/equality before the law*
	pluralism as supreme values', (Preamble) 'The Republic of Moldova is a democratic and governed by the rule of law State, in which human dignity, his/ her rights and freedoms, the free development of human personality, justice and political pluralism represent supreme values and shall be guaranteed'. (Article 1.3)		'For the tenure of their mandate the judges of the Constitutional Court shall be irremovable, independent and shall obey only the Constitution'. (Article 137)		'In the Republic of Moldova no law may be adopted which might curtail or restrict the fundamental rights and liberties of the person and citizen. The pursuit of the rights and freedoms may not be subdued to other restrictions unless for those provided for by the law, which are in compliance with the unanimously recognised norms of the international law and are requested in such cases as: the defense of national security, territorial integrity, economic welfare of the State, public order, with the view to prevent the mass revolt and felonies, protect other persons' rights, liberties and dignity, impede the disclosure of confidential information or guarantee the power and impartiality of justice'. (Article 54.1–2)	

Russia	–	'The Constitution of the Russian Federation and federal laws shall have supremacy on the entire territory of the Russian Federation'. (Article 4) 'The Constitution of the Russian Federation shall have supreme legal force, direct effect and shall be applicable on the entire territory of the Russian Federation. Laws and other legal acts, which are adopted in the Russian Federation, must not contradict the Constitution of the Russian Federation'. (Article 15.1)	'State power in the Russian Federation shall be exercised on the basis of its division into legislative, executive and judicial authority. Bodies of legislative, executive and judicial authority shall be independent'. (Article 10)	'Judges shall be independent and shall be subordinate only to the Constitution of the Russian Federation and federal law'. (Article 120.1) 'Judges shall be irremovable'. 'The powers of a judge may be terminated or suspended only on the grounds and in accordance with the procedure established by federal law'. (Article 121.1, 121.2)	'Man, his rights and freedoms shall be the supreme value. The recognition, observance and protection of human and civil rights and freedoms shall be an obligation of the State'. (Article 2) 'In the Russian Federation human and civil rights and freedoms shall be recognised and guaranteed according to the universally recognised principles and norms of international law and this Constitution'. 'Basic human rights and freedoms shall be inalienable and shall be enjoyed by everyone from birth'. (Article 17.1, 17.2) 'Human dignity shall be protected by the State. Nothing may serve as a basis for its derogation'. (Article 21.1) Human and civil rights and freedoms may be limited by federal law only to the extent necessary for the protection of the basis of the constitutional order,	'All persons shall be equal before the law and the court'. (Article 19.1) 'The State guarantees the equality of human and civil rights and freedoms regardless of sex, race, nationality, language, origin, material and official status, place of residence, attitude to religion, convictions, membership of public associations, or of other circumstances. All forms of limitations of human rights on social, racial, national, language or religious grounds shall be prohibited'. 'Men and women shall enjoy equal rights and freedoms and equal opportunities to exercise them'. (Article 19.1, 19.2)

(*Continued*)

Annex 1 (Continued)

Country	*Rule of law provision with direct mentioning of the term*	*Supremacy of the law/ the constitution*	*Separation of powers*	*Independence of the judiciary/courts*	*Respect for fundamental rights*	*Equal rights/equality before the law*
					'morality, health, rights and lawful interests of other people, and for ensuring the defense of the country and the security of the State'. (Article 55.3) 'The rights and freedoms specified in Articles 20, 21, 23 (part 1), 24, 28, 34 (part1), 40 (part 1), and 46–54 of the Constitution of the Russian Federation might not be restricted'. (Article 56.3)	
Tajikistan	–	'The Constitution of Tajikistan has the supreme juridical force [and] its norms have direct effect. Laws and other legal acts contradicting the Constitution have no juridical force'. (Article 10)	'The State power is based on the principle of its division into legislative, executive, and judicial'. (Article 9)	'Judicial power, being independent, is exercised in the name of the State by courts. Judicial power protects the rights and freedoms of individual and citizen, interests of the State, organisations, institutions, lawfulness, and justice'. (Article 84)	'Man, his rights and freedoms are the highest value. The life, honour, dignity and other natural rights of man are inviolable'. (Article 5) 'The rights and freedoms of man and citizen are regulated and protected by the Constitution, laws of the Republic, [and] international legal acts recognised by Tajikistan'. (Article 14)	'All are equal before the law and court. The State guarantees the rights and freedoms of everyone regardless of his nationality, race, gender, language, religious beliefs, political persuasion,

				'The President: Presents to the Majlisi Milli candidates for election and recall of Chairman, Deputy Chairmen, and judges of the Constitutional Court, Supreme Court and Higher Economic Court'. (Article 69)	'During a state of emergency the rights and freedoms provided in Articles 16, 17, 18, 19, 20, 22, 25 and 28 of the Constitution may not be limited'. (Article 47)	education, [and] social and property status. Men and women have equal rights'. (Article 17)
Turkmenistan	–	'The Constitution of Turkmenistan is the Basic Law of the State. Rules and regulations laid down in it are unswervingly applicable. The laws and other legal acts that contradict the Constitution are null and void'. (Article 5)	'State power is based on the principle of separation of powers between the legislative, executive and judicial branches, which operate independently, balancing each other'. (Article 4)	'Judges are independent; they are subject only to law and are guided by inner belief. Interference in the work of judges, by whichever side, is unacceptable and punishable by law. The immunity of judges is guaranteed by law'. (Article 101) 'Judges are appointed by the President of Turkmenistan. The order of appointment and dismissal, and	'In Turkmenistan, the people are the highest value of the society and the state'. (Article 3) 'The rights and freedoms of the individual are inviolable and inalienable.' (Article 18) 'The implementation of the rights and freedoms of citizens may be suspended only in a state of emergency or martial law in a manner and within the limits established by the Constitution and laws'. (Article 47)	'Turkmenistan guarantees the equality of rights and freedoms of individual and citizen, and also the equality of the individual and citizen before the law regardless of their nationality, race, gender, origin, property and official status, place of residence, language, religion, political beliefs, party affiliation or lack of affiliation to any party'. (Article 19)

(*Continued*)

Annex 1 (Continued)

Country	*Rule of law provision with direct mentioning of the term*	*Supremacy of the law/ the constitution*	*Separation of powers*	*Independence of the judiciary/courts*	*Respect for fundamental rights*	*Equal rights/equality before the law*
				the terms of their office, are determined by law. Judges can be removed from office prior to the expiration of their term only on grounds specified by law'. (Article 102)		'Men and Women in Turkmenistan have equal civil rights. Violation of equality on the basis of gender is punishable by law'. (Article 20) 'The implementation of the rights and freedoms of citizens may be suspended only in a state of emergency or martial law in a manner and within the limits established by the Constitution and laws'. (Article 47)
Ukraine	'In Ukraine, the principle of the rule of law is recognised and effective'. (Article 8)	'Ukraine is a sovereign and independent, democratic, social, law-based state'. (Article 1)	'State power in Ukraine is exercised on the principles of its division into legislative, executive and judicial power'. (Article 6)	'The independence and immunity of judges are guaranteed by the Constitution and the laws of Ukraine . . . A judge is dismissed from office by the body that elected or appointed him or her . . .' (Article 126)	'The human being, his or her life and health, honour and dignity, inviolability and security are recognised in Ukraine as the highest social value. Human rights and freedoms and their guarantees determine the essence and orientation of	'Citizens have equal constitutional rights and freedoms and are equal before the law. There shall be no privileges or restrictions based on race, colour of skin, political

	'The Constitution of Ukraine has the highest legal force. Laws and other normative legal acts are adopted on the basis of the Constitution of Ukraine and shall conform to it'. (Article 8)		the activity of the State. The State is answerable to the individual for its activity. To affirm and ensure human rights and freedoms is the main duty of the State'. 'All people are free and equal in their dignity and rights. Human rights and freedoms are inalienable and inviolable'. (Article 31) 'Everyone has the right to respect of his or her dignity'. (Article 28) 'Constitutional human and citizens' rights and freedoms shall not be restricted, except in cases envisaged by the Constitution of Ukraine. Under conditions of martial law or a state of emergency, specific restrictions on rights and freedoms may be established with the indication of the period of effectiveness of these	religious and other beliefs, sex, ethnic and social origin, property status, place of residence, linguistic or other characteristics. Equality of the rights of women and men is ensured: by providing women with opportunities equal to those of men, in public and political, and cultural activity, in obtaining education and in professional training, in work and its remuneration; by special measures for the protection of work and health of women; by establishing pension privileges, by creating conditions that allow women to

(*Continued*)

Annex 1 (Continued)

Country	*Rule of law provision with direct mentioning of the term*	*Supremacy of the law/ the constitution*	*Separation of powers*	*Independence of the judiciary/courts*	*Respect for fundamental rights*	*Equal rights/equality before the law*
					restrictions. The rights and freedoms envisaged in Articles 24, 25, 2 7, 28, 29, 40, 47, 51, 52, 55, 56, 57, 58, 59, 60, 61, 62 and 63 of this Constitution shall not be restricted'. (Article 64)	combine work and motherhood; by legal protection, material and moral support of motherhood and childhood, including the provision of paid leaves and other privileges to pregnant women and mothers'. (Article 24)
Uzbekistan	–	'The Constitution and laws of the Republic of Uzbekistan shall have absolute supremacy in the Republic of Uzbekistan'. (Article 15)	'The principle of separation of powers into the legislative, executive and judicial shall underlie the system of state authority of the Republic of Uzbekistan'. (Article 11)	'The judicial authority in the Republic of Uzbekistan shall function independently from the legislative and executive authorities, political parties, other public associations'. (Article 106)	'Democracy in the Republic of Uzbekistan shall be based on the principles common to all mankind according to which the ultimate value is a human being, his life, freedom, honour, dignity and other inalienable rights'. (Article 13)	'All citizens of the Republic of Uzbekistan shall have equal rights and freedoms, and shall be equal before law without discrimination by sex, race, nationality, language, religion, social origin,

	'Judges shall be independent and subject solely to law. Any interference in the work of judges in administering law shall be inadmissible and punishable by law'. (Article 112) 'The President of the Republic of Uzbekistan shall: appoint and relieve judges of regional, interdistrict, district, city, martial and economic courts of their posts'. (Article 14)	'A citizen of the Republic of Uzbekistan and the state shall be bound by mutual rights and mutual responsibility. Citizens' rights and freedoms, established by the Constitution and laws, shall be inalienable. No one shall have the right to deprive or limit them without a court'. (Article 19) 'Citizens shall be obliged to observe the Constitution and laws, and to respect the rights, freedoms, honour and dignity of others'. (Article 48)	convictions, individual and social status. Any privileges may be granted solely by law and must conform to the principles of social justice'. (Article 18) 'Women and men shall have equal rights'. (Article 46) 'Children shall be equal before law regardless of the origin and civic status of parents'. (Article 65)

Note

1 For this table, the latest versions of post-Soviet constitutions were reviewed, with all amendments currently in force.

Annex 2

Constitutional provisions on the protection of national sovereignty

Country	*Protection of national sovereignty (how/by which mechanisms is it guaranteed)*
Armenia	'The armed forces of the Republic of Armenia ensure security, defence and territorial integrity of the Republic of Armenia, as well as the inviolability of its borders. The armed forces shall maintain neutrality in political matters and remain under civilian control'. (Article 8.2) 'The President of the Republic shall be the guarantor of the independence, territorial integrity and security of the Republic of Armenia'. (Article 49)
Azerbaijan	'The President of the Republic of Azerbaijan guarantees independence, territorial integrity and fulfilment of international agreements to which the Republic of Azerbaijan is a party'. (Article 8.III) 'The Republic of Azerbaijan establishes its Armed Forces and other military troops to ensure its security and protection'. (Article 9.I) 'The territory of the Republic of Azerbaijan may not be torn away. The Republic of Azerbaijan shall not yield its territory, or part of it, in any form, to anyone; borders can be specified only by the Decree of the Milli Majlis of the Republic of Azerbaijan on the basis of the will of the people of Azerbaijan'. (Article 11.III)
Belarus	'The Republic of Belarus exercises supreme control and absolute authority over the whole of its territory, and shall implement an independent internal and foreign policy. The Republic of Belarus shall defend its independence and territorial integrity, its constitutional system, and safeguard legality and law and order'. (Article 1) 'The President of the Republic of Belarus shall provide the protection of the sovereignty of the Republic of Belarus, its national security and territorial integrity, shall ensure its political and economic stability, continuity and interaction of bodies of state power, shall maintain the intermediation among the bodies of state power'. (Article 79) 'The President of the Republic of Belarus shall impose, in the event of military threat or attack, martial law in the territory of the Republic of Belarus and announce general or partial mobilisation with the submission within 3 days of the taken decision for approval of the Council of the Republic'. (Article 84.29)

Country	*Protection of national sovereignty (how/by which mechanisms is it guaranteed)*
Georgia	'The following shall fall within the exclusive competence of supreme state authorities of Georgia: b. status, regime, and protection of the state borders, status and protection of territorial waters, airspace, continental shelf and Exclusive Economic Zone c. issues of war and peace, determination and introduction of legal regime of state of emergency and martial law'. (Article 3) '[The President shall] . . . have the right to suspend, on the recommendation of the Government and with the consent of Parliament, the activity of self-government bodies or other representative institutions of territorial units or dismiss them if their activities jeopardise the sovereignty, territorial integrity of the country, or the exercise of constitutional powers by state bodies'. (Article 73.j) 'Defensive war shall be a sovereign right of Georgia." "Georgia shall have the Armed Forces to protect the independence, sovereignty, and territorial integrity of the country, also to fulfil its international obligations'. (Article 98.1–2)
Kazakhstan	'The sovereignty of the Republic extends to its entire territory. The state ensures the integrity, inviolability and inalienability of its territory'. (Article 2.2) ' . . . in the event of serious and immediate threat to the democratic institutions of the Republic, its independence and territorial integrity, political stability of the Republic, security of its citizens and the disruption of normal functioning of the Constitutional bodies of the state, the President shall have official consultation with Prime Minister and Chairpersons of the Parliamentary Chambers of the Republic and take measures, caused by state of emergency on the entire territory or in particular areas of Kazakhstan, and immediately inform the Parliament of the use of the Armed Forces of the Republic'; 'in the case of aggression against the Republic or immediate external threat to its security, the President shall impose martial law on the entire territory of the Republic or in particular areas, declare partial or total mobilisation and immediately inform the Parliament of the Republic to the effect'. (Article 44.16–17)
Kyrgyzstan	'The right to wage war shall not be recognised except in cases of aggression against Kyrgyzstan and other States bound by obligations of collective defense. The permission in each instance of displacement of the units of the Armed Forces of the Kyrgyz Republic beyond the territory of Kyrgyzstan shall be granted by decision of the Jogorku Kenesh adopted by a majority of not less than two thirds of the total number of deputies'. (Article 14.2) 'The Government . . . shall ensure the implementation of measures aimed at protecting the sovereignty of the state; territorial integrity, protection of the constitutional order, as well as measures to strengthen defense capacity, national security and law and order'. (Article 88.1.4)

(*Continued*)

Annex 2 (Continued)

Country	*Protection of national sovereignty (how/by which mechanisms is it guaranteed)*
Moldova	'The President of the Republic of Moldova shall represent the State and shall be the guarantor of the national sovereignty and independence, as well as of the territorial unity and integrity of the State'. (Article 77) 'The armed forces shall be exclusively subordinated to the will of people as to safeguard the sovereignty, independence, unity and territorial integrity of the country and constitutional democracy'. (Article 108) 'The provisions regarding the sovereignty, independence and unity of the State, as well as those regarding the permanent neutrality of the State may be revised only by referendum based on a majority vote of the registered voting citizens'. (Article 142.1)
Russia	'The Russian Federation shall ensure the integrity and inviolability of its territory'. (Article 4) 'The President of the Russian Federation shall be the guarantor of the Constitution of the Russian Federation and of human and civil rights and freedoms. In accordance with the procedure established by the Constitution of the Russian Federation, he (she) shall adopt measures to protect the sovereignty of the Russian Federation, its independence and State integrity, and shall ensure the coordinated functioning and interaction of State government bodies'. (Article 80.2)
Tajikistan	'The State secures the sovereignty, independence and territorial integrity of the Republic. Propaganda and actions aimed to divide the unity of the State are prohibited'. (Article 7) 'The President is the guarantor of the Constitution and the laws, rights and freedoms of man and citizen, national independence, unity and territorial integrity, continuity of the long-lived State, functioning and interaction of the State organs in concord, [and] observance of international treaties of Tajikistan'. (Article 64)
Turkmenistan	'The State protects the independence, territorial integrity of Turkmenistan, and constitutional system, and provides law and order'. (Article 1) "In order to protect the state sovereignty and security, Turkmenistan has its own armed forces'. (Article 13) 'The President of Turkmenistan is the head of the state and executive power, the highest official of Turkmenistan, acting as guarantor of the state independence and the status of neutrality of Turkmenistan, its territorial integrity, respect for the Constitution and fulfilment of international obligations'. (Article 50)

Country	*Protection of national sovereignty (how/by which mechanisms is it guaranteed)*
Ukraine	'The people are the bearers of sovereignty and the only source of power in Ukraine. The people exercise power directly and through bodies of state power and bodies of local self-government'. (Article 5) 'To protect the sovereignty and territorial indivisibility of Ukraine, and to ensure its economic and informational security are the most important functions of the State and a matter of concern for all the Ukrainian people. The defence of Ukraine and the protection of its sovereignty, territorial indivisibility and inviolability, are entrusted to the Armed Forces of Ukraine. Ensuring state security and protecting the state border of Ukraine are entrusted to the respective military formations and law enforcement bodies of the State, whose organisation and operational procedure are determined by law'. (Article 17) 'The President of Ukraine is the guarantor of state sovereignty and territorial indivisibility of Ukraine, the observance of the Constitution of Ukraine and human and citizens' rights and freedoms'. (Article 102) 'The President of Ukraine: ensures state independence, national security and the legal succession of the state'. (Article 106.1)
Uzbekistan	'The President of the Republic of Uzbekistan shall: take necessary measures on the protection of sovereignty, security and territorial integrity of the Republic of Uzbekistan, implementation of decisions regarding its national-state structure'. (Article 93.2)

Table of cases

European Court of Justice

European Court of Human Rights

Economic Court of the Commonwealth of Independent States

Consultative Opinion of the CIS Economic Court on the request of the Integration Committee of the Eurasian Economic Community about interpretation of Articles 1(2) and 14(2) of the Treaty on the establishment of the Eurasian Economic Community of 10 October 2000), in *Resheniia Ekonomicheskogo Suda Sodruzhestva Niezavisimykh Gosudarstv, 1992–2006*, Minsk: Kovcheg, 2007, 540 165n27

Court of the Eurasian Economic Community

Judgment of 10 July 2013, *Biulleten' Suda Evraziiskogo ekonomicheskogo soobshchestva* (2013) No.2, 7–17. 167n68

Court of the Eurasian Economic Union

Judgment of 4 April 2016, Case No CE-1–2/2–16-KC '*ZAO General Fright*' 179n39

Advisory Opinion on 4 April 2017, Case No SE-2–1/1–17-BK, '*Vertical agreements*' 179n40, 180n45

Constitutional Court of Federal Republic of Germany

BVerfG, Judgment of the Second Senate of 30 June 2009–2 BvE 2/08 (*Lisbon judgment*), BVerGE 123, 267; ECLI:DE:BVerfG: 2009 167n67

Constitutional Court of Czech Republic

Pl. ÚS 50/04: *Sugar Quotas III* 2006/03/08 16, 25n74

Pl. ÚS 66/04: *European Arrest Warrant* 2006/05/03 16

Pl. ÚS 5/12: *Holubec* 2012/01/31 16

Pl ÚS 19/08: *Lisbon I* 2008/11/26 16

Pl ÚS 26/06: *Lisbon II* 2009/11/03 16

Constitutional Court of Hungary

Decision 17/2004 (V. 25) AB: *Sugar Surplus Duty* 16, 25n80

Constitutional Court of Armenia

Decision "*Case on Conformity of the Obligations Stipulated in the Treaty on 'The Accession to the Treaty of May 20, 2014 on "The Eurasian Economic Union" signed by the Republic of Armenia' Signed on October 10, 2014 in*

Minsk with the Constitution of the Republic of Armenia," November 14, 2014 DCC – 1175 149n57

Constitutional Court of Belarus

Decision '*On conformity of the Law of the Republic of Belarus "On technical requirements conformity assessment and accreditation of conformity assessment bodies" to the Constitution of the Republic of Belarus)*, adopted on 13 October 2016, No R-1069/2016 165n28

Constitutional and Supreme Court of Georgia

Decision of the Constitutional Court of Georgia, N 8/177/2, 21 May 2002 116n34

Decision of the Constitutional Court of Georgia, N 1/5/224, 16 November 2004 117n57

Decision of the First Panel of the Constitutional Court of Georgia, N 1/1/374, 379, 9 February 2007 117n58

Decision of the Supreme Court of Georgia, N AS-1210–1139–2012, 2 May 2013 117n59

Decision of the Constitutional Court of Georgia, N 2/3/630, 31 July 2015 117n64

Constitutional Court of Moldova

Decision of 5 December 2013, No. 36, *On the interpretation of Article 13, para 1 of the Constitution in correlation with the Preamble of the Constitution and the Declaration of Independence of the Republic of Moldova* 128n27

Decision of 9 October 2014, No. 24, *On the constitutionality of the Association Agreement between the Republic of Moldova of the one part and the European Union, the European Atomic Energy Community and their Member States of the other part* 129n47

Constitutional Court of the Russian Federation

Order of of 3 July 1997 No. 87-O, Bulletin of the Constitutional Court of the Russian Federation, 1997, No. 5 178n27

Order of 27 June 2000, No 92-O, SZ RF of 17 July 2000. No 29 178n25

Judgment of the Constitutional Court of the Russian Federation of 7 June 2000, No 10-P, *on the case concerning the review of constitutionality of certain provisions of the Constitution of the Republic of Altai and the Federal Law 'On the General Principles of Organisation of Legislative (Representative) and Executive Bodies of State Power of Subjects of the Russian Federation'*, SZ RF of 19 June 2000, No 25 178n25

Supreme Courts of the Russian Federation

Constitutional Court of Ukraine

Case law of Ukrainian courts

United States of America

Index

For Product Safety Concerns and Information please contact our EU representative GPSR@taylorandfrancis.com
Taylor & Francis Verlag GmbH, Kaufingerstraße 24, 80331 München, Germany

www.ingramcontent.com/pod-product-compliance
Ingram Content Group UK Ltd.
Pitfield, Milton Keynes, MK11 3LW, UK
UKHW011003180926
475701UK00004B/537

* 9 7 8 0 3 6 7 8 7 5 4 6 6 *